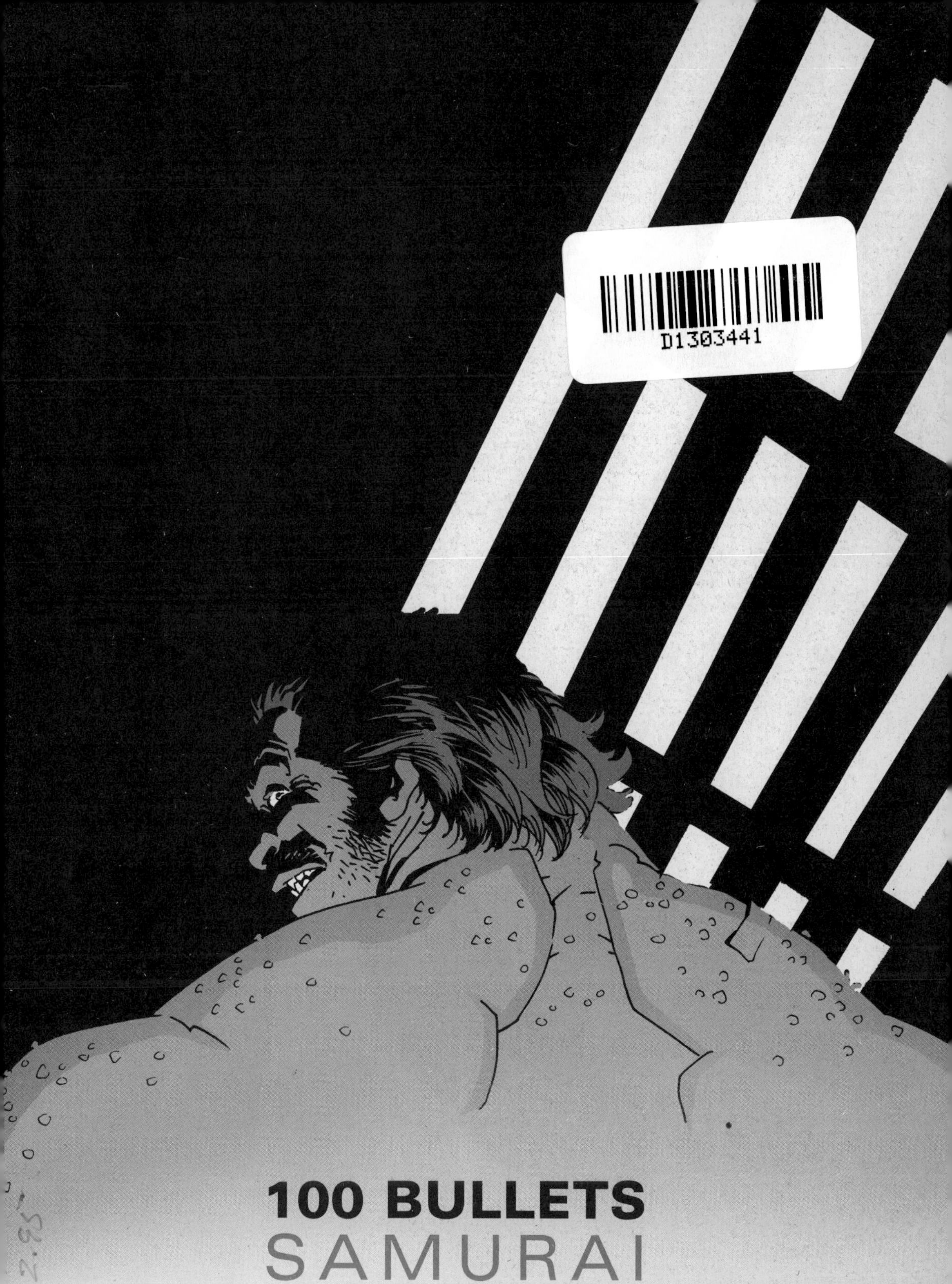

100 BULLETS
SAMURAI

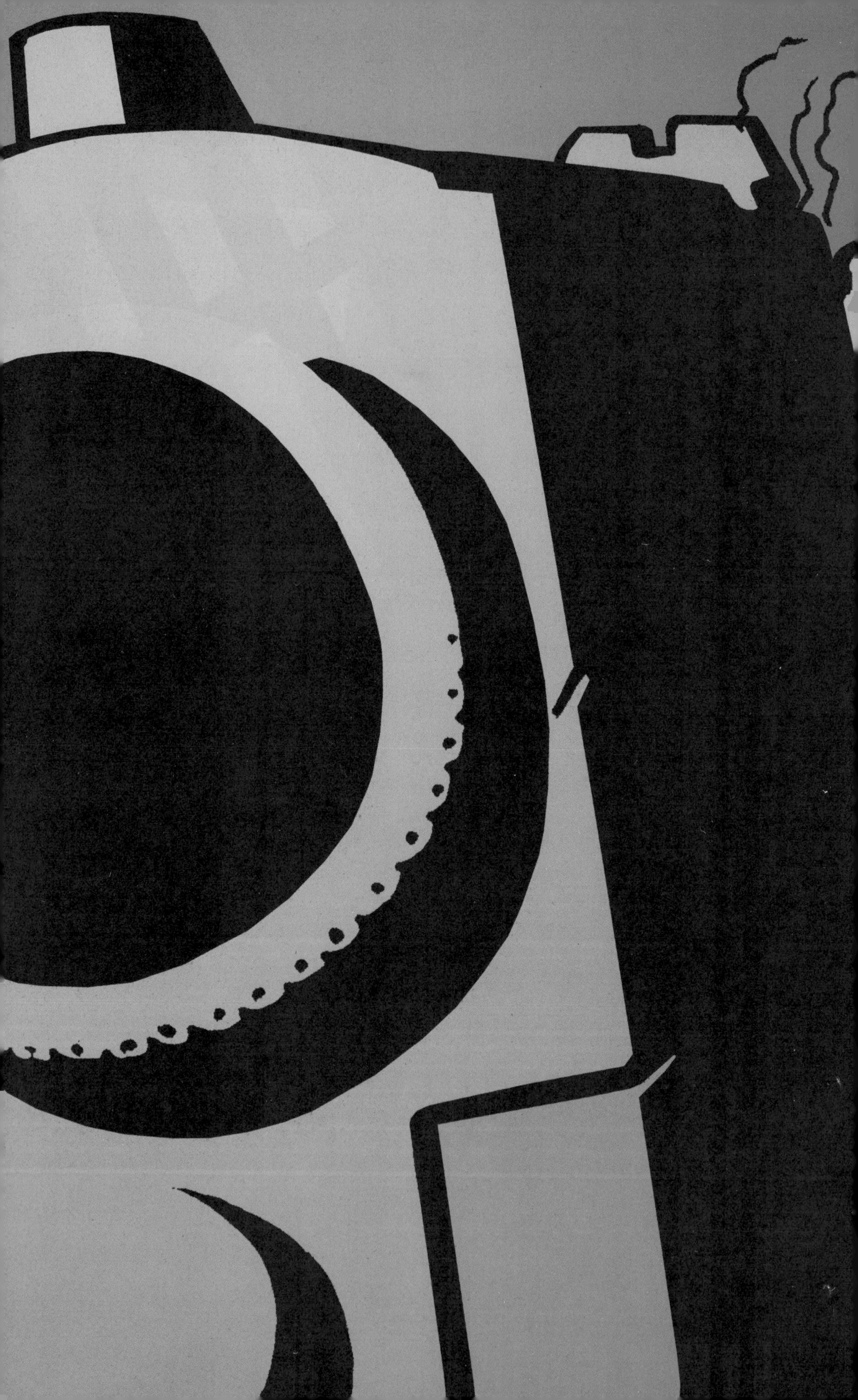

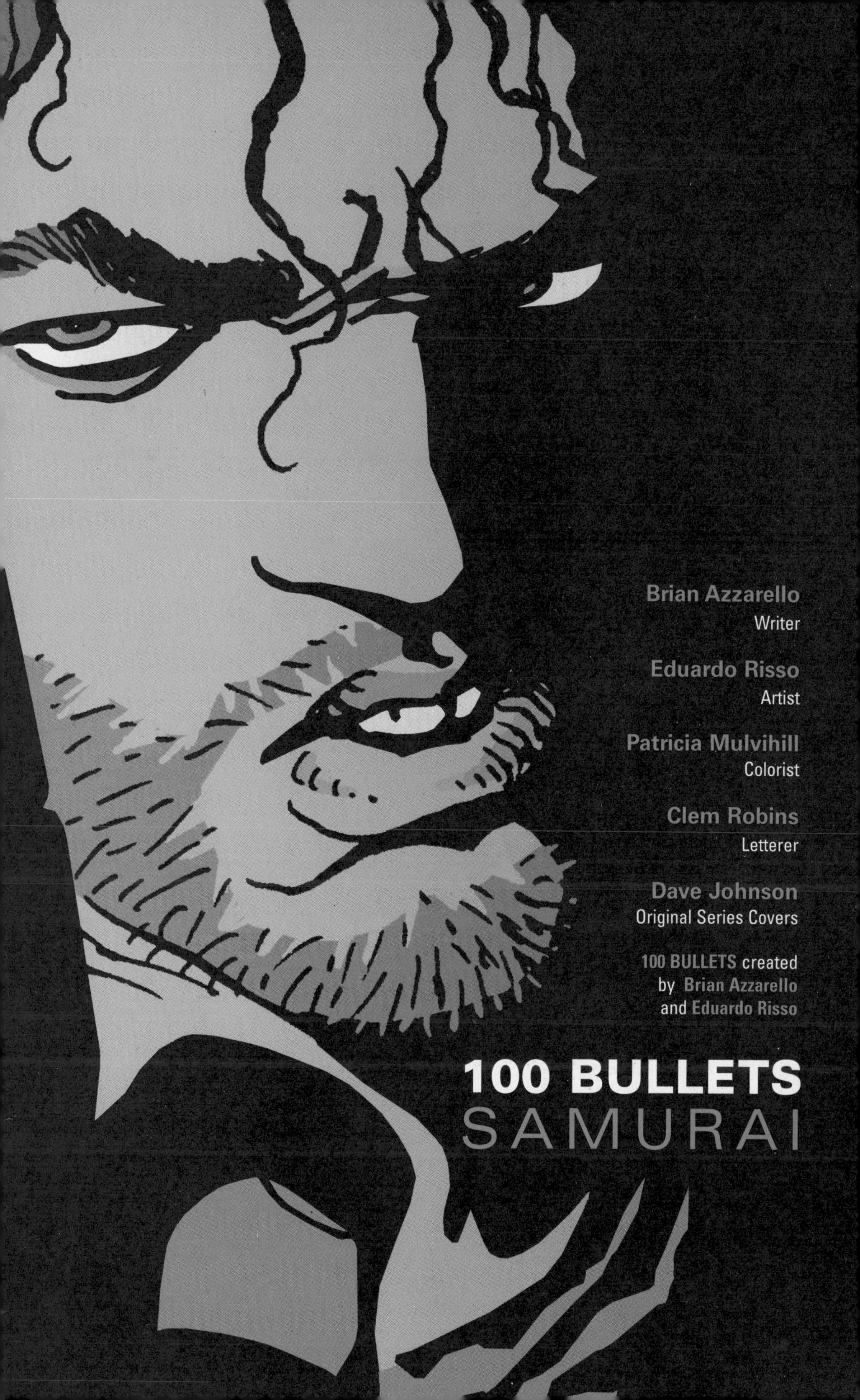

Brian Azzarello
Writer

Eduardo Risso
Artist

Patricia Mulvihill
Colorist

Clem Robins
Letterer

Dave Johnson
Original Series Covers

100 BULLETS created
by Brian Azzarello
and Eduardo Risso

100 BULLETS
SAMURAI

100 BULLETS: SAMURAI.
Published by DC Comics. Cover, introduction and compilation copyright © 2004 DC Comics. All Rights Reserved. Originally published in single magazine form as 100 BULLETS 43-49. Copyright © 2003, 2004 Brian Azzarello, Eduardo Risso and DC Comics. All Rights Reserved. All characters, their distinctive likenesses and related elements featured in this publication are trademarks of DC Comics. The stories, characters and incidents featured in this publication are entirely fictional. DC Comics does not read or accept unsolicited submissions of ideas, stories or artwork.
DC Comics, 1700 Broadway, New York, NY 10019.   A Warner Bros. Entertainment Company.
Printed in Canada. First Printing. ISBN: 1-4012-0189-X.
Cover illustration by Dave Johnson. Publication design by Peter Hamboussi.
Special thanks to Eduardo A. Santillan Marcus for his translating assistance.

Introduction by Carlos Trillo

When, in 1926, "Captain" Joseph T. Shaw took over the management of *Black Mask* magazine, he had already decided to offer his readers a new way of facing up to the old detective genre, with all its mystery and enigmatic ways, which had been so abused by many English and some American authors.

It is probable that "Cap'n" Shaw had noticed that, in that year alone, three million emigrants arrived in New York. They came from all over Europe and the whole entertainment industry was trying to figure out what type of cultural food they had to give this enormous mass of potential consumers of entertainment. Radio and the music hall had already found the way of communicating with this new audience, an audience so much in need of diversion. Meanwhile, literary magazines calmly continued with their stories of butlers, assassinations in the library, and almost mathematical mysteries populated only by millionaires in drawing rooms where expensive drinks were well served, and women in dresses from refined dressmakers.

Shaw undoubtedly realized that, amongst the readers that he could capture for his badly printed and not very refined publication, there were none with butlers, nor libraries, nor fortunes, and if you wanted to address the immigrant, with this huge mass of poor workers, you had to tell life as it was being lived on the streets, as it was perceived from the icy cold, concerning those well wrapped-up rich people who wrote the laws and armed the police so as to feel less fear of those ever-increasing-in-number, politicized, and aggressive foreigners who were spreading like a fungus, putting at risk their property and their power.

In the stories published in "Cap'n" Shaw's *Black Mask* there was no place for the classic mystery story which followed mechanical processes and which were credible and likely in their construction. Neither was there space for police stories with intrigue and suspense which involved the playing up and later resolution of a distressing situation; nor for stories with simple plots which favor adventure.

No, there was nothing of that type. The "Cap'n" — a prize fencer, drinker of corn whiskey, and compulsive poker player — set out the basis for his literary project calling on his authors to distance themselves as much as possible from the outline explained by Edgar Allan Poe in 1841 which, from that time, had been faithfully adhered to by all authors of the detective story until it became a repetitive and oppressive genre.

"Get out on the streets, boys, and preferably at night!" it seems the "Cap'n" shouted at his writers.

I am in no doubt that the oldest predecessors of the adult, bitter, and brutal approach chosen by Brian Azzarello and Eduardo Risso for their 100 BULLETS are to be found in those old stories from *Black Mask* and in the writers who followed that path.

There is always something of 100 BULLETS in the dry violence of James Cain, in the bitter observations on the corruption of power of Dashiell Hammett, in the romantic disenchantment of Raymond Chandler, and in the beastly descriptions of Mickey Spillane. Not to forget, of course, in the gratuitous violence cultivated by Samuel Fuller, or in the philosophical observation of the black part of the soul which John Huston wanted to construct.

Into this huge spring of North American fiction Azzarello and Risso's comic has arrived to add to a literary category which had been able to cross over the literature of the United States, all the time modifying itself, at a time when this same is incessantly expanding into so many other western countries.

The French decided to call this type of narration *serie noir*, "the black series," and also *polar* (due to its darkness and coldness). Italians, on the other hand, prefer to call it *giallo*, "yellow," as this is the color of corruption and of the lies which are shouted out so that those around might believe them. However, all the time what is being referred to is a literary genre which decided to grab the mystery novel by the neck and shake it up, kick the hell out of its mathematical and abstract construction and, once it is on its death bed, shove it violently into the middle of a dirty back street, bloodied and pissed on by the dogs.

In that back street, as in the depths of the jungle, pity is nowhere to be seen. The beasts and the rats are capable of eating whoever falls asleep. Passions are naked, without clothes to hide them. The lot is rotten, there's no perfume to hide bad smells, and feelings always end up being drowned in money.

In the making of this genre of fiction in the 20th century — which has now come through unscathed into the 21st century — great literary figures and potboiler writers, directors of quality cinema and B-movie directors have been involved.

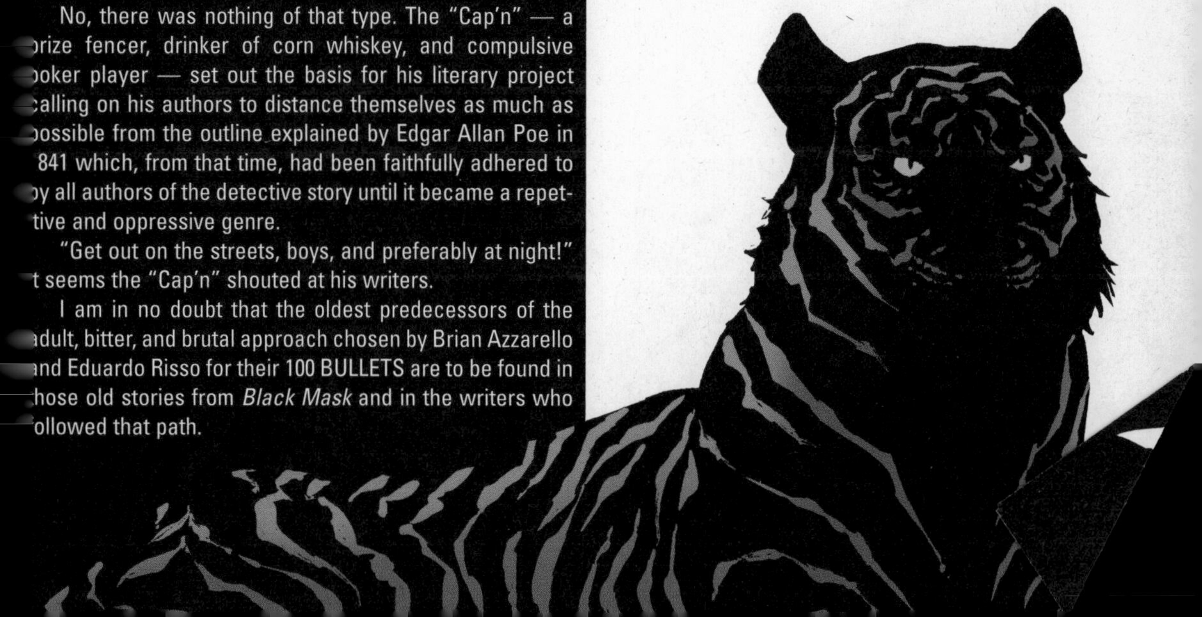

It is necessary to pay attention to all of these to find the origins of 100 BULLETS. From the outset, these are not only to be found in the instructions and editing that "Cap'n" Shaw carried out while at *Black Mask*, but also, for example, in that seminal text of Hemingway's, The *Assassins* (also, by chance, from 1926, the same year that Shaw took charge of *Black Mask*), that one in which two paid bullies arrive in Chicago to kill a former boxer that they don't know, in a place where corruption and eagerness to corrupt had already taken hold, this time in the world of sport.

In that long road, contributions piled up, amongst which mixed the refined writing of William Faulkner, in his *Sanctuary* (1931) for example, and the dizzy writing of James Hadley Chase in *No Orchids for Miss Blandish* (1939), which is, no more nor less, a rewriting of Faulkner's novel in a brutal style.

With some highs and lows along the way the genre continues with some of the aforementioned authors, and with David Goodis, James M. Cain, William Blake, continuing on and arriving at Patricia Highsmith, James Ellroy, Walter Mosley, and Michael Connelly.

And, in the comic, at 100 BULLETS, which comes with two sample stories from the series in the present volume. One of these, "Chill in the Oven," takes place in the closed world of a jail where, following the principles of the *noir* genre, the police abuse their power with an asphyxiating violence and where there is a typical intervention of the now legendary Agent Graves who then proceeds to open the doors to the answers for the victims. The other, "In Stinked," situated in a zoo at night, with fierce beings both inside and outside of the cages, shows us that there is always something hidden behind the crime, and that there is always the same old resilient troika that has moved the history of mankind: money, sex, and power.

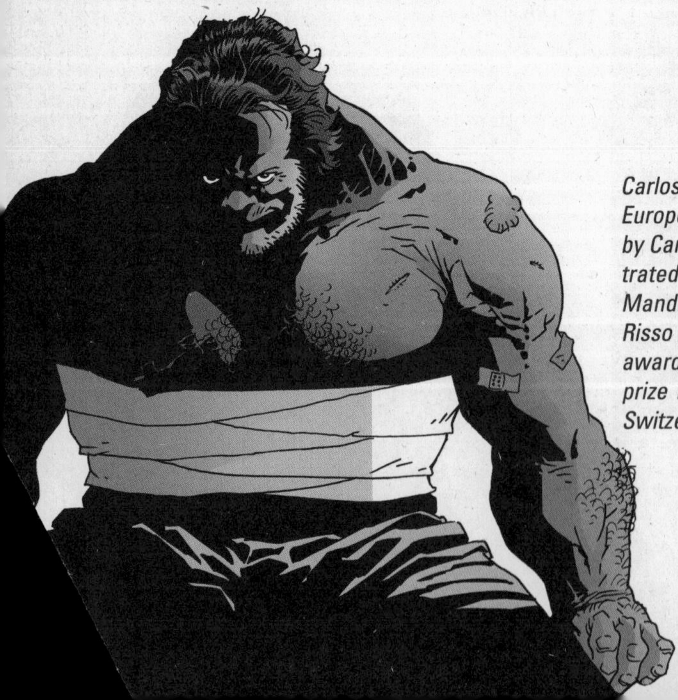

To these stories presented here, and to others in the 100 BULLETS series that we have read during the last few years, can be applied to perfection the thoughts of Raymond Chandler in his book *The Simple Art of Murder* (1950):

"The realist in murder writes of a world in which gangsters can rule nations and almost rule cities, in which hotels and apartment houses and celebrated restaurants are owned by rich men who made their money out of brothels, in which a screen star can be the finger man for a mob, and the nice man down the hall is a boss of the numbers racket; a world where a judge with a cellar full of bootleg liquor can send a man to jail for having a pint in his pocket, where the mayor of your town may have condoned murder as an instrument of money making, where no man can walk down a dark street in safety because law and order are things we talk about but refrain from practicing; a world where you may witness a hold-up in broad daylight and see who did it, but you will fade quickly back into the crowd rather than tell anyone, because the hold-up men may have friends with long guns, or the police may not like your testimony, and in any case the shyster for the defense will be allowed to abuse and vilify you in open court, before a jury of selected morons, without any but the most perfunctory interference from a political judge. It is not a very fragrant world, but it is the world you live in, and certain writers with tough minds and a cool spirit of detachment can make very interesting and even amusing patterns out of it. It is not funny that a man should be killed, but it is sometimes funny that he should be killed for so little, and that his death should be the coin of what we call civilization."

— Carlos Trillo
Buenos Aires
April, 2004

Carlos Trillo is a comics scriptwriter who works for the European market. He is the author of Cybersix, *illustrated by Carlos Meglia;* Clara de Noche *("Clara by Night"), illustrated by Jordi Bernet;* The Big Hoax, *illustrated by Mandrafina; and various collaborations with Eduardo Risso (*Fulú, Chicanos, Video Noir, Borderline*). He has been awarded the Yellow Kid prize in Lucca, Italy; the Alph Art prize in Angoulême, France; the Grand Prix d'Humour in Switzerland; and the Gaudi in Spain.*

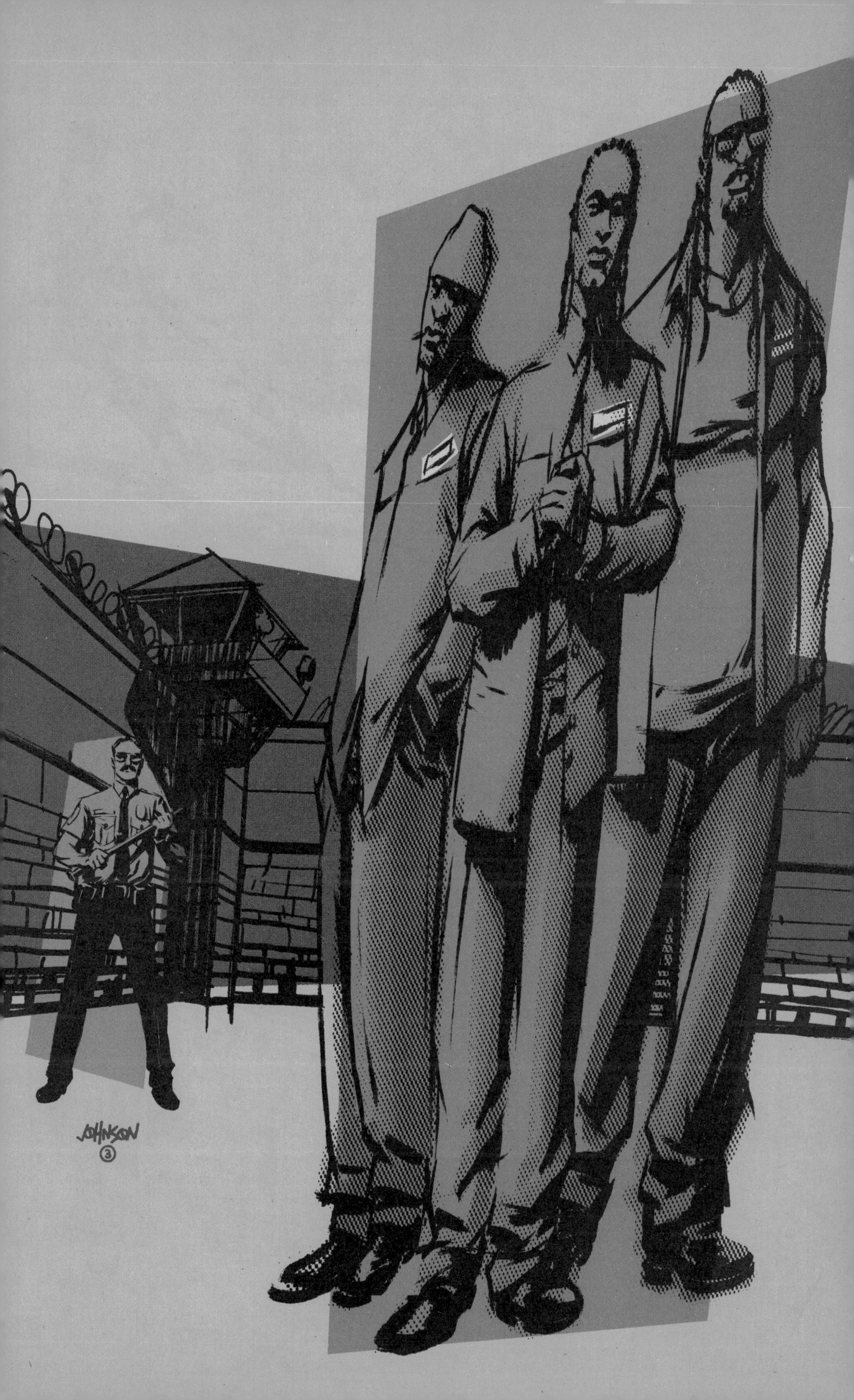
JOHNSON
3

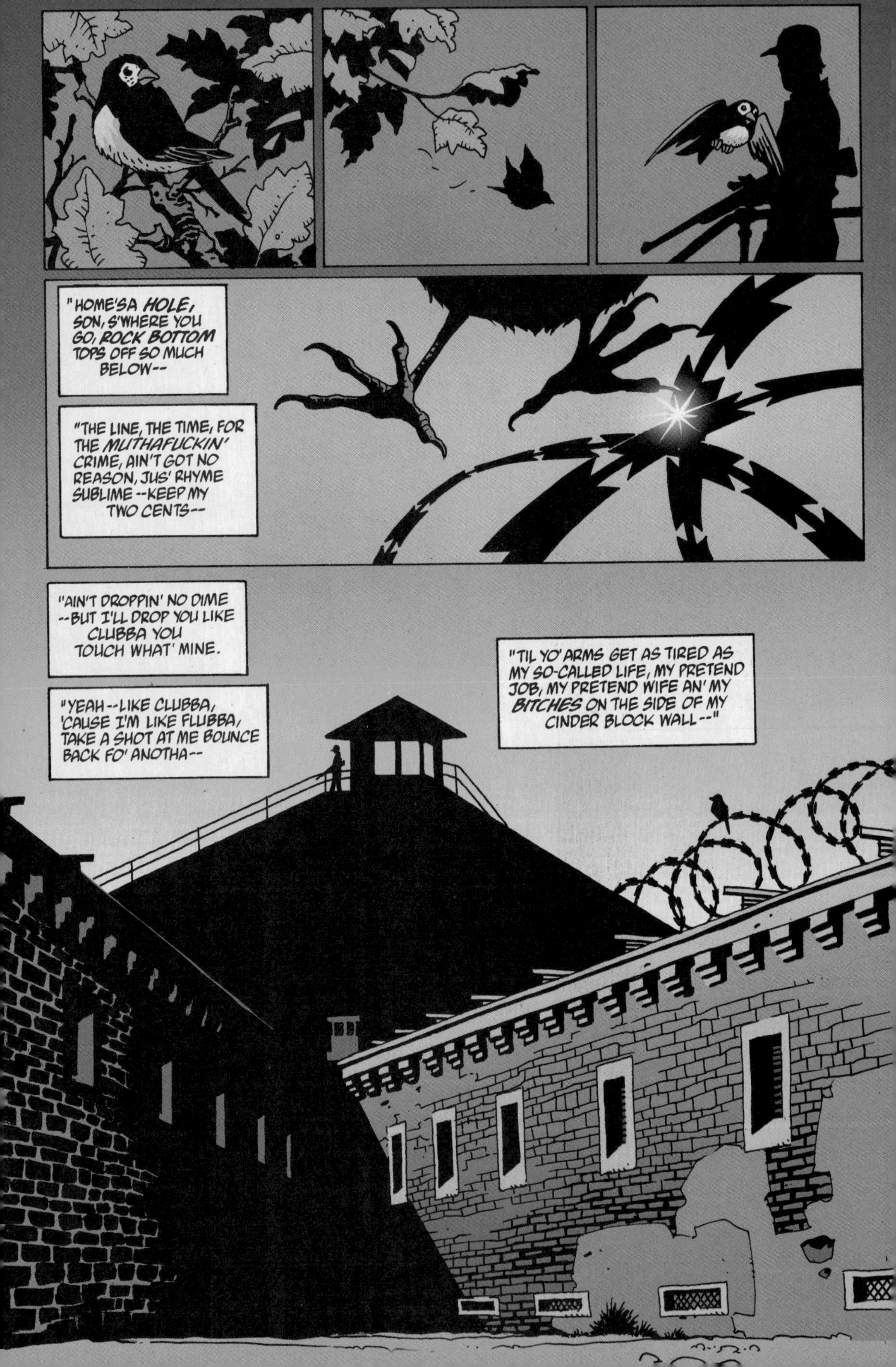
"HOME'SA HOLE, SON, S'WHERE YOU GO, ROCK BOTTOM TOPS OFF SO MUCH BELOW--
"THE LINE, THE TIME, FOR THE MUTHAFUCKIN' CRIME, AIN'T GOT NO REASON, JUS' RHYME SUBLIME --KEEP MY TWO CENTS--
"AIN'T DROPPIN' NO DIME --BUT I'LL DROP YOU LIKE CLUBBA YOU TOUCH WHAT' MINE.
"YEAH --LIKE CLUBBA, 'CAUSE I'M LIKE FLUBBA, TAKE A SHOT AT ME BOUNCE BACK FO' ANOTHA--
"TIL YO' ARMS GET AS TIRED AS MY SO-CALLED LIFE, MY PRETEND JOB, MY PRETEND WIFE AN' MY BITCHES ON THE SIDE OF MY CINDER BLOCK WALL--"

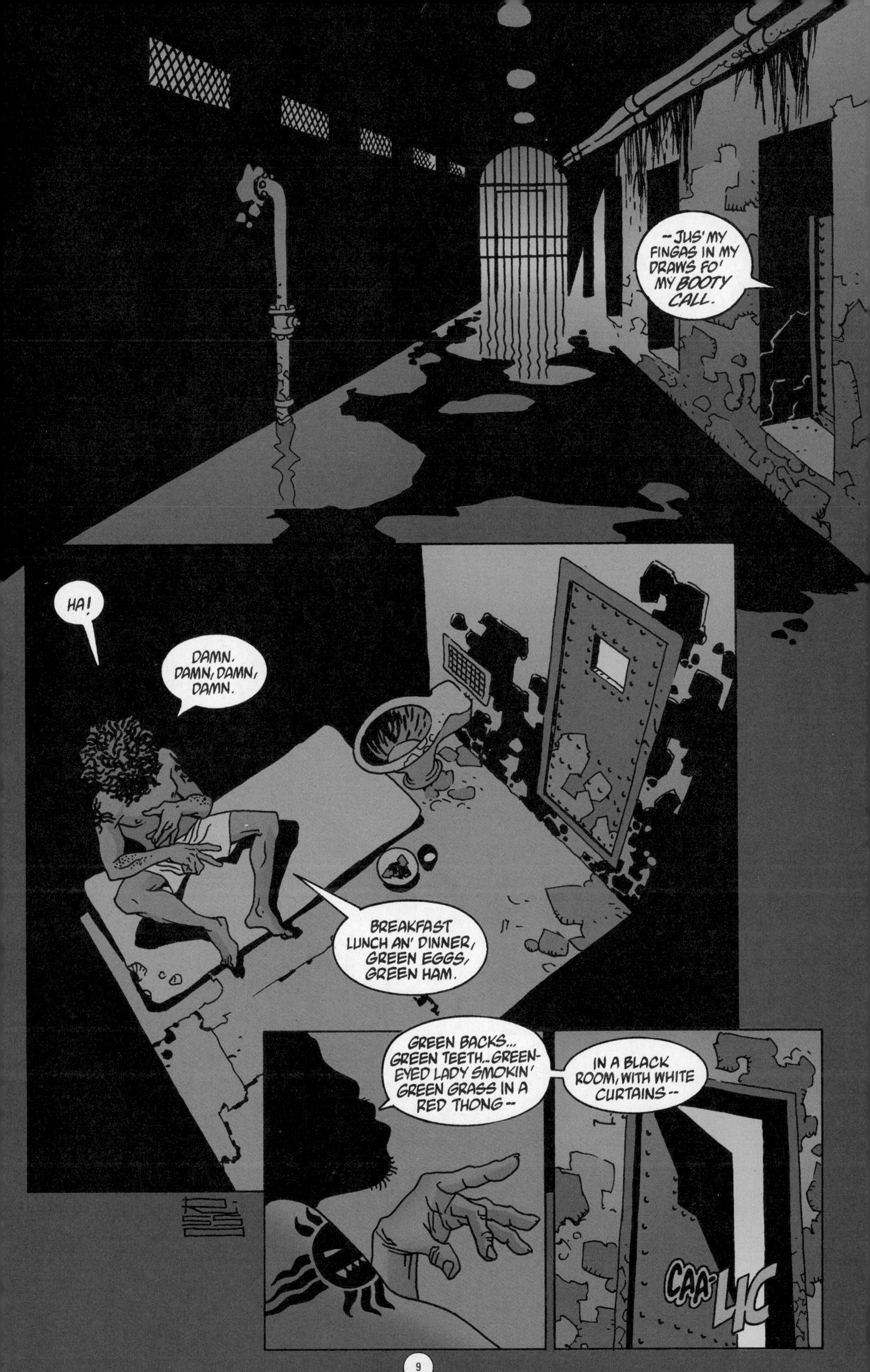
-- JUS' MY FINGAS IN MY DRAWS FO' MY BOOTY CALL.
HA!
DAMN. DAMN, DAMN, DAMN.
BREAKFAST LUNCH AN' DINNER, GREEN EGGS, GREEN HAM.
GREEN BACKS... GREEN TEETH... GREEN-EYED LADY SMOKIN' GREEN GRASS IN A RED THONG --
IN A BLACK ROOM, WITH WHITE CURTAINS --
CAA-LIC

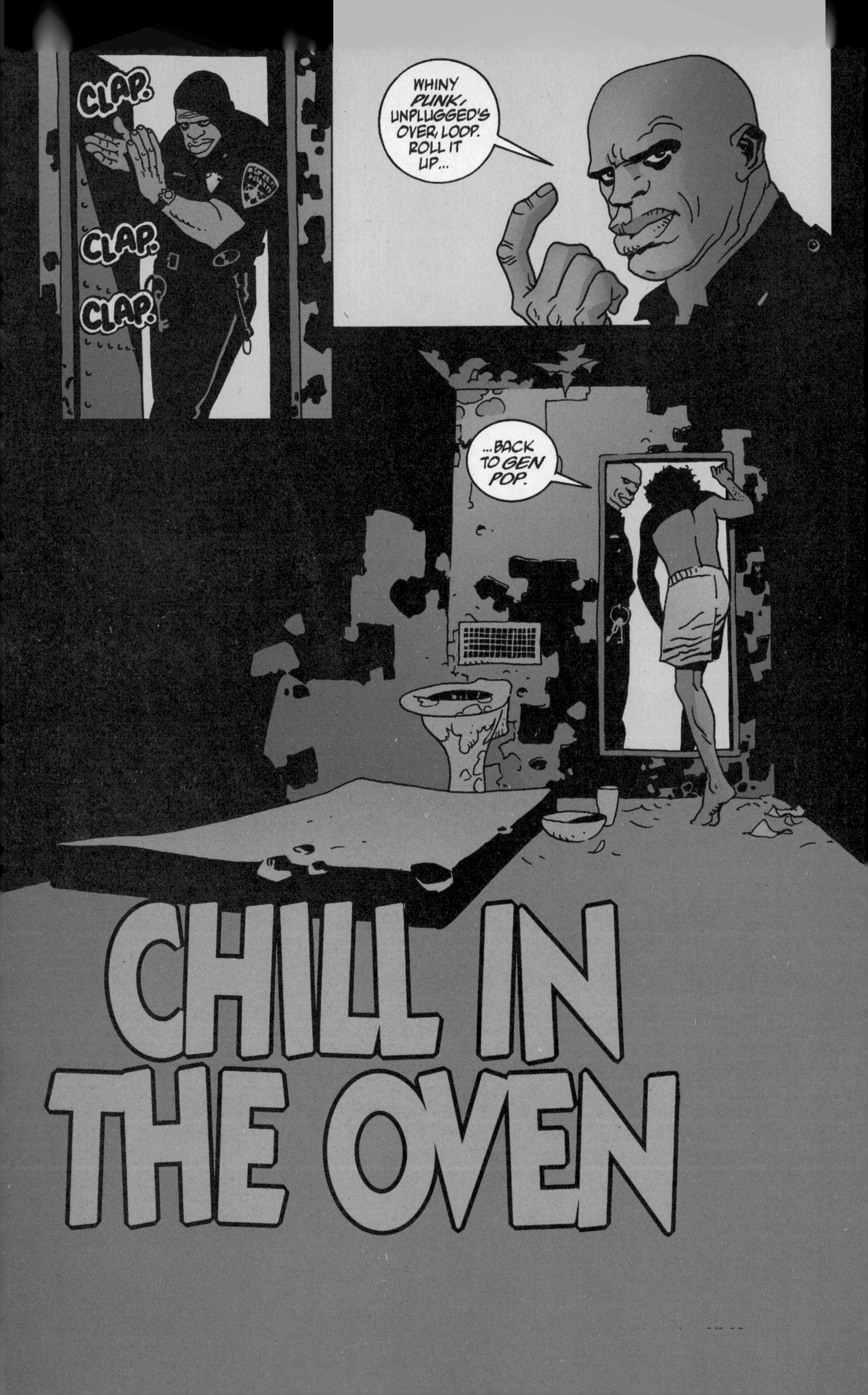
CLAP.
CLAP.
CLAP.
WHINY PUNK, UNPLUGGED'S OVER, LOOP. ROLL IT UP...
...BACK TO GEN POP.
CHILL IN THE OVEN

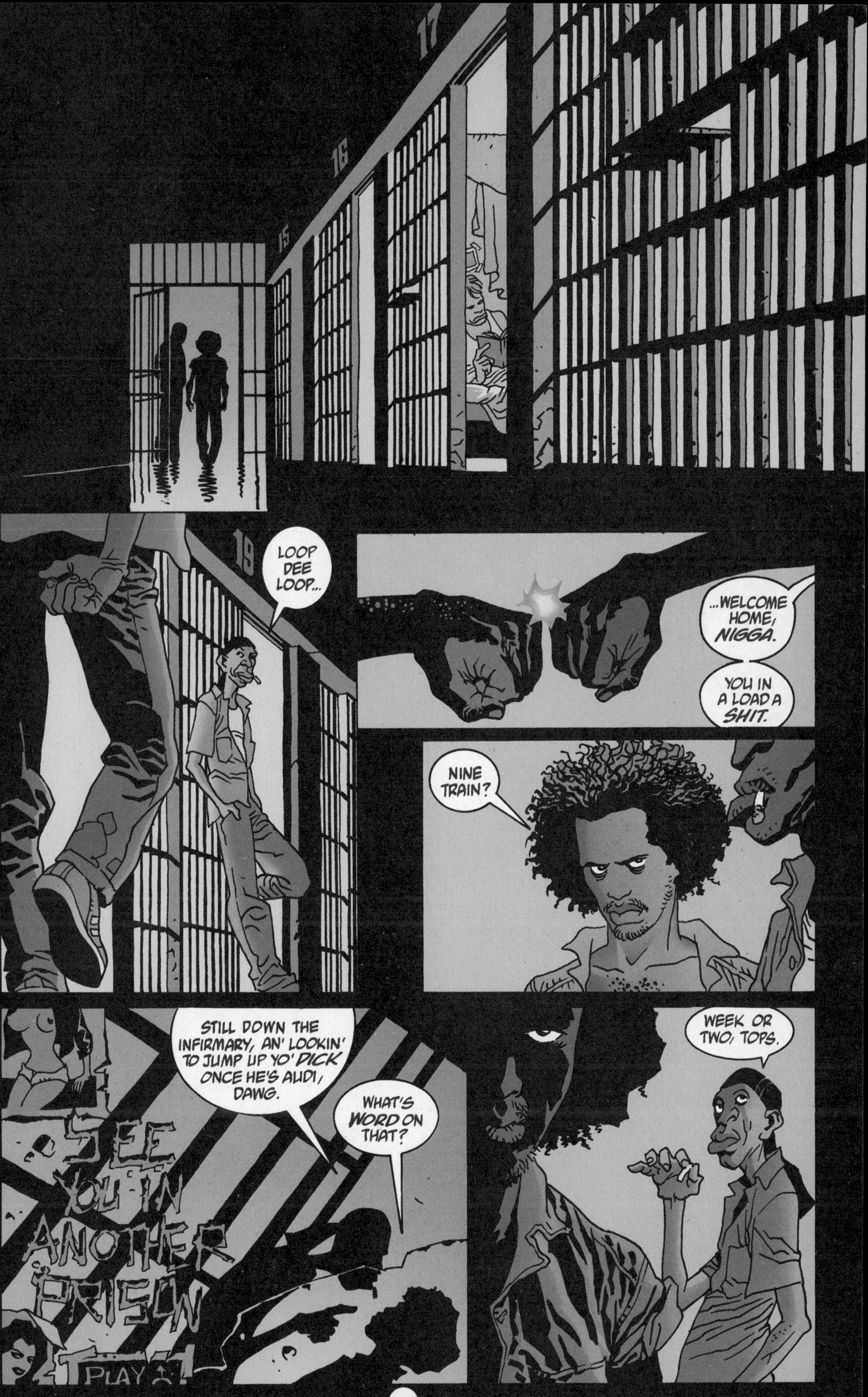
17
16
15
19
LOOP DEE LOOP...
...WELCOME HOME, NIGGA.
YOU IN A LOAD A SHIT.
NINE TRAIN?
STILL DOWN THE INFIRMARY, AN' LOOKIN' TO JUMP UP YO' DICK ONCE HE'S AUDI, DAWG.
WHAT'S WORD ON THAT?
WEEK OR TWO, TOPS.
SEE YOU IN ANOTHER PRISON
PLAY

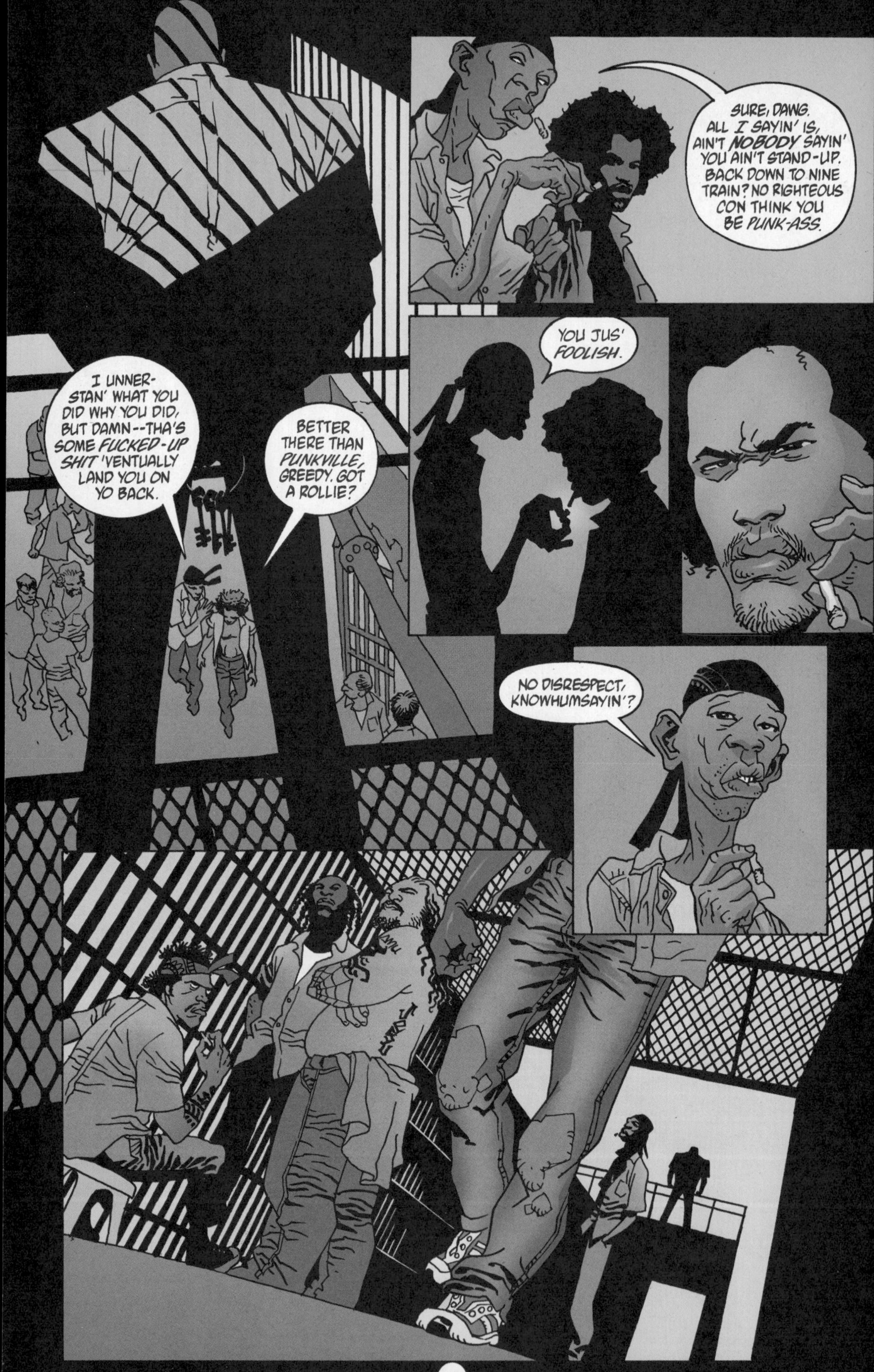
SURE, DAWG. ALL I SAYIN' IS, AIN'T NOBODY SAYIN' YOU AIN'T STAND-UP. BACK DOWN TO NINE TRAIN? NO RIGHTEOUS CON THINK YOU BE PUNK-ASS.
I UNNER-STAN' WHAT YOU DID WHY YOU DID, BUT DAMN--THA'S SOME FUCKED-UP SHIT 'VENTUALLY LAND YOU ON YO BACK.
BETTER THERE THAN PUNKVILLE, GREEDY. GOT A ROLLIE?
YOU JUS' FOOLISH.
NO DISRESPECT, KNOWHUMSAYIN'?

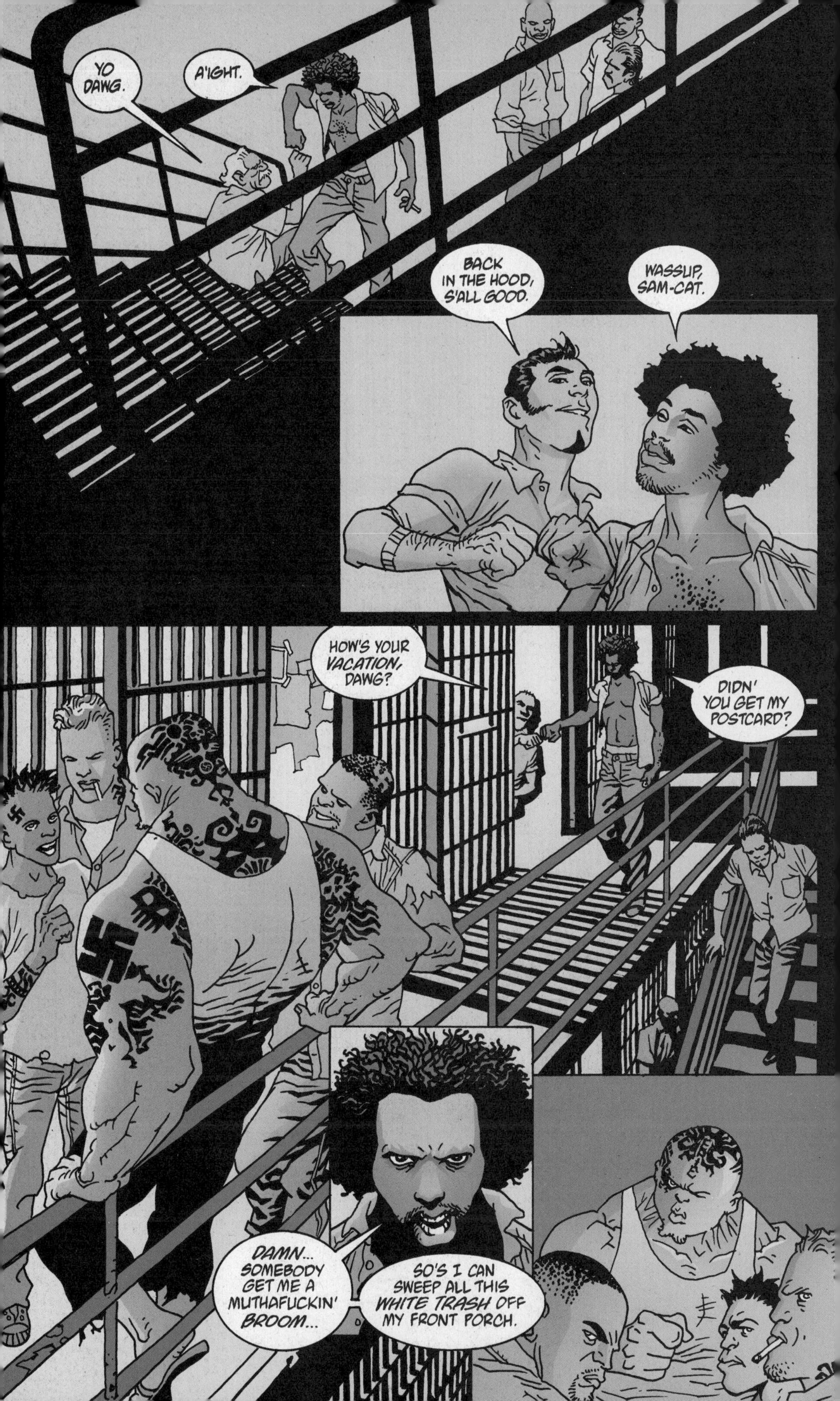
YO DAWG.
A'IGHT.
BACK IN THE HOOD, S'ALL GOOD.
WASSUP, SAM-CAT.
HOW'S YOUR VACATION, DAWG?
DIDN' YOU GET MY POSTCARD?
DAMN... SOMEBODY GET ME A MUTHAFUCKIN' BROOM...
SO'S I CAN SWEEP ALL THIS WHITE TRASH OFF MY FRONT PORCH.

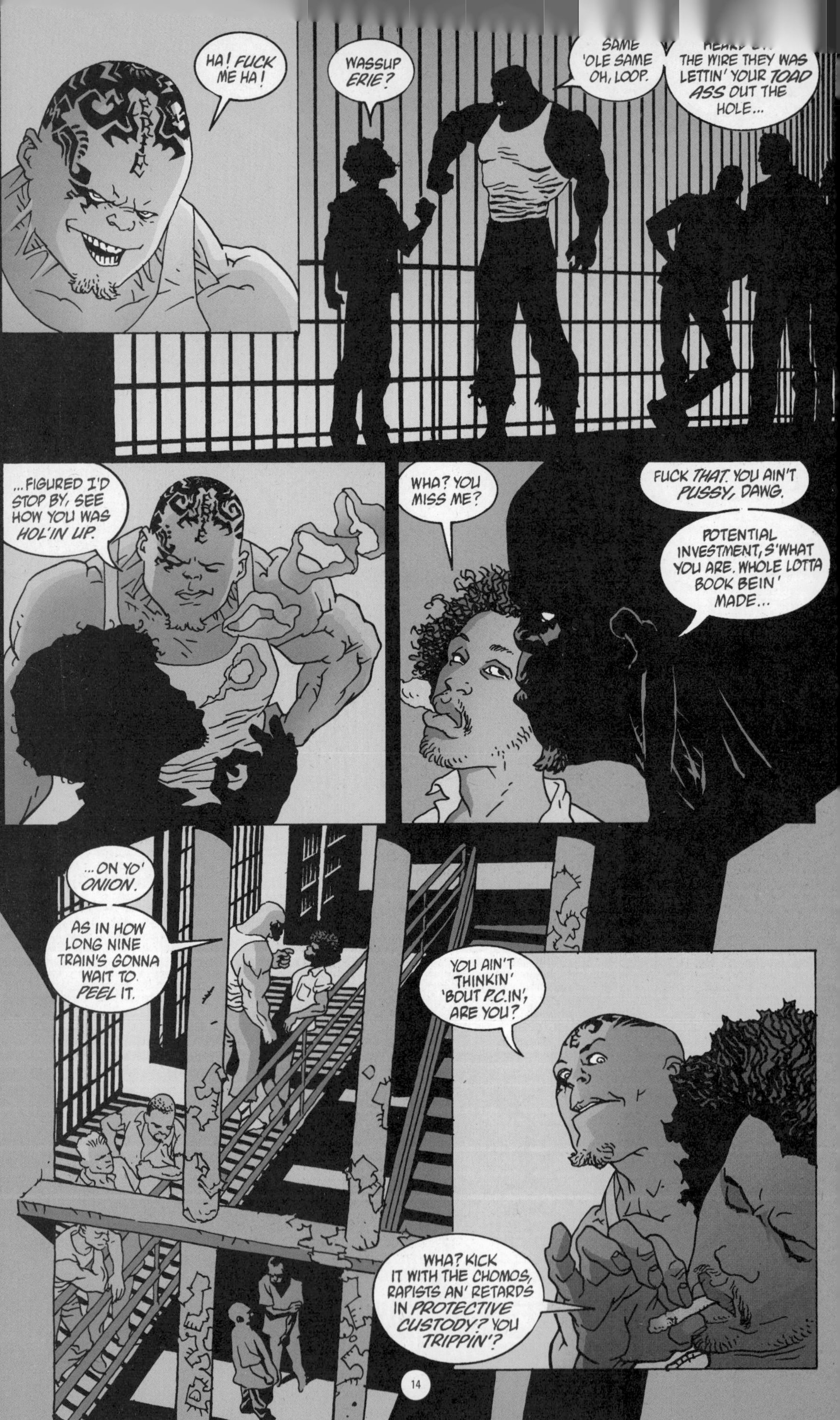
HA! FUCK ME HA!
WASSUP ERIE?
SAME 'OLE SAME OH, LOOP.
THE WIRE THEY WAS LETTIN' YOUR TOAD ASS OUT THE HOLE...
...FIGURED I'D STOP BY, SEE HOW YOU WAS HOL'IN UP.
WHA? YOU MISS ME?
FUCK THAT. YOU AIN'T PUSSY, DAWG.
POTENTIAL INVESTMENT, S'WHAT YOU ARE. WHOLE LOTTA BOOK BEIN' MADE...
...ON YO' ONION.
AS IN HOW LONG NINE TRAIN'S GONNA WAIT TO PEEL IT.
YOU AIN'T THINKIN' 'BOUT P.C.IN', ARE YOU?
WHA? KICK IT WITH THE CHOMOS, RAPISTS AN' RETARDS IN PROTECTIVE CUSTODY? YOU TRIPPIN'?

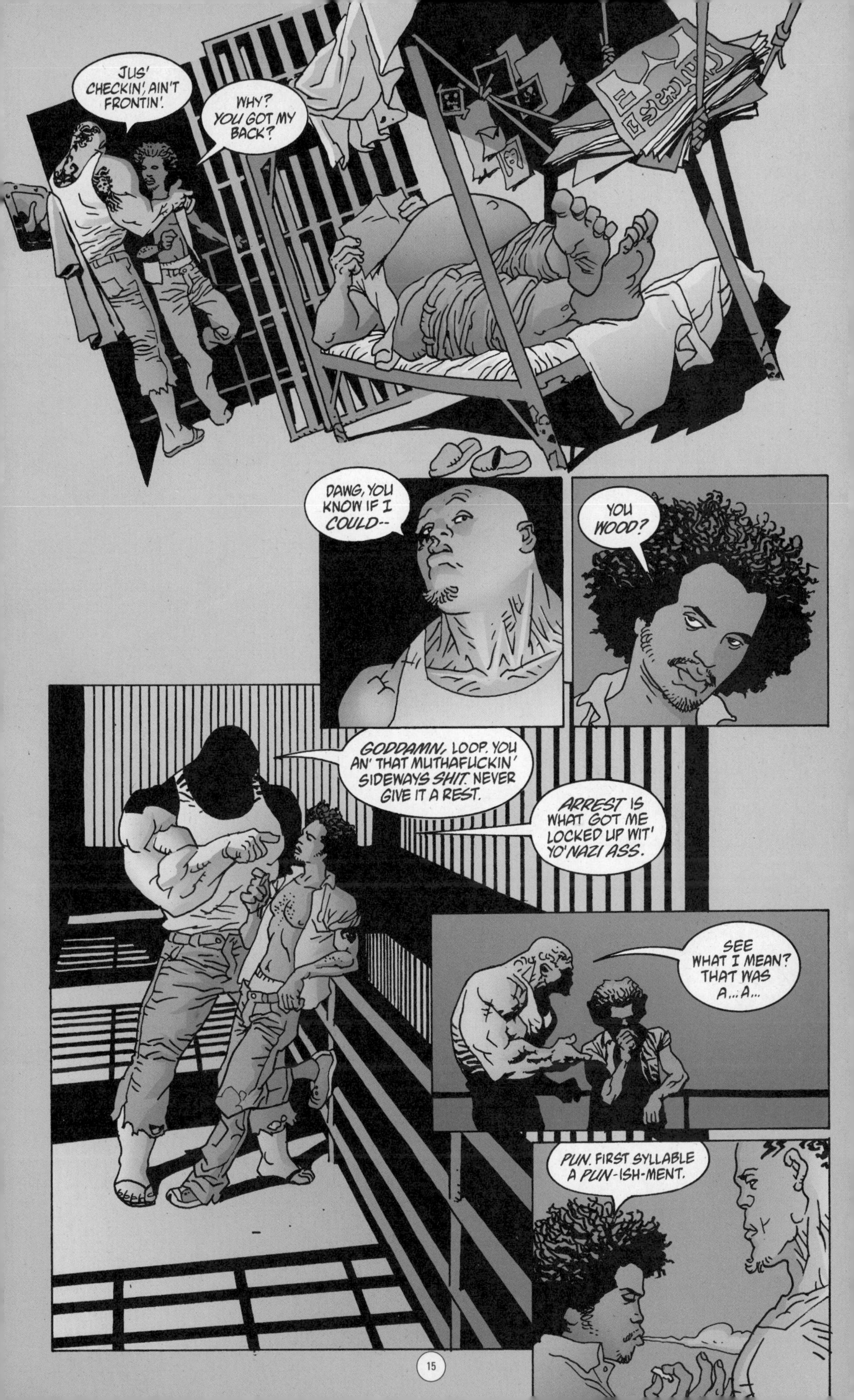
JUS' CHECKIN', AIN'T FRONTIN'.
WHY? YOU GOT MY BACK?
DAWG, YOU KNOW IF I COULD--
YOU WOOD?
GODDAMN, LOOP. YOU AN' THAT MUTHAFUCKIN' SIDEWAYS SHIT. NEVER GIVE IT A REST.
ARREST IS WHAT GOT ME LOCKED UP WIT' YO' NAZI ASS.
SEE WHAT I MEAN? THAT WAS A...A...
PUN. FIRST SYLLABLE A PUN-ISH-MENT.

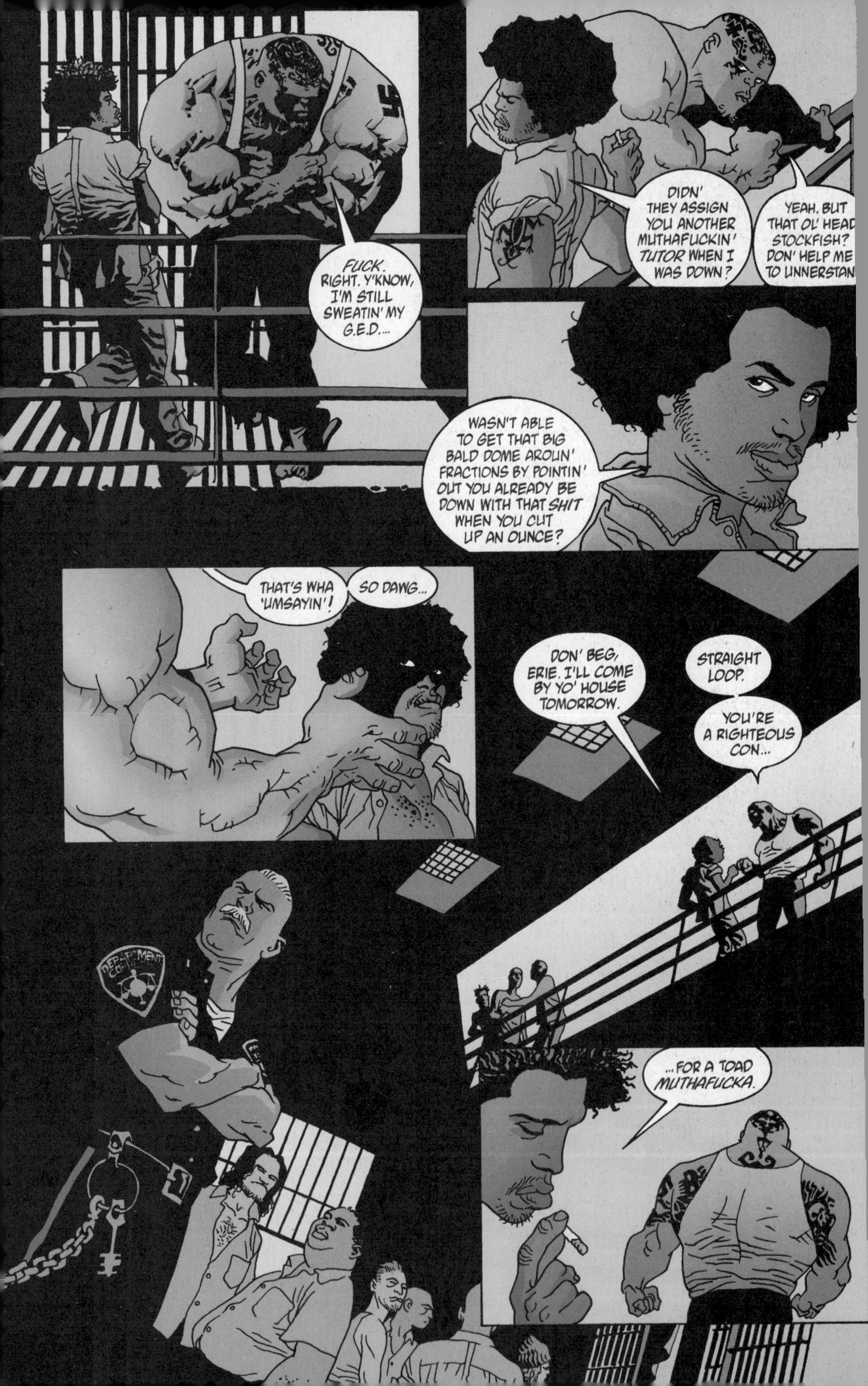
FUCK. RIGHT. Y'KNOW, I'M STILL SWEATIN' MY G.E.D....
DIDN' THEY ASSIGN YOU ANOTHER MUTHAFUCKIN' TUTOR WHEN I WAS DOWN?
YEAH, BUT THAT OL' HEAD STOCKFISH? DON' HELP ME TO UNNERSTAN
WASN'T ABLE TO GET THAT BIG BALD DOME AROUN' FRACTIONS BY POINTIN' OUT YOU ALREADY BE DOWN WITH THAT SHIT WHEN YOU CUT UP AN OUNCE?
THAT'S WHA 'UMSAYIN'!
SO DAWG...
DON' BEG, ERIE. I'LL COME BY YO' HOUSE TOMORROW.
STRAIGHT LOOP.
YOU'RE A RIGHTEOUS CON...
...FOR A TOAD MUTHAFUCKA.

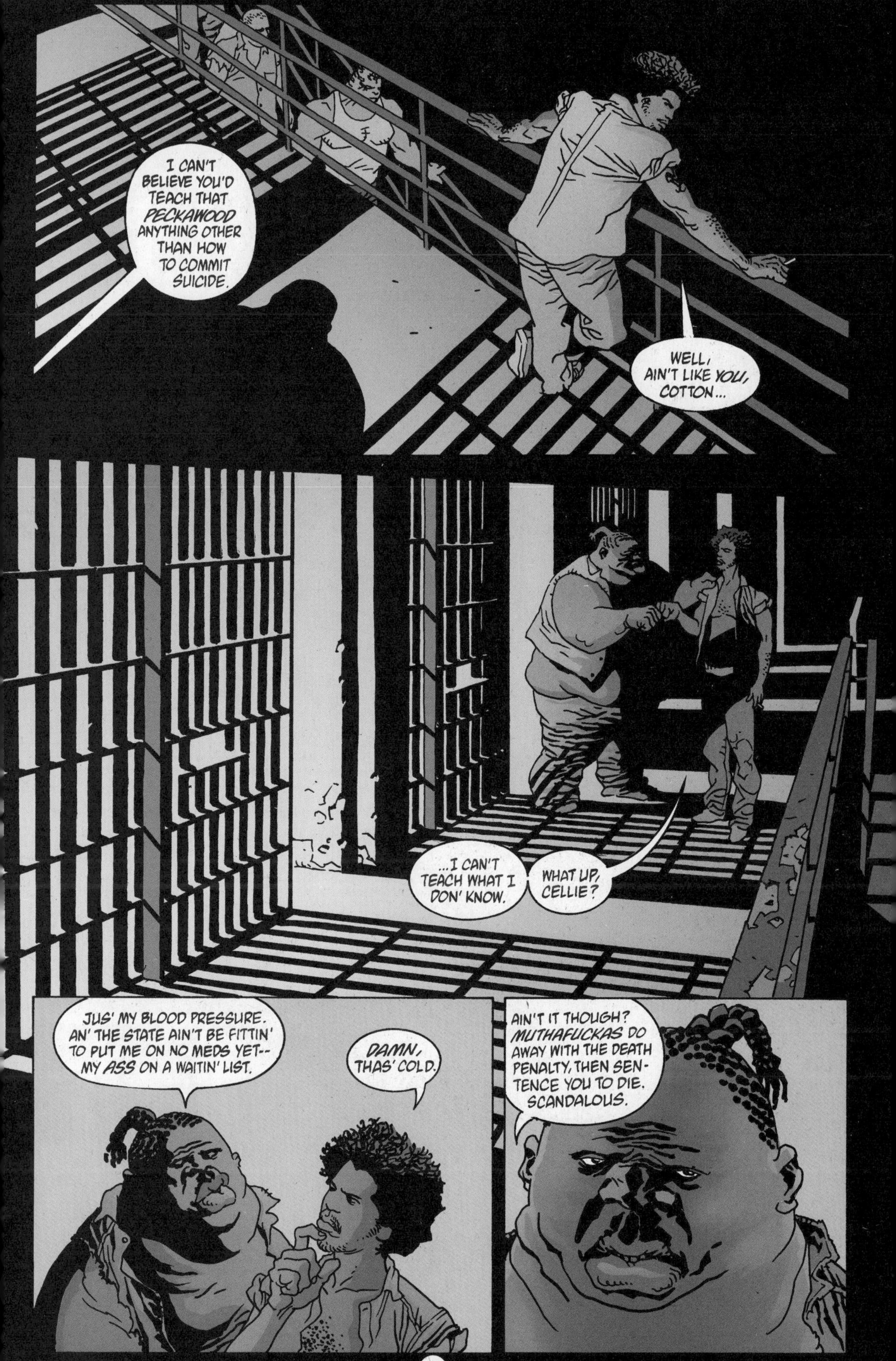

I CAN'T BELIEVE YOU'D TEACH THAT PECKAWOOD ANYTHING OTHER THAN HOW TO COMMIT SUICIDE.
WELL, AIN'T LIKE YOU, COTTON...
...I CAN'T TEACH WHAT I DON' KNOW.
WHAT UP, CELLIE?
JUS' MY BLOOD PRESSURE. AN' THE STATE AIN'T BE FITTIN' TO PUT ME ON NO MEDS YET-- MY ASS ON A WAITIN' LIST.
DAMN, THAS' COLD.
AIN'T IT THOUGH? MUTHAFUCKAS DO AWAY WITH THE DEATH PENALTY, THEN SENTENCE YOU TO DIE. SCANDALOUS.

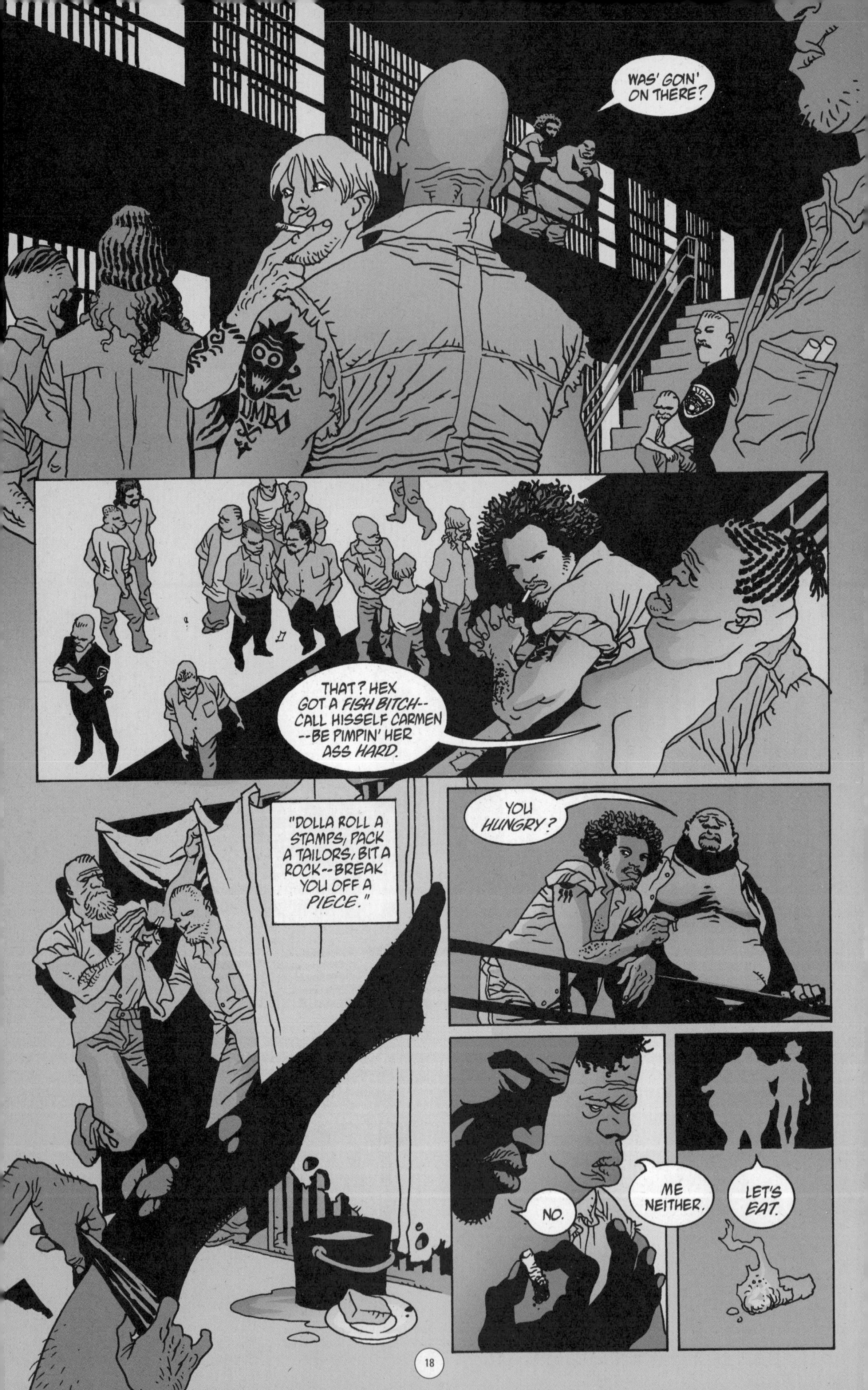
WAS' GOIN' ON THERE?
THAT? HEX GOT A FISH BITCH-- CALL HISSELF CARMEN --BE PIMPIN' HER ASS HARD.
"DOLLA ROLL A STAMPS, PACK A TAILORS, BIT A ROCK--BREAK YOU OFF A PIECE."
YOU HUNGRY?
NO.
ME NEITHER.
LET'S EAT.

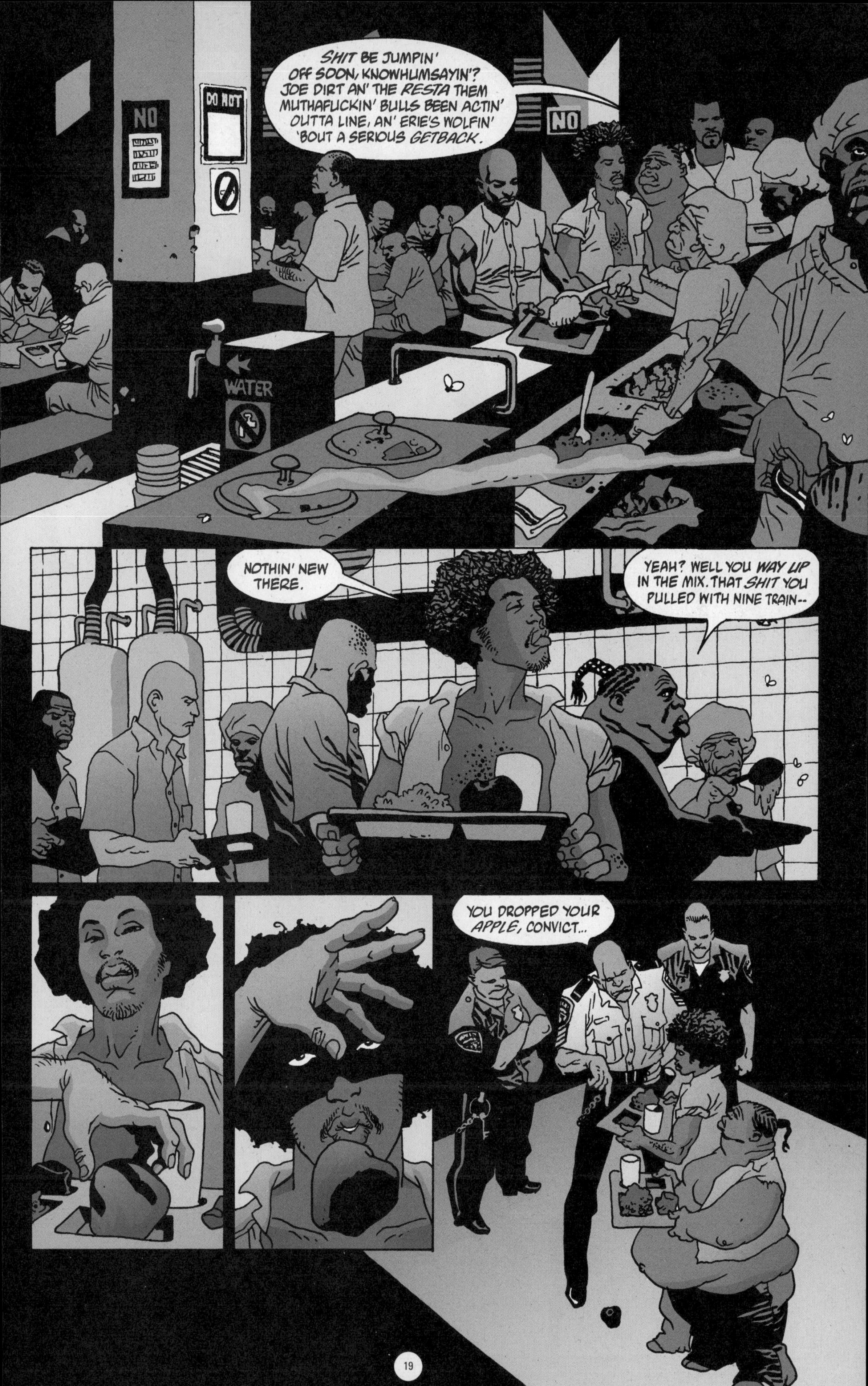

NO
DO NOT
SHIT BE JUMPIN' OFF SOON, KNOWHUMSAYIN'? JOE DIRT AN' THE RESTA THEM MUTHAFUCKIN' BULLS BEEN ACTIN' OUTTA LINE, AN' ERIE'S WOLFIN' 'BOUT A SERIOUS GETBACK.
NO
WATER
NOTHIN' NEW THERE.
YEAH? WELL YOU WAY UP IN THE MIX. THAT SHIT YOU PULLED WITH NINE TRAIN--
YOU DROPPED YOUR APPLE, CONVICT...

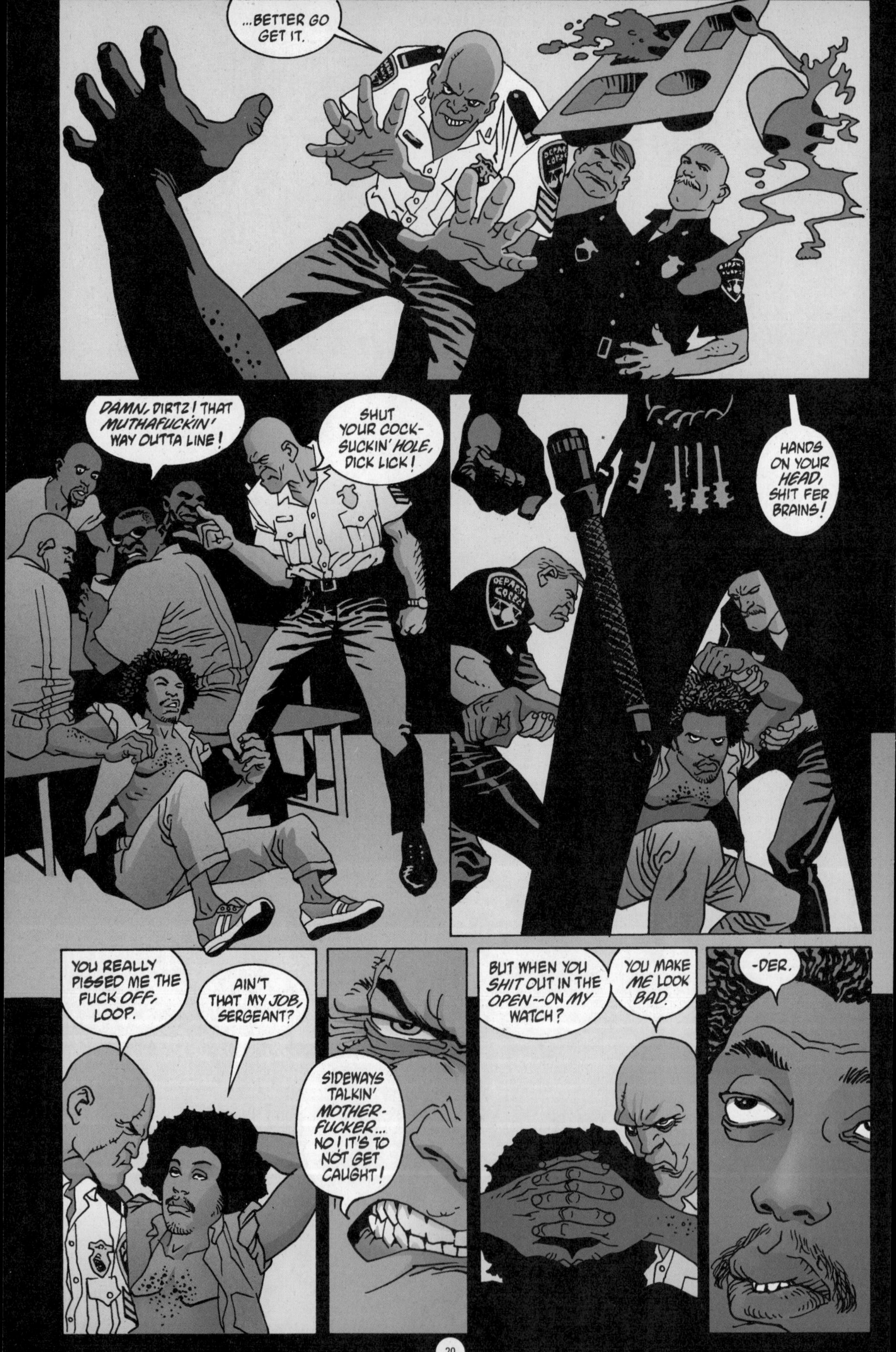
...BETTER GO GET IT.
DAMN, DIRTZ! THAT MUTHAFUCKIN' WAY OUTTA LINE!
SHUT YOUR COCK-SUCKIN' HOLE, DICK LICK!
HANDS ON YOUR HEAD, SHIT FER BRAINS!
YOU REALLY PISSED ME THE FUCK OFF, LOOP.
AIN'T THAT MY JOB, SERGEANT?
SIDEWAYS TALKIN' MOTHER-FUCKER... NO! IT'S TO NOT GET CAUGHT!
BUT WHEN YOU SHIT OUT IN THE OPEN--ON MY WATCH?
YOU MAKE ME LOOK BAD.
-DER.

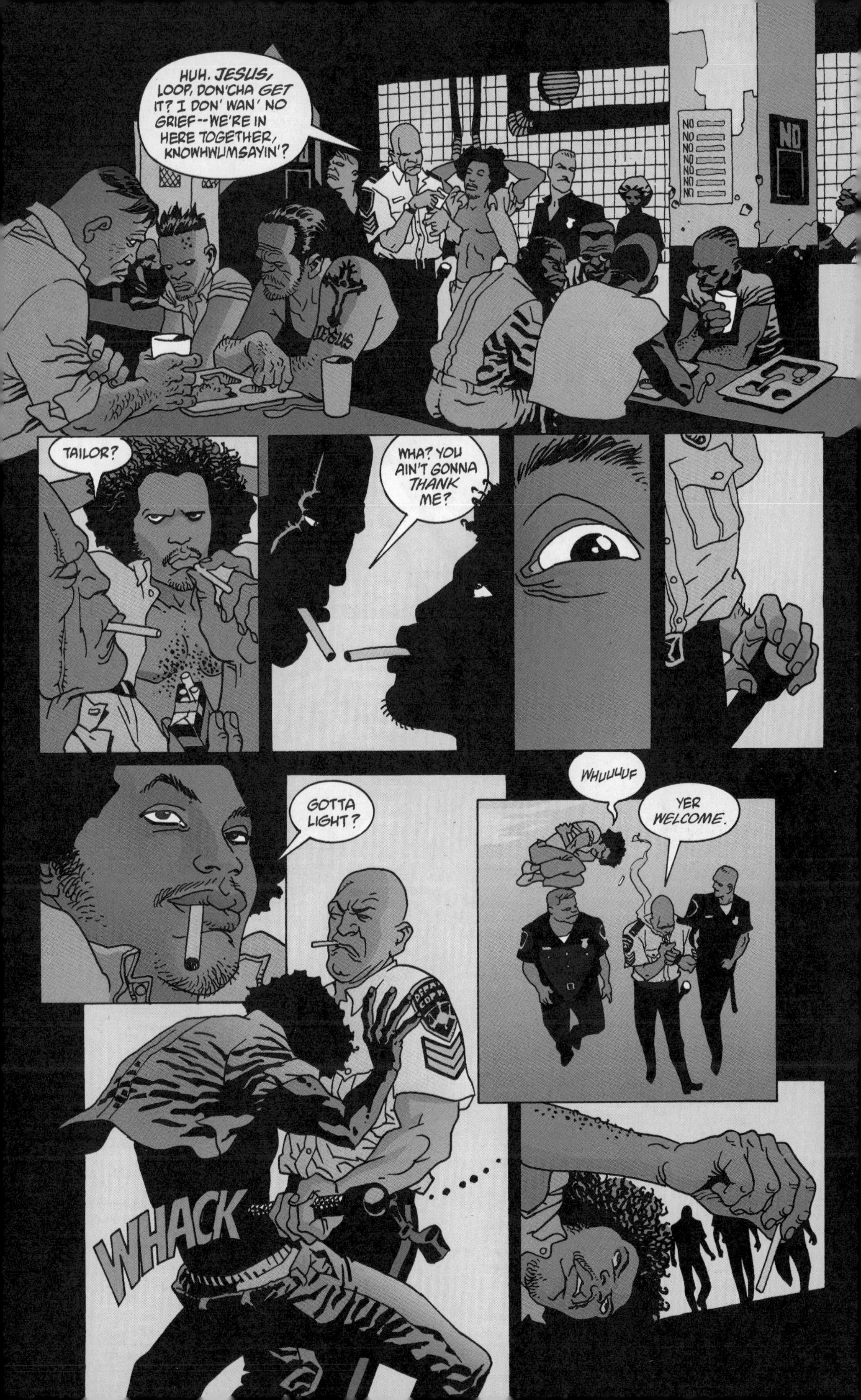
HUH. JESUS, LOOP, DON'CHA GET IT? I DON' WAN' NO GRIEF--WE'RE IN HERE TOGETHER, KNOWHWUMSAYIN'?
NO
TAILOR?
WHA? YOU AIN'T GONNA THANK ME?
GOTTA LIGHT?
WHUUUUF
YER WELCOME.
WHACK

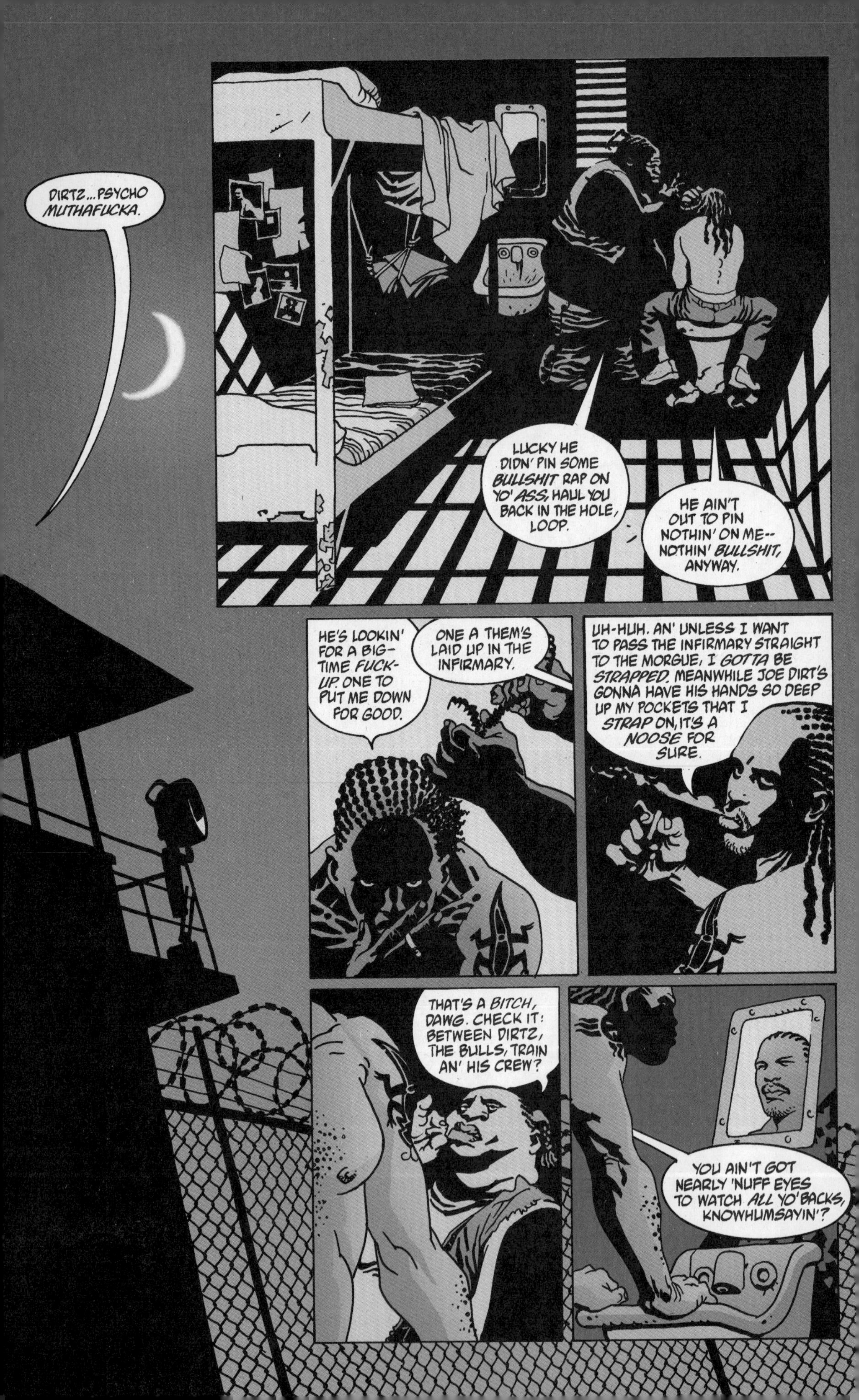
DIRTZ...PSYCHO MUTHAFUCKA.
LUCKY HE DIDN' PIN SOME BULLSHIT RAP ON YO' ASS, HAUL YOU BACK IN THE HOLE, LOOP.
HE AIN'T OUT TO PIN NOTHIN' ON ME-- NOTHIN' BULLSHIT, ANYWAY.
HE'S LOOKIN' FOR A BIG-TIME FUCK-UP. ONE TO PUT ME DOWN FOR GOOD.
ONE A THEM'S LAID UP IN THE INFIRMARY.
UH-HUH. AN' UNLESS I WANT TO PASS THE INFIRMARY STRAIGHT TO THE MORGUE, I GOTTA BE STRAPPED. MEANWHILE JOE DIRT'S GONNA HAVE HIS HANDS SO DEEP UP MY POCKETS THAT I STRAP ON, IT'S A NOOSE FOR SURE.
THAT'S A BITCH, DAWG. CHECK IT: BETWEEN DIRTZ, THE BULLS, TRAIN AN' HIS CREW?
YOU AIN'T GOT NEARLY 'NUFF EYES TO WATCH ALL YO' BACKS, KNOWHUMSAYIN'?

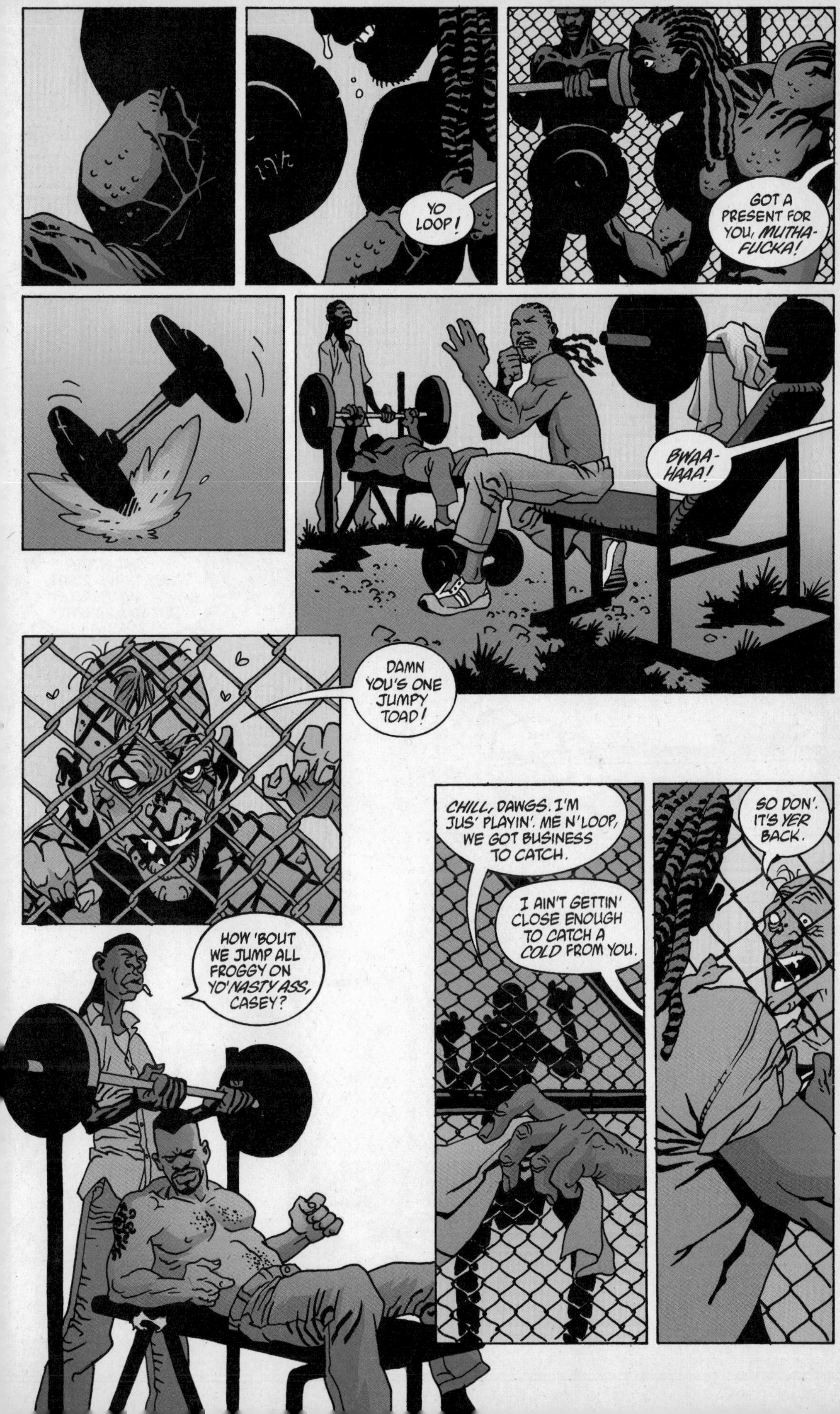
YO LOOP!
GOT A PRESENT FOR YOU, MUTHA-FUCKA!
BWAA-HAAA!
DAMN YOU'S ONE JUMPY TOAD!
HOW 'BOUT WE JUMP ALL FROGGY ON YO' NASTY ASS, CASEY?
CHILL, DAWGS. I'M JUS' PLAYIN'. ME N' LOOP, WE GOT BUSINESS TO CATCH.
I AIN'T GETTIN' CLOSE ENOUGH TO CATCH A COLD FROM YOU.
SO DON'. IT'S YER BACK.

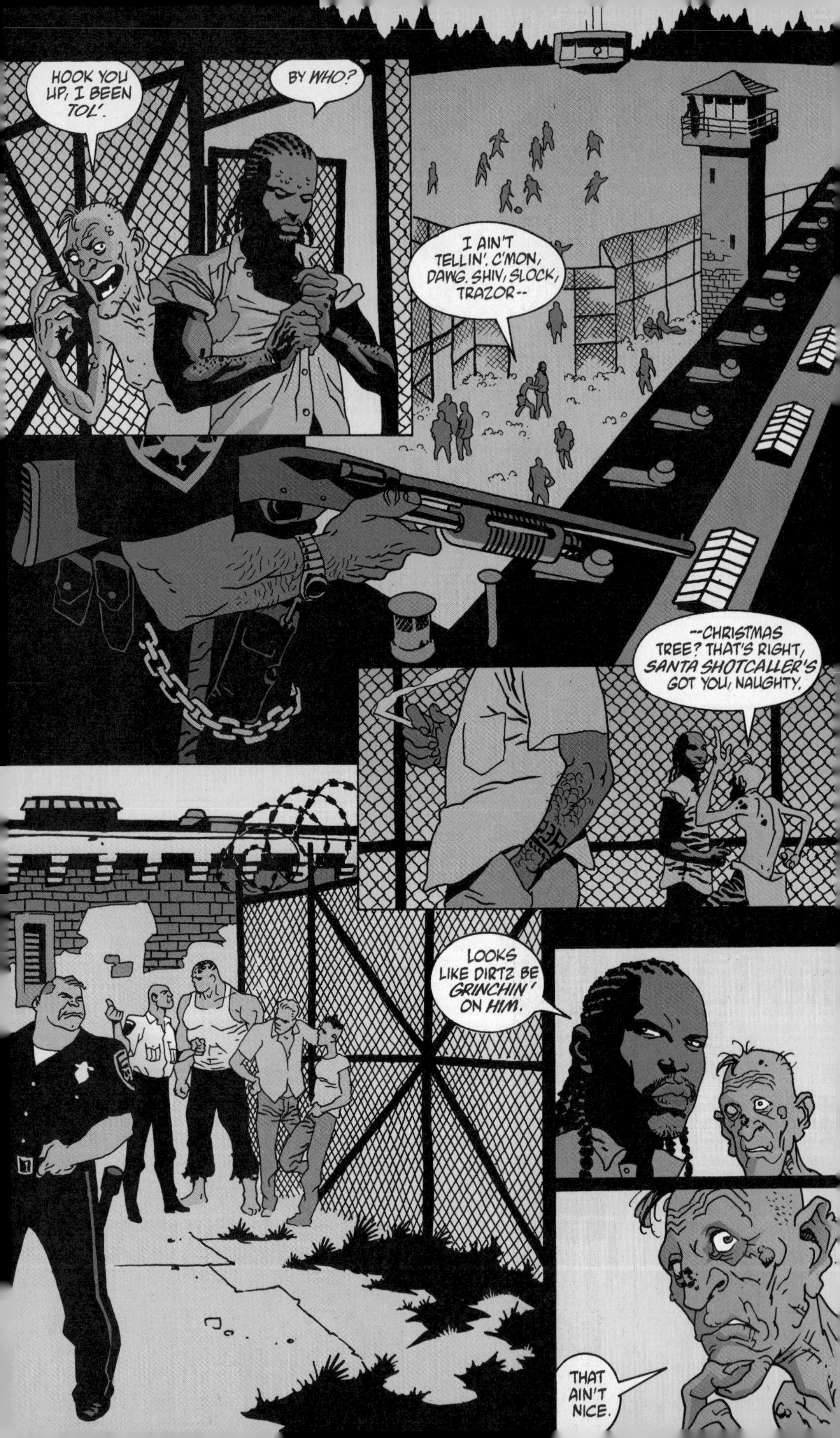
HOOK YOU UP, I BEEN TOL'.
BY WHO?
I AIN'T TELLIN'. C'MON, DAWG. SHIV, SLOCK, TRAZOR--
--CHRISTMAS TREE? THAT'S RIGHT, SANTA SHOTCALLER'S GOT YOU, NAUGHTY.
LOOKS LIKE DIRTZ BE GRINCHIN' ON HIM.
THAT AIN'T NICE.

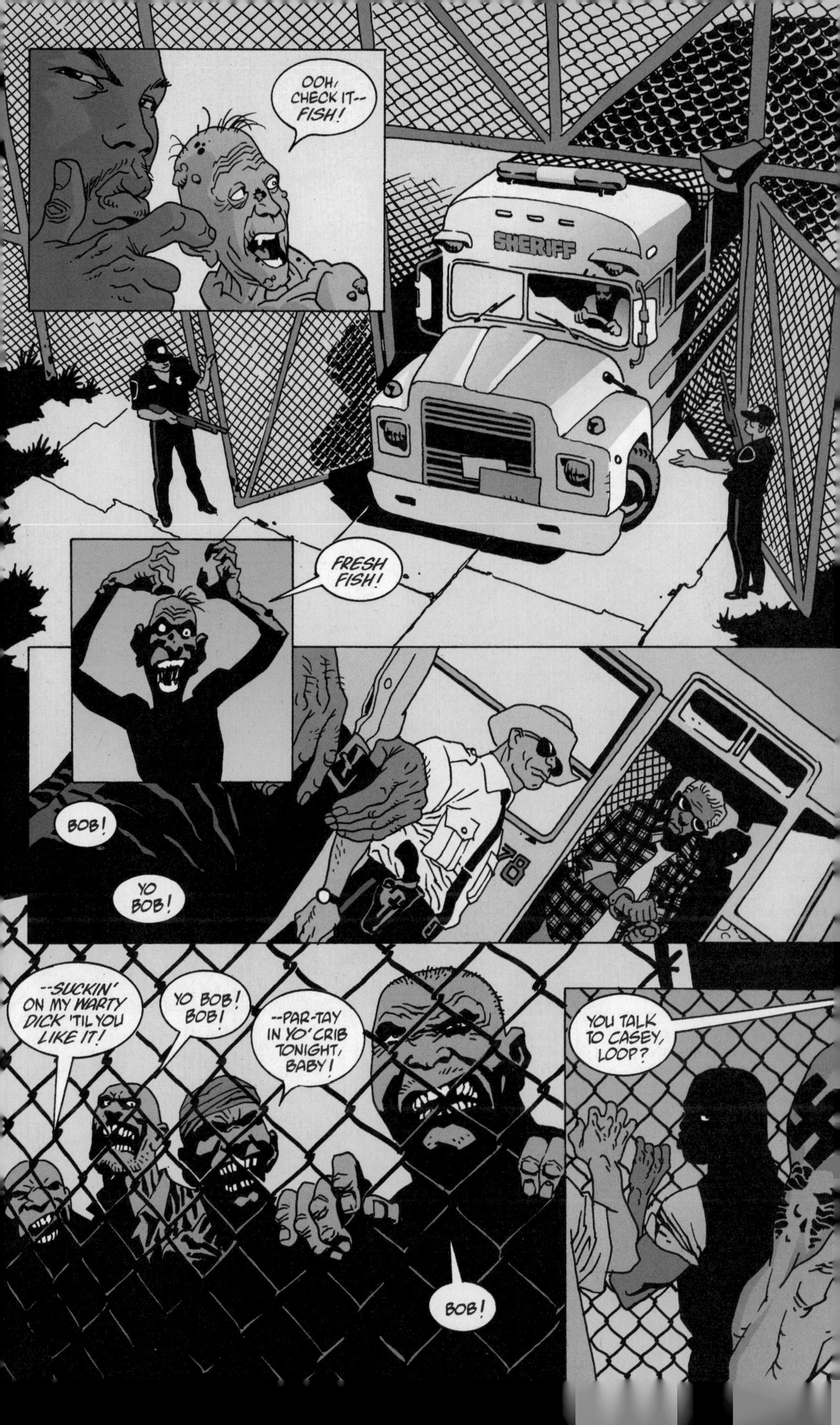
OOH, CHECK IT-- FISH!
FRESH FISH!
BOB!
YO BOB!
--SUCKIN' ON MY WARTY DICK 'TIL YOU LIKE IT!
YO BOB! BOB!
--PAR-TAY IN YO' CRIB TONIGHT, BABY!
BOB!
YOU TALK TO CASEY, LOOP?
SHERIFF

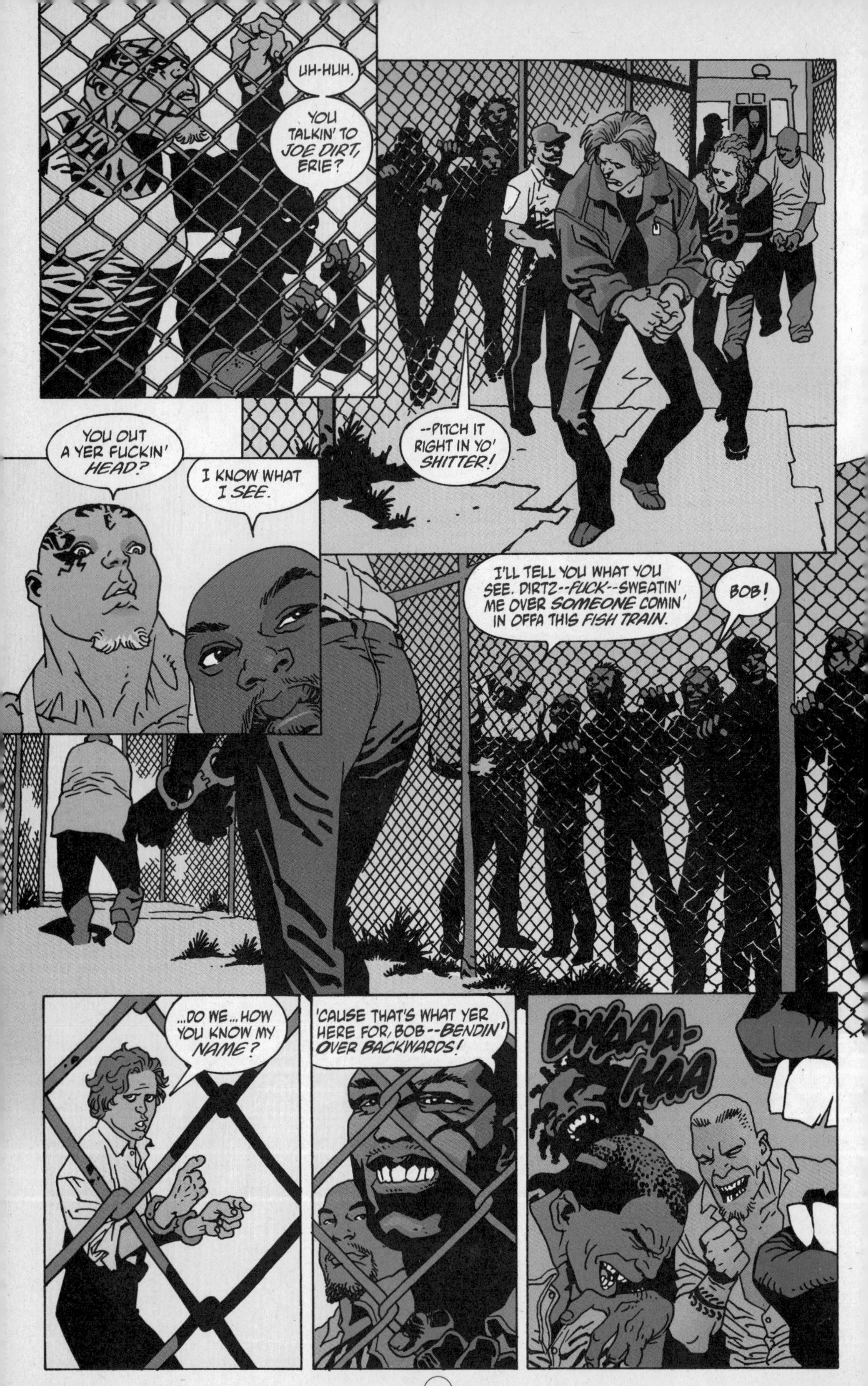
UH-HUH.
YOU TALKIN' TO JOE DIRT, ERIE?
YOU OUT A YER FUCKIN' HEAD?
I KNOW WHAT I SEE.
--PITCH IT RIGHT IN YO' SHITTER!
I'LL TELL YOU WHAT YOU SEE. DIRTZ--FUCK--SWEATIN' ME OVER SOMEONE COMIN' IN OFFA THIS FISH TRAIN.
BOB!
...DO WE... HOW YOU KNOW MY NAME?
'CAUSE THAT'S WHAT YER HERE FOR, BOB--BENDIN' OVER BACKWARDS!
BWAAA-HAA

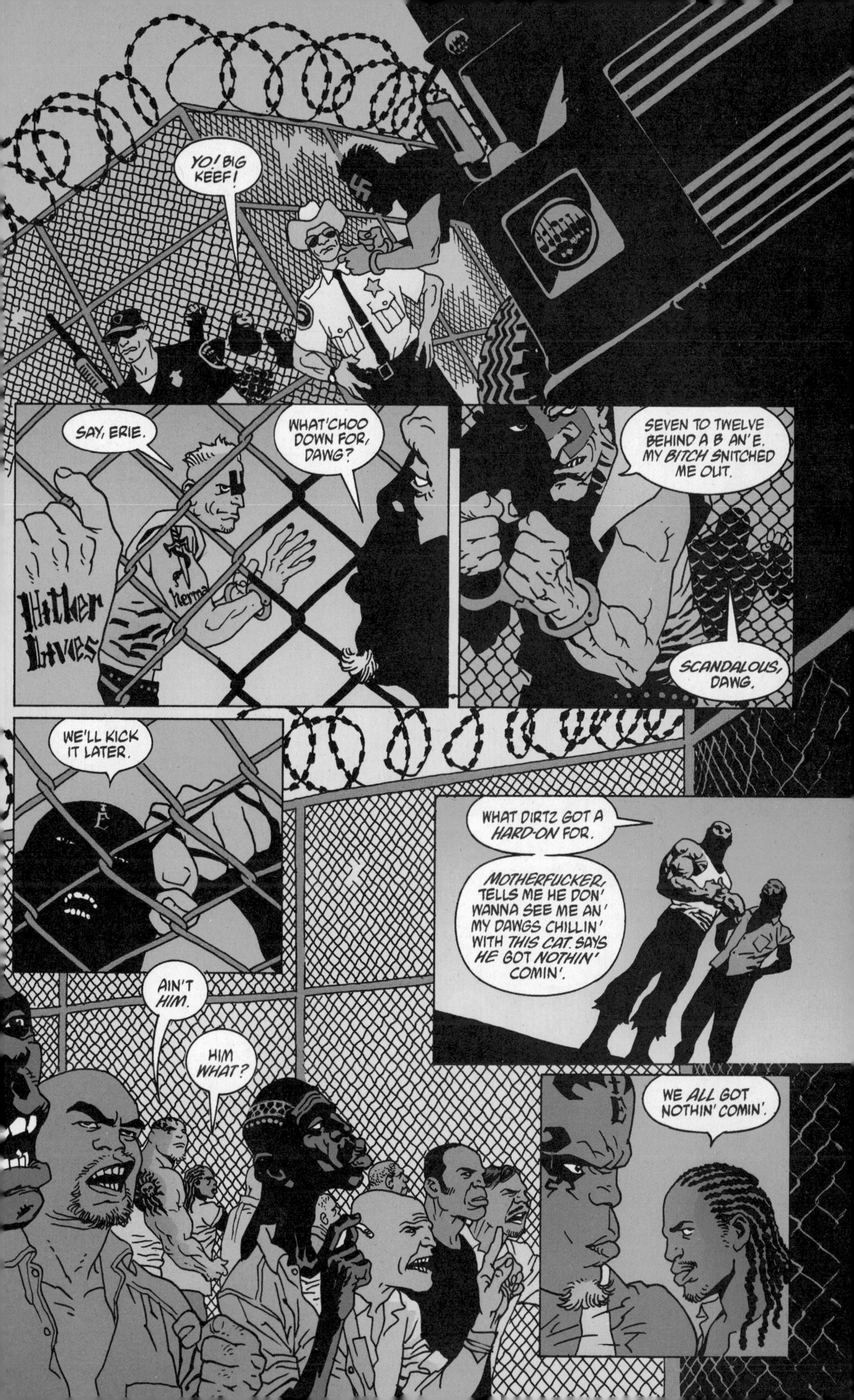
YO! BIG KEEF!
SAY, ERIE.
WHAT'CHOO DOWN FOR, DAWG?
Hitler Lives
SEVEN TO TWELVE BEHIND A B AN' E. MY BITCH SNITCHED ME OUT.
SCANDALOUS, DAWG.
WE'LL KICK IT LATER.
WHAT DIRTZ GOT A HARD-ON FOR.
MOTHERFUCKER, TELLS ME HE DON' WANNA SEE ME AN' MY DAWGS CHILLIN' WITH THIS CAT. SAYS HE GOT NOTHIN' COMIN'.
AIN'T HIM.
HIM WHAT?
WE ALL GOT NOTHIN' COMIN'.

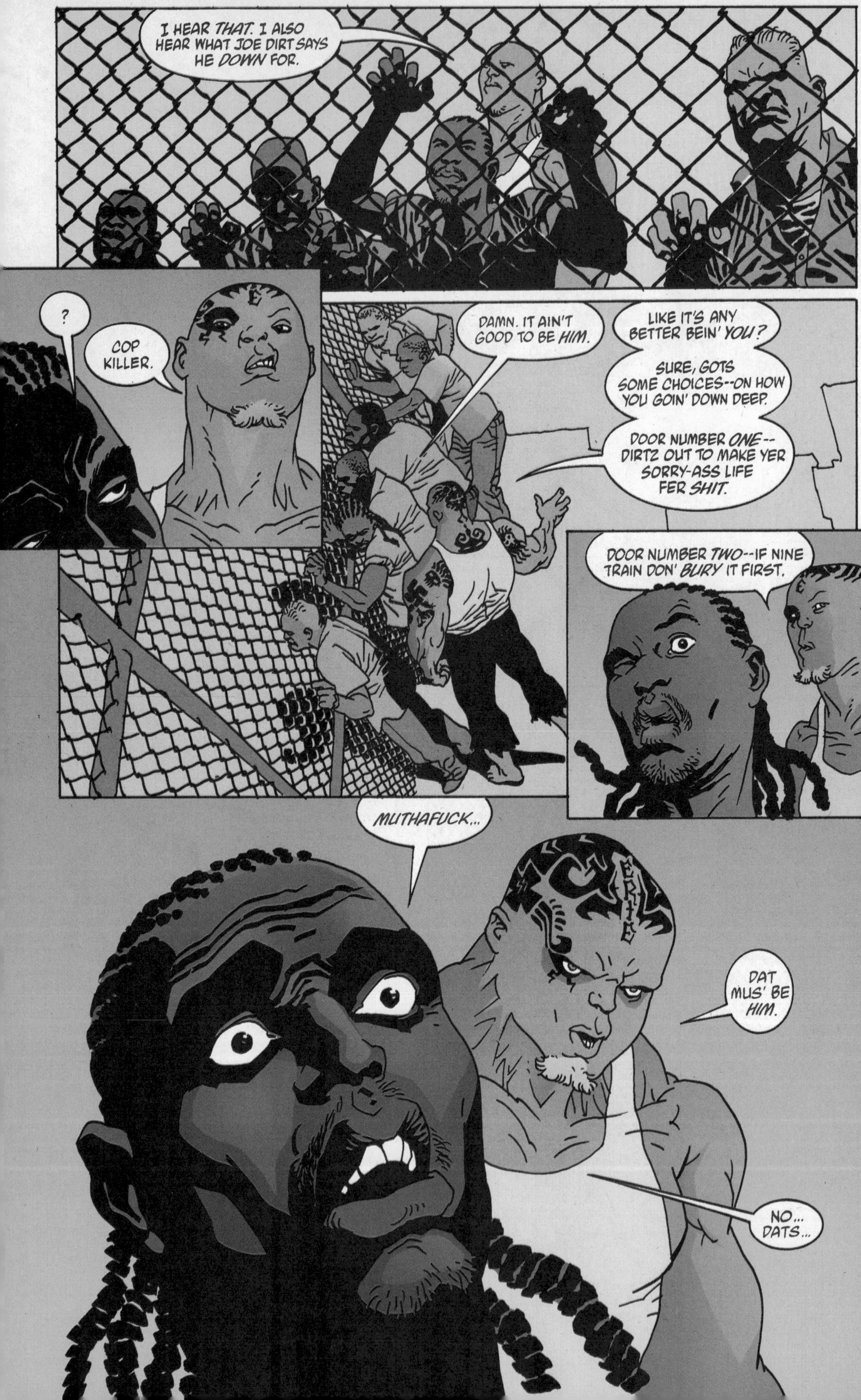
I HEAR THAT. I ALSO HEAR WHAT JOE DIRT SAYS HE DOWN FOR.
?
COP KILLER.
DAMN. IT AIN'T GOOD TO BE HIM.
LIKE IT'S ANY BETTER BEIN' YOU?
SURE, GOTS SOME CHOICES--ON HOW YOU GOIN' DOWN DEEP.
DOOR NUMBER ONE--DIRTZ OUT TO MAKE YER SORRY-ASS LIFE FER SHIT.
DOOR NUMBER TWO--IF NINE TRAIN DON' BURY IT FIRST.
MUTHAFUCK...
ERIE
DAT MUS' BE HIM.
NO... DATS...

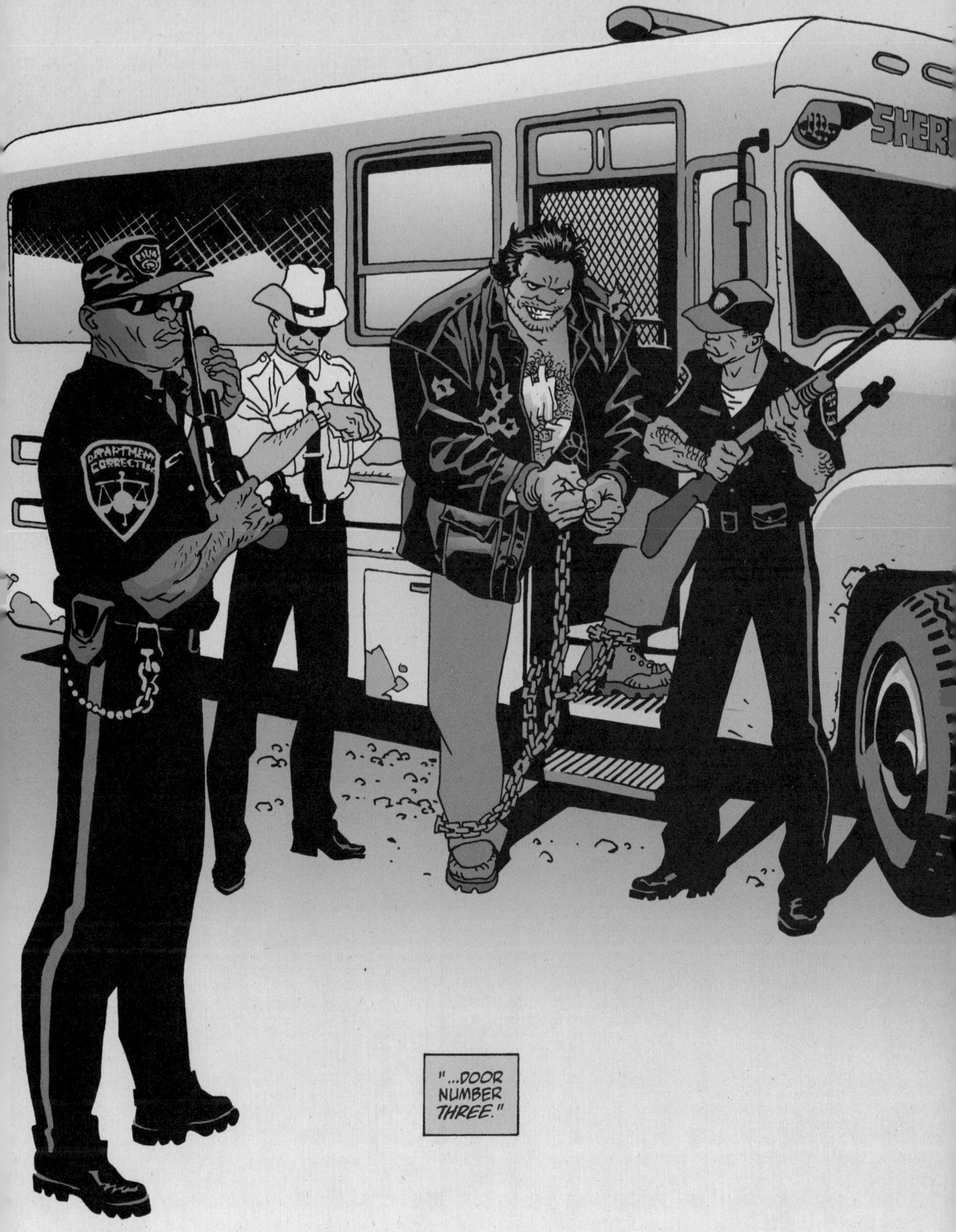
"...DOOR NUMBER THREE."

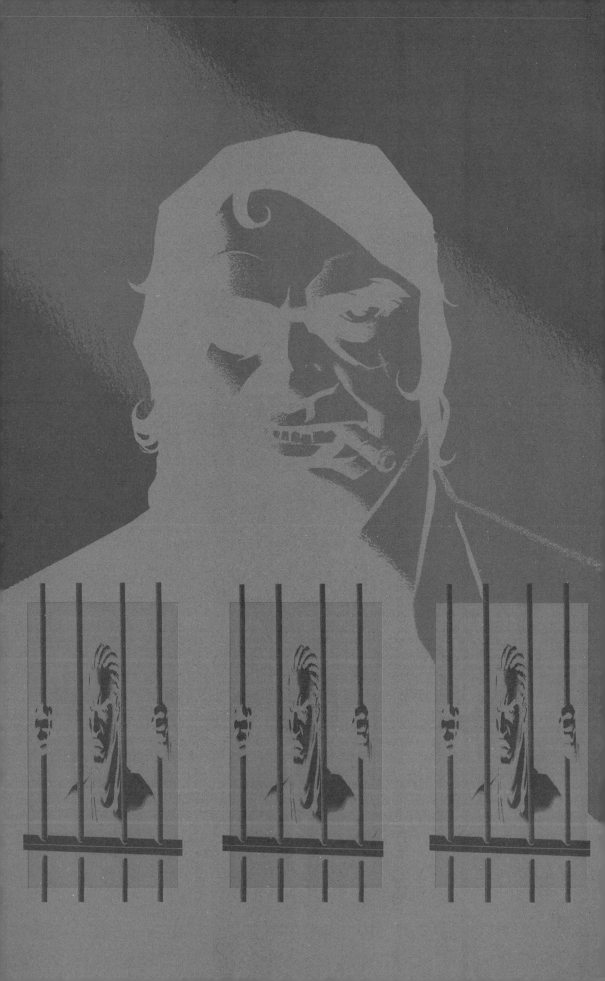

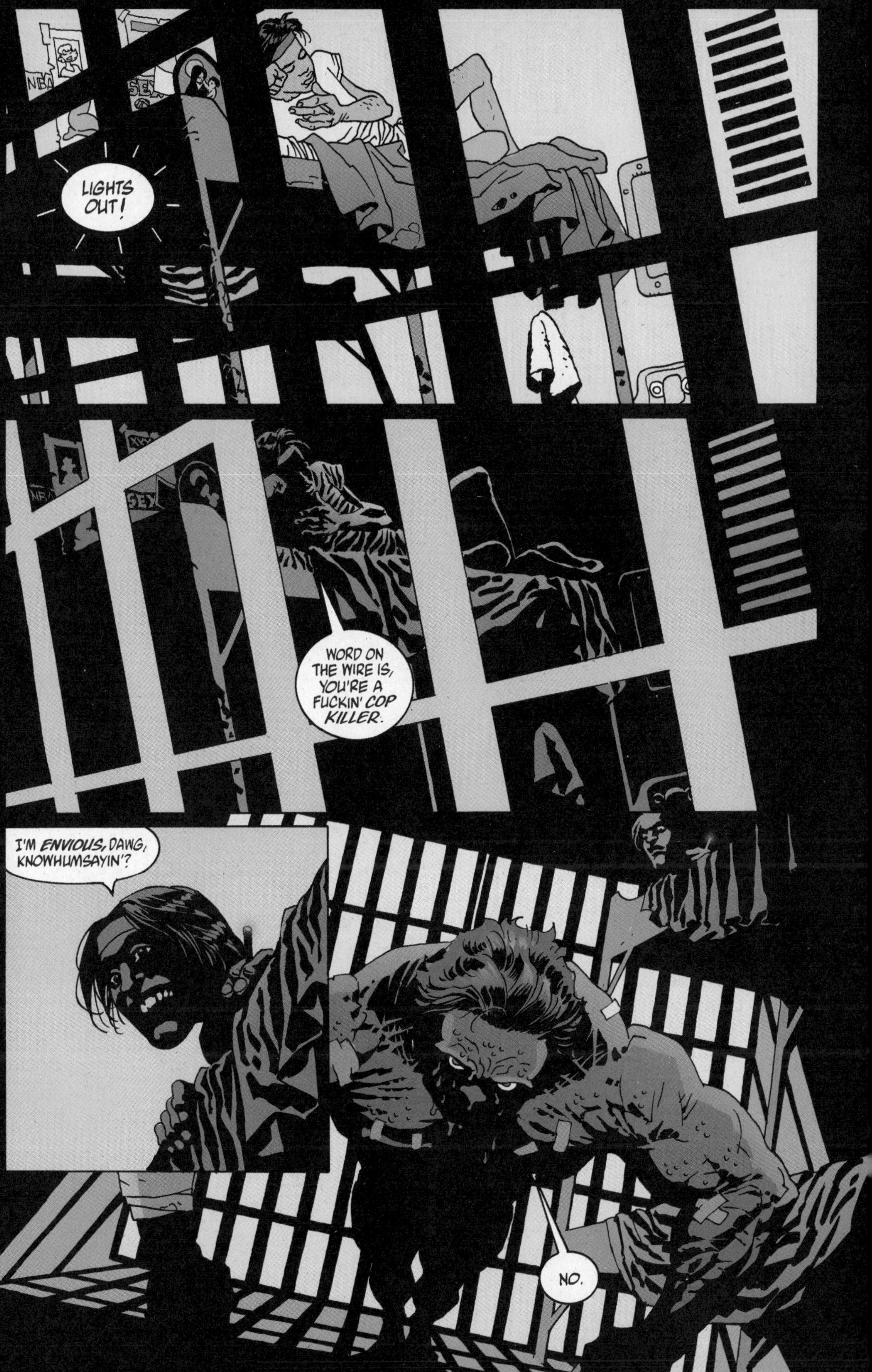
LIGHTS OUT!
WORD ON THE WIRE IS, YOU'RE A FUCKIN' COP KILLER.
I'M ENVIOUS, DAWG, KNOWHUMSAYIN'?
NO.

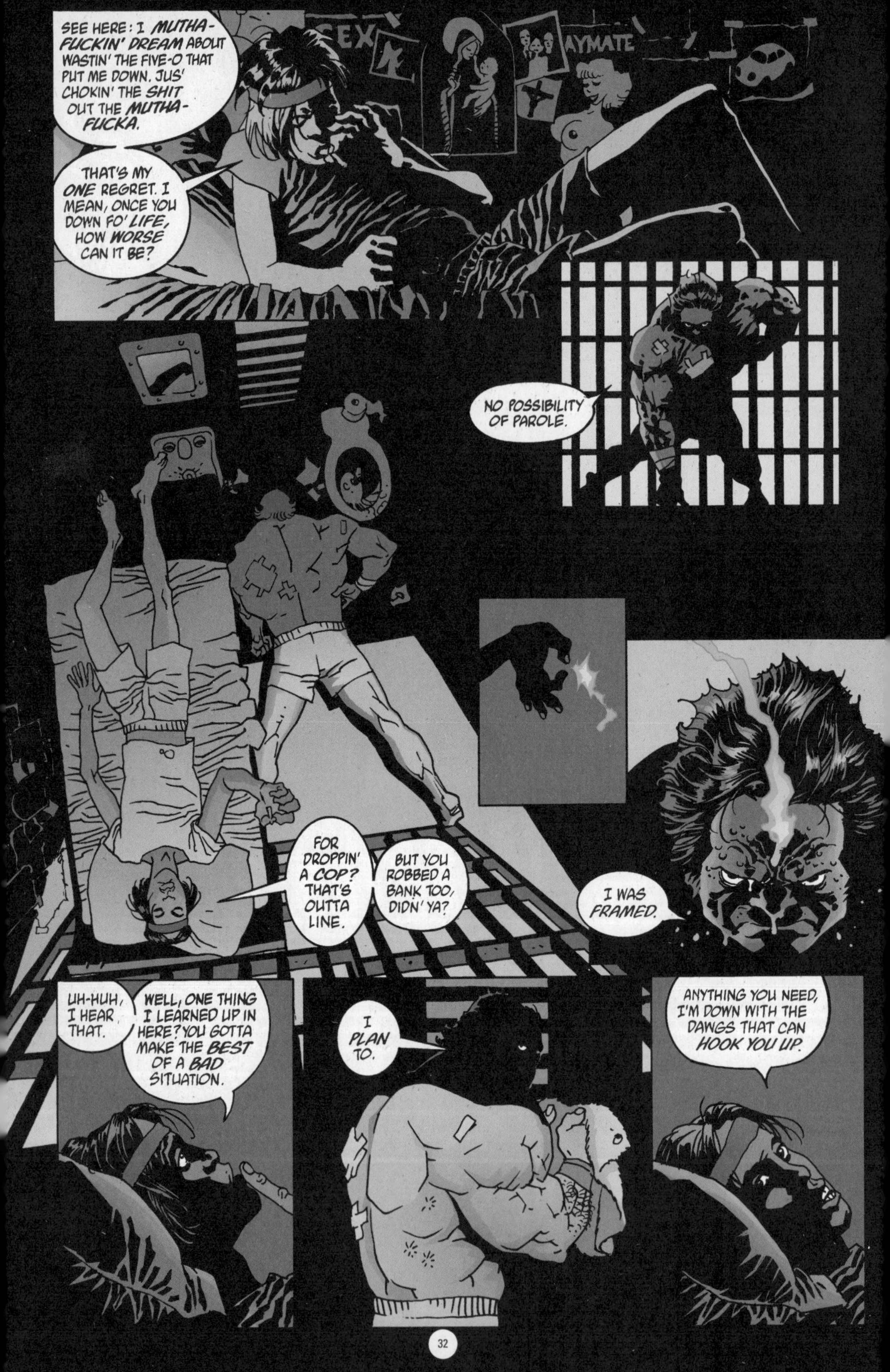
SEE HERE: I MUTHA-FUCKIN' DREAM ABOUT WASTIN' THE FIVE-O THAT PUT ME DOWN. JUS' CHOKIN' THE SHIT OUT THE MUTHA-FUCKA.
THAT'S MY ONE REGRET. I MEAN, ONCE YOU DOWN FO' LIFE, HOW WORSE CAN IT BE?
NO POSSIBILITY OF PAROLE.
FOR DROPPIN' A COP? THAT'S OUTTA LINE.
BUT YOU ROBBED A BANK TOO, DIDN' YA?
I WAS FRAMED.
UH-HUH, I HEAR THAT.
WELL, ONE THING I LEARNED UP IN HERE? YOU GOTTA MAKE THE BEST OF A BAD SITUATION.
I PLAN TO.
ANYTHING YOU NEED, I'M DOWN WITH THE DAWGS THAT CAN HOOK YOU UP.

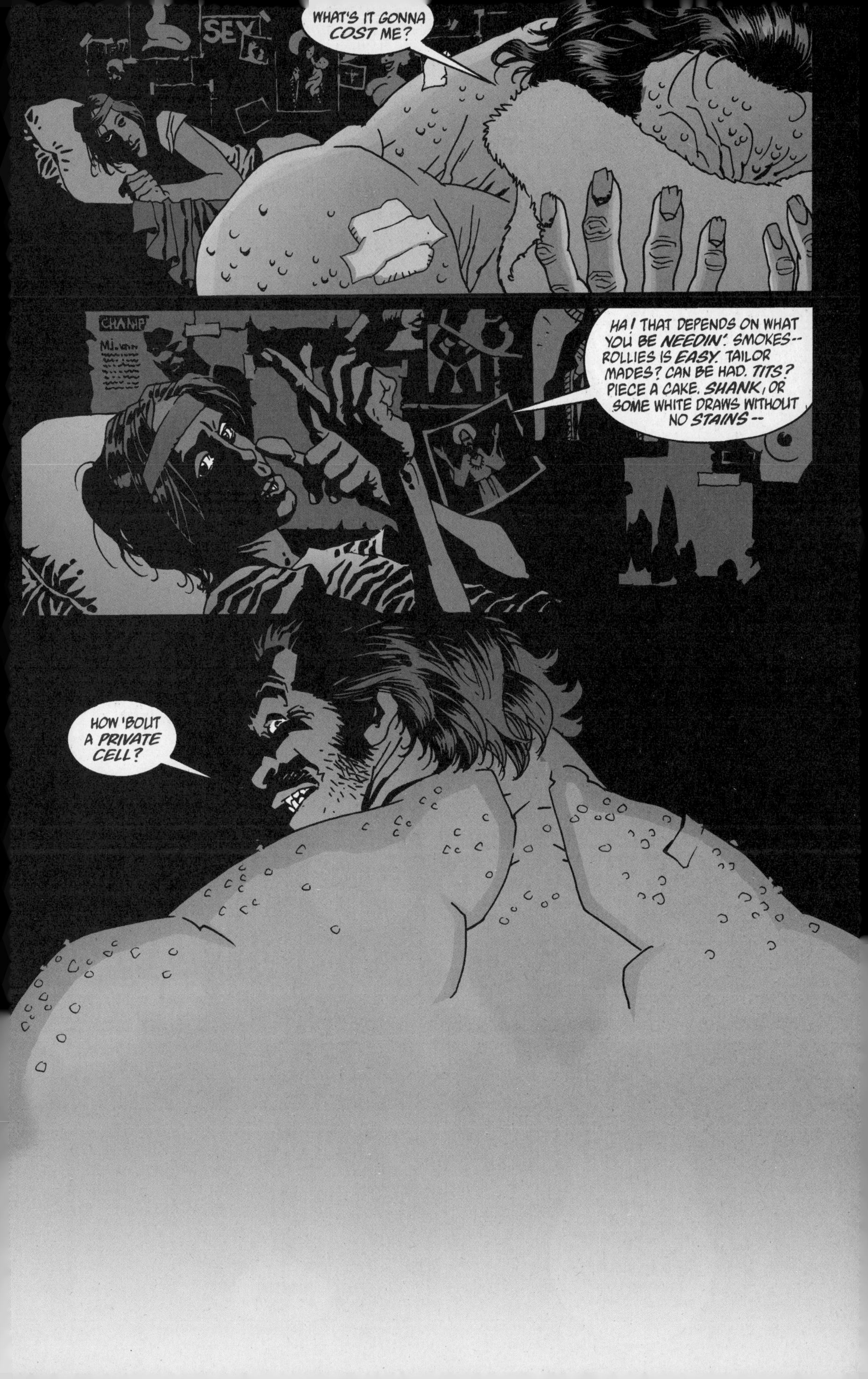
WHAT'S IT GONNA COST ME?
HA! THAT DEPENDS ON WHAT YOU BE NEEDIN'. SMOKES-- ROLLIES IS EASY. TAILOR MADES? CAN BE HAD. TITS? PIECE A CAKE. SHANK, OR SOME WHITE DRAWS WITHOUT NO STAINS --
HOW 'BOUT A PRIVATE CELL?

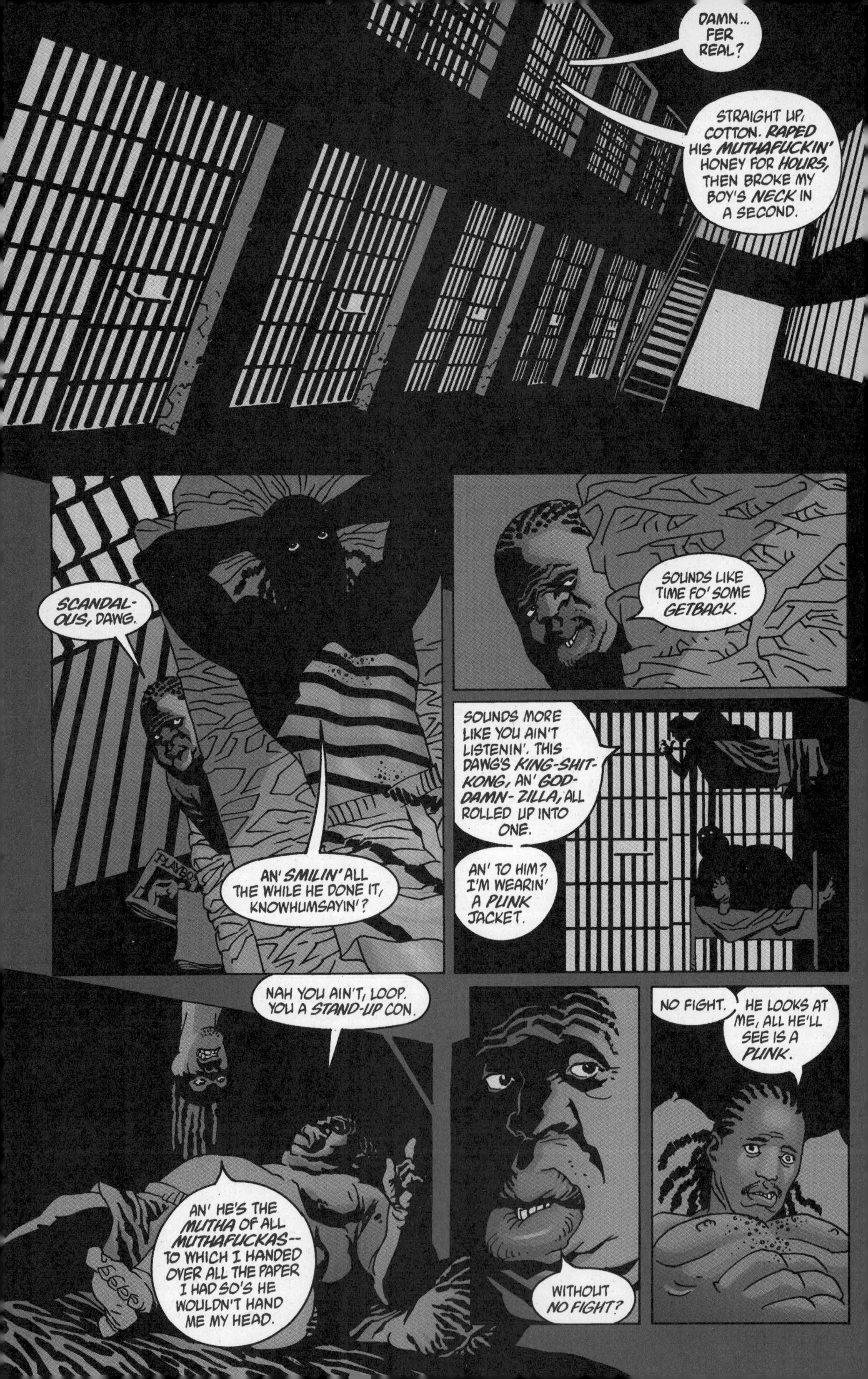
DAMN... FER REAL?
STRAIGHT UP, COTTON. RAPED HIS MUTHAFUCKIN' HONEY FOR HOURS, THEN BROKE MY BOY'S NECK IN A SECOND.
SCANDAL-OUS, DAWG.
AN' SMILIN' ALL THE WHILE HE DONE IT, KNOWHUMSAYIN'?
PLAYBOY
SOUNDS LIKE TIME FO' SOME GETBACK.
SOUNDS MORE LIKE YOU AIN'T LISTENIN'. THIS DAWG'S KING-SHIT-KONG, AN' GOD-DAMN-ZILLA, ALL ROLLED UP INTO ONE.
AN' TO HIM? I'M WEARIN' A PUNK JACKET.
NAH YOU AIN'T, LOOP. YOU A STAND-UP CON.
AN' HE'S THE MUTHA OF ALL MUTHAFUCKAS-- TO WHICH I HANDED OVER ALL THE PAPER I HAD SO'S HE WOULDN'T HAND ME MY HEAD.
WITHOUT NO FIGHT?
NO FIGHT.
HE LOOKS AT ME, ALL HE'LL SEE IS A PUNK.

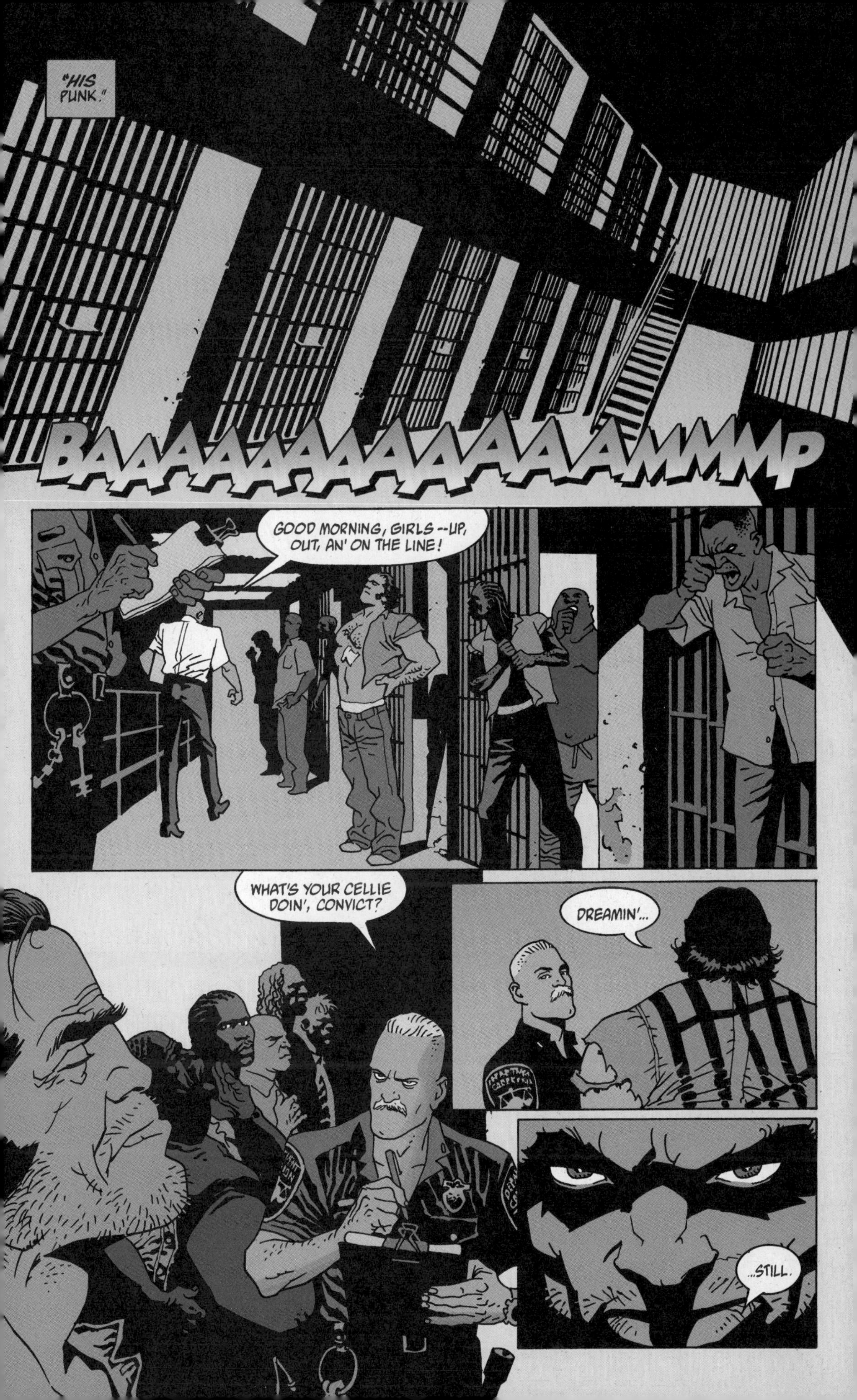
"HIS PUNK."
BAAAAAAAAAAAAMMMP
GOOD MORNING, GIRLS --UP, OUT, AN' ON THE LINE!
WHAT'S YOUR CELLIE DOIN', CONVICT?
DREAMIN'...
...STILL.

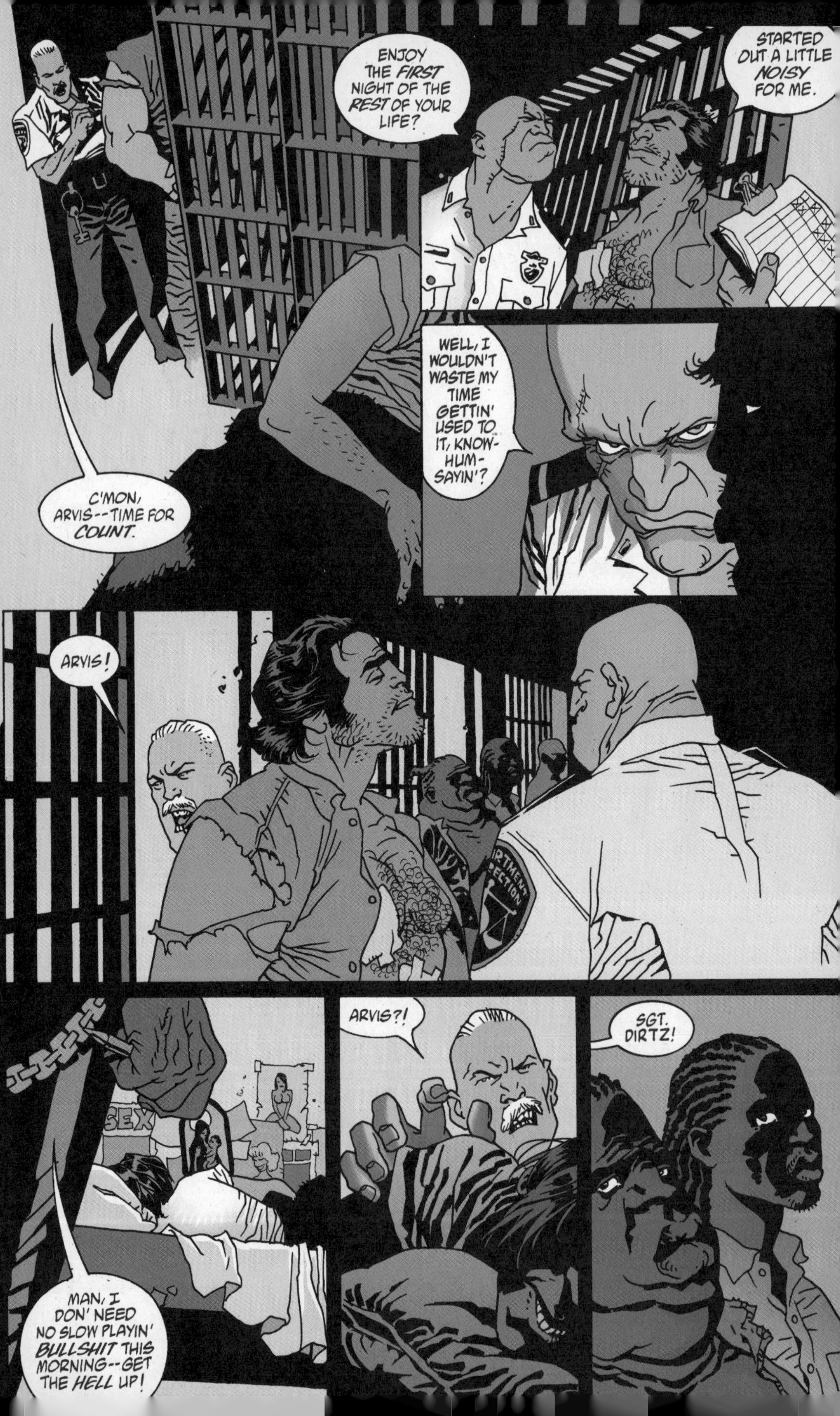
ENJOY THE FIRST NIGHT OF THE REST OF YOUR LIFE?
STARTED OUT A LITTLE NOISY FOR ME.
WELL, I WOULDN'T WASTE MY TIME GETTIN' USED TO IT, KNOW-HUM-SAYIN'?
C'MON, ARVIS--TIME FOR COUNT.
ARVIS!
MAN, I DON' NEED NO SLOW PLAYIN' BULLSHIT THIS MORNING--GET THE HELL UP!
SEX
ARVIS?!
SGT. DIRTZ!

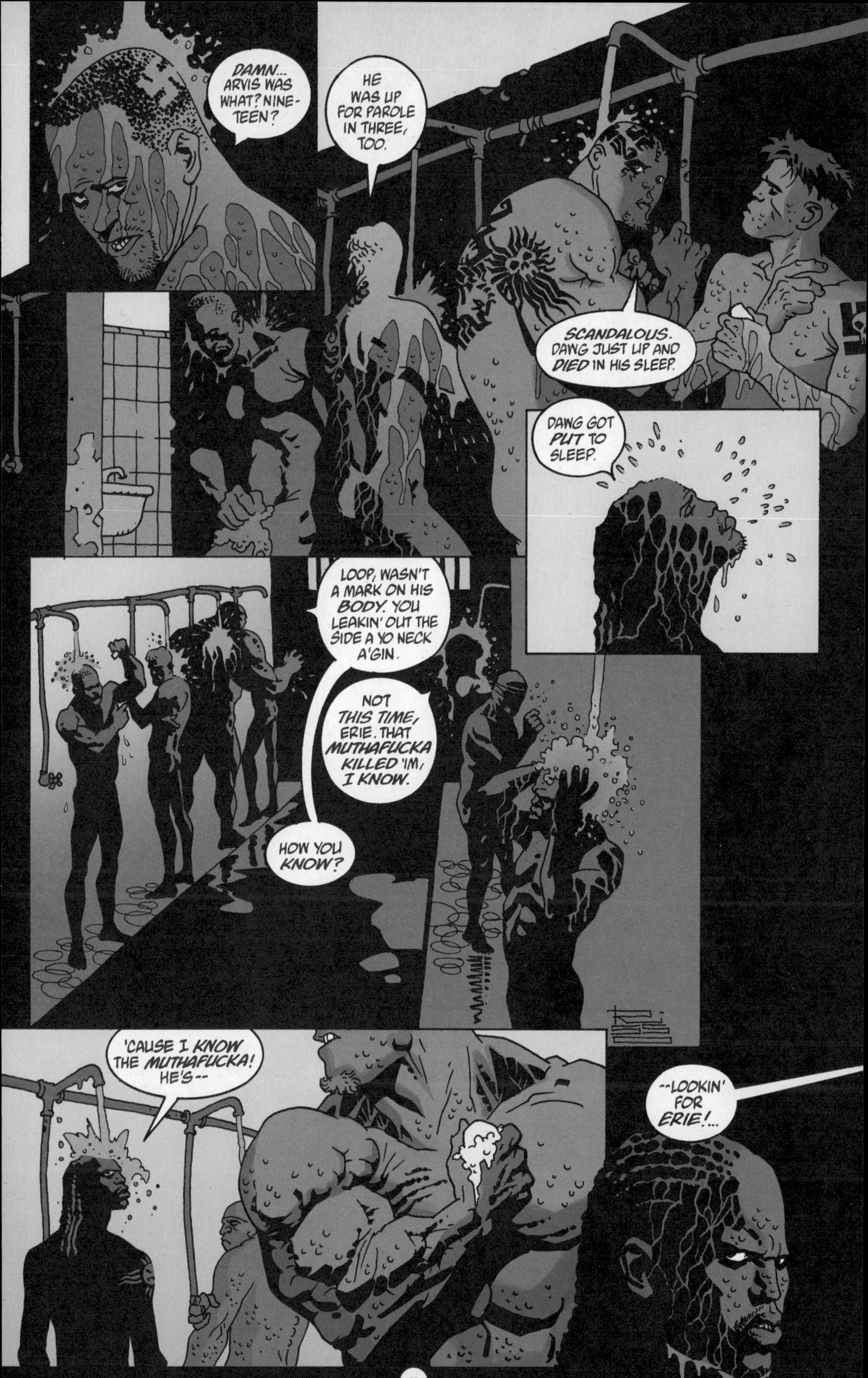
DAMN... ARVIS WAS WHAT? NINE-TEEN?
HE WAS UP FOR PAROLE IN THREE, TOO.
SCANDALOUS. DANG JUST UP AND DIED IN HIS SLEEP.
DANG GOT PUT TO SLEEP.
LOOP, WASN'T A MARK ON HIS BODY. YOU LEAKIN' OUT THE SIDE A YO NECK A'GIN.
NOT THIS TIME, ERIE. THAT MUTHAFUCKA KILLED 'IM, I KNOW.
HOW YOU KNOW?
'CAUSE I KNOW THE MUTHAFUCKA! HE'S--
--LOOKIN' FOR ERIE!...

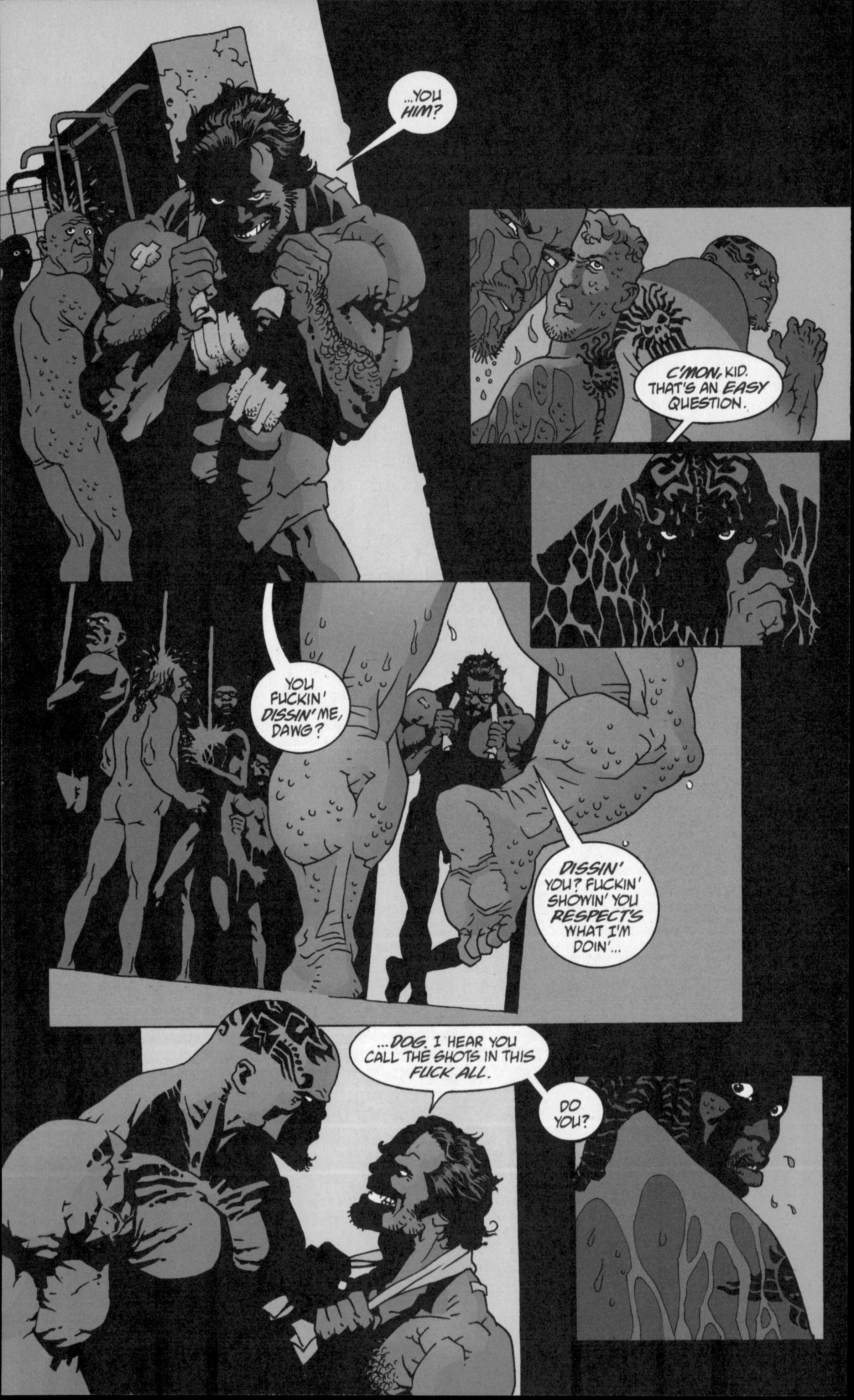
...YOU HIM?
C'MON, KID. THAT'S AN EASY QUESTION.
YOU FUCKIN' DISSIN' ME, DAWG?
DISSIN' YOU? FUCKIN' SHOWIN' YOU RESPECT'S WHAT I'M DOIN'...
...DOG. I HEAR YOU CALL THE SHOTS IN THIS FUCK ALL.
DO YOU?

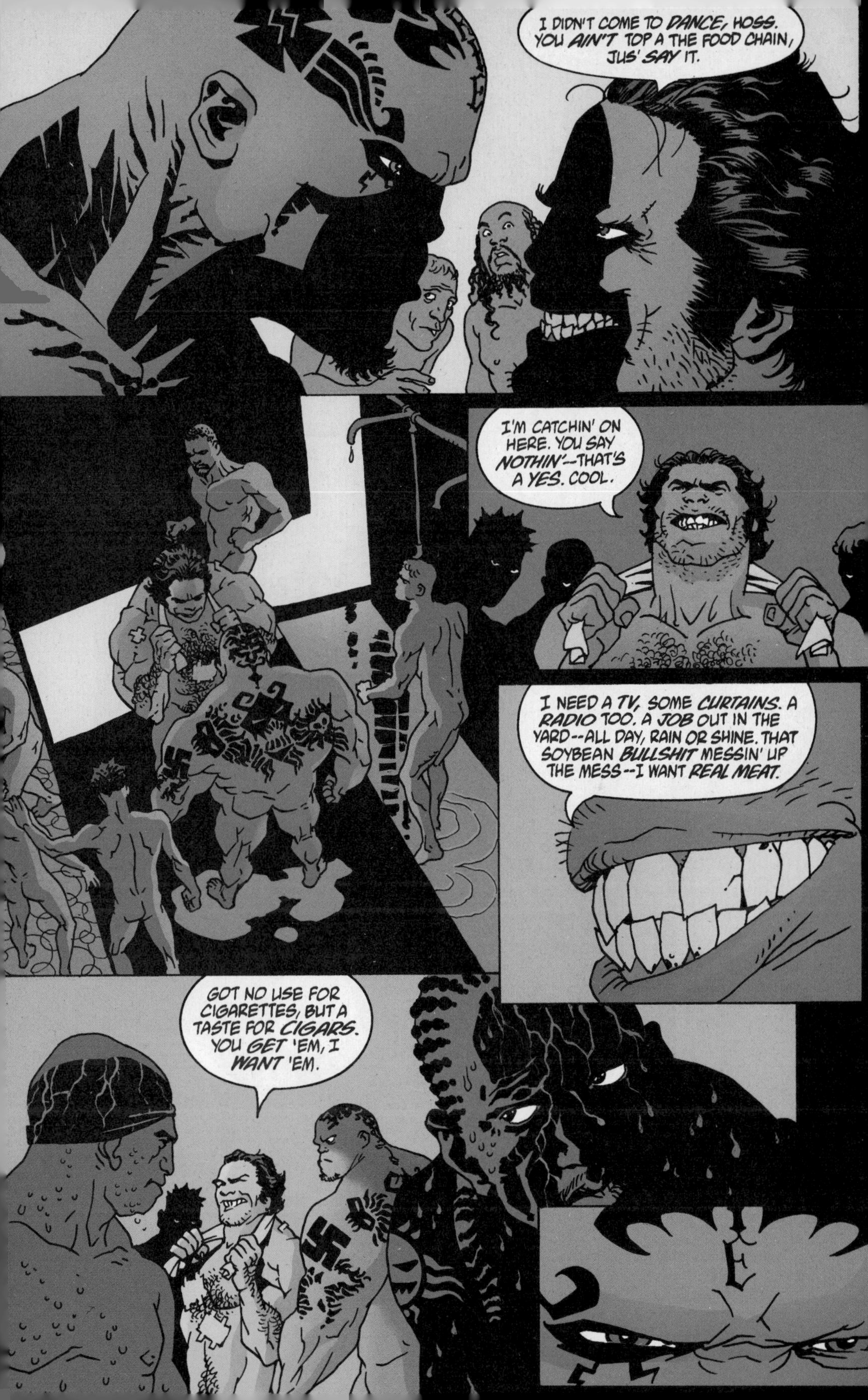
I DIDN'T COME TO DANCE, HOSS. YOU AIN'T TOP A THE FOOD CHAIN, JUS' SAY IT.
I'M CATCHIN' ON HERE. YOU SAY NOTHIN'--THAT'S A YES. COOL.
I NEED A TV, SOME CURTAINS. A RADIO TOO. A JOB OUT IN THE YARD--ALL DAY, RAIN OR SHINE. THAT SOYBEAN BULLSHIT MESSIN' UP THE MESS--I WANT REAL MEAT.
GOT NO USE FOR CIGARETTES, BUT A TASTE FOR CIGARS. YOU GET 'EM, I WANT 'EM.

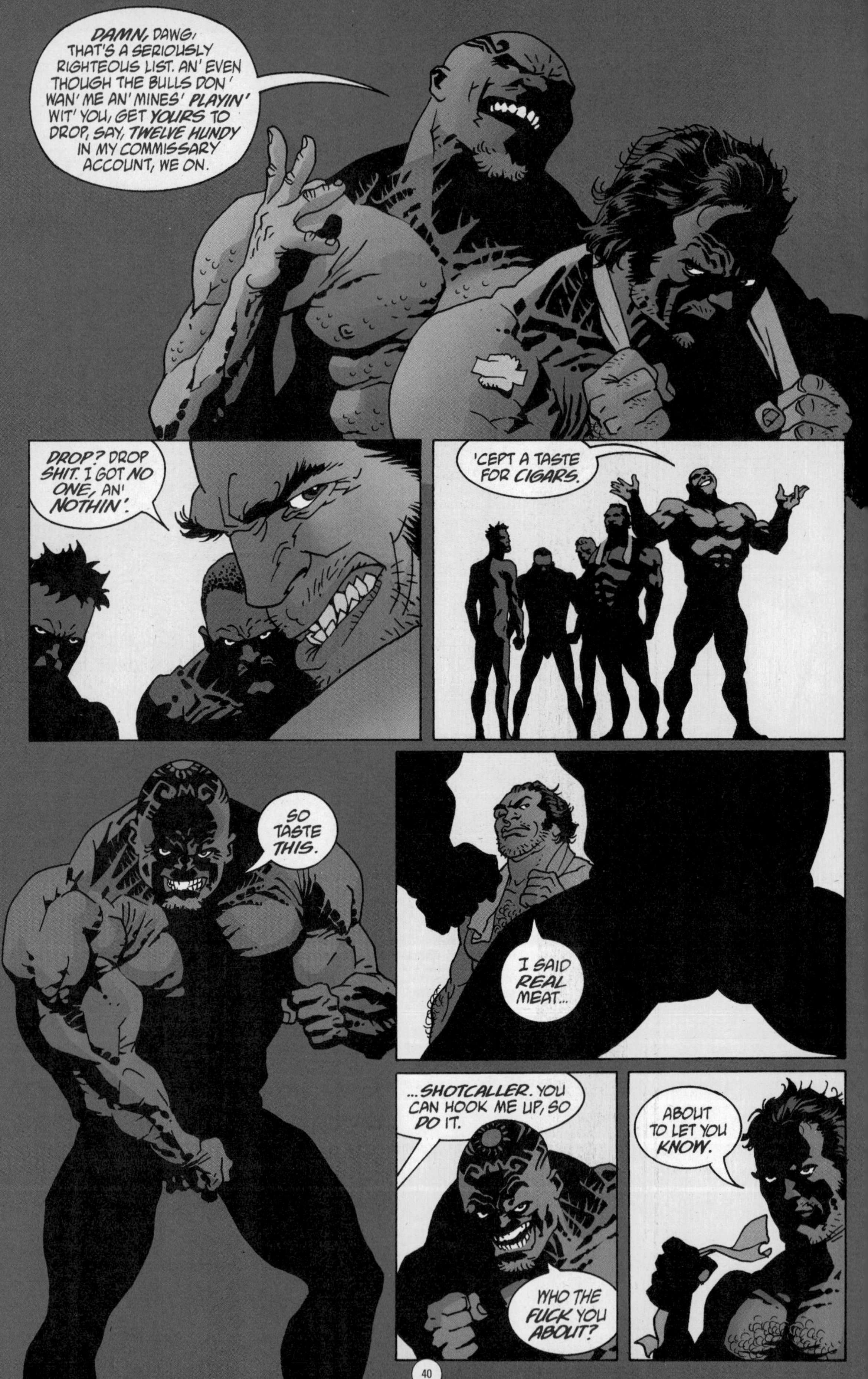
DAMN, DAWG, THAT'S A SERIOUSLY RIGHTEOUS LIST. AN' EVEN THOUGH THE BULLS DON' WAN' ME AN' MINES' PLAYIN' WIT' YOU, GET YOURS TO DROP, SAY, TWELVE HUNDY IN MY COMMISSARY ACCOUNT, WE ON.
DROP? DROP SHIT. I GOT NO ONE, AN' NOTHIN'.
'CEPT A TASTE FOR CIGARS.
SO TASTE THIS.
I SAID REAL MEAT...
...SHOTCALLER. YOU CAN HOOK ME UP, SO DO IT.
WHO THE FUCK YOU ABOUT?
ABOUT TO LET YOU KNOW.

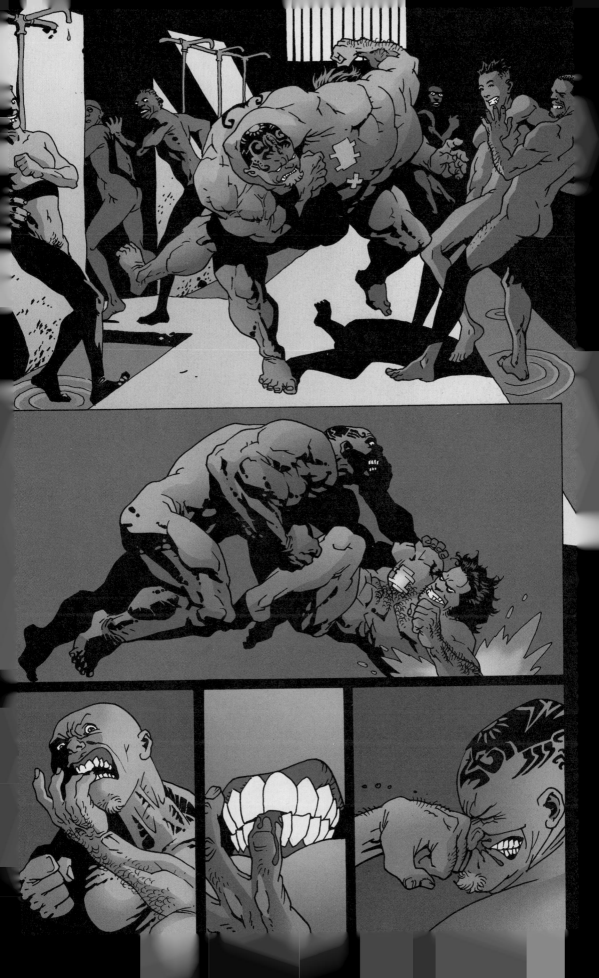

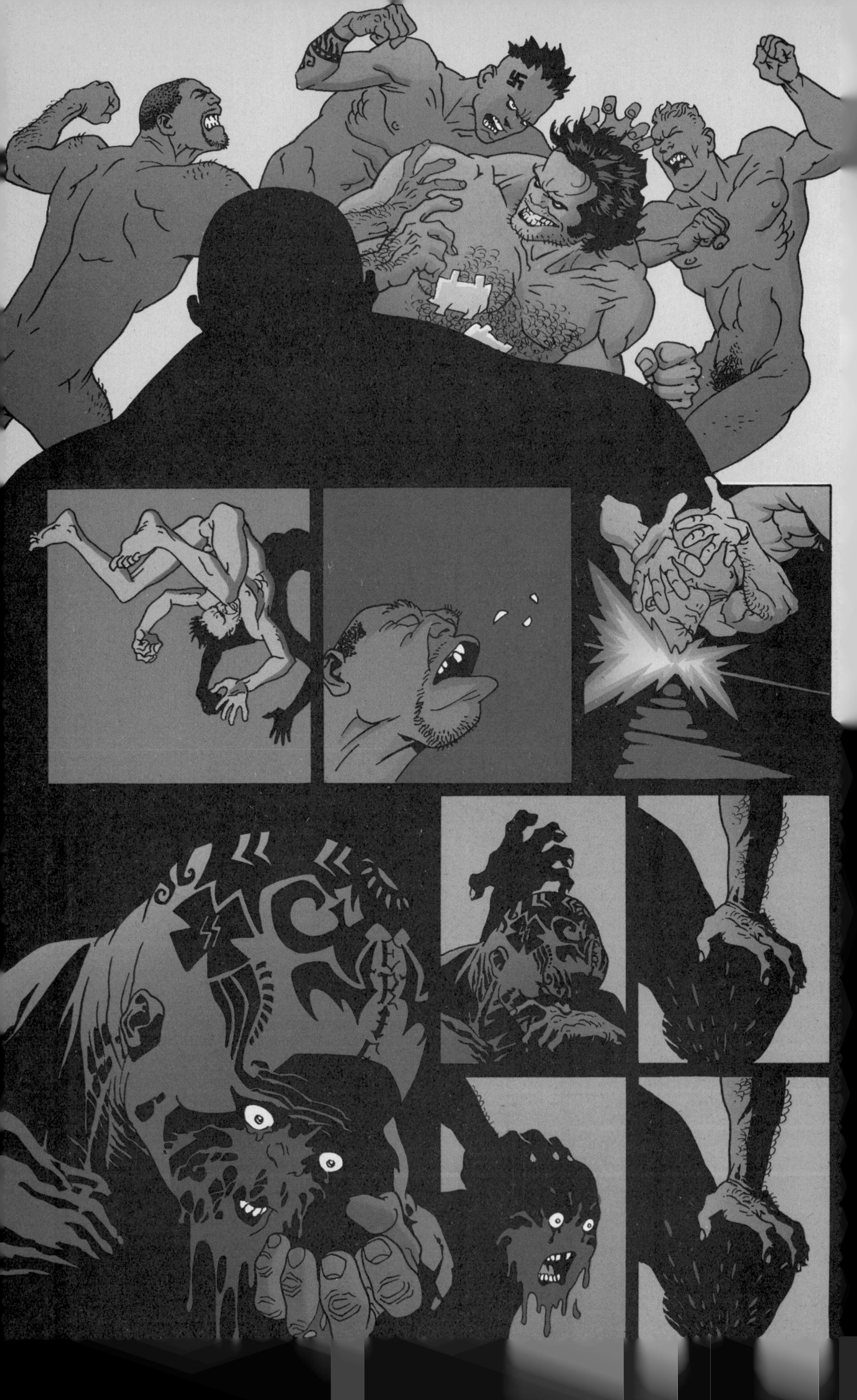

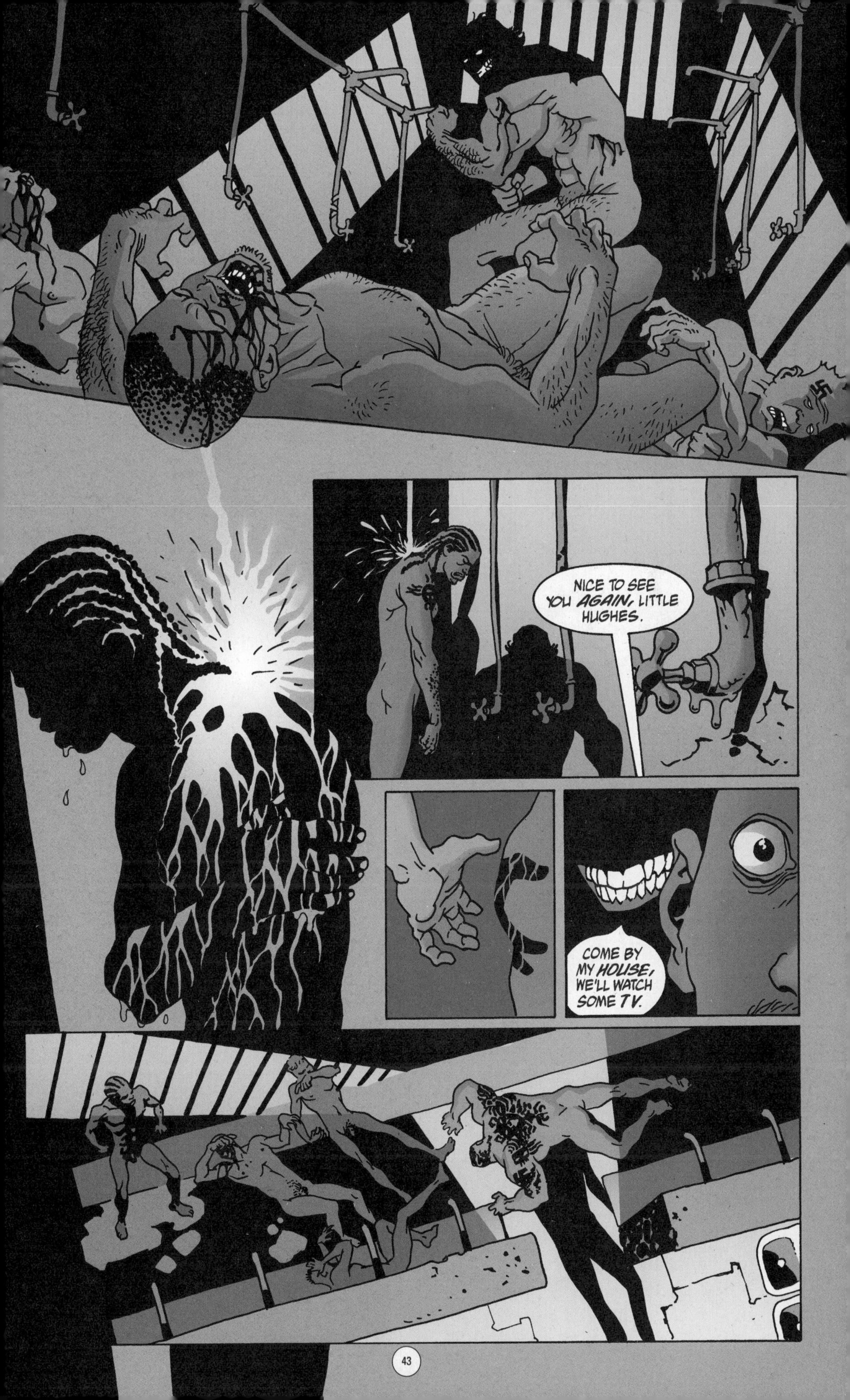
NICE TO SEE YOU AGAIN, LITTLE HUGHES.
COME BY MY HOUSE, WE'LL WATCH SOME TV.

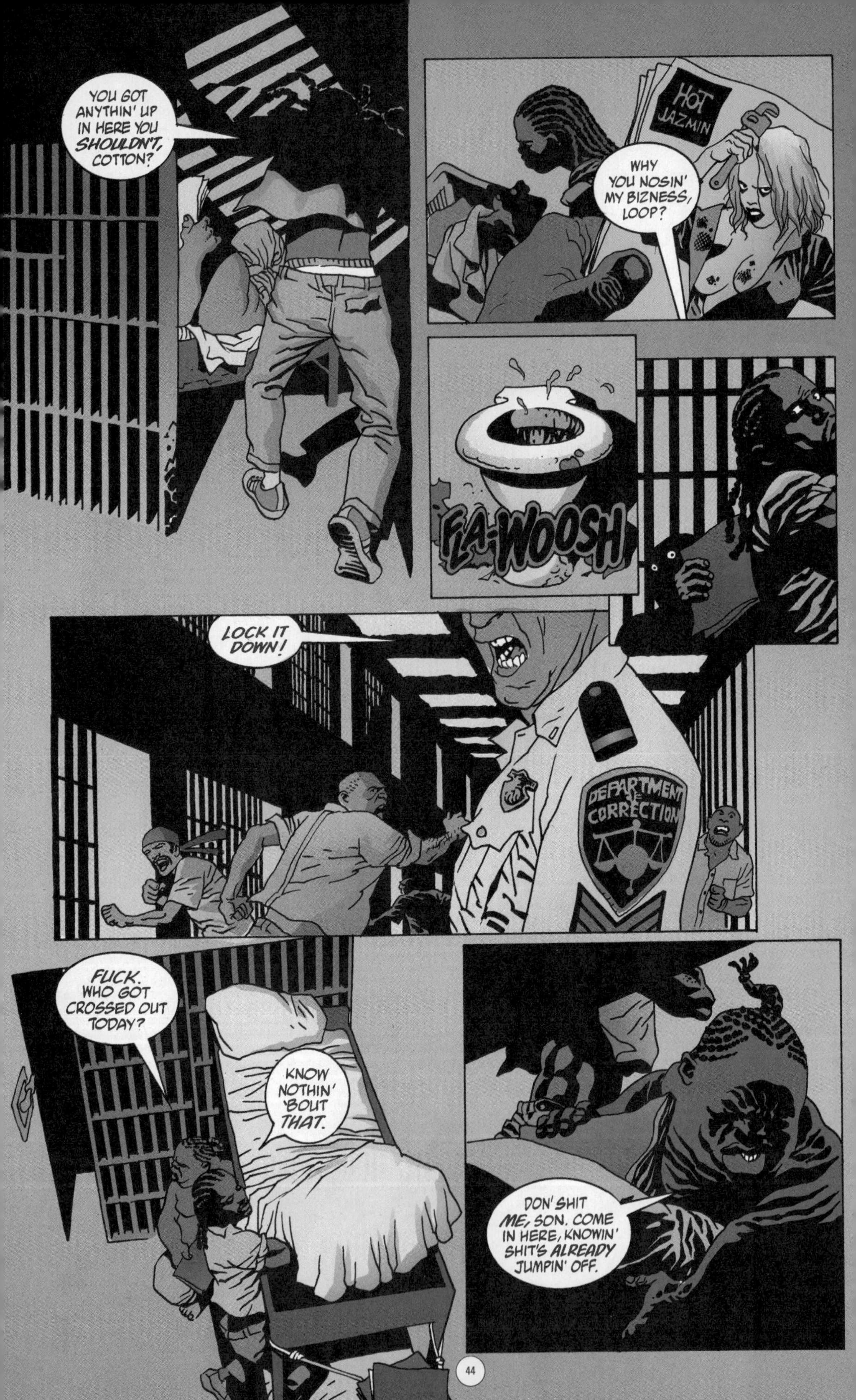
YOU GOT ANYTHIN' UP IN HERE YOU SHOULDN'T, COTTON?
HOT JAZMIN
WHY YOU NOSIN' MY BIZNESS, LOOP?
FLA-WOOSH
LOCK IT DOWN!
DEPARTMENT OF CORRECTION
FUCK. WHO GOT CROSSED OUT TODAY?
KNOW NOTHIN' 'BOUT THAT.
DON' SHIT ME, SON. COME IN HERE, KNOWIN' SHIT'S ALREADY JUMPIN' OFF.

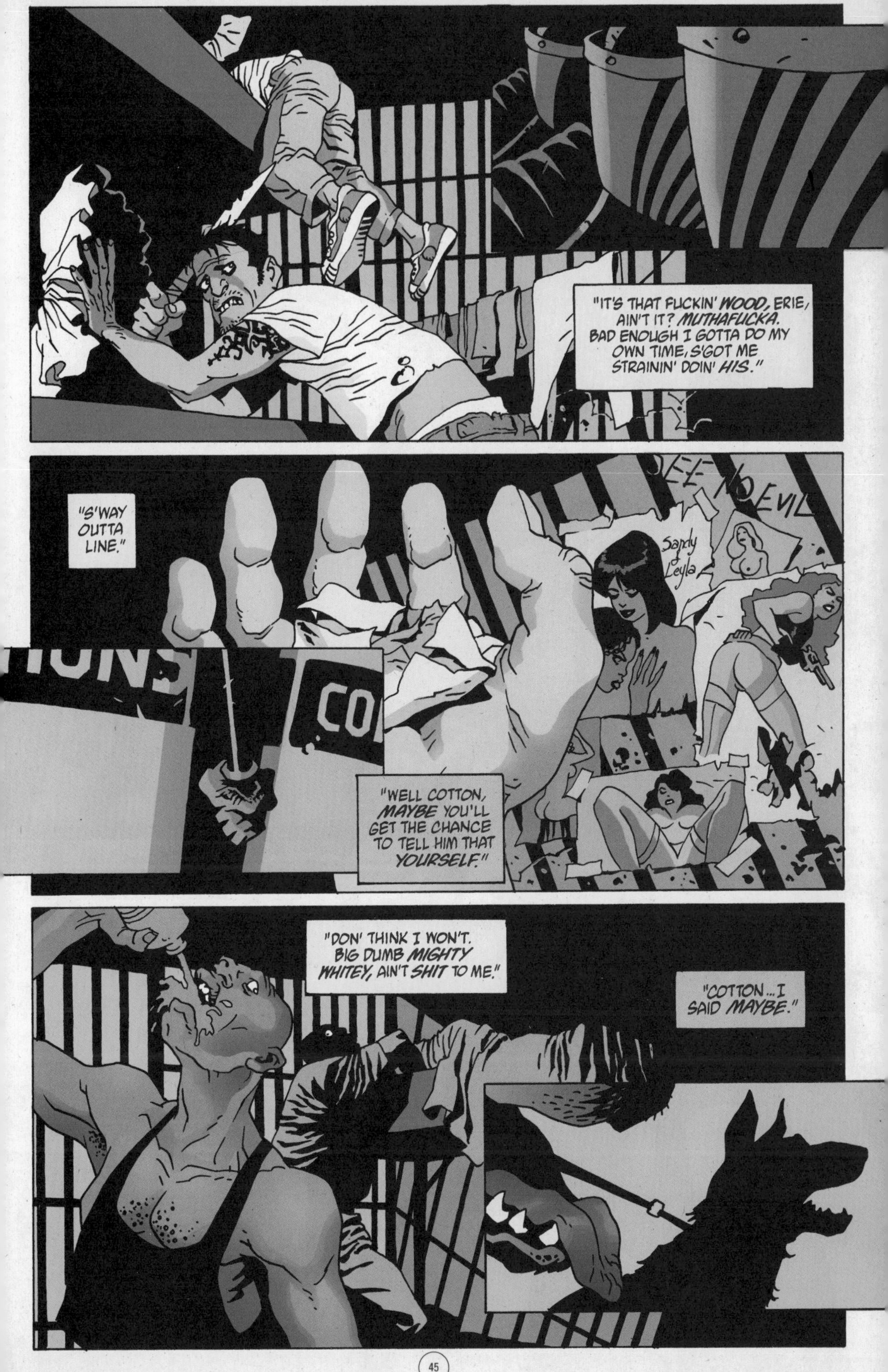
"IT'S THAT FUCKIN' WOOD, ERIE, AIN'T IT? MUTHAFUCKA. BAD ENOUGH I GOTTA DO MY OWN TIME, S'GOT ME STRAININ' DOIN' HIS."
"S'WAY OUTTA LINE."
SEE NO EVIL
Sandy
Leyla
"WELL COTTON, MAYBE YOU'LL GET THE CHANCE TO TELL HIM THAT YOURSELF."
"DON' THINK I WON'T. BIG DUMB MIGHTY WHITEY, AIN'T SHIT TO ME."
"COTTON... I SAID MAYBE."

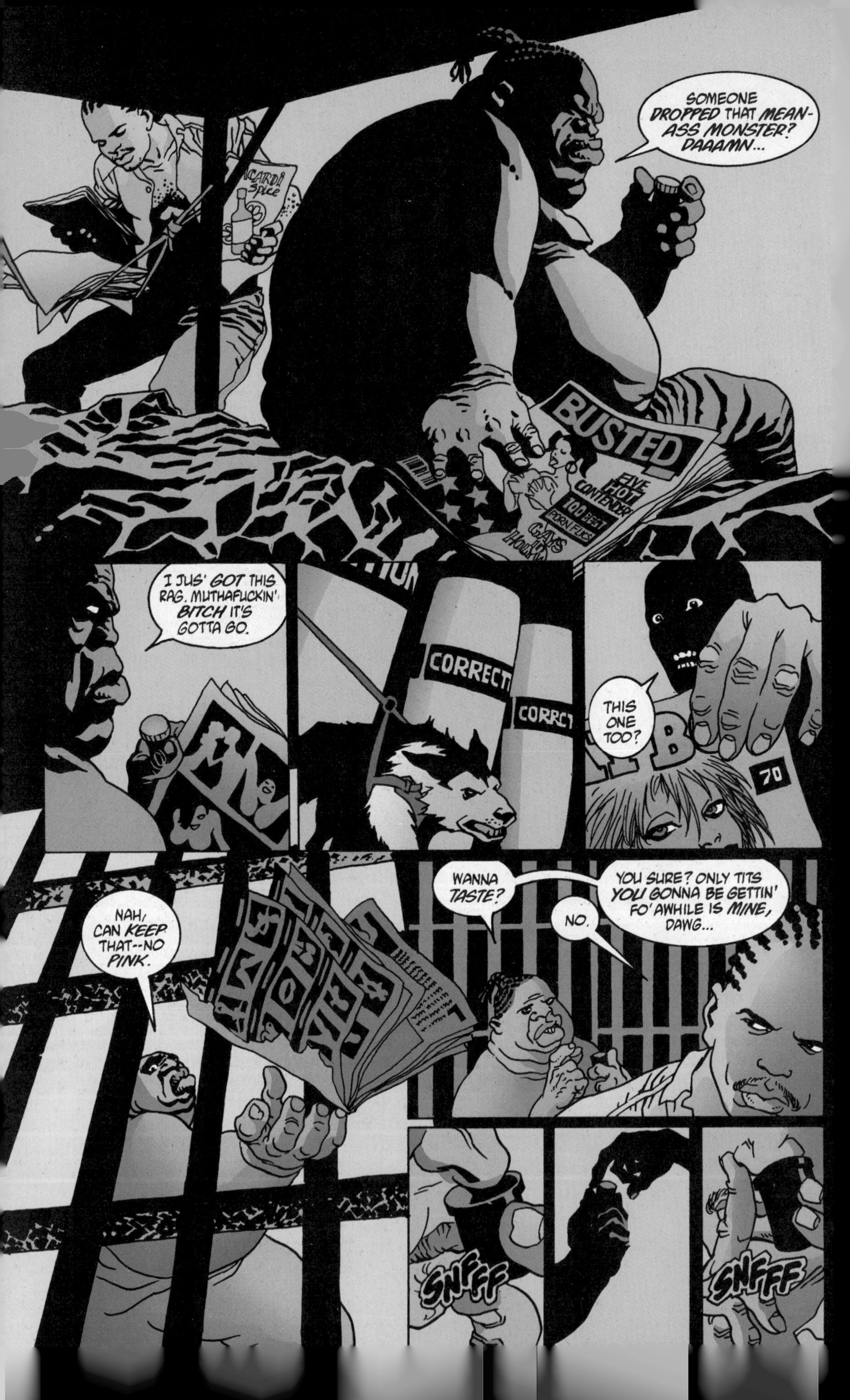
SOMEONE DROPPED THAT MEAN-ASS MONSTER? DAAAMN...
BUSTED
FIVE HOT CONTENDERS
100 BEST PORN FLICS
I JUS' GOT THIS RAG. MUTHAFUCKIN' BITCH IT'S GOTTA GO.
CORRECT
CORRCT
THIS ONE TOO?
70
NAH, CAN KEEP THAT--NO PINK.
WANNA TASTE?
NO.
YOU SURE? ONLY TITS YOU GONNA BE GETTIN' FO'AWHILE IS MINE, DAWG...
SNFFF
SNFFF

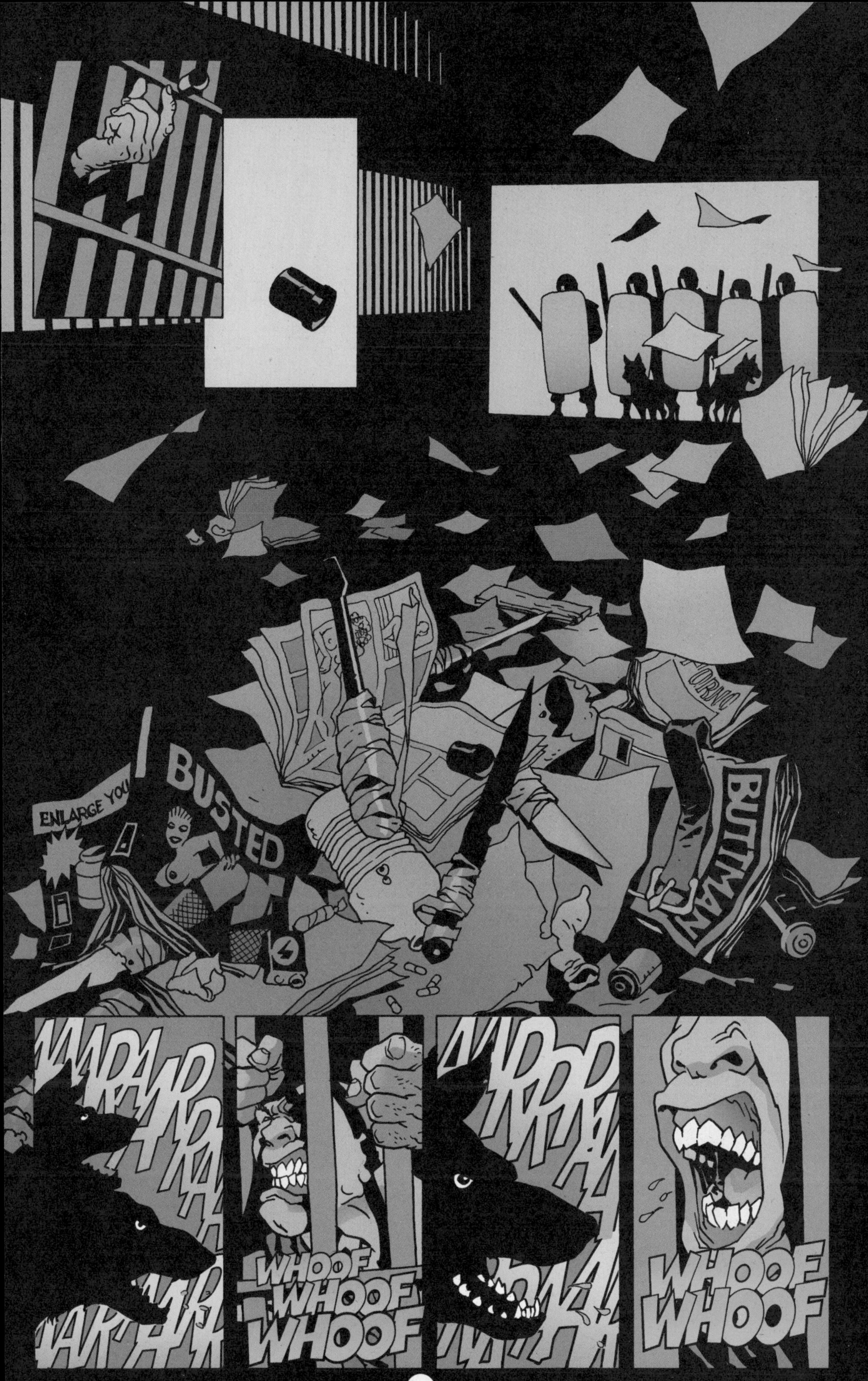

ENLARGE YOU
BUSTED
BUTTMAN
WHOOF
WHOOF
WHOOF
WHOOF
WHOOF

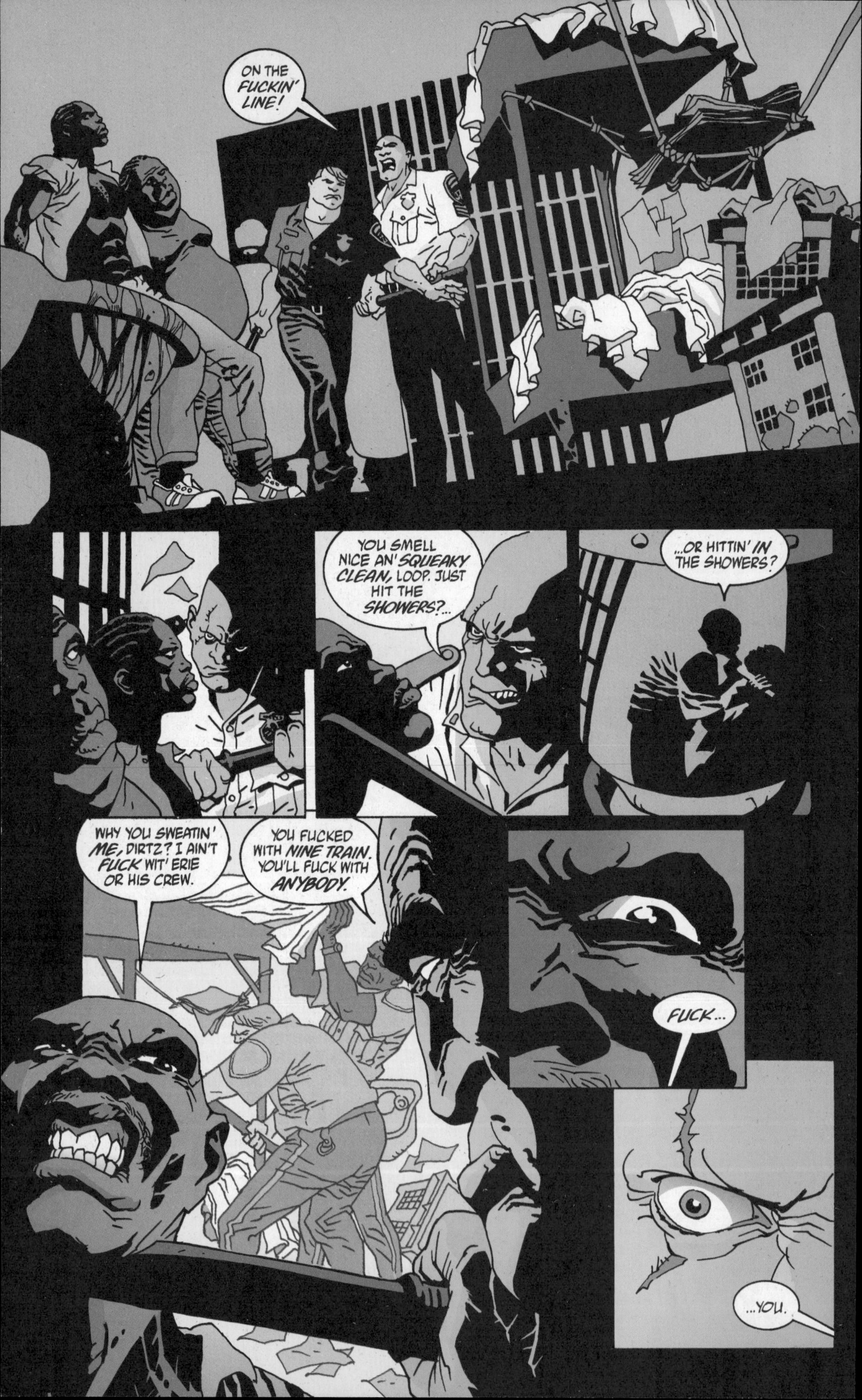

ON THE FUCKIN' LINE!
YOU SMELL NICE AN' SQUEAKY CLEAN, LOOP. JUST HIT THE SHOWERS?...
...OR HITTIN' IN THE SHOWERS?
WHY YOU SWEATIN' ME, DIRTZ? I AIN'T FUCK WIT' ERIE OR HIS CREW.
YOU FUCKED WITH NINE TRAIN. YOU'LL FUCK WITH ANYBODY.
FUCK...
...YOU.

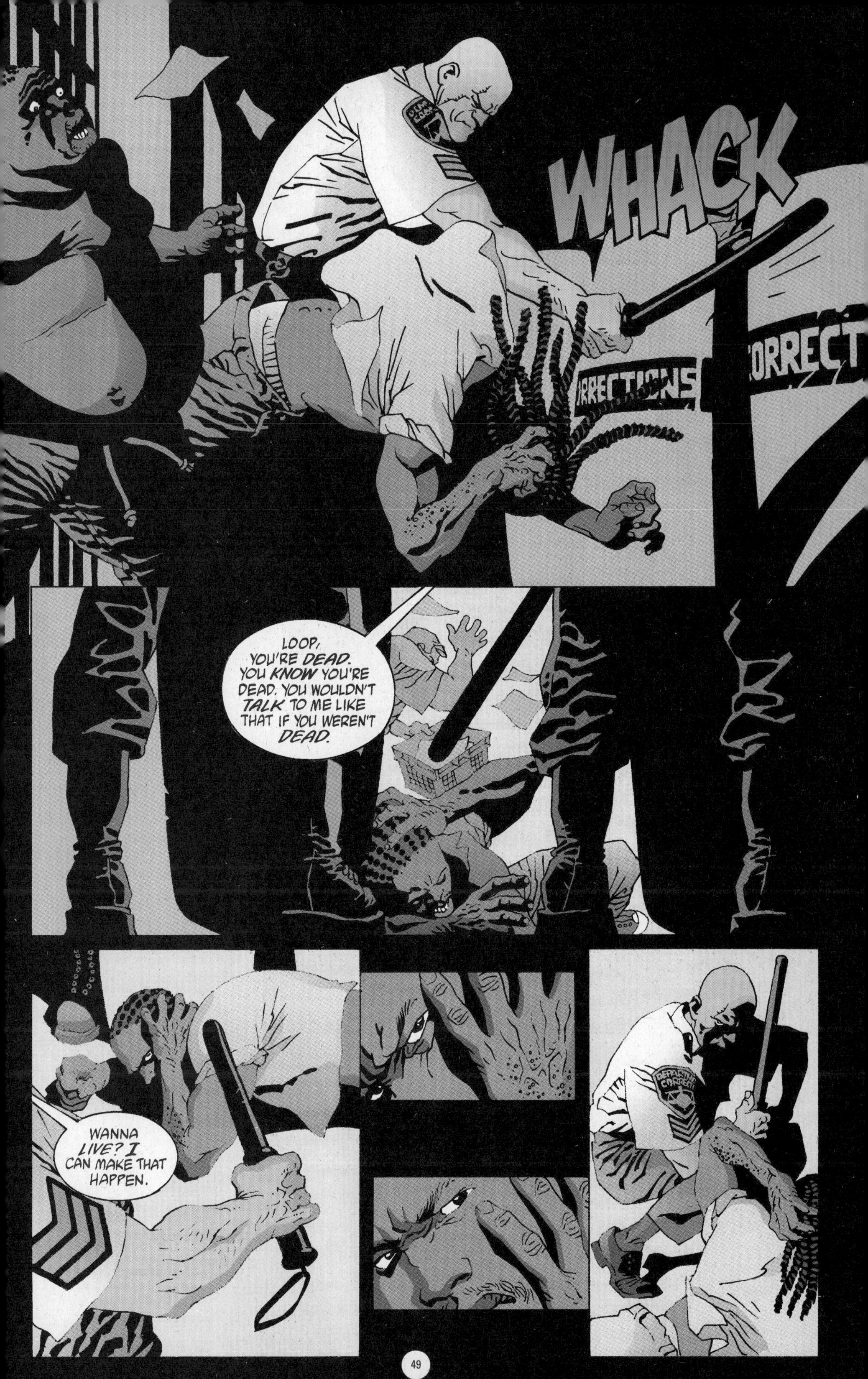
WHACK
LOOP, YOU'RE *DEAD*. YOU *KNOW* YOU'RE DEAD. YOU WOULDN'T *TALK* TO ME LIKE THAT IF YOU WEREN'T *DEAD*.
WANNA *LIVE*? *I* CAN MAKE THAT HAPPEN.

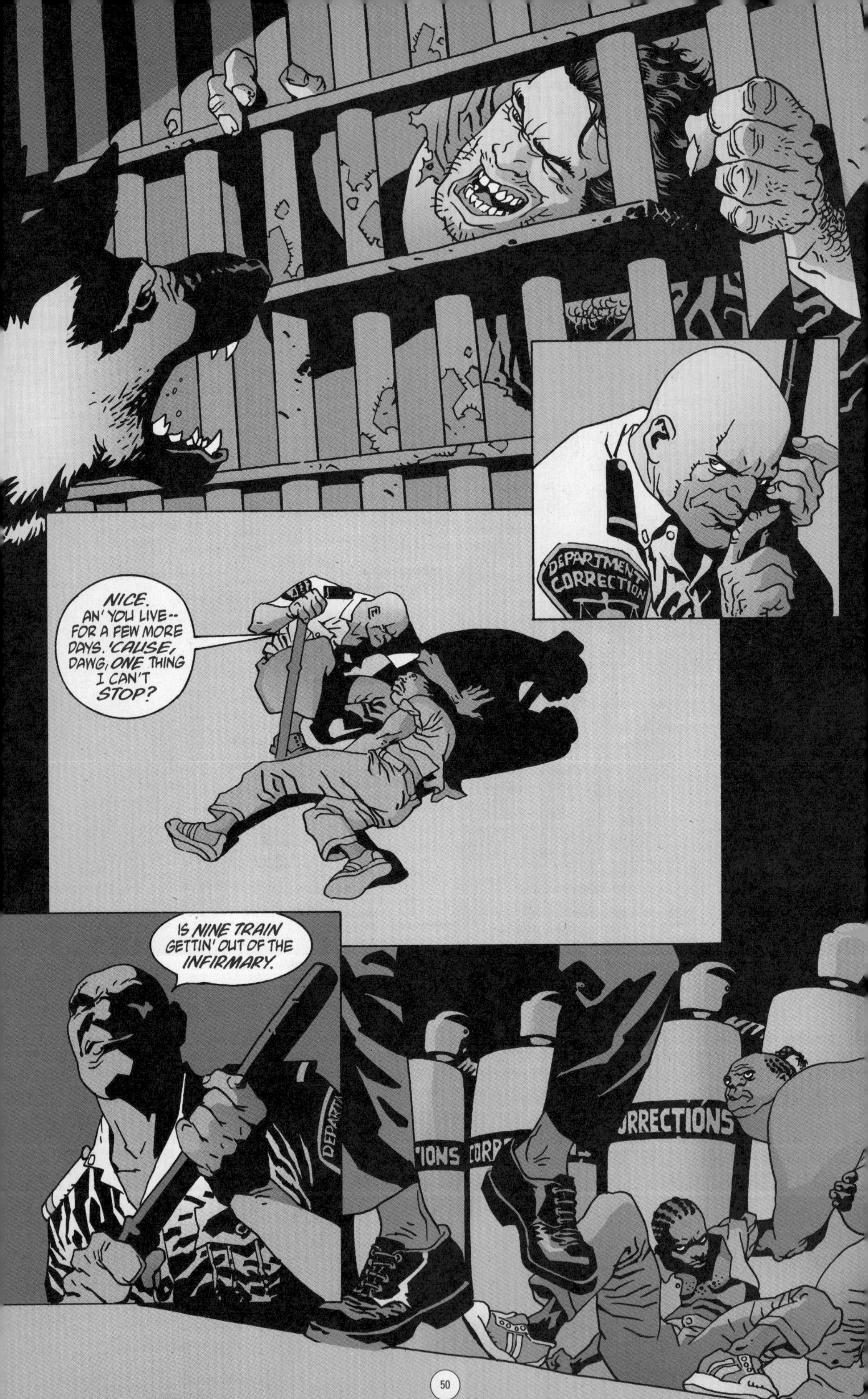
DEPARTMENT CORRECTION
NICE. AN' YOU LIVE-- FOR A FEW MORE DAYS. 'CAUSE, DAWG, ONE THING I CAN'T STOP?
IS NINE TRAIN GETTIN' OUT OF THE INFIRMARY.
DEPARTM
TIONS
CORRE
RRECTIONS

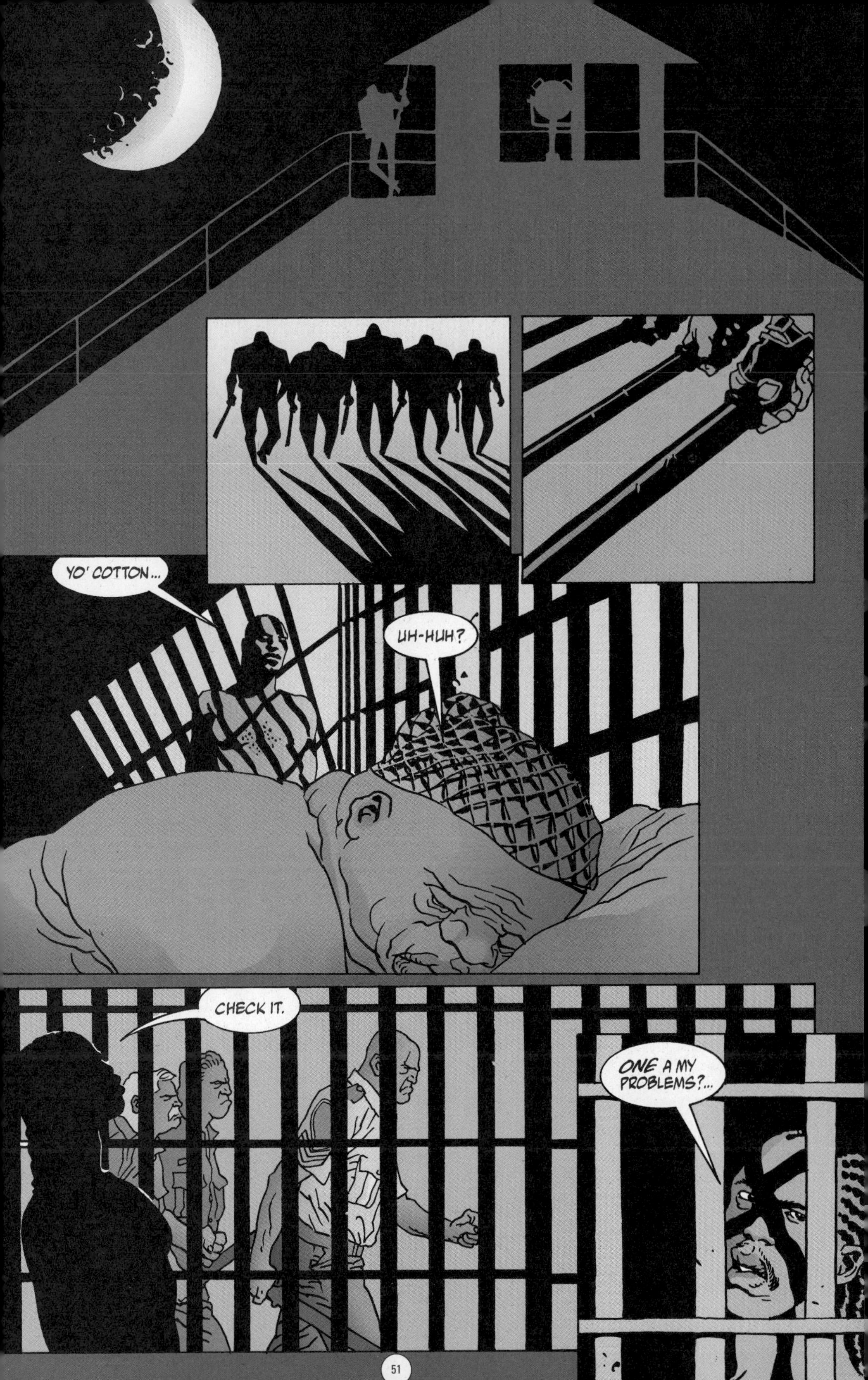
YO' COTTON...
UH-HUH?
CHECK IT.
ONE A MY PROBLEMS?...

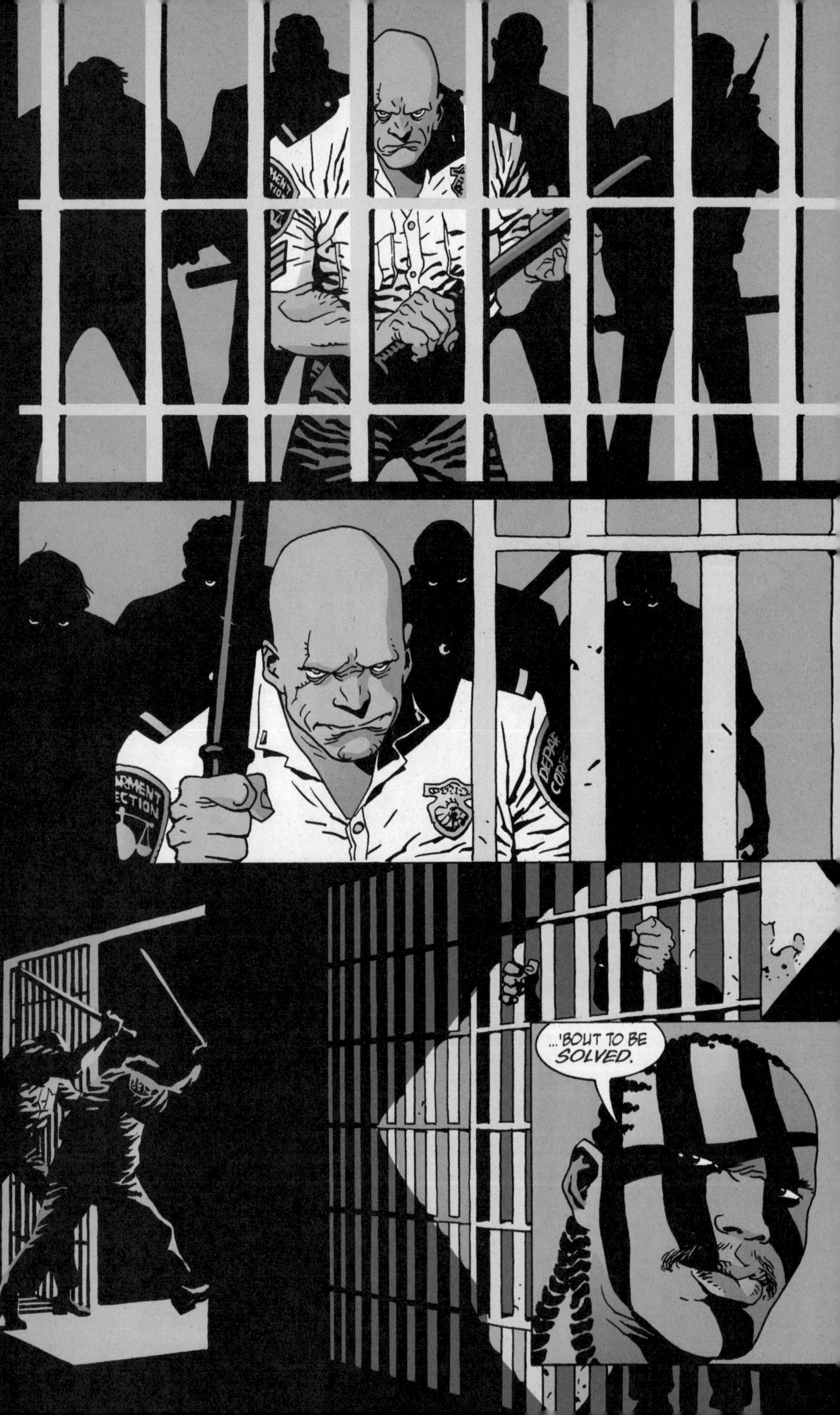
...'BOUT TO BE SOLVED.

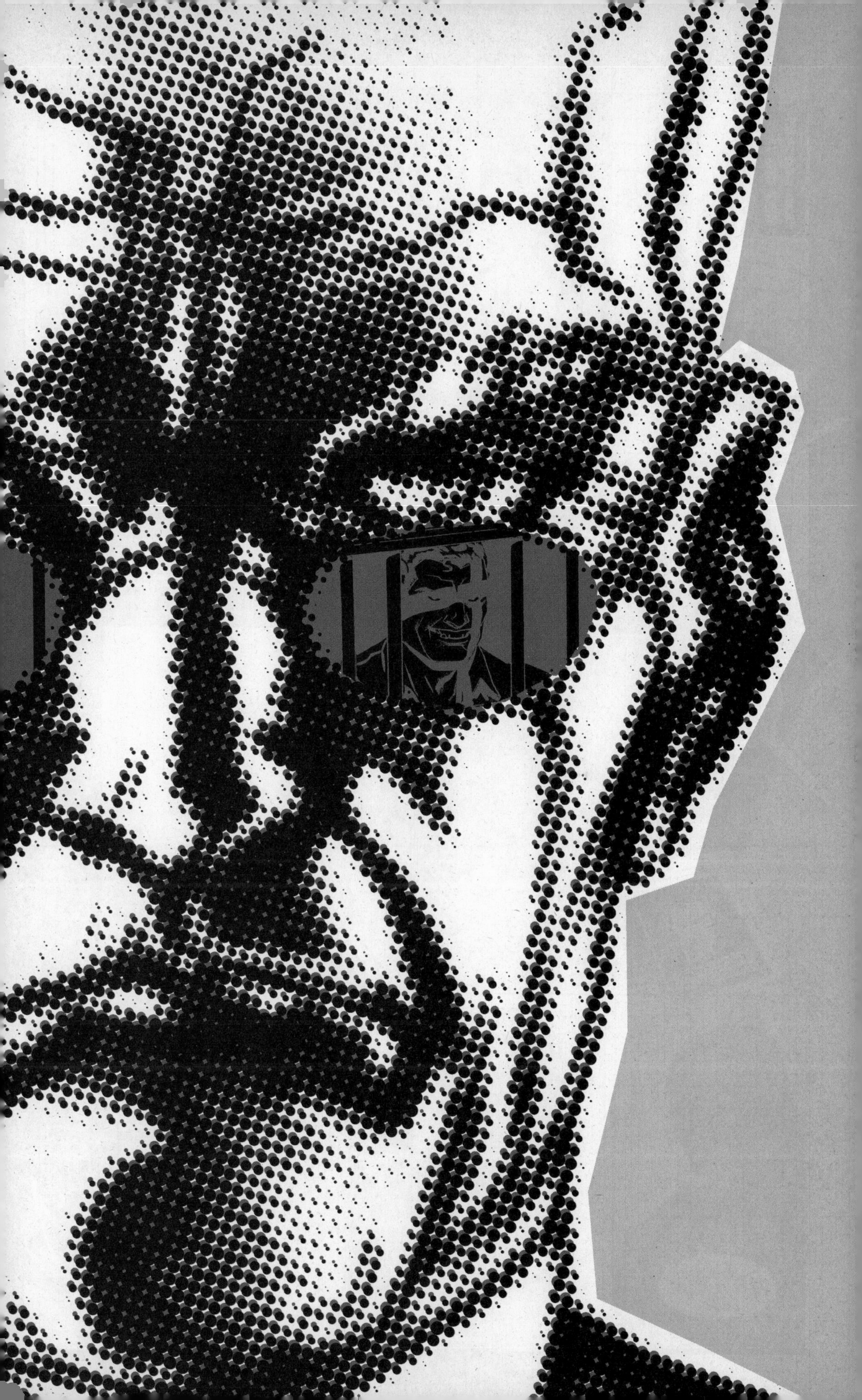

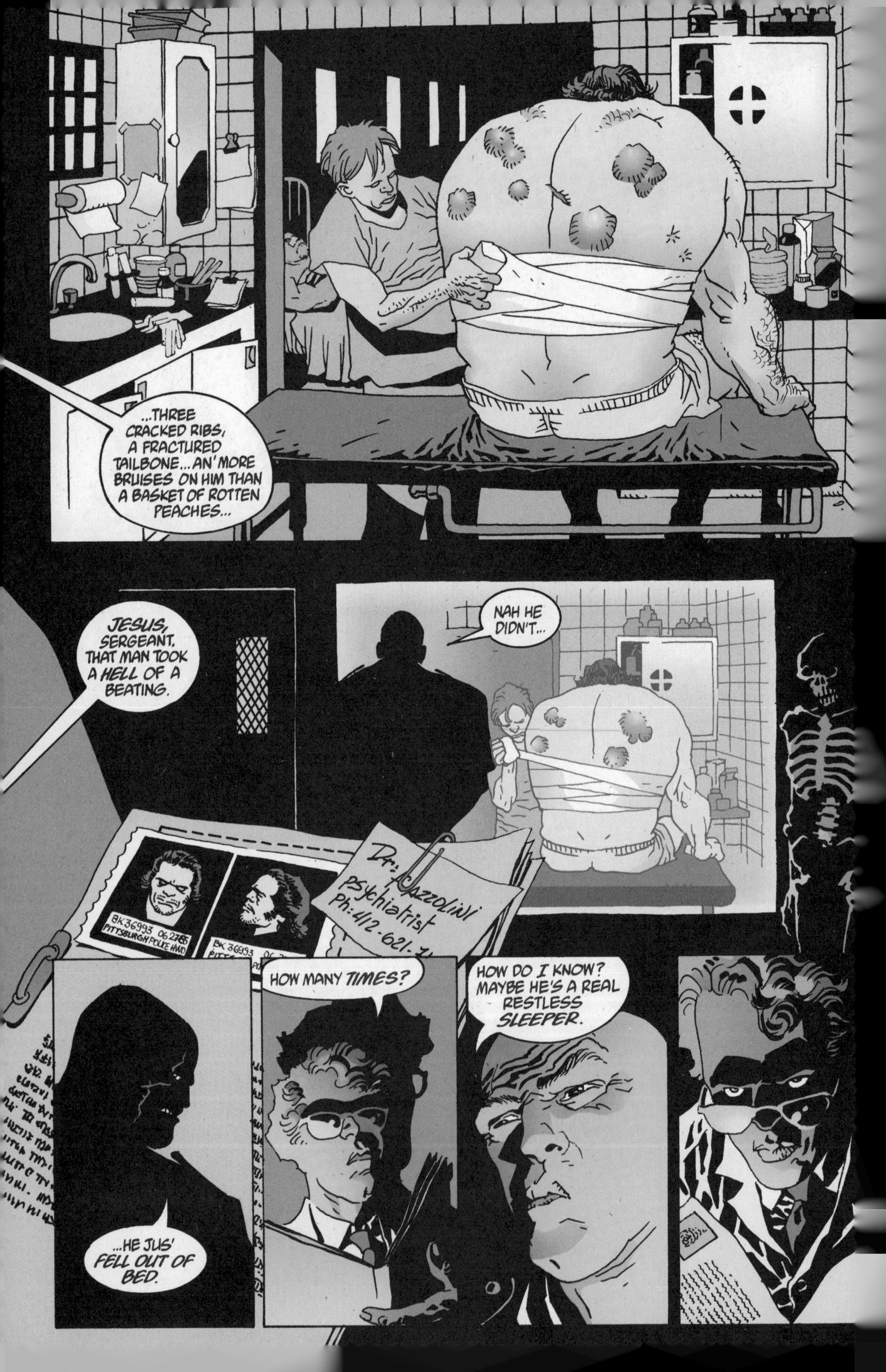
...THREE CRACKED RIBS, A FRACTURED TAILBONE... AN' MORE BRUISES ON HIM THAN A BASKET OF ROTTEN PEACHES...
JESUS, SERGEANT, THAT MAN TOOK A HELL OF A BEATING.
NAH HE DIDN'T...
...HE JUS' FELL OUT OF BED.
HOW MANY TIMES?
HOW DO I KNOW? MAYBE HE'S A REAL RESTLESS SLEEPER.

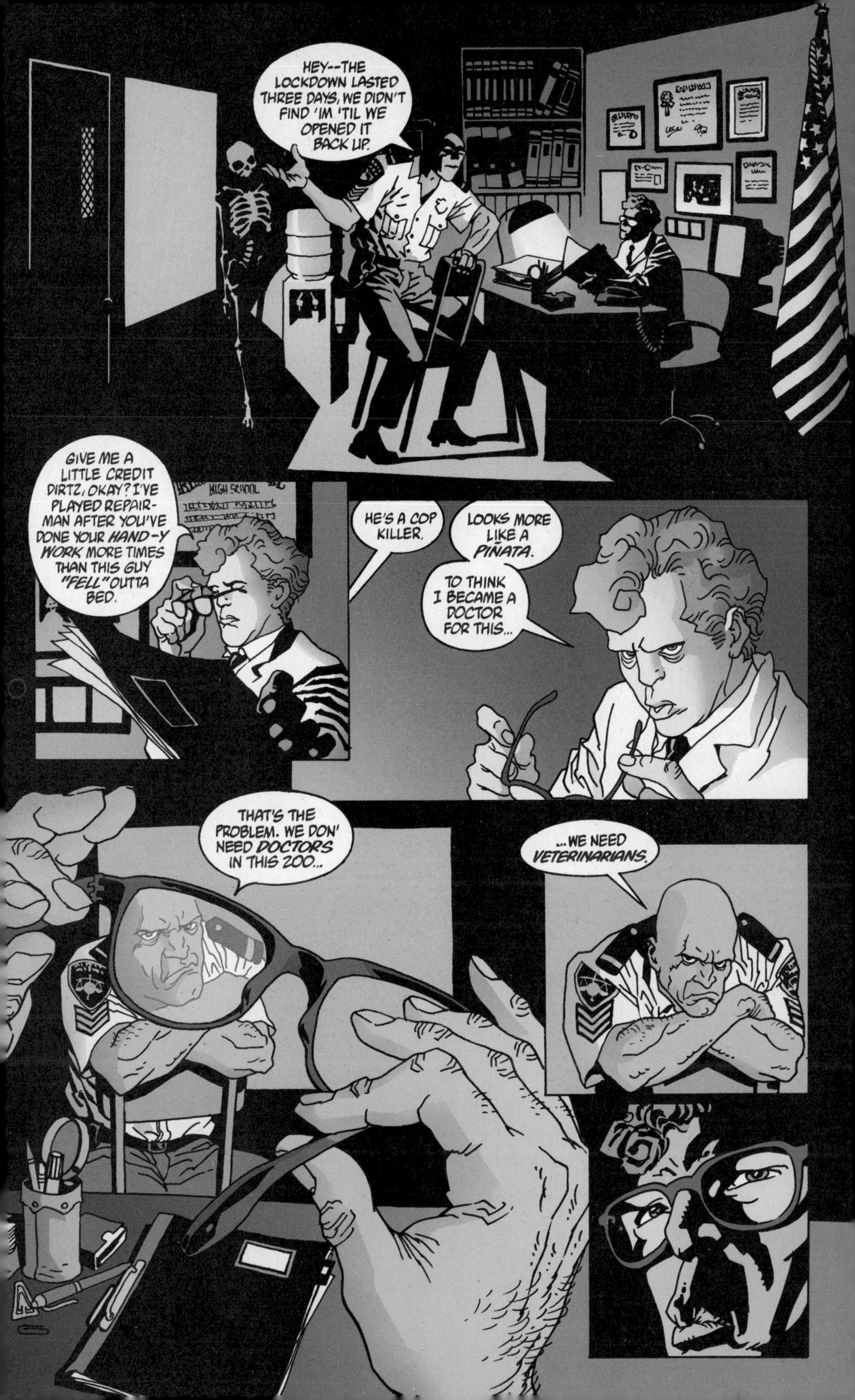
HEY--THE LOCKDOWN LASTED THREE DAYS, WE DIDN'T FIND 'IM 'TIL WE OPENED IT BACK UP.
GIVE ME A LITTLE CREDIT DIRTZ, OKAY? I'VE PLAYED REPAIR-MAN AFTER YOU'VE DONE YOUR HAND-Y WORK MORE TIMES THAN THIS GUY "FELL" OUTTA BED.
HE'S A COP KILLER.
LOOKS MORE LIKE A PIÑATA.
TO THINK I BECAME A DOCTOR FOR THIS...
THAT'S THE PROBLEM. WE DON' NEED DOCTORS IN THIS ZOO...
...WE NEED VETERINARIANS.

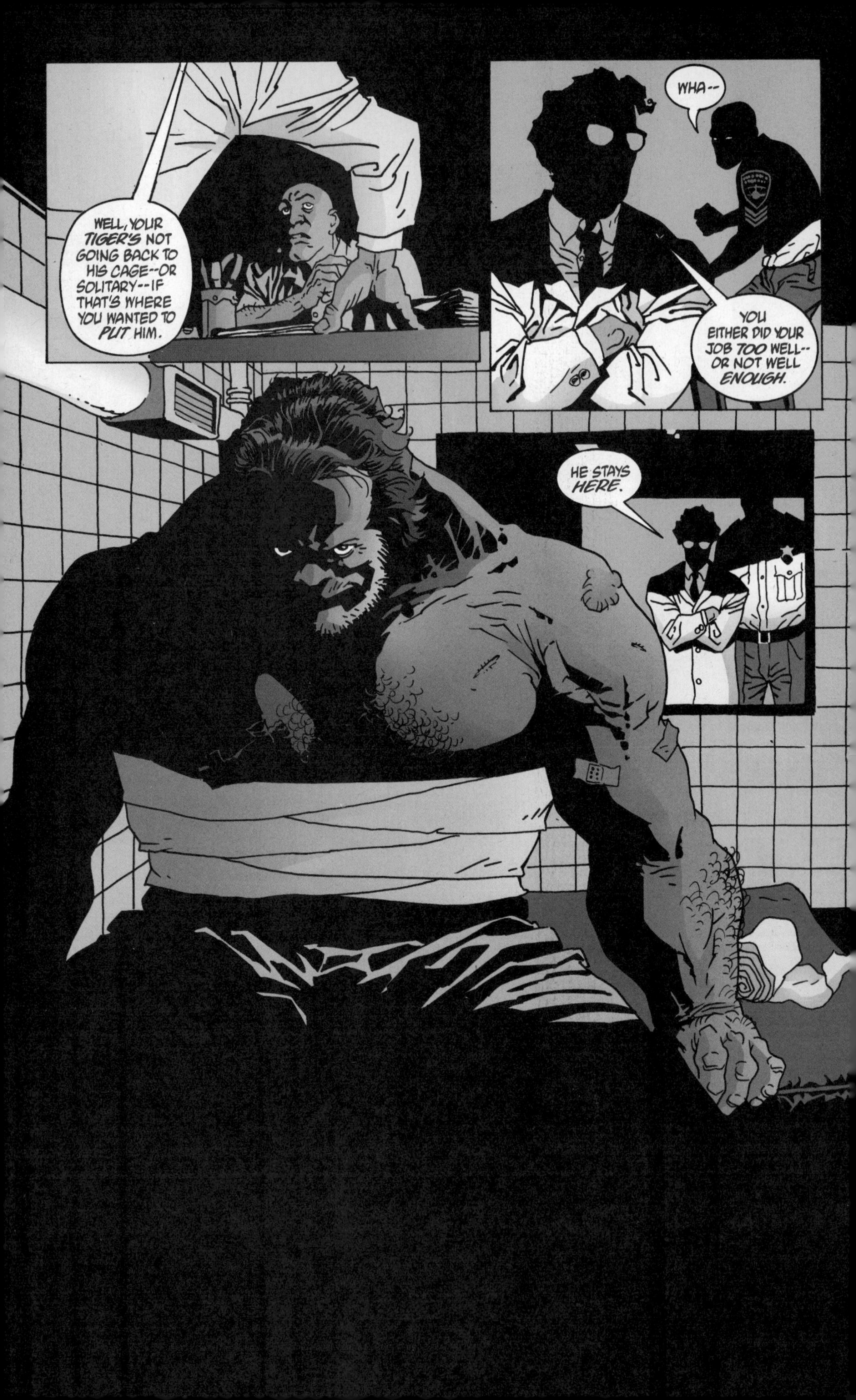
WELL, YOUR TIGER'S NOT GOING BACK TO HIS CAGE--OR SOLITARY--IF THAT'S WHERE YOU WANTED TO PUT HIM.
WHA--
YOU EITHER DID YOUR JOB TOO WELL--OR NOT WELL ENOUGH.
HE STAYS HERE.

NICE MOVE, YOUNG BLOOD. YOU BEEN LEARNIN' SOMETHIN' FINALLY.

UH-HUH. I BEEN STUDYIN' YO' ASS, OLD HEAD. HOW MANY GAMES WE PLAY?

HUN'RED.

AN' HOW MANY I WON?

YOU AIN'T.

SO MAYBE IT'S TIME I GOT LUCKY.

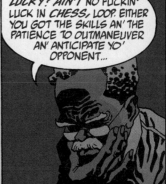

LUCKY? AIN'T NO FUCKIN' LUCK IN CHESS, LOOP. EITHER YOU GOT THE SKILLS AN' THE PATIENCE TO OUTMANEUVER AN' ANTICIPATE YO' OPPONENT...

...OR YOU AIN'T. CHECK-MATE.

ONE-OH-ONE TO NONE.

YO' LOOPY LOOP...

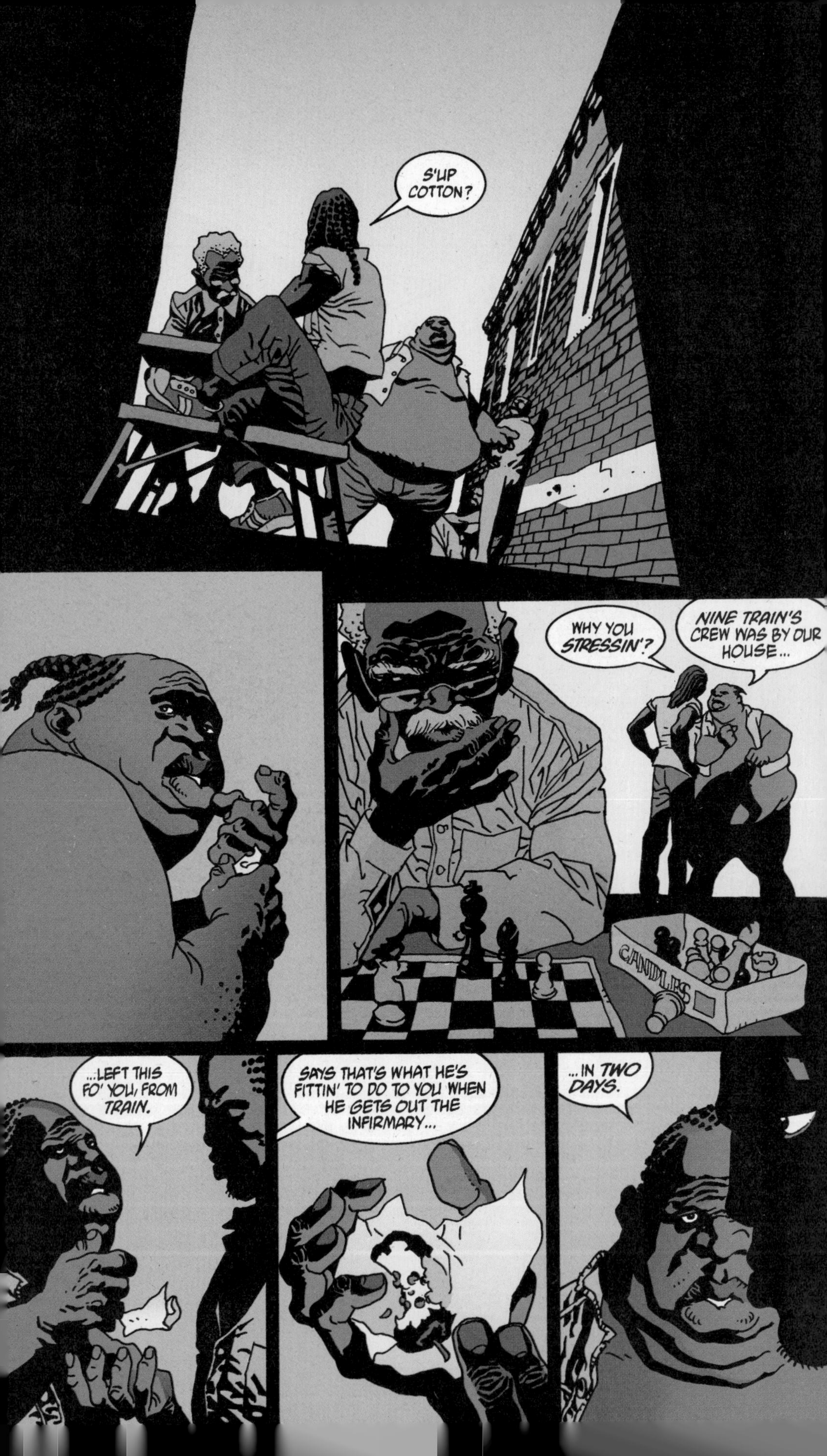
S'UP COTTON?
WHY YOU STRESSIN'?
NINE TRAIN'S CREW WAS BY OUR HOUSE...
...LEFT THIS FO' YOU, FROM TRAIN.
SAYS THAT'S WHAT HE'S FITTIN' TO DO TO YOU WHEN HE GETS OUT THE INFIRMARY...
...IN TWO DAYS.
CANDLES

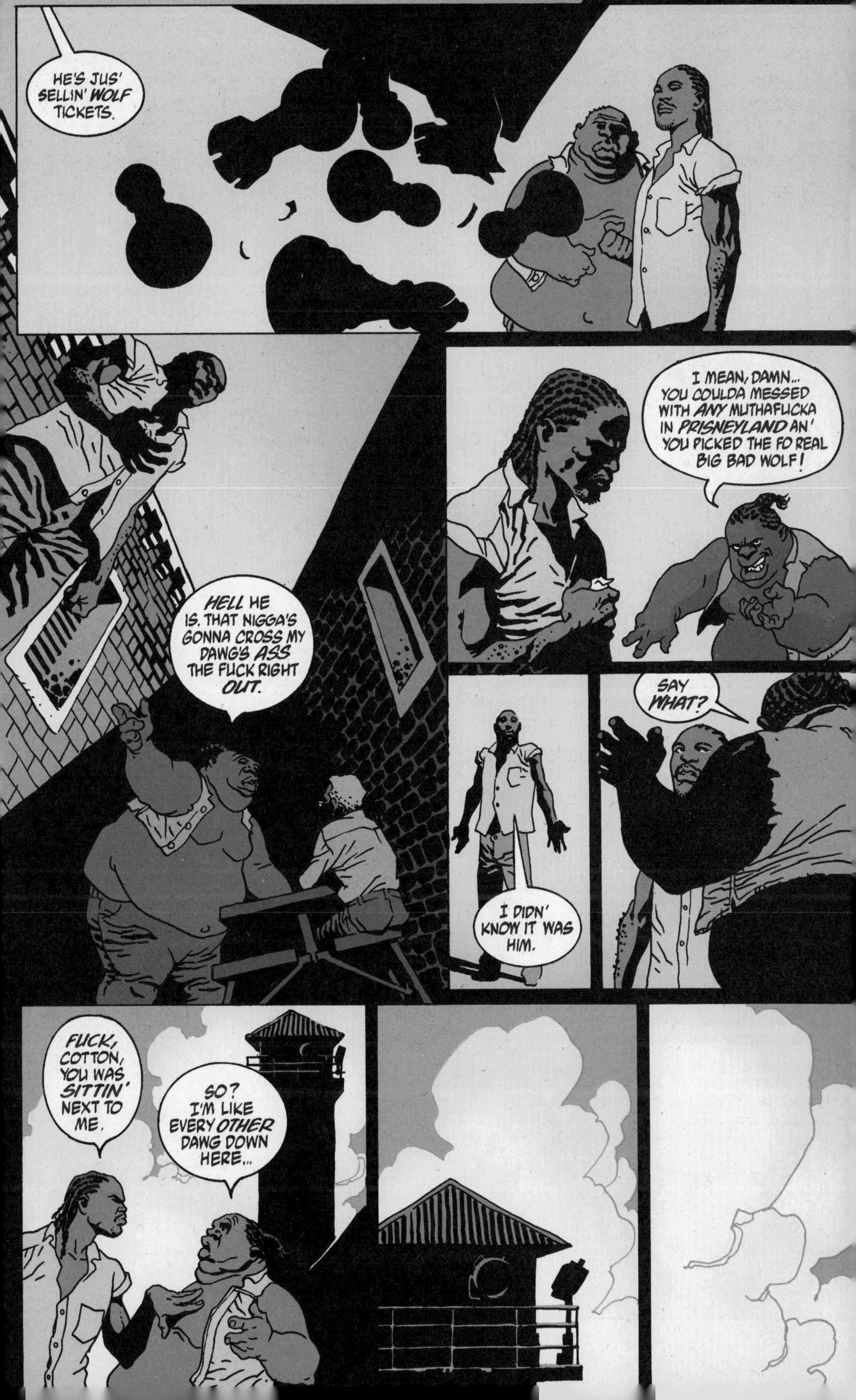
HE'S JUS' SELLIN' WOLF TICKETS.
HELL HE IS. THAT NIGGA'S GONNA CROSS MY DAWG'S ASS THE FUCK RIGHT OUT.
I MEAN, DAMN... YOU COULDA MESSED WITH ANY MUTHAFUCKA IN PRISNEYLAND AN' YOU PICKED THE FO REAL BIG BAD WOLF!
I DIDN' KNOW IT WAS HIM.
SAY WHAT?
FUCK, COTTON, YOU WAS SITTIN' NEXT TO ME.
SO? I'M LIKE EVERY OTHER DAWG DOWN HERE...

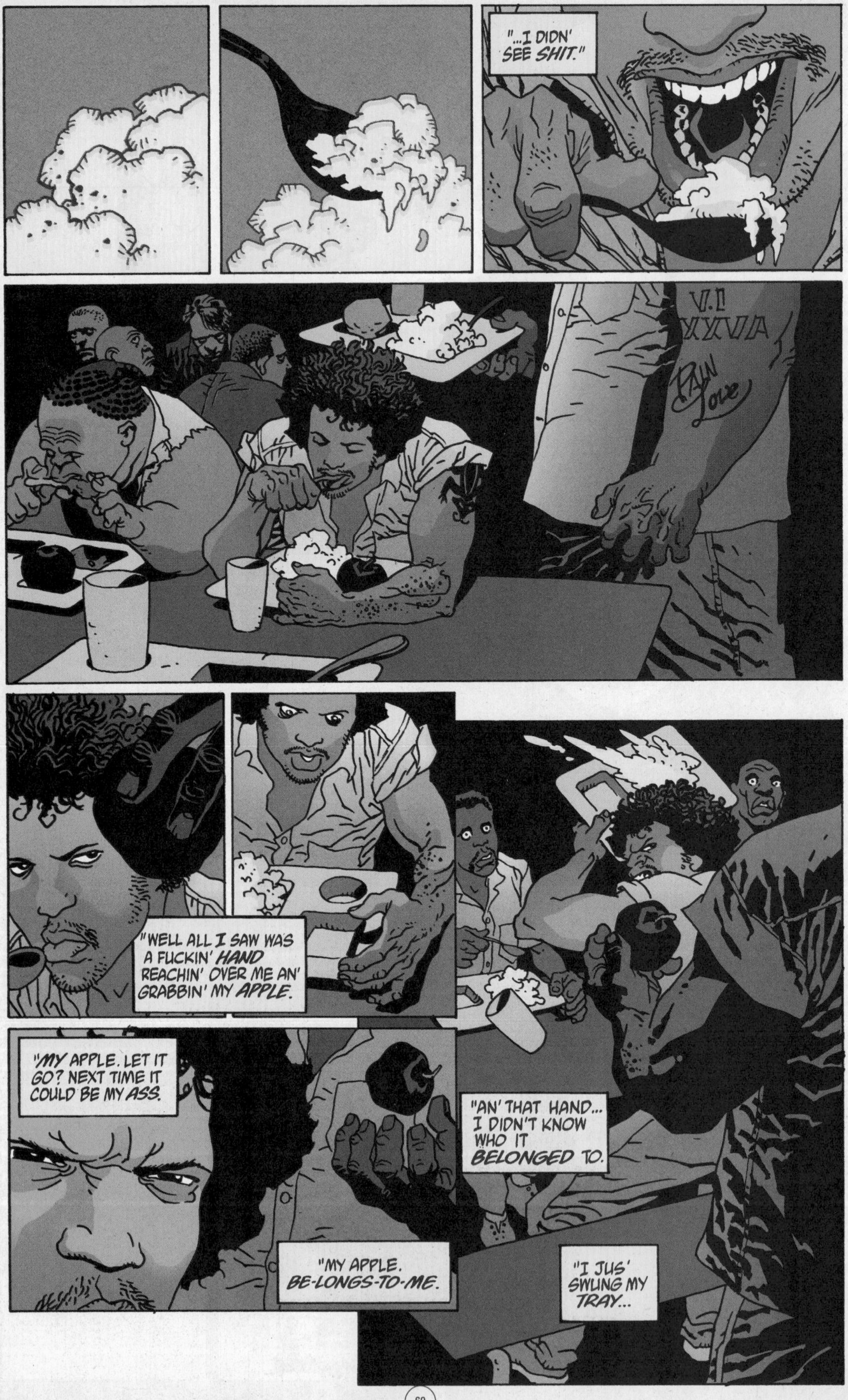
"...I DIDN' SEE SHIT."
V.I
XXVIA
PAIN
LOVE
"WELL ALL I SAW WAS A FUCKIN' HAND REACHIN' OVER ME AN' GRABBIN' MY APPLE.
"MY APPLE. LET IT GO? NEXT TIME IT COULD BE MY ASS.
"MY APPLE. BE-LONGS-TO-ME.
"AN' THAT HAND... I DIDN'T KNOW WHO IT BELONGED TO.
"I JUS' SWUNG MY TRAY...

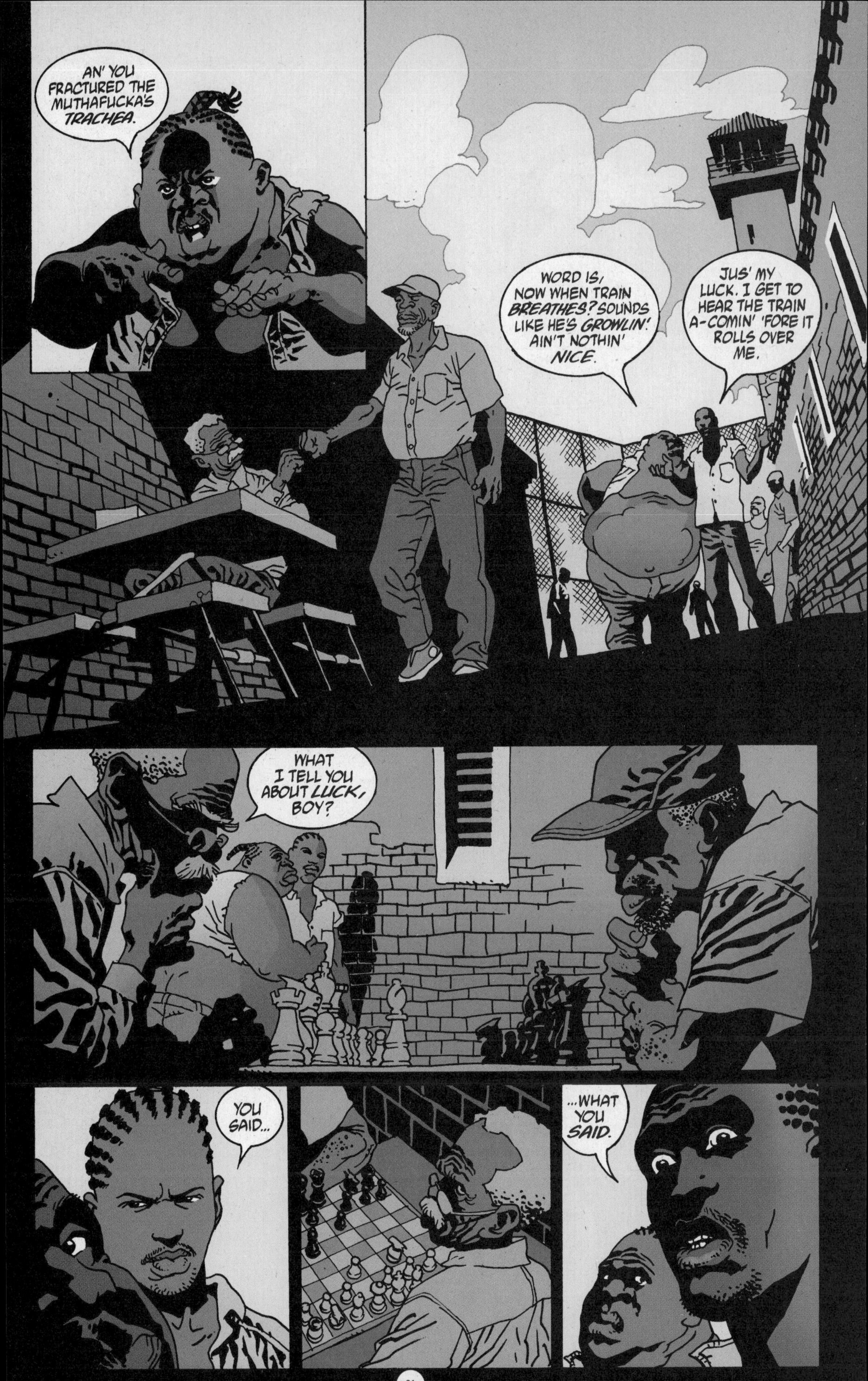
AN' YOU FRACTURED THE MUTHAFUCKA'S TRACHEA.
WORD IS, NOW WHEN TRAIN BREATHES? SOUNDS LIKE HE'S GROWLIN'. AIN'T NOTHIN' NICE.
JUS' MY LUCK. I GET TO HEAR THE TRAIN A-COMIN' 'FORE IT ROLLS OVER ME.
WHAT I TELL YOU ABOUT LUCK, BOY?
YOU SAID...
...WHAT YOU SAID.

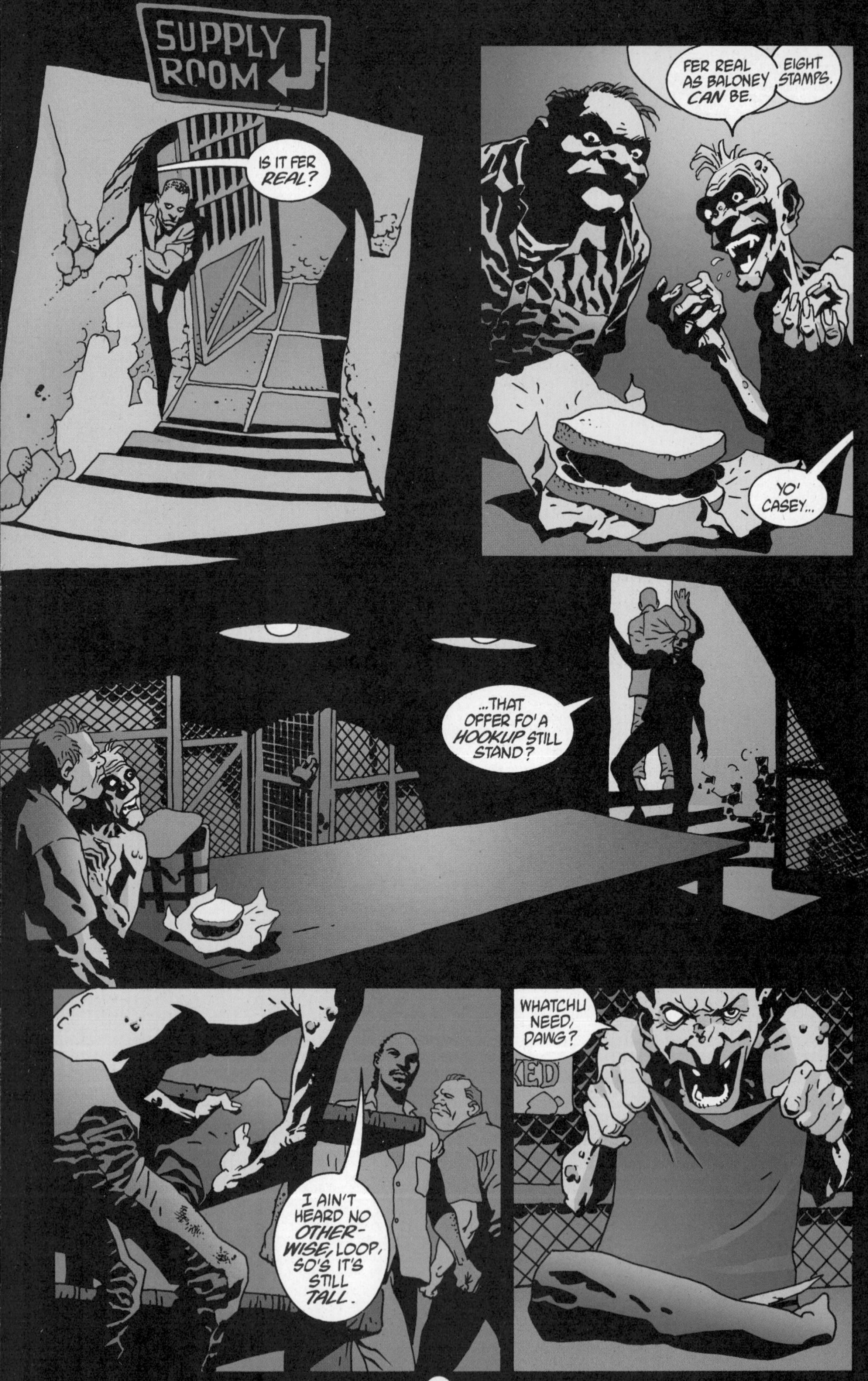
SUPPLY ROOM
IS IT FER REAL?
FER REAL AS BALONEY CAN BE.
EIGHT STAMPS.
YO' CASEY...
...THAT OFFER FO'A HOOKUP STILL STAND?
I AIN'T HEARD NO OTHER-WISE, LOOP, SO'S IT'S STILL TALL.
WHATCHU NEED, DANG?

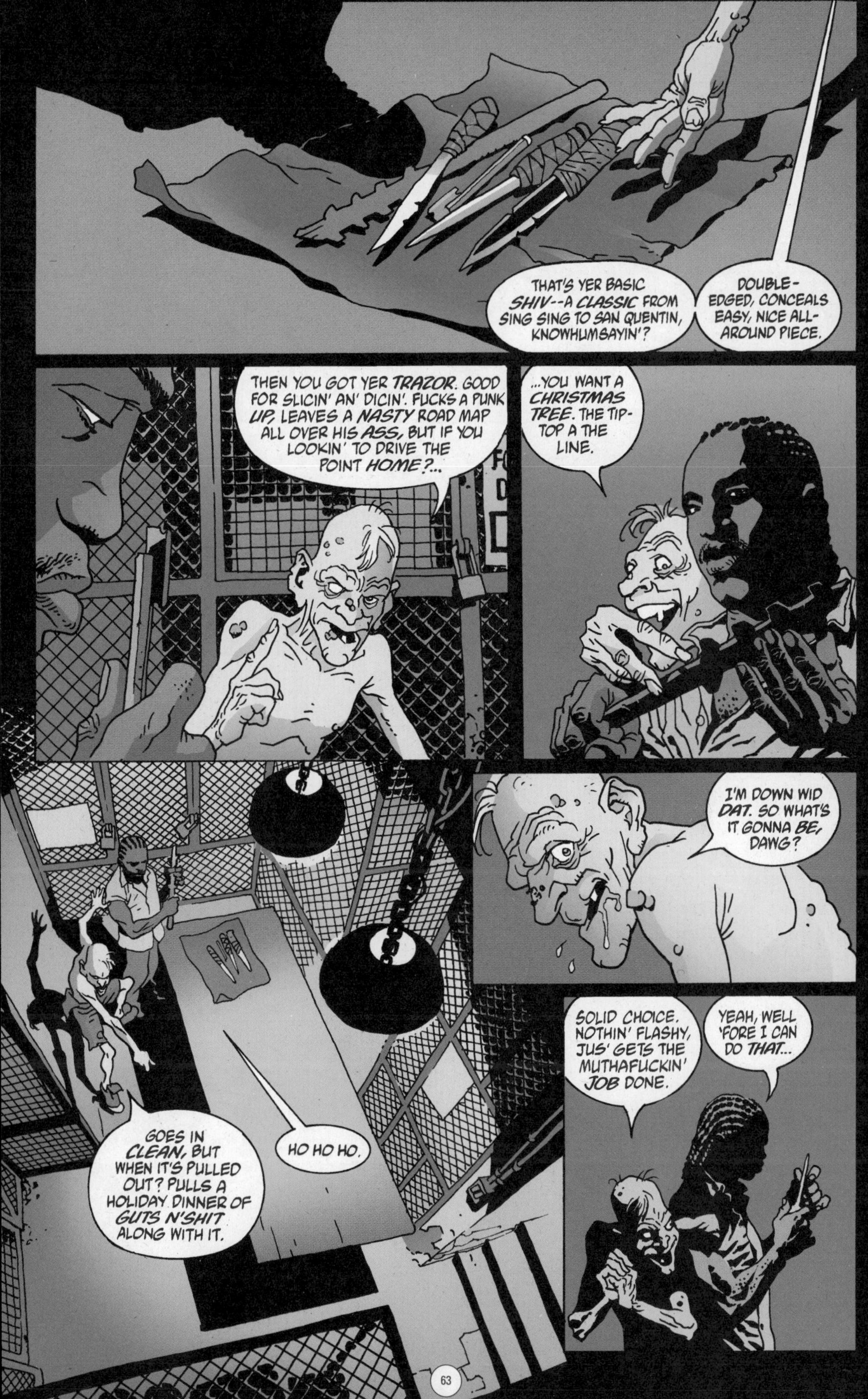
THAT'S YER BASIC SHIV--A CLASSIC FROM SING SING TO SAN QUENTIN, KNOWHUMSAYIN'?
DOUBLE-EDGED, CONCEALS EASY, NICE ALL-AROUND PIECE.
THEN YOU GOT YER TRAZOR. GOOD FOR SLICIN' AN' DICIN'. FUCKS A PUNK UP, LEAVES A NASTY ROAD MAP ALL OVER HIS ASS, BUT IF YOU LOOKIN' TO DRIVE THE POINT HOME?...
...YOU WANT A CHRISTMAS TREE. THE TIP-TOP A THE LINE.
GOES IN CLEAN, BUT WHEN IT'S PULLED OUT? PULLS A HOLIDAY DINNER OF GUTS N'SHIT ALONG WITH IT.
HO HO HO.
I'M DOWN WID DAT. SO WHAT'S IT GONNA BE, DAWG?
SOLID CHOICE. NOTHIN' FLASHY, JUS' GETS THE MUTHAFUCKIN' JOB DONE.
YEAH, WELL 'FORE I CAN DO THAT...

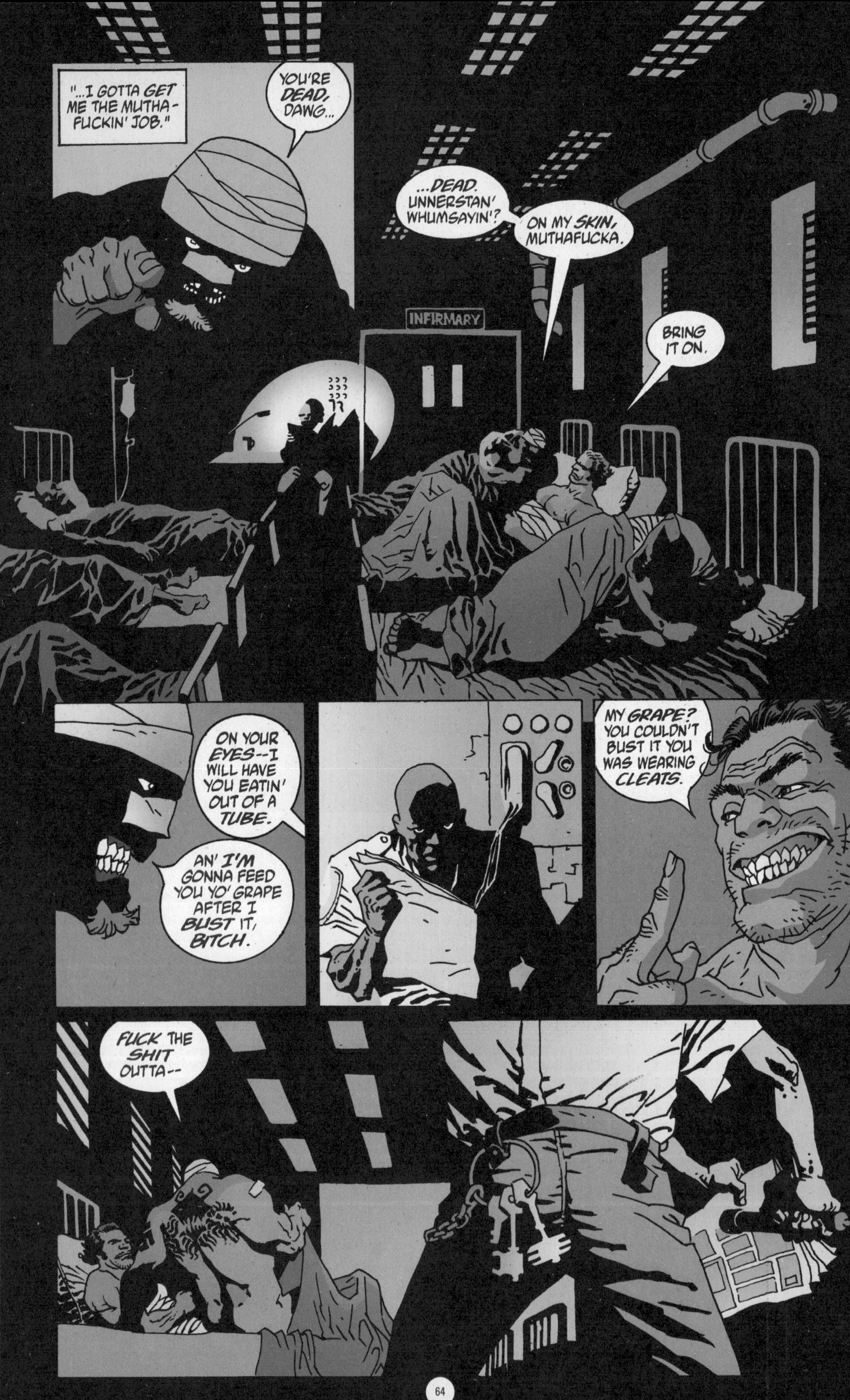

"...I GOTTA GET ME THE MUTHA-FUCKIN' JOB."
YOU'RE DEAD, DAWG...
...DEAD. UNNERSTAN' WHUMSAYIN'?
ON MY SKIN, MUTHAFUCKA.
INFIRMARY
BRING IT ON.
ON YOUR EYES--I WILL HAVE YOU EATIN' OUT OF A TUBE.
AN' I'M GONNA FEED YOU YO' GRAPE AFTER I BUST IT, BITCH.
MY GRAPE? YOU COULDN'T BUST IT YOU WAS WEARING CLEATS.
FUCK THE SHIT OUTTA--

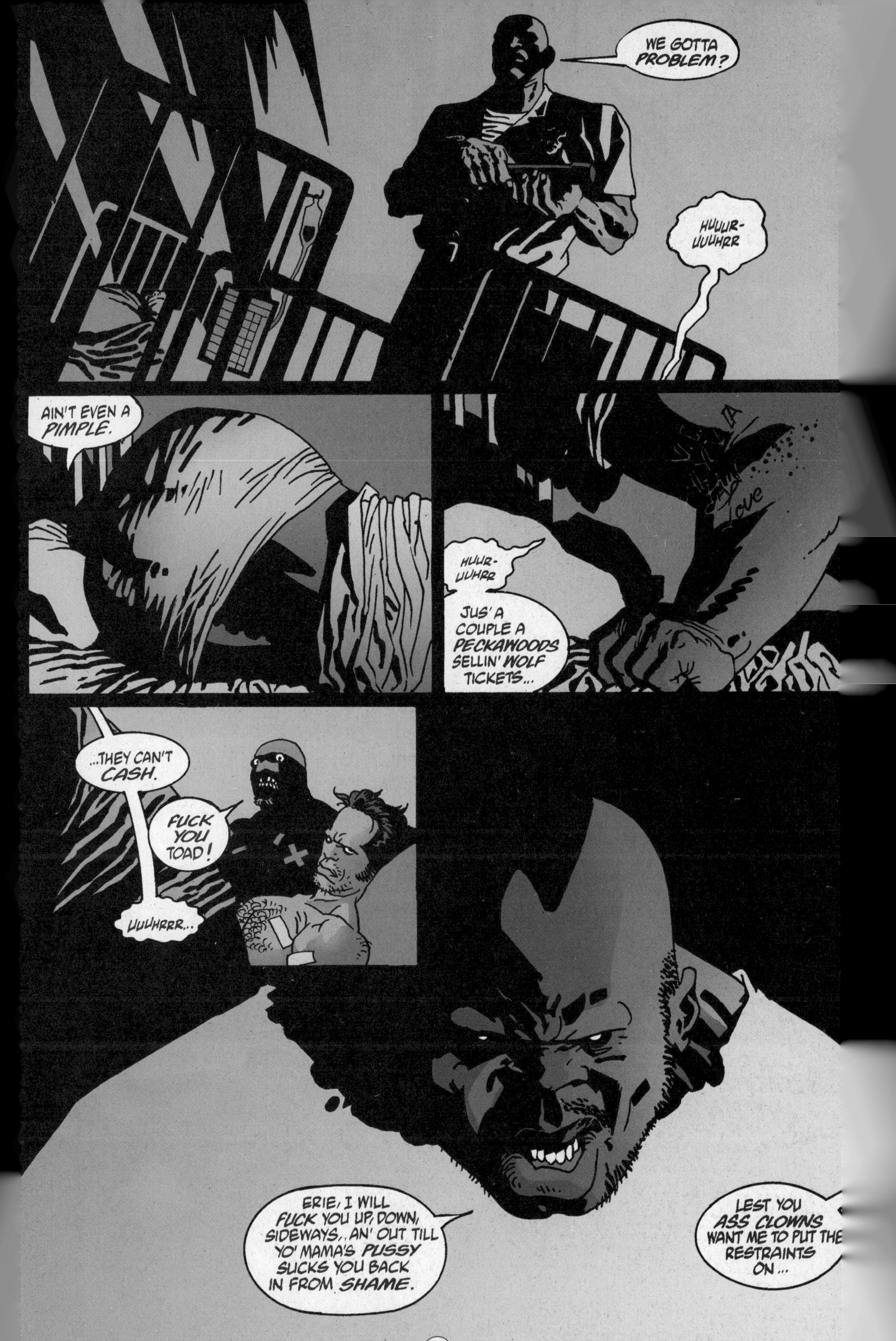
WE GOTTA PROBLEM?
HUUUR-UUUHRR
AIN'T EVEN A PIMPLE.
HUUR-UUHRR
JUS' A COUPLE A PECKAWOODS SELLIN' WOLF TICKETS...
...THEY CAN'T CASH.
FUCK YOU TOAD!
UUUHRRR...
ERIE, I WILL FUCK YOU UP, DOWN, SIDEWAYS... AN' OUT TILL YO' MAMA'S PUSSY SUCKS YOU BACK IN FROM SHAME.
LEST YOU ASS CLOWNS WANT ME TO PUT THE RESTRAINTS ON...

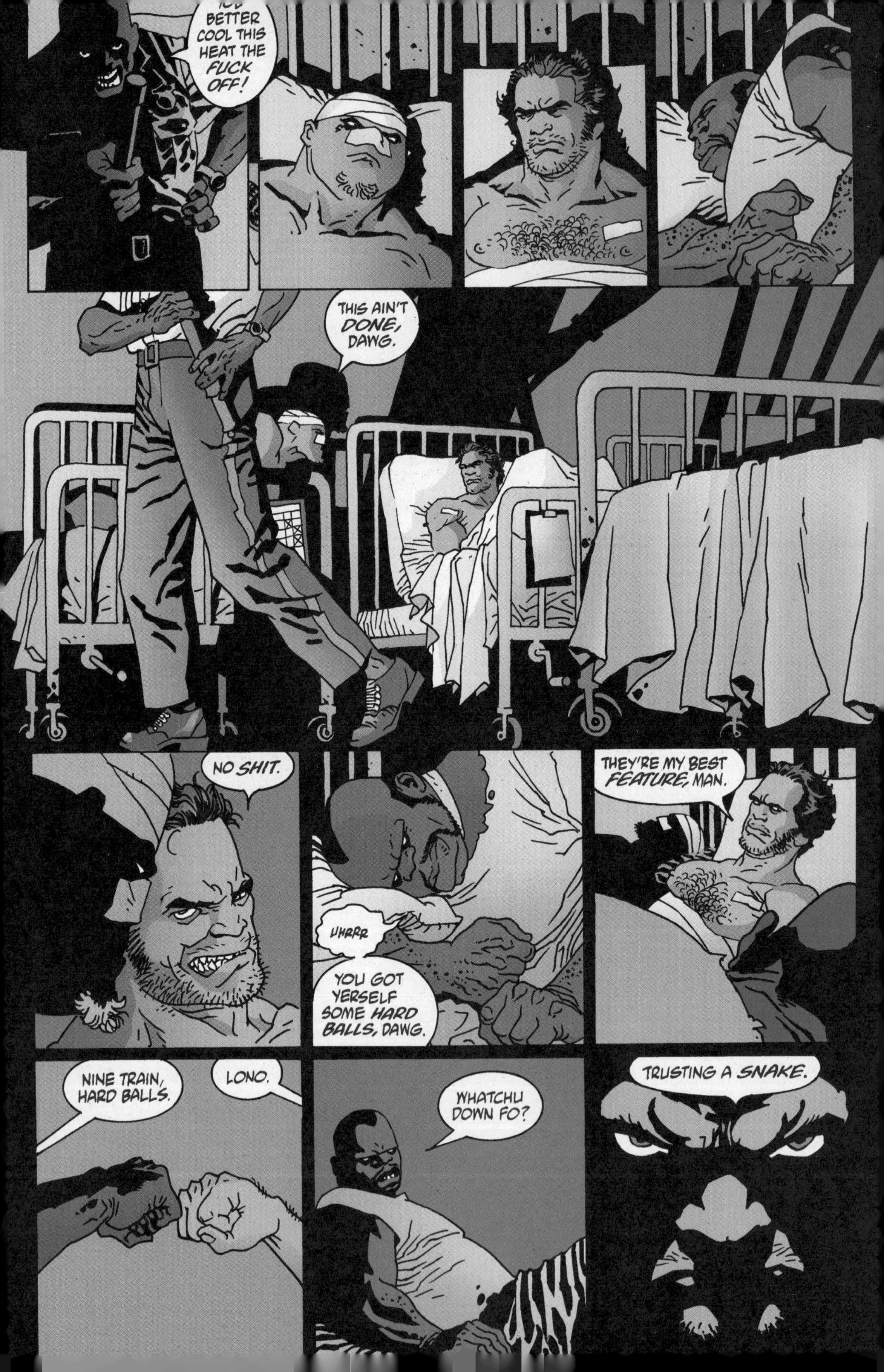

YOU BETTER COOL THIS HEAT THE *FUCK* OFF!
THIS AIN'T *DONE*, DAWG.
NO *SHIT*.
UHRRR
YOU GOT YERSELF SOME *HARD BALLS*, DAWG.
THEY'RE MY BEST *FEATURE*, MAN.
NINE TRAIN, HARD BALLS.
LONO.
WHATCHU DOWN FO?
TRUSTING A *SNAKE*.

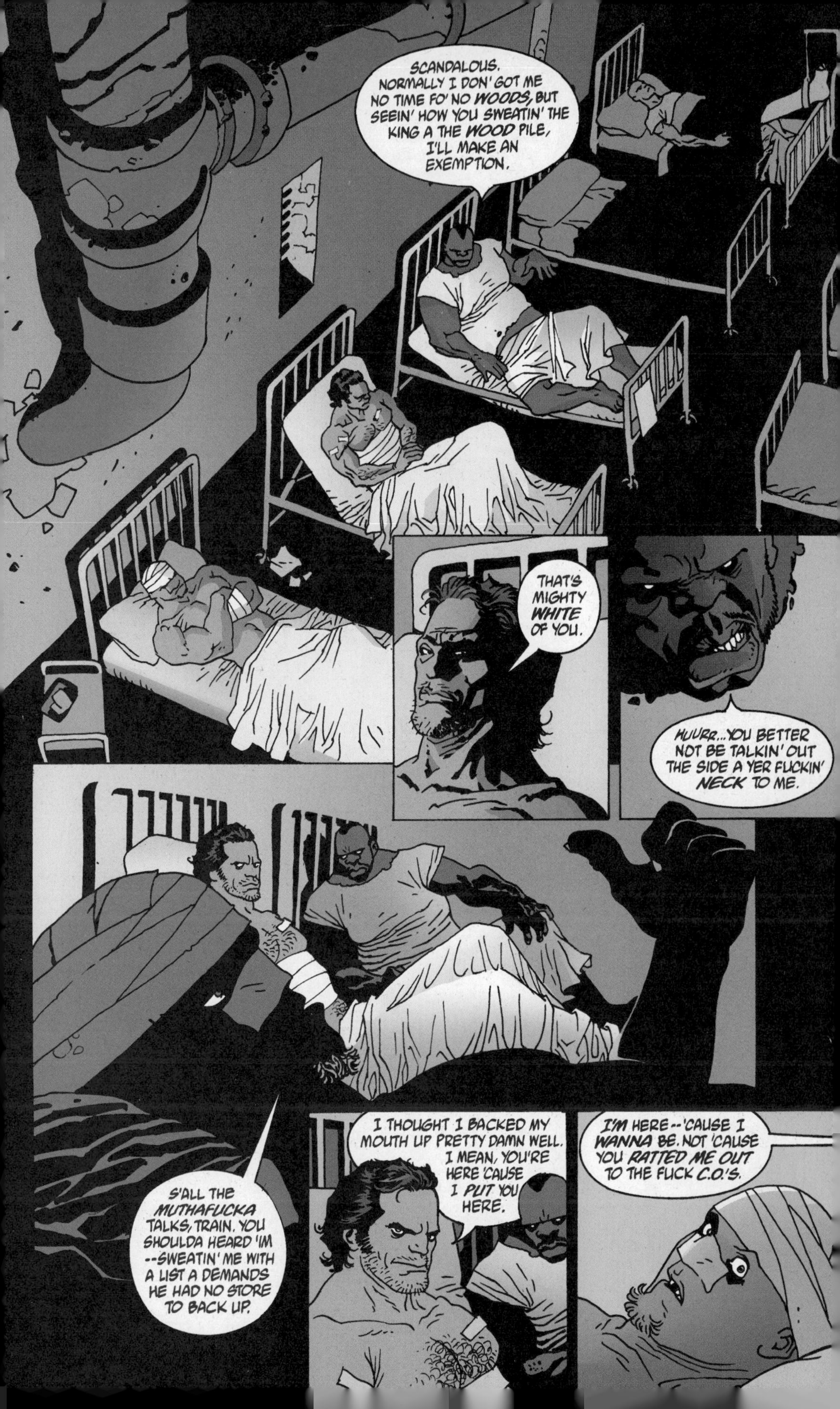
SCANDALOUS. NORMALLY I DON' GOT ME NO TIME FO' NO WOODS, BUT SEEIN' HOW YOU SWEATIN' THE KING A THE WOOD PILE, I'LL MAKE AN EXEMPTION.
THAT'S MIGHTY WHITE OF YOU.
HUURR...YOU BETTER NOT BE TALKIN' OUT THE SIDE A YER FUCKIN' NECK TO ME.
S'ALL THE MUTHAFUCKA TALKS, TRAIN. YOU SHOULDA HEARD 'IM --SWEATIN' ME WITH A LIST A DEMANDS HE HAD NO STORE TO BACK UP.
I THOUGHT I BACKED MY MOUTH UP PRETTY DAMN WELL. I MEAN, YOU'RE HERE 'CAUSE I PUT YOU HERE.
I'M HERE--'CAUSE I WANNA BE. NOT 'CAUSE YOU RATTED ME OUT TO THE FUCK C.O.'S.

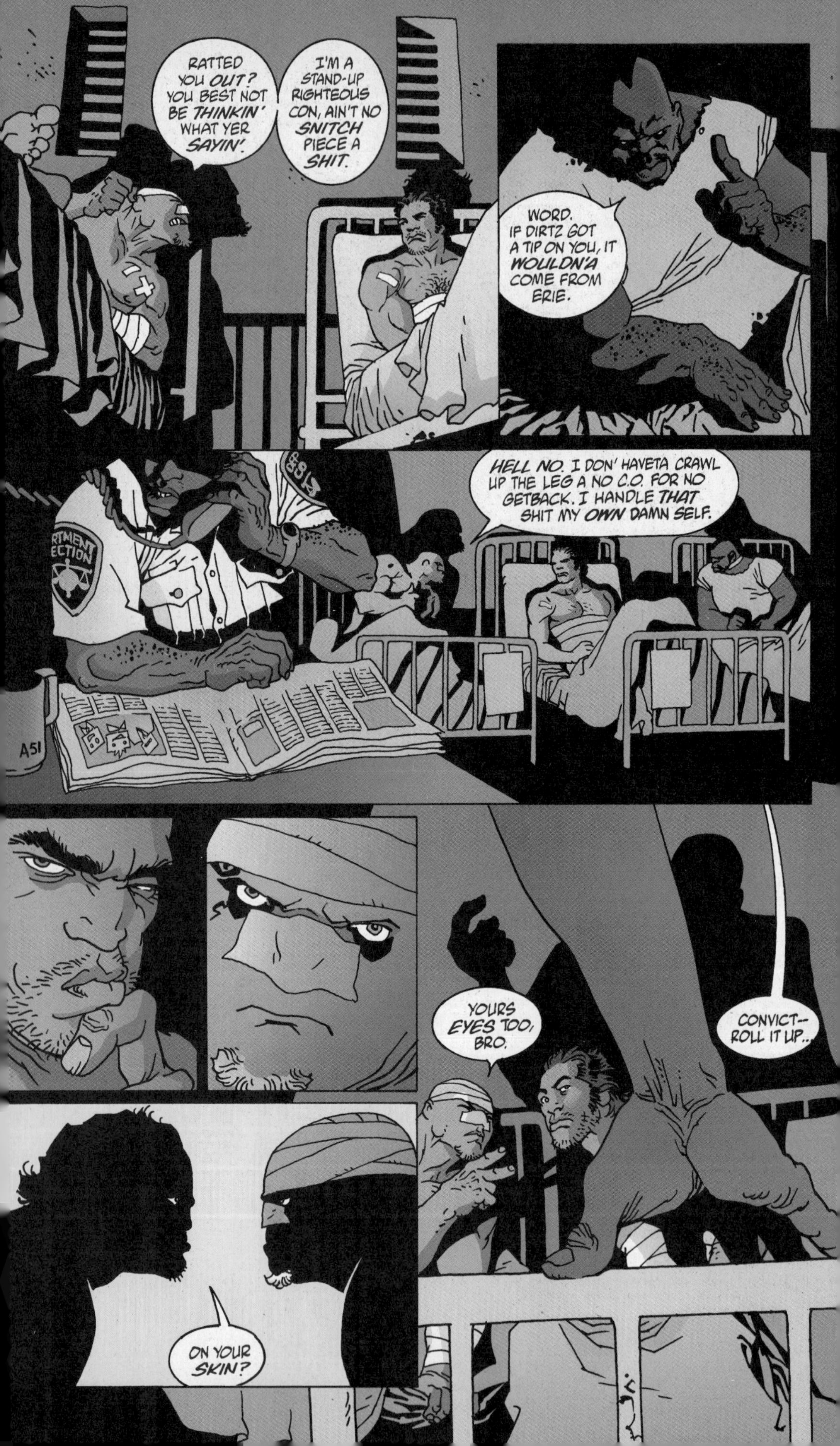
RATTED YOU OUT? YOU BEST NOT BE THINKIN' WHAT YER SAYIN'.
I'M A STAND-UP RIGHTEOUS CON, AIN'T NO SNITCH PIECE A SHIT.
WORD. IF DIRTZ GOT A TIP ON YOU, IT WOULDN'A COME FROM ERIE.
HELL NO. I DON' HAVETA CRAWL UP THE LEG A NO C.O. FOR NO GETBACK. I HANDLE THAT SHIT MY OWN DAMN SELF.
YOURS EYES TOO, BRO.
CONVICT-- ROLL IT UP...
ON YOUR SKIN?

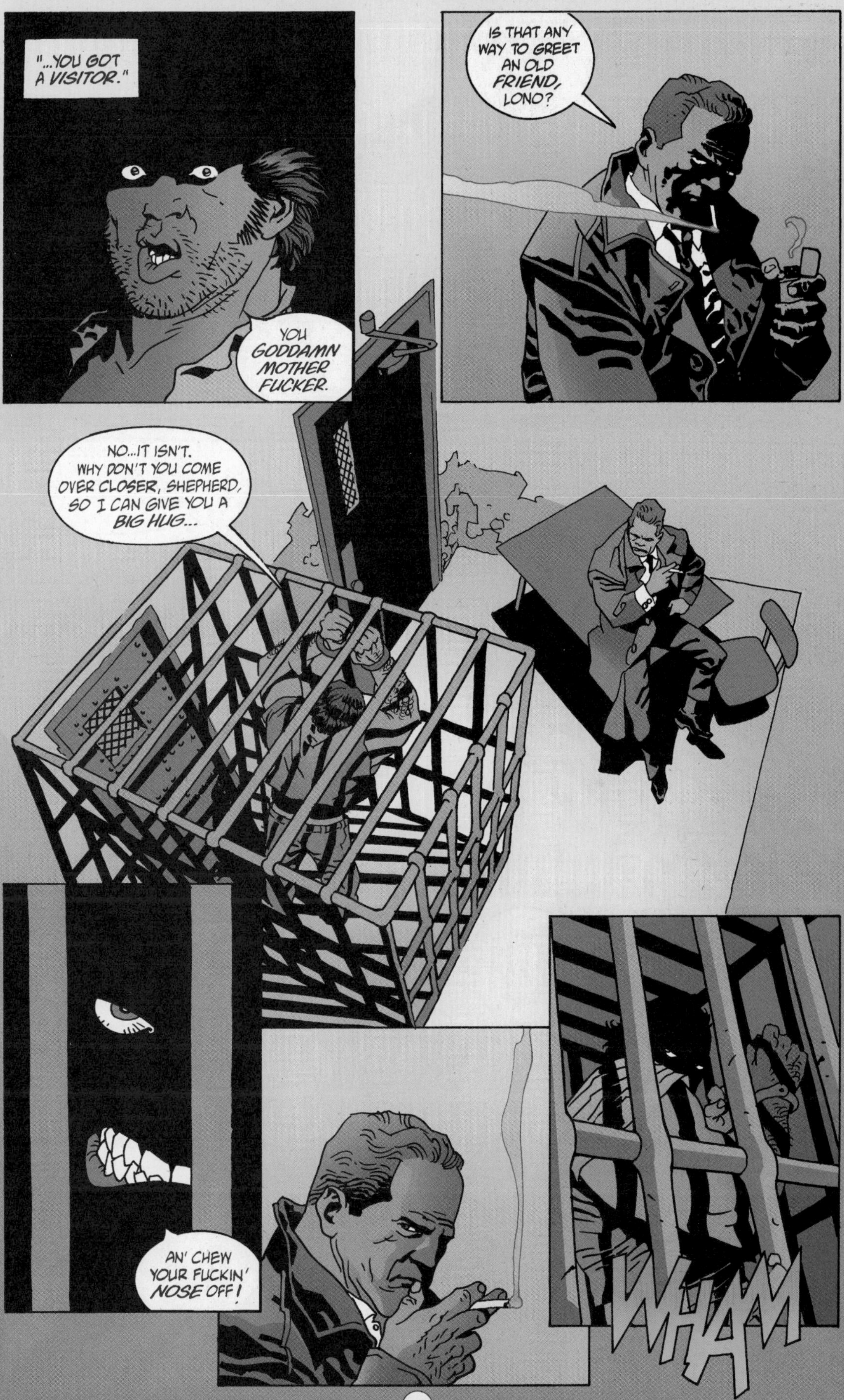
"...YOU GOT A VISITOR."
YOU GODDAMN MOTHER FUCKER.
IS THAT ANY WAY TO GREET AN OLD FRIEND, LONO?
NO...IT ISN'T. WHY DON'T YOU COME OVER CLOSER, SHEPHERD, SO I CAN GIVE YOU A BIG HUG...
AN' CHEW YOUR FUCKIN' NOSE OFF!
WHAM

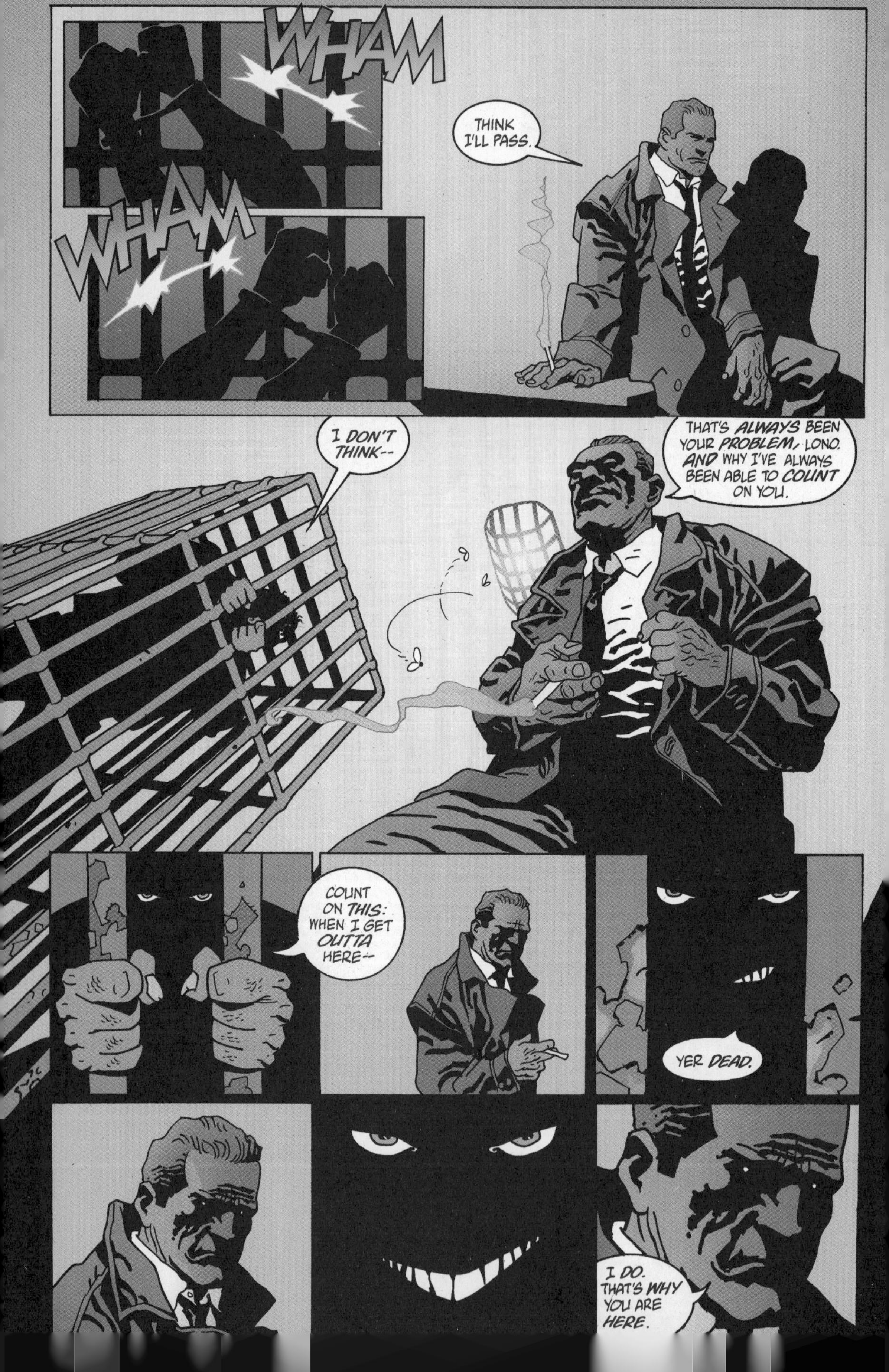
WHAM
THINK I'LL PASS.
WHAM
I DON'T THINK--
THAT'S ALWAYS BEEN YOUR PROBLEM, LONO. AND WHY I'VE ALWAYS BEEN ABLE TO COUNT ON YOU.
COUNT ON THIS: WHEN I GET OUTTA HERE--
YER DEAD.
I DO. THAT'S WHY YOU ARE HERE.

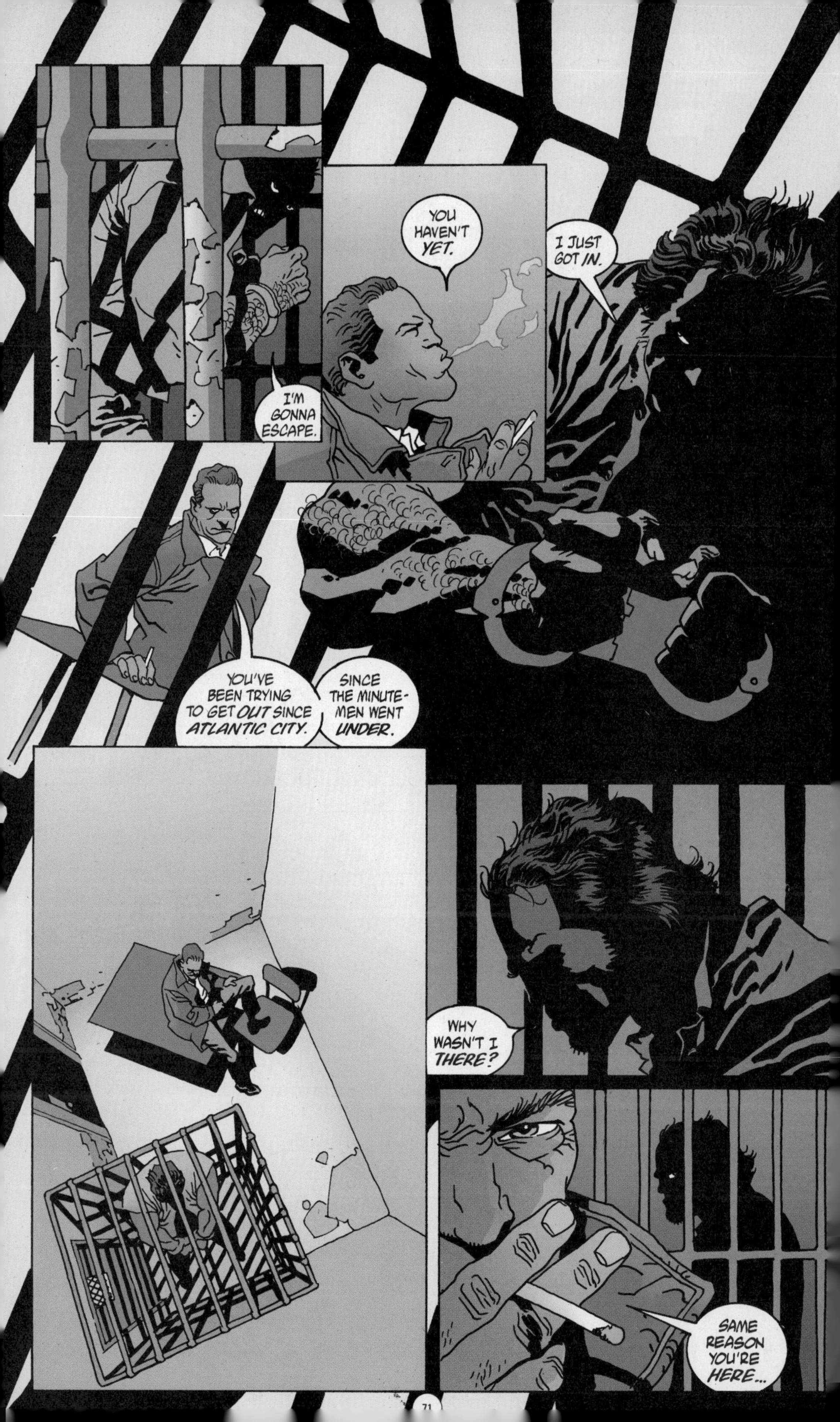
I'M GONNA ESCAPE.
YOU HAVEN'T YET.
I JUST GOT IN.
YOU'VE BEEN TRYING TO GET OUT SINCE ATLANTIC CITY.
SINCE THE MINUTE-MEN WENT UNDER.
WHY WASN'T I THERE?
SAME REASON YOU'RE HERE...

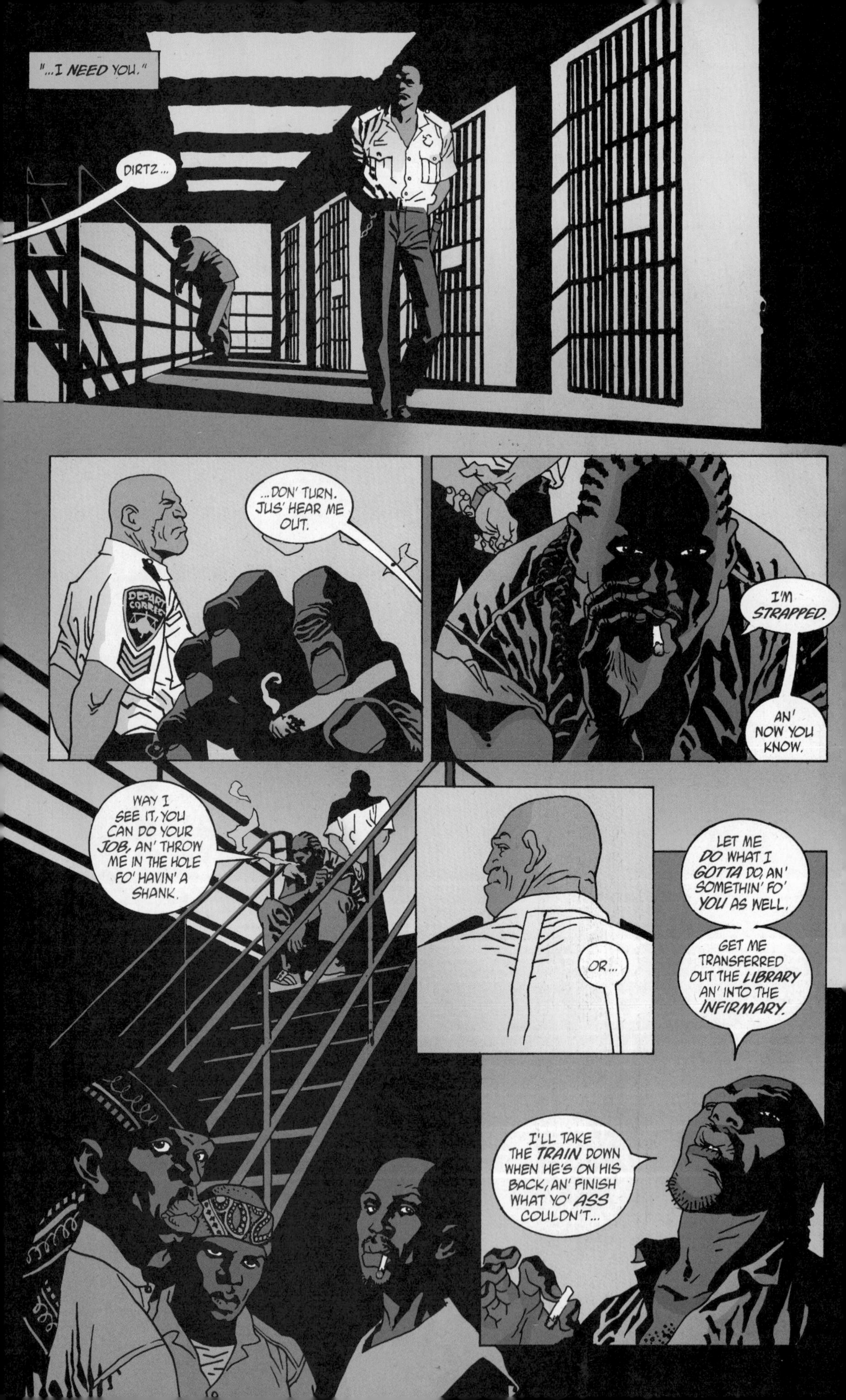
"...I NEED YOU."
DIRTZ...
...DON' TURN. JUS' HEAR ME OUT.
I'M STRAPPED.
AN' NOW YOU KNOW.
WAY I SEE IT, YOU CAN DO YOUR JOB, AN' THROW ME IN THE HOLE FO' HAVIN' A SHANK.
OR...
LET ME DO WHAT I GOTTA DO, AN' SOMETHIN' FO' YOU AS WELL.
GET ME TRANSFERRED OUT THE LIBRARY AN' INTO THE INFIRMARY.
I'LL TAKE THE TRAIN DOWN WHEN HE'S ON HIS BACK, AN' FINISH WHAT YO' ASS COULDN'T...

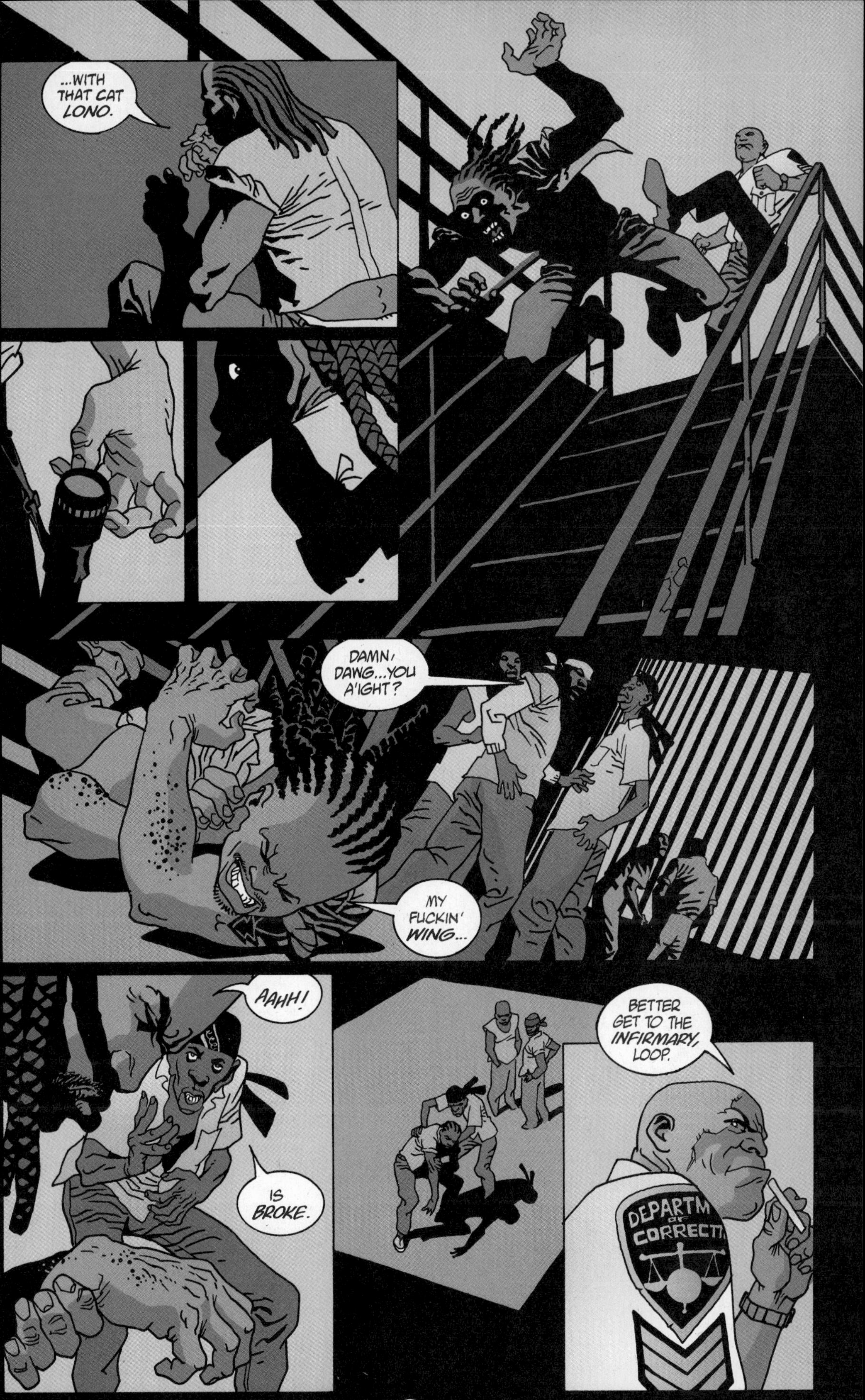
...WITH THAT CAT LONO.
DAMN, DAWG...YOU A'IGHT?
MY FUCKIN' WING...
AAHH!
IS BROKE.
BETTER GET TO THE INFIRMARY, LOOP.
DEPARTM
CORRECTI

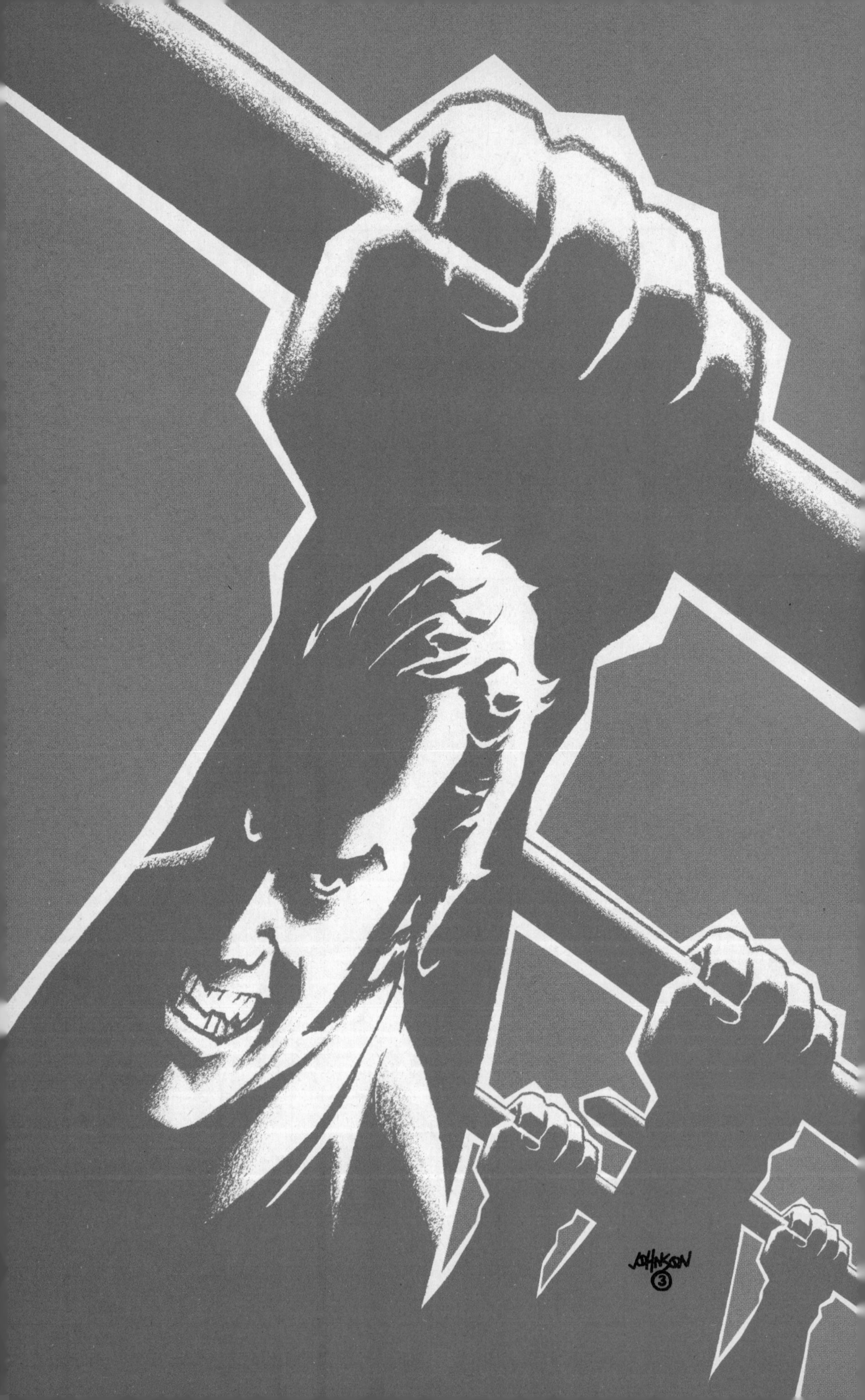
JOHNSON
3

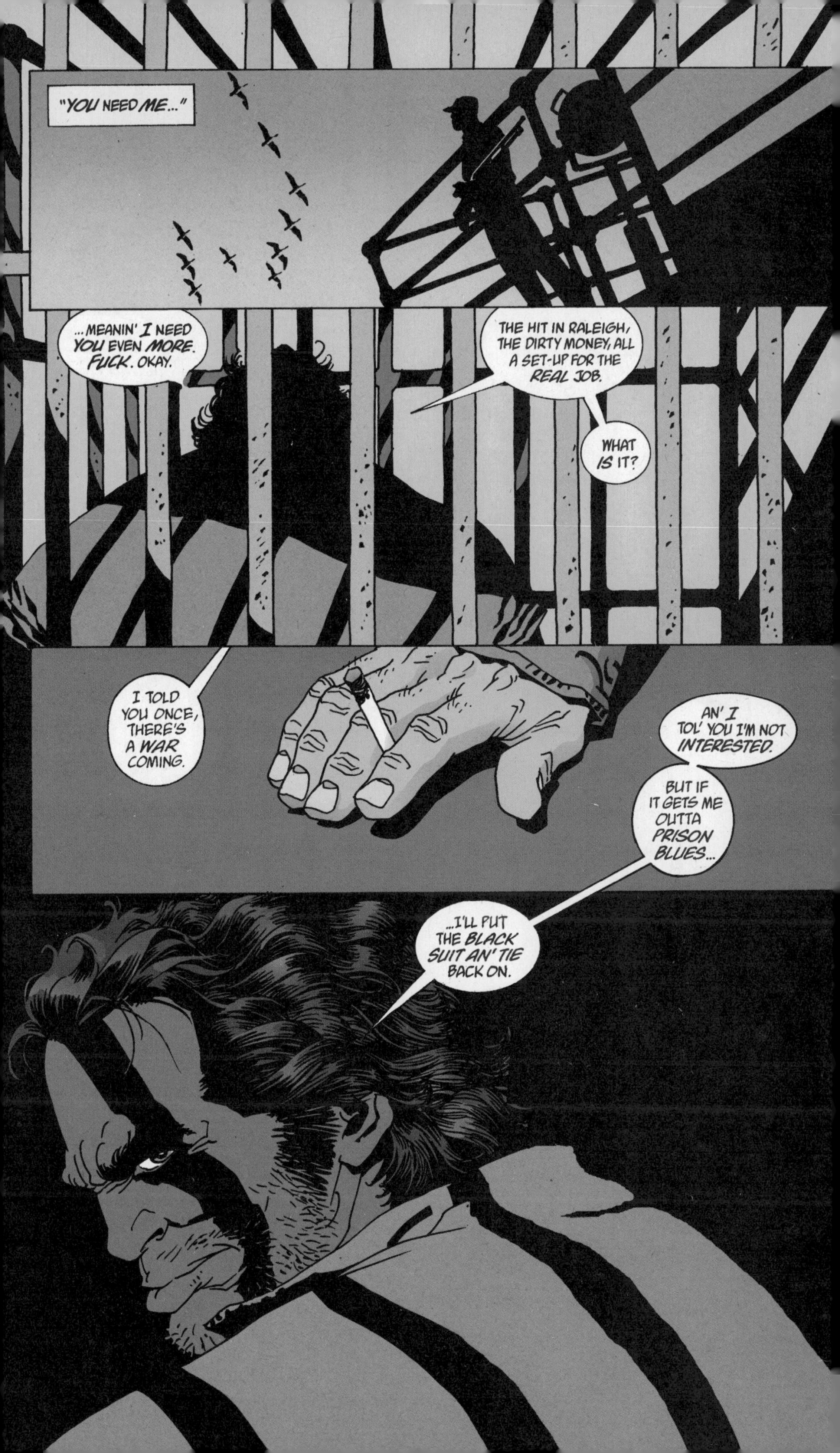
"YOU NEED ME..."
...MEANIN' I NEED YOU EVEN MORE. FUCK. OKAY.
THE HIT IN RALEIGH, THE DIRTY MONEY, ALL A SET-UP FOR THE REAL JOB.
WHAT IS IT?
I TOLD YOU ONCE, THERE'S A WAR COMING.
AN' I TOL' YOU I'M NOT INTERESTED.
BUT IF IT GETS ME OUTTA PRISON BLUES...
...I'LL PUT THE BLACK SUIT AN' TIE BACK ON.

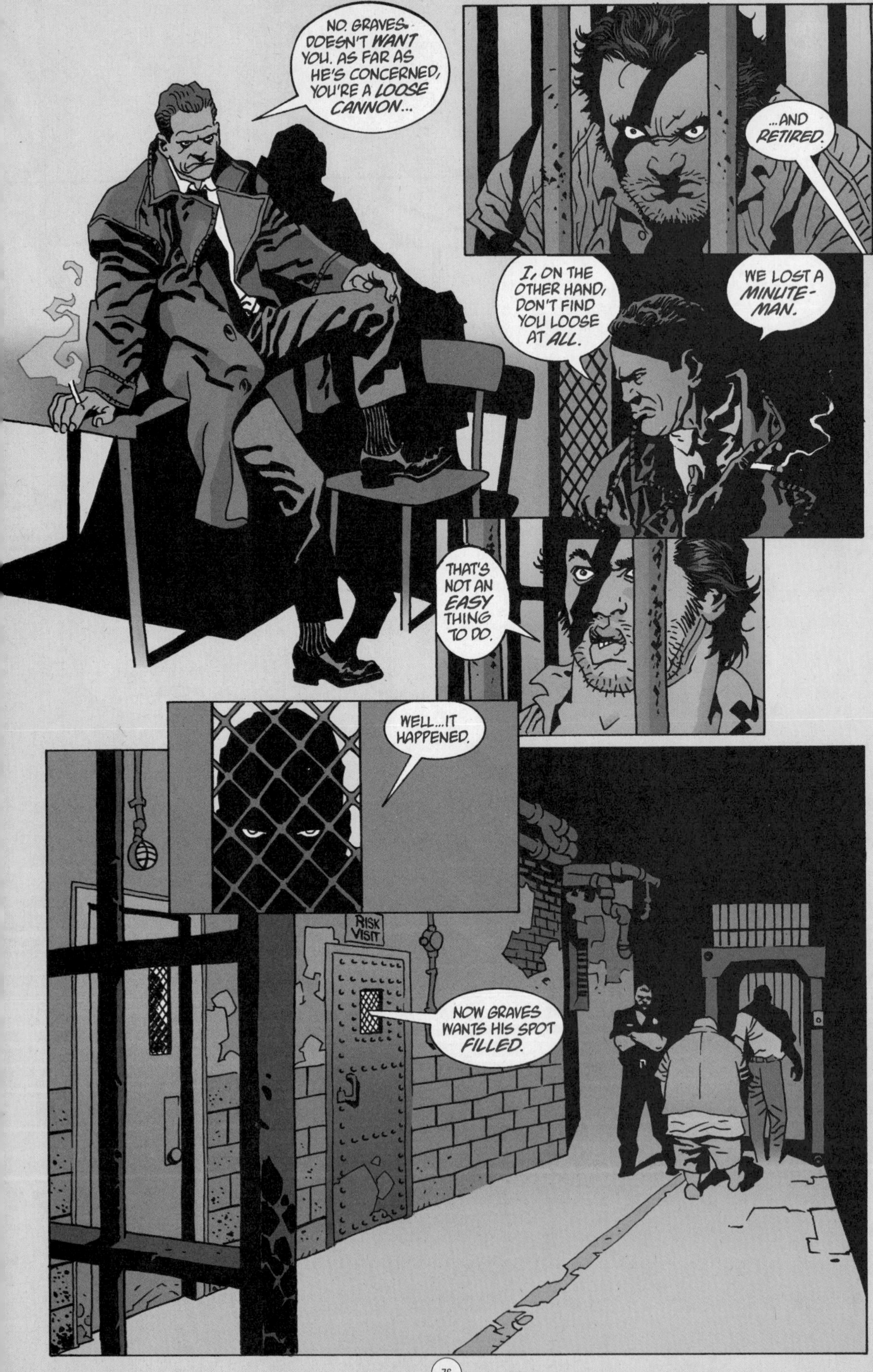
NO, GRAVES DOESN'T WANT YOU. AS FAR AS HE'S CONCERNED, YOU'RE A LOOSE CANNON...
...AND RETIRED.
I, ON THE OTHER HAND, DON'T FIND YOU LOOSE AT ALL.
WE LOST A MINUTE-MAN.
THAT'S NOT AN EASY THING TO DO.
WELL...IT HAPPENED.
RISK VISIT
NOW GRAVES WANTS HIS SPOT FILLED.

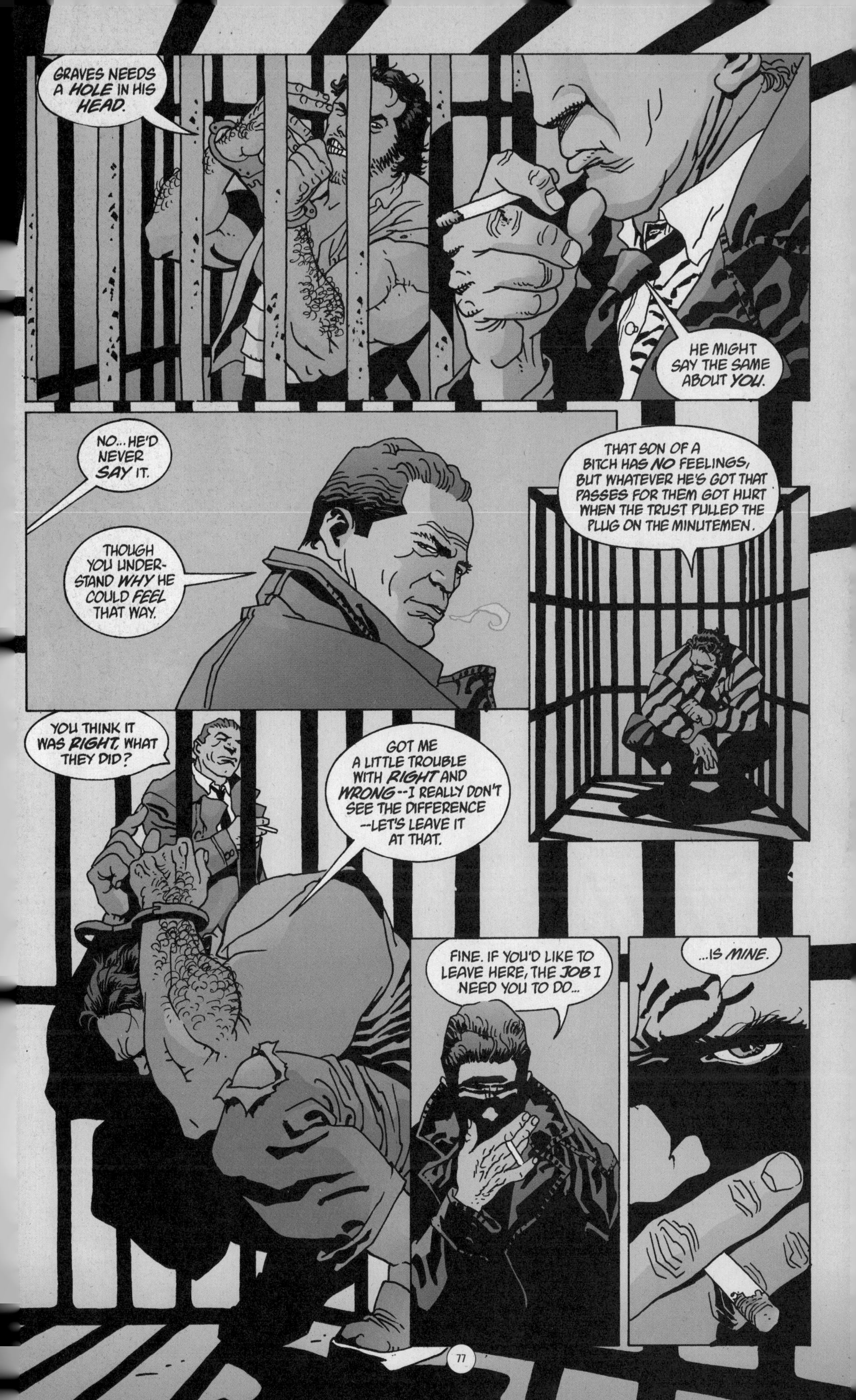
GRAVES NEEDS A HOLE IN HIS HEAD.
HE MIGHT SAY THE SAME ABOUT YOU.
NO... HE'D NEVER SAY IT.
THOUGH YOU UNDERSTAND WHY HE COULD FEEL THAT WAY.
THAT SON OF A BITCH HAS NO FEELINGS, BUT WHATEVER HE'S GOT THAT PASSES FOR THEM GOT HURT WHEN THE TRUST PULLED THE PLUG ON THE MINUTEMEN.
YOU THINK IT WAS RIGHT, WHAT THEY DID?
GOT ME A LITTLE TROUBLE WITH RIGHT AND WRONG--I REALLY DON'T SEE THE DIFFERENCE --LET'S LEAVE IT AT THAT.
FINE. IF YOU'D LIKE TO LEAVE HERE, THE JOB I NEED YOU TO DO...
...IS MINE.

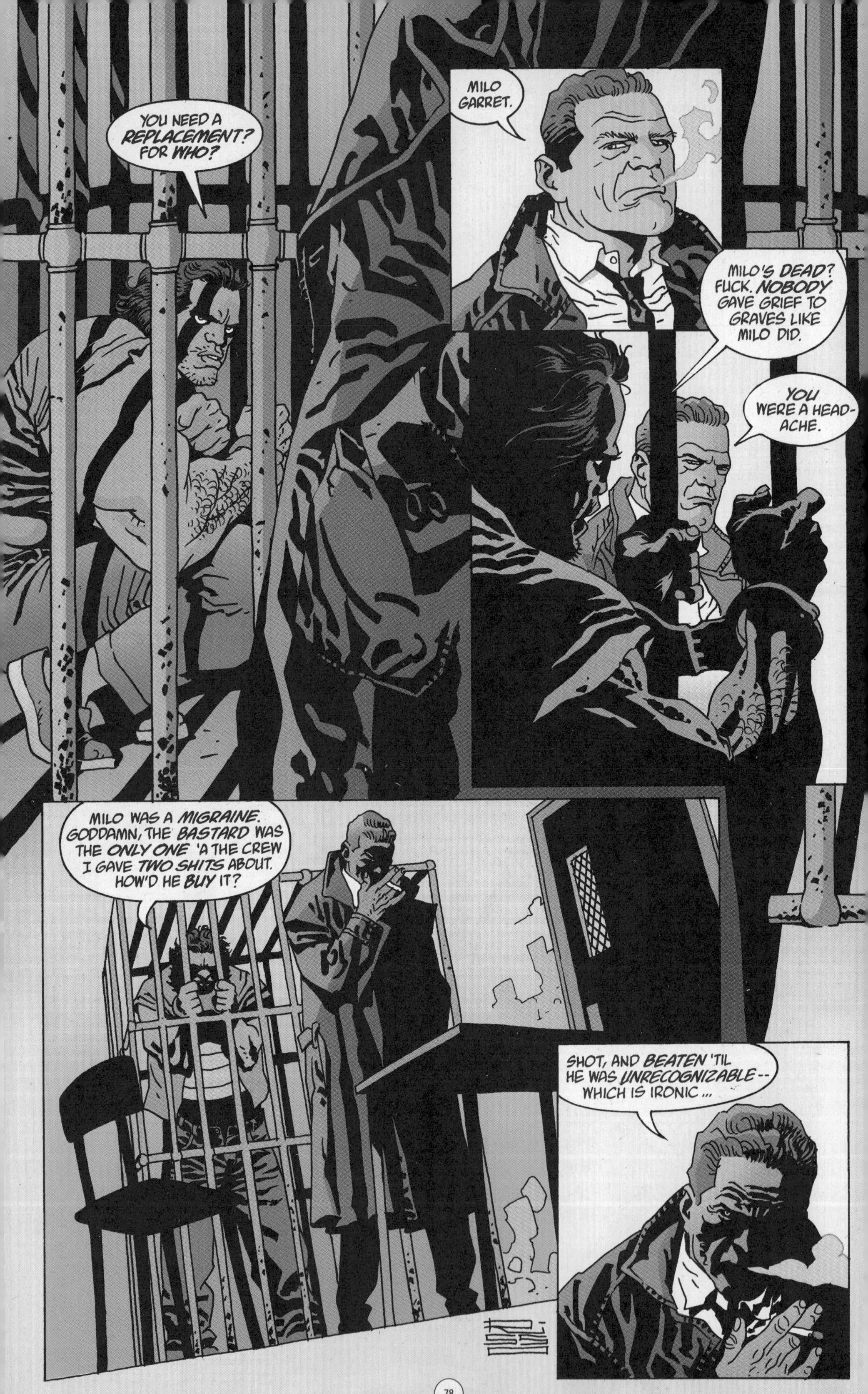

YOU NEED A REPLACEMENT? FOR WHO?
MILO GARRET.
MILO'S DEAD? FUCK. NOBODY GAVE GRIEF TO GRAVES LIKE MILO DID.
YOU WERE A HEAD-ACHE.
MILO WAS A MIGRAINE. GODDAMN, THE BASTARD WAS THE ONLY ONE 'A THE CREW I GAVE TWO SHITS ABOUT. HOW'D HE BUY IT?
SHOT, AND BEATEN 'TIL HE WAS UNRECOGNIZABLE-- WHICH IS IRONIC ...

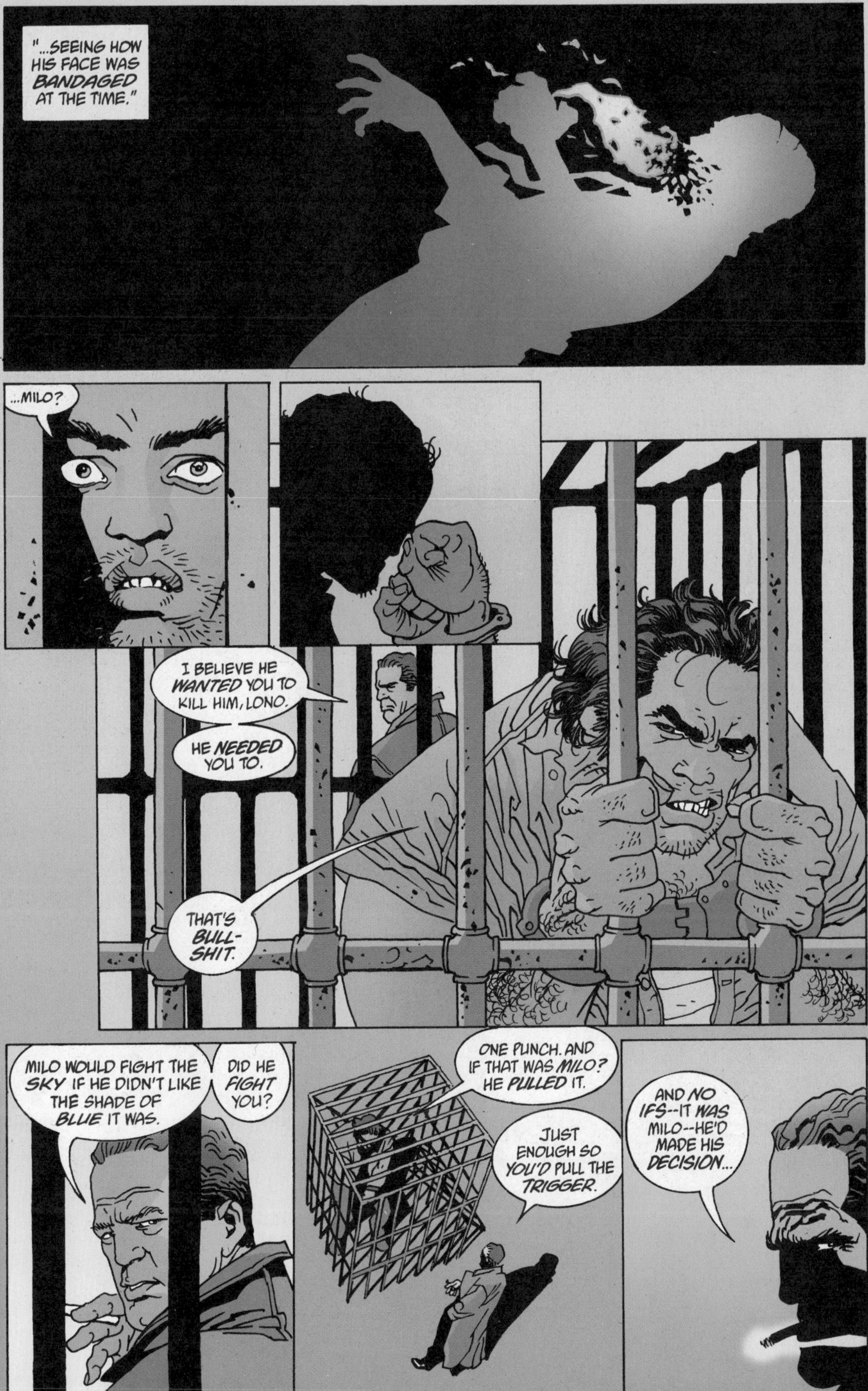
"...SEEING HOW HIS FACE WAS BANDAGED AT THE TIME."
...MILO?
I BELIEVE HE WANTED YOU TO KILL HIM, LONO.
HE NEEDED YOU TO.
THAT'S BULL-SHIT.
MILO WOULD FIGHT THE SKY IF HE DIDN'T LIKE THE SHADE OF BLUE IT WAS.
DID HE FIGHT YOU?
ONE PUNCH. AND IF THAT WAS MILO? HE PULLED IT.
JUST ENOUGH SO YOU'D PULL THE TRIGGER.
AND NO IFS--IT WAS MILO--HE'D MADE HIS DECISION...

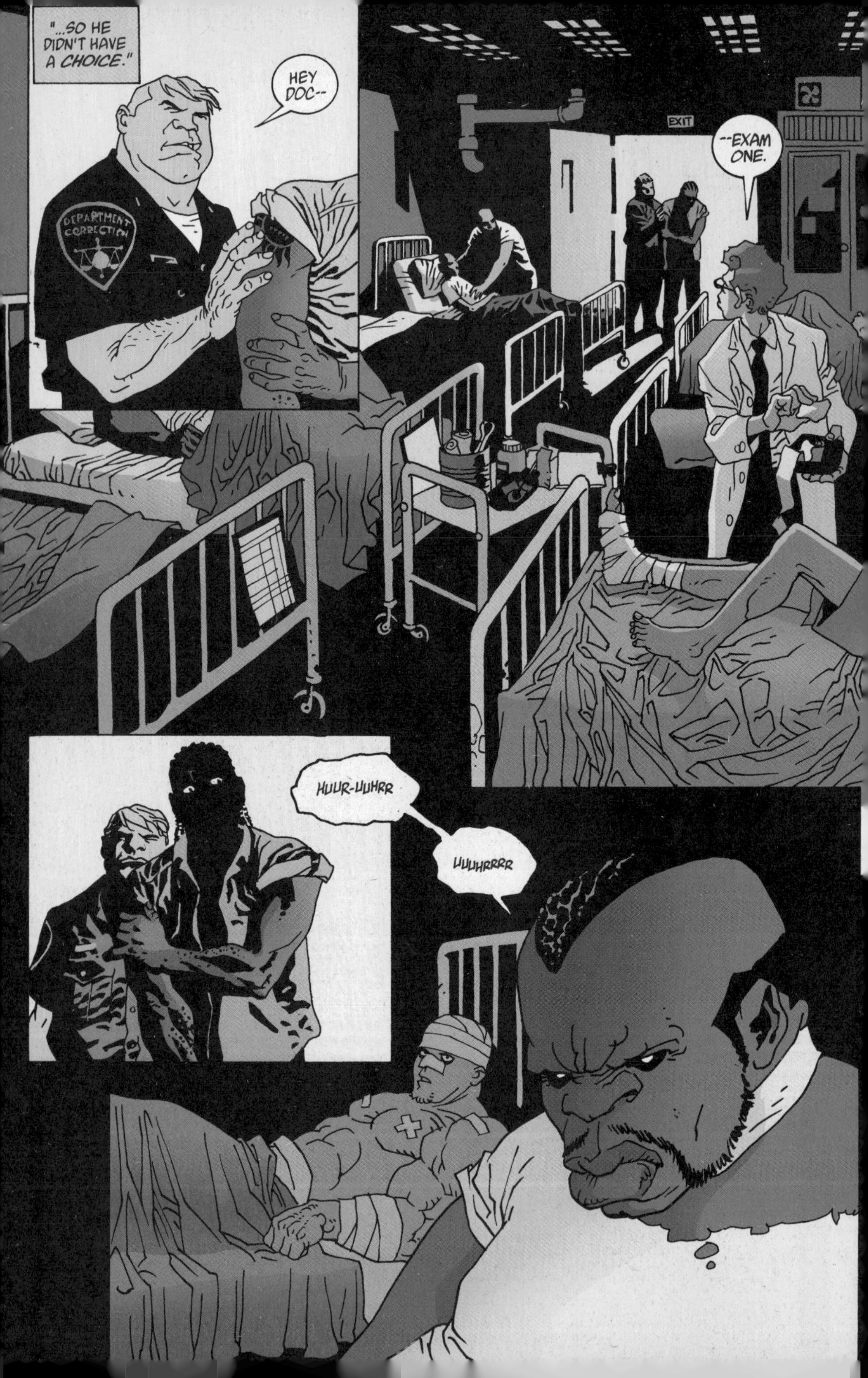

"...SO HE DIDN'T HAVE A CHOICE."
HEY DOC--
--EXAM ONE.
HUUR-UUHRR
UUUHRRRR

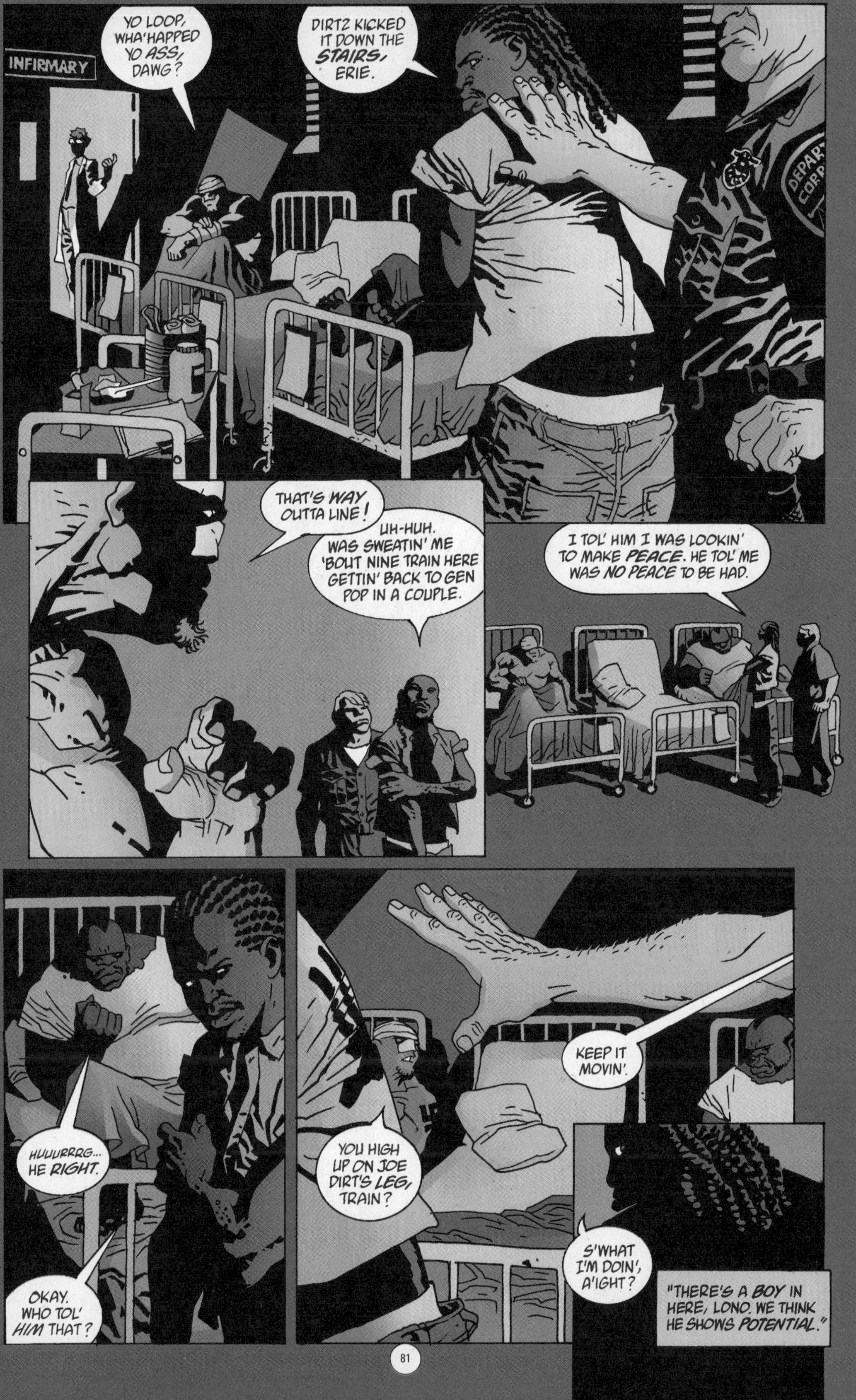
INFIRMARY
YO LOOP, WHA'HAPPED YO ASS, DAWG?
DIRTZ KICKED IT DOWN THE STAIRS, ERIE.
THAT'S WAY OUTTA LINE!
UH-HUH. WAS SWEATIN' ME 'BOUT NINE TRAIN HERE GETTIN' BACK TO GEN POP IN A COUPLE.
I TOL' HIM I WAS LOOKIN' TO MAKE PEACE. HE TOL' ME WAS NO PEACE TO BE HAD.
HUUURRRG... HE RIGHT.
OKAY. WHO TOL' HIM THAT?
YOU HIGH UP ON JOE DIRT'S LEG, TRAIN?
KEEP IT MOVIN'.
S'WHAT I'M DOIN', A'IGHT?
"THERE'S A BOY IN HERE, LONO. WE THINK HE SHOWS POTENTIAL."

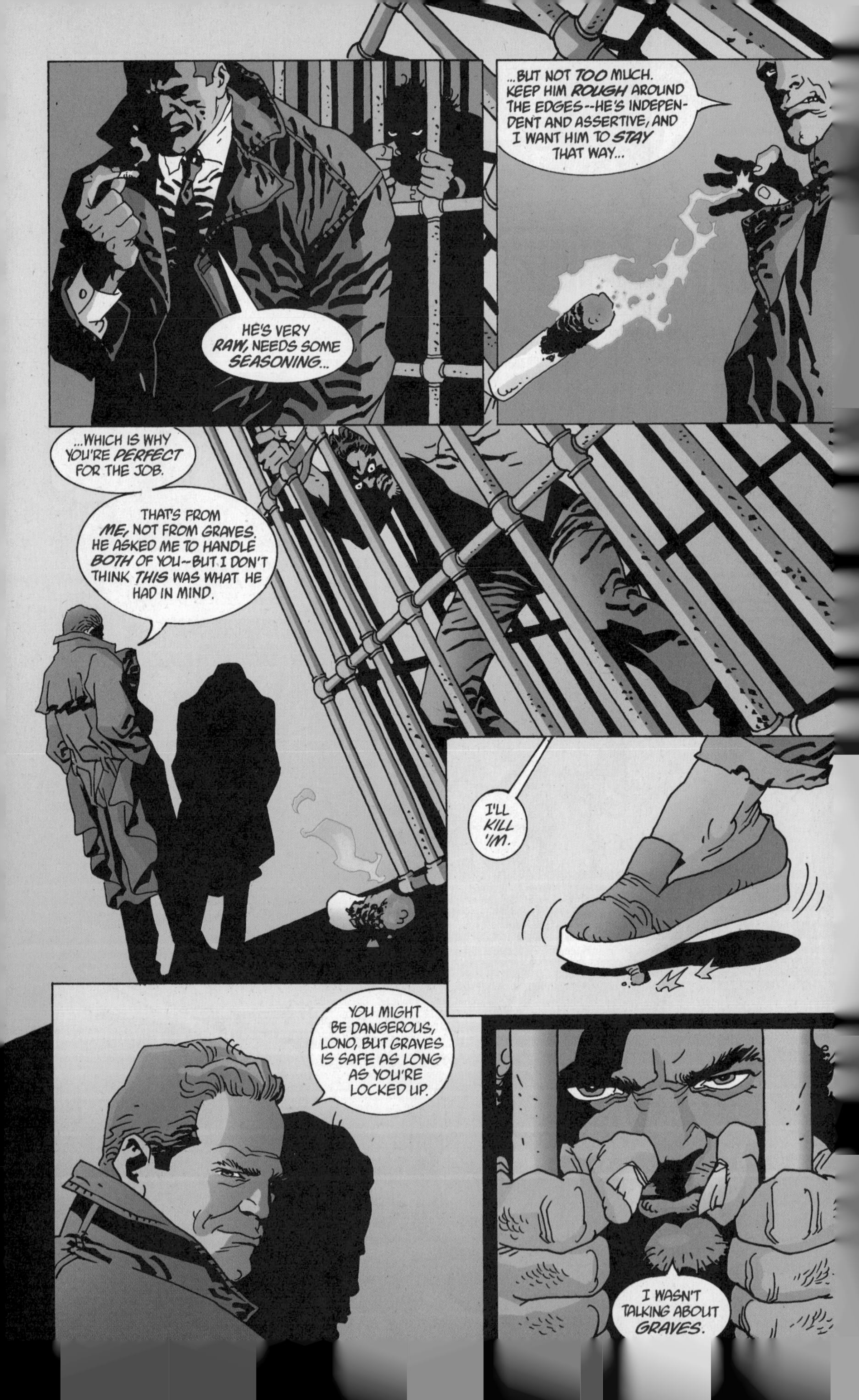
HE'S VERY RAW, NEEDS SOME SEASONING...
...BUT NOT TOO MUCH. KEEP HIM ROUGH AROUND THE EDGES--HE'S INDEPENDENT AND ASSERTIVE, AND I WANT HIM TO STAY THAT WAY...
...WHICH IS WHY YOU'RE PERFECT FOR THE JOB.
THAT'S FROM ME, NOT FROM GRAVES. HE ASKED ME TO HANDLE BOTH OF YOU--BUT I DON'T THINK THIS WAS WHAT HE HAD IN MIND.
I'LL KILL 'IM.
YOU MIGHT BE DANGEROUS, LONO, BUT GRAVES IS SAFE AS LONG AS YOU'RE LOCKED UP.
I WASN'T TALKING ABOUT GRAVES.

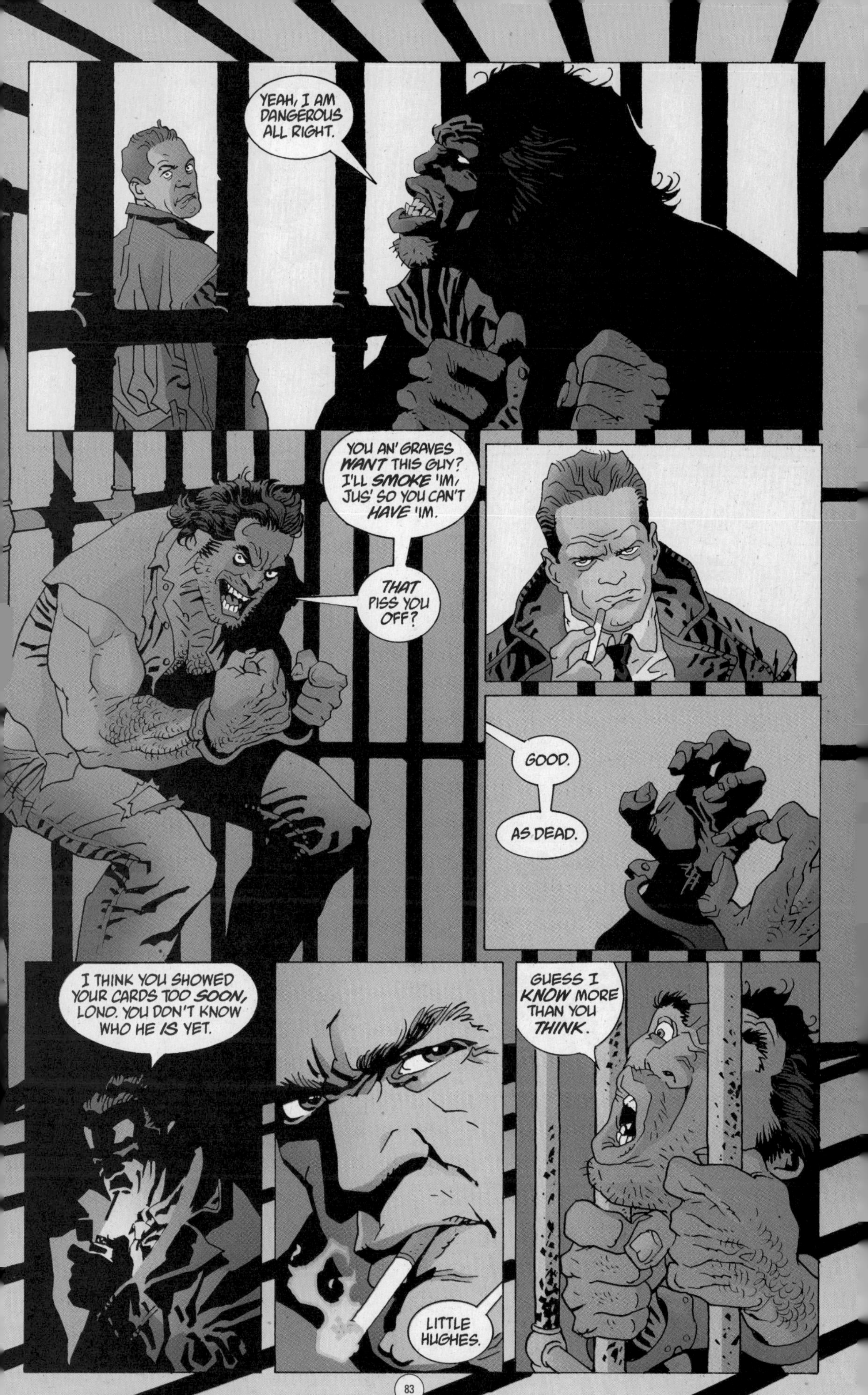
YEAH, I AM DANGEROUS ALL RIGHT.
YOU AN' GRAVES WANT THIS GUY? I'LL SMOKE 'IM, JUS' SO YOU CAN'T HAVE 'IM.
THAT PISS YOU OFF?
GOOD.
AS DEAD.
I THINK YOU SHOWED YOUR CARDS TOO SOON, LONO. YOU DON'T KNOW WHO HE IS YET.
LITTLE HUGHES.
GUESS I KNOW MORE THAN YOU THINK.

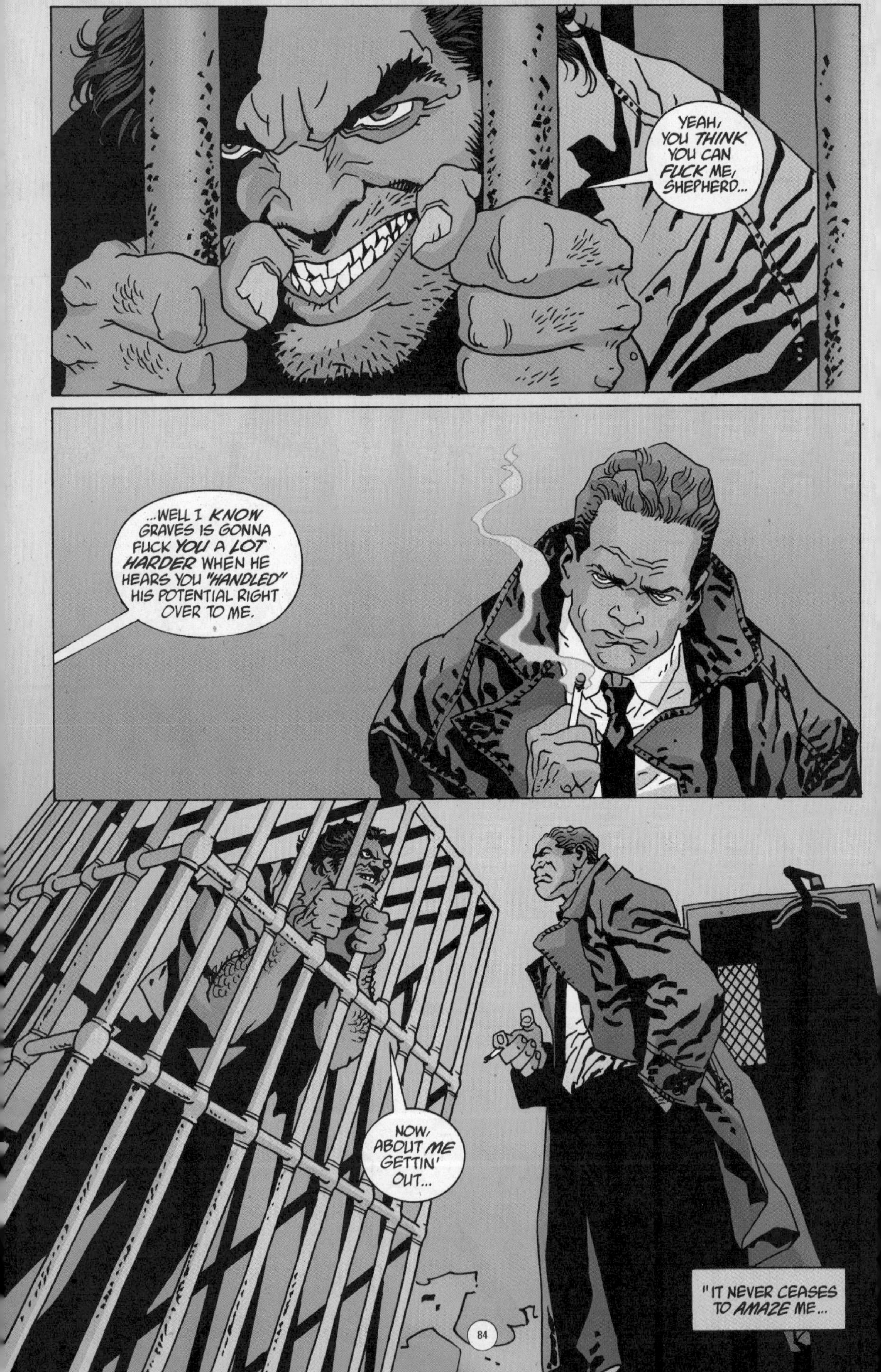
YEAH, YOU THINK YOU CAN FUCK ME, SHEPHERD...
...WELL I KNOW GRAVES IS GONNA FUCK YOU A LOT HARDER WHEN HE HEARS YOU "HANDLED" HIS POTENTIAL RIGHT OVER TO ME.
NOW, ABOUT ME GETTIN' OUT...
"IT NEVER CEASES TO AMAZE ME...

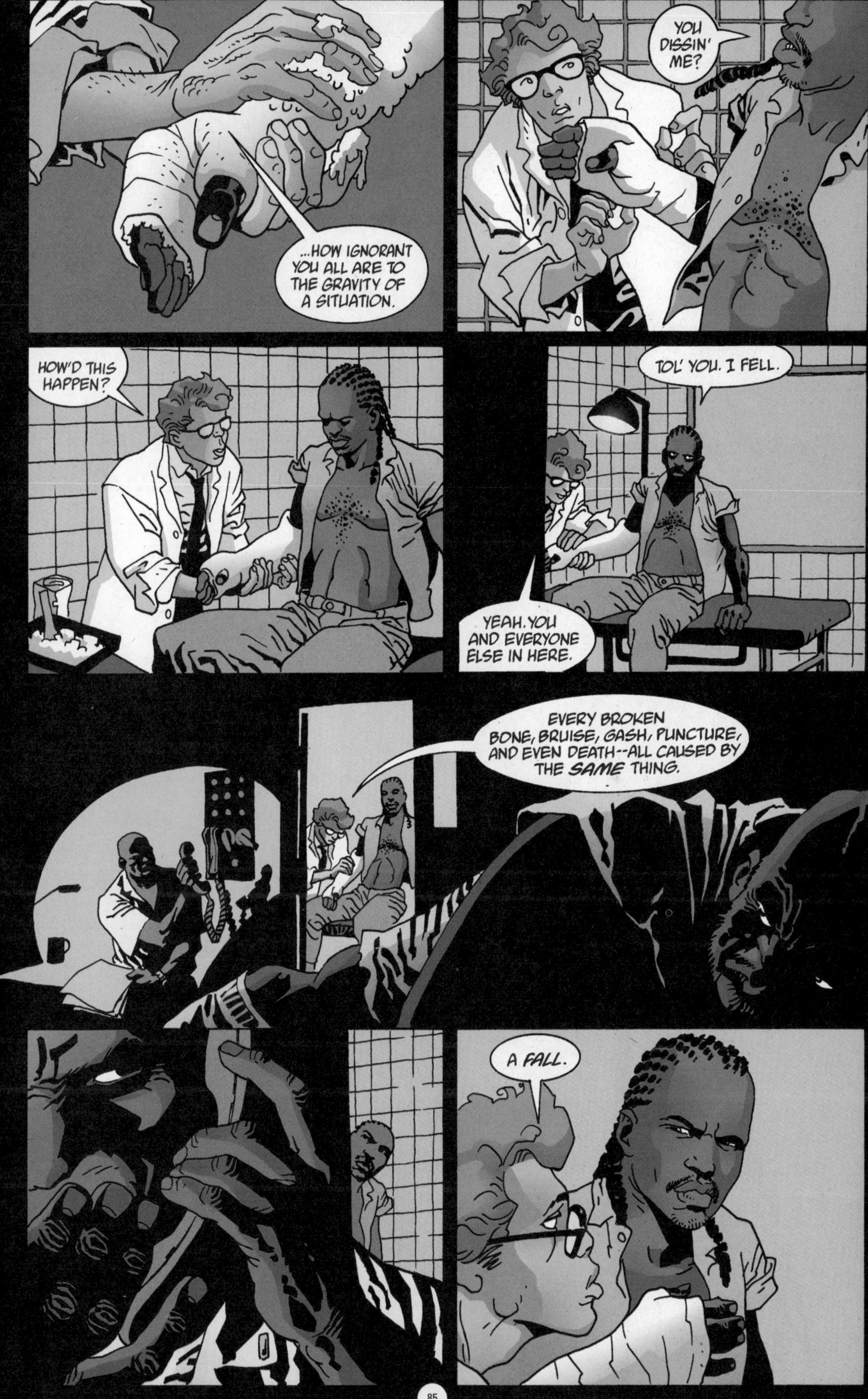
...HOW IGNORANT YOU ALL ARE TO THE GRAVITY OF A SITUATION.
YOU DISSIN' ME?
HOW'D THIS HAPPEN?
TOL' YOU. I FELL.
YEAH. YOU AND EVERYONE ELSE IN HERE.
EVERY BROKEN BONE, BRUISE, GASH, PUNCTURE, AND EVEN DEATH--ALL CAUSED BY THE SAME THING.
A FALL.

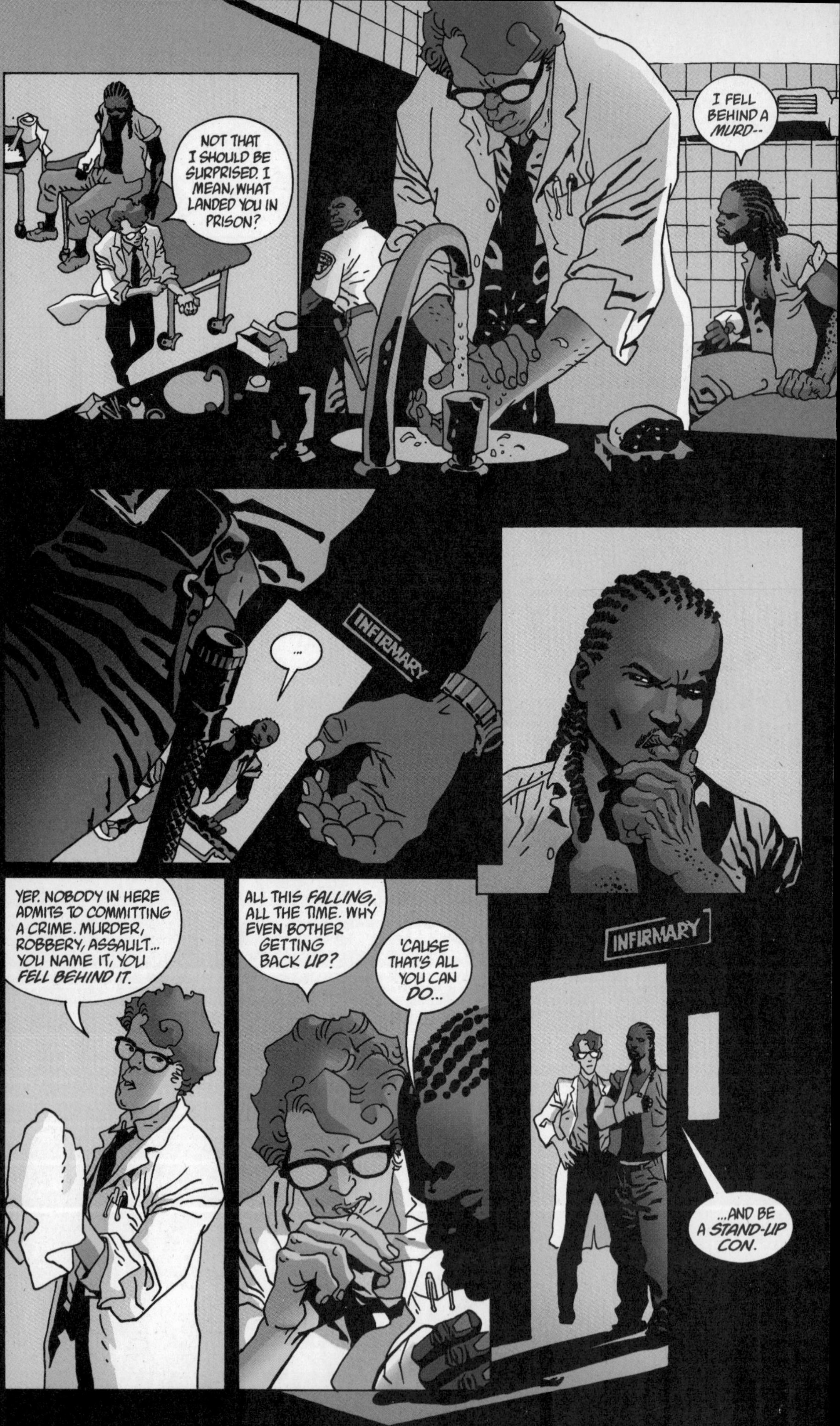
NOT THAT I SHOULD BE SURPRISED. I MEAN, WHAT LANDED YOU IN PRISON?
I FELL BEHIND A MURD--
...
INFIRMARY
YEP. NOBODY IN HERE ADMITS TO COMMITTING A CRIME. MURDER, ROBBERY, ASSAULT... YOU NAME IT, YOU FELL BEHIND IT.
ALL THIS FALLING, ALL THE TIME. WHY EVEN BOTHER GETTING BACK UP?
'CAUSE THAT'S ALL YOU CAN DO...
INFIRMARY
...AND BE A STAND-UP CON.

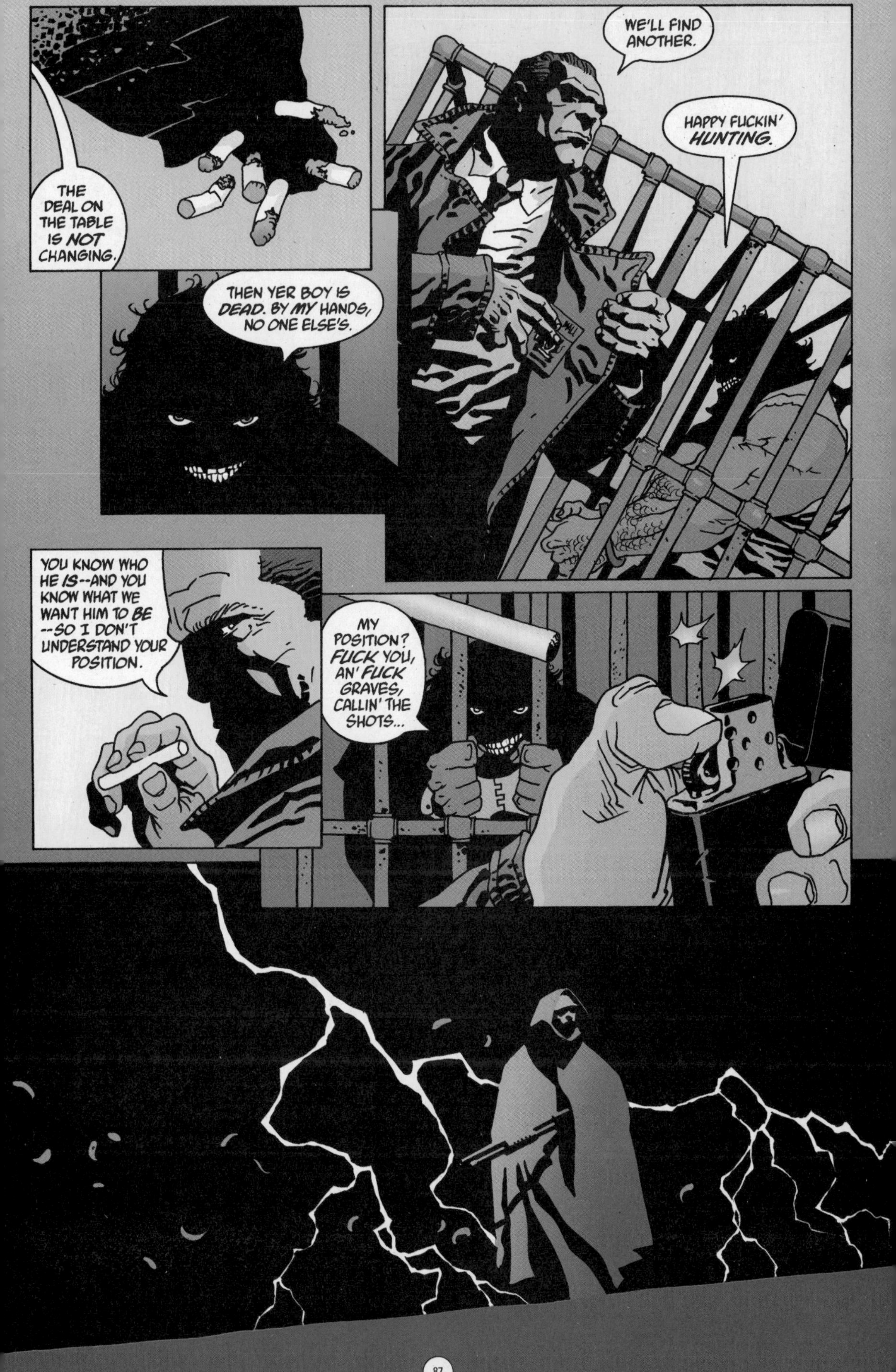
THE DEAL ON THE TABLE IS NOT CHANGING.
THEN YER BOY IS DEAD. BY MY HANDS, NO ONE ELSE'S.
WE'LL FIND ANOTHER.
HAPPY FUCKIN' HUNTING.
YOU KNOW WHO HE IS--AND YOU KNOW WHAT WE WANT HIM TO BE --SO I DON'T UNDERSTAND YOUR POSITION.
MY POSITION? FUCK YOU, AN' FUCK GRAVES, CALLIN' THE SHOTS...

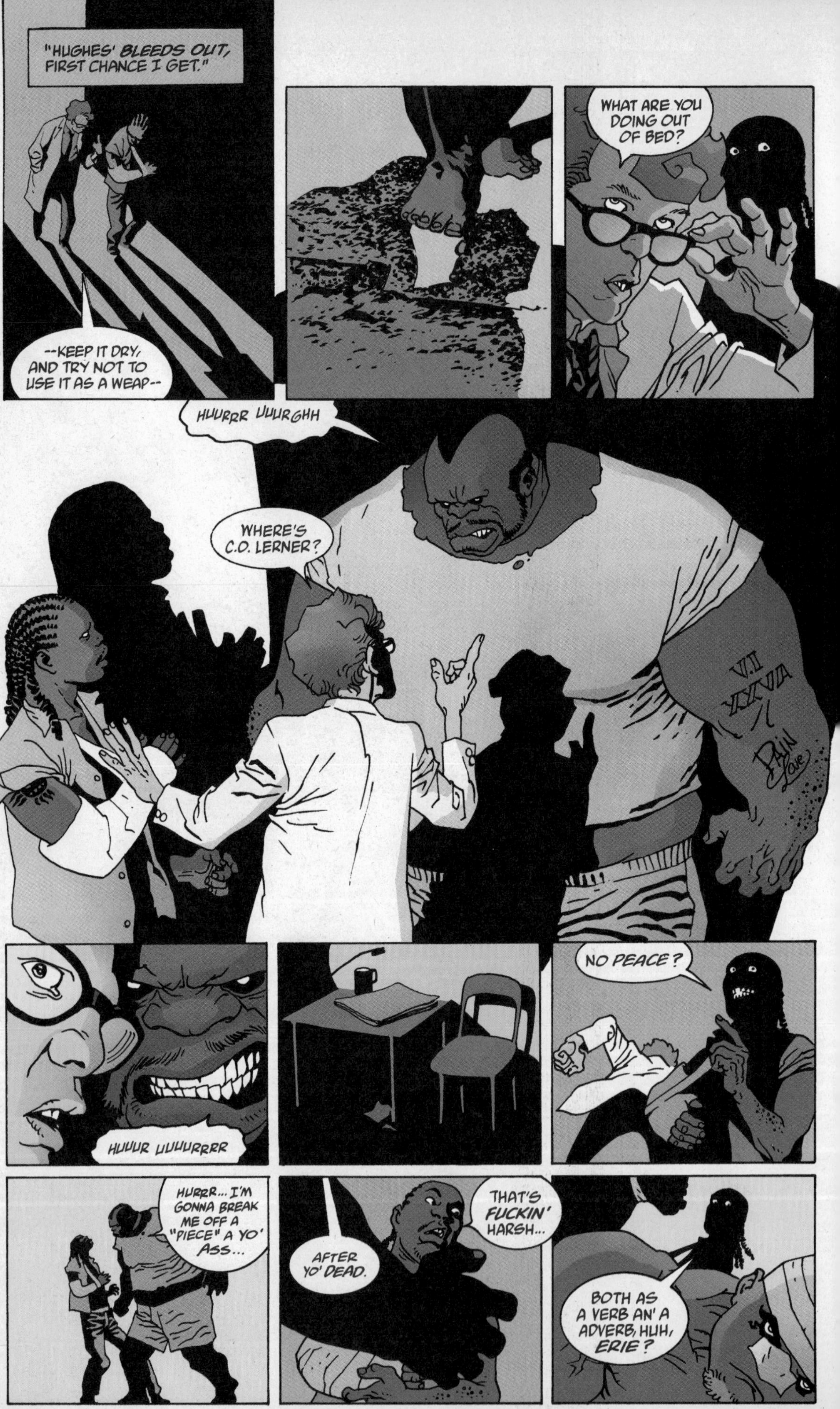
"HUGHES' BLEEDS OUT, FIRST CHANCE I GET."
--KEEP IT DRY, AND TRY NOT TO USE IT AS A WEAP--
WHAT ARE YOU DOING OUT OF BED?
HUURRR UUURGHH
WHERE'S C.O. LERNER?
HUUUR UUUURRRR
NO PEACE?
HURRR... I'M GONNA BREAK ME OFF A "PIECE" A YO' ASS...
THAT'S FUCKIN' HARSH...
AFTER YO' DEAD.
BOTH AS A VERB AN' A ADVERB, HUH, ERIE?

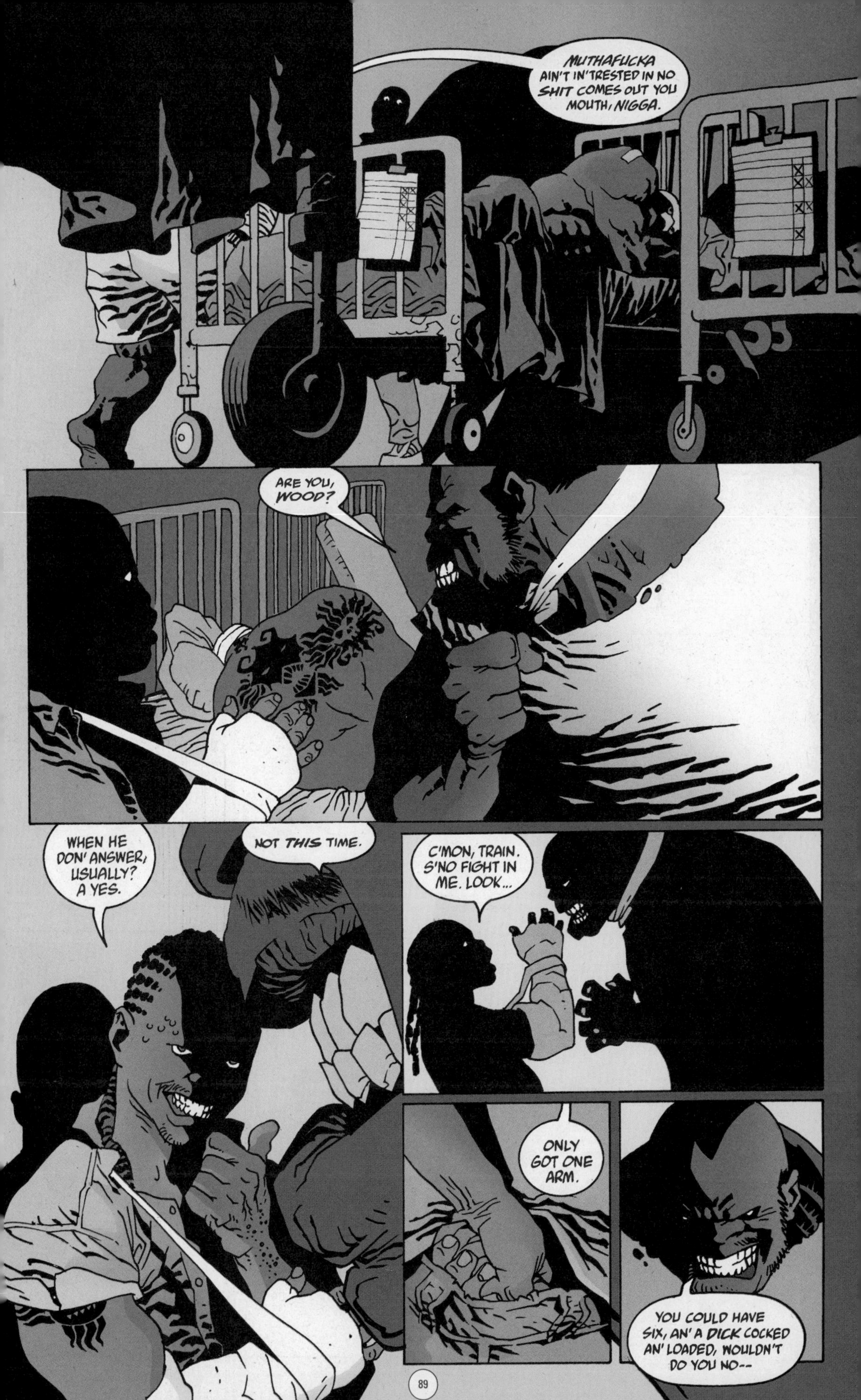
MUTHAFUCKA AIN'T IN'TRESTED IN NO SHIT COMES OUT YOU MOUTH, NIGGA.
ARE YOU, WOOD?
WHEN HE DON' ANSWER, USUALLY? A YES.
NOT THIS TIME.
C'MON, TRAIN. S'NO FIGHT IN ME. LOOK...
ONLY GOT ONE ARM.
YOU COULD HAVE SIX, AN' A DICK COCKED AN' LOADED, WOULDN'T DO YOU NO--

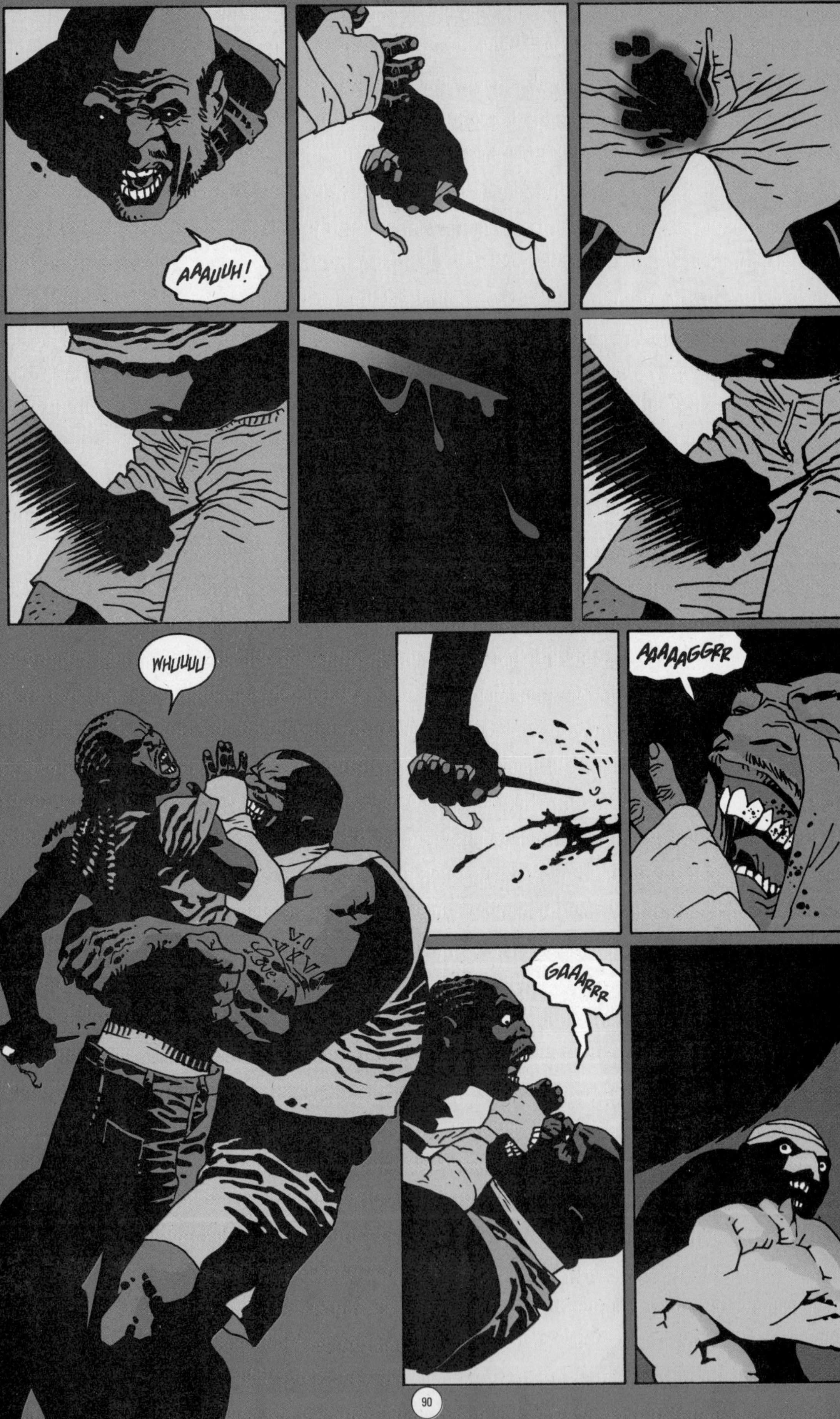
AAAUUH!
WHUUUU
AAAAAGGRR
GAAARRR

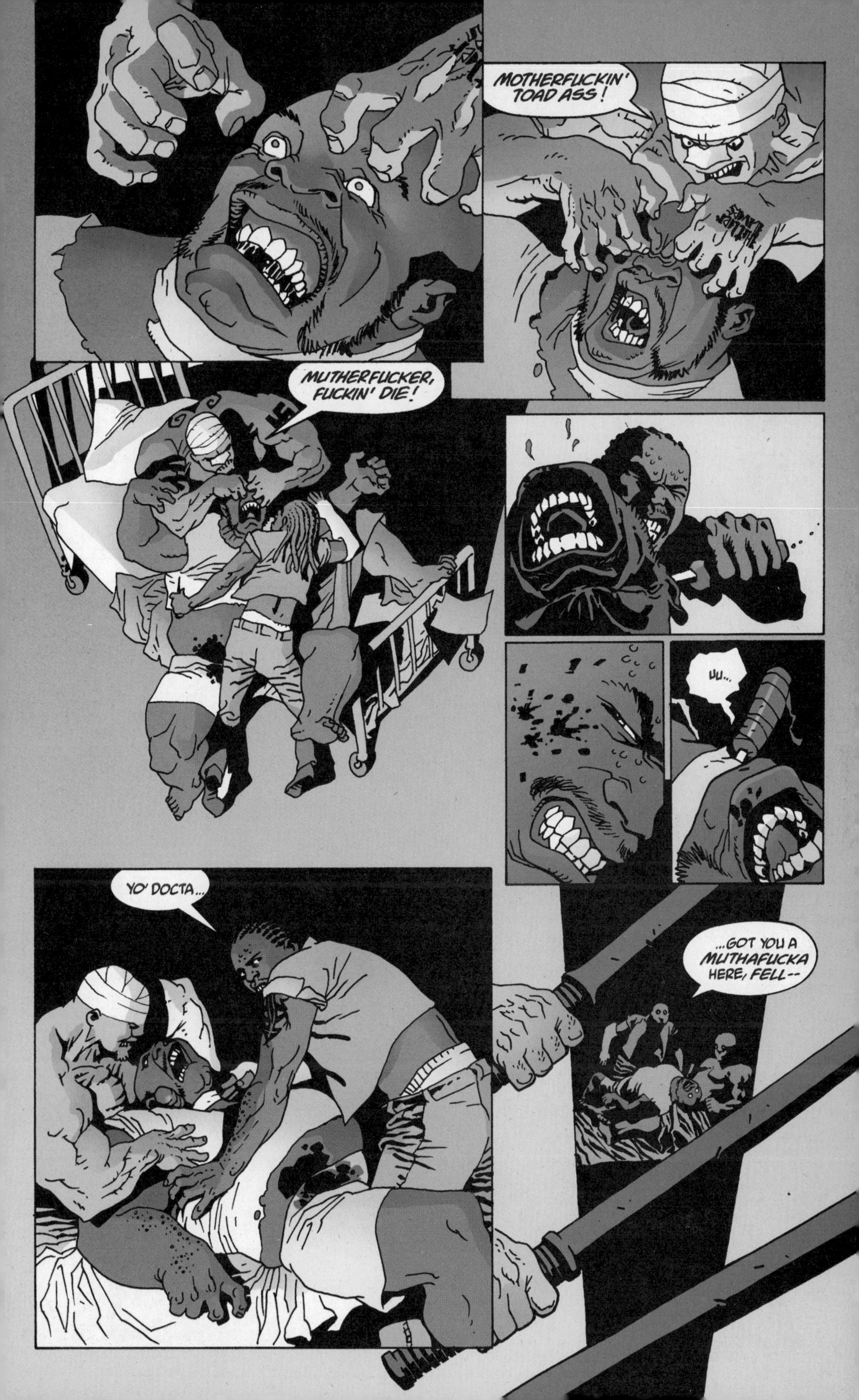
MOTHERFUCKIN' TOAD ASS!
MUTHERFUCKER, FUCKIN' DIE!
UU...
YO' DOCTA...
...GOT YOU A MUTHAFUCKA HERE, FELL--

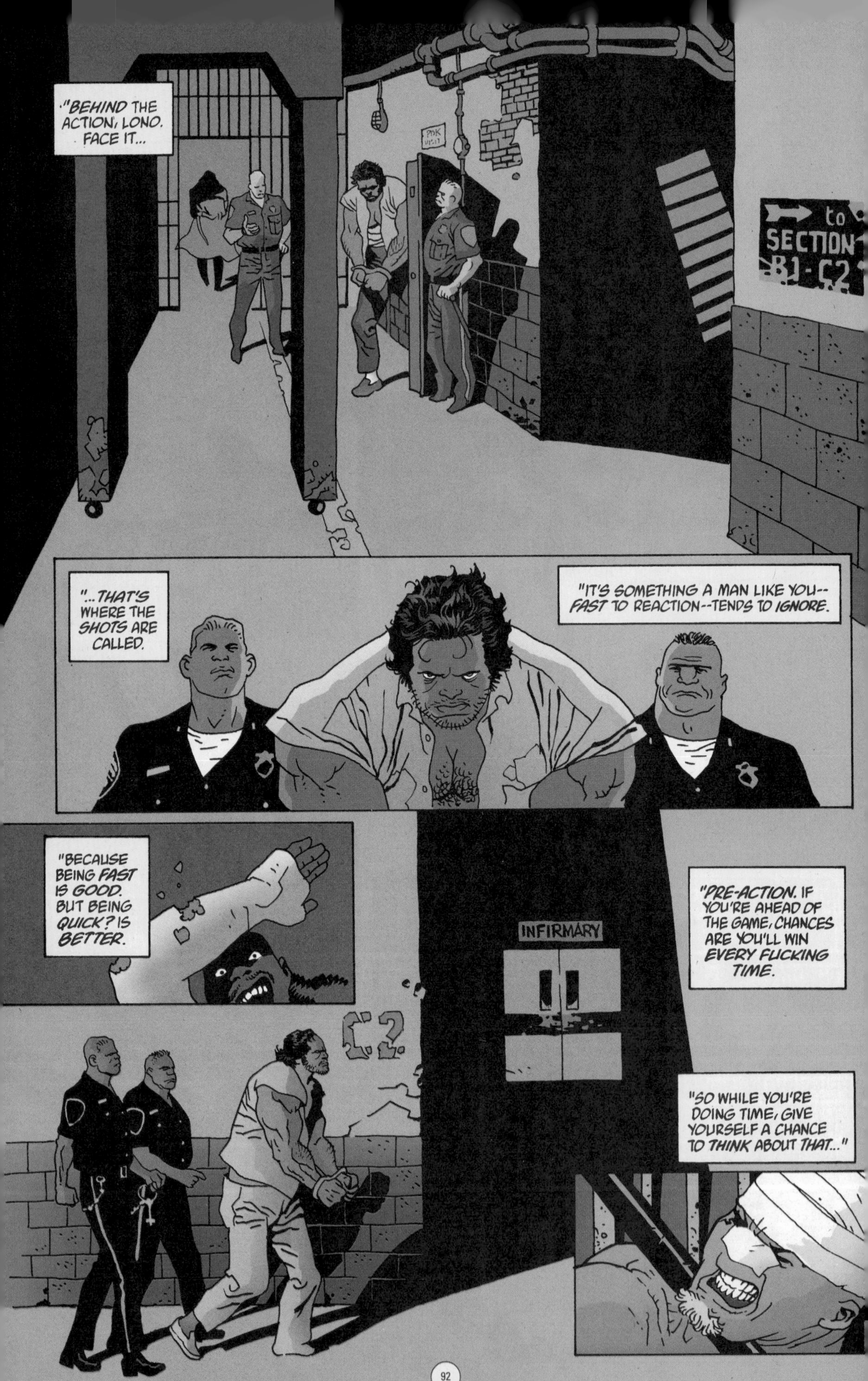
"BEHIND THE ACTION," LONO. FACE IT...
to SECTION B1-C2
"...THAT'S WHERE THE SHOTS ARE CALLED.
"IT'S SOMETHING A MAN LIKE YOU-- FAST TO REACTION--TENDS TO IGNORE.
"BECAUSE BEING FAST IS GOOD. BUT BEING QUICK? IS BETTER.
INFIRMARY
"PRE-ACTION. IF YOU'RE AHEAD OF THE GAME, CHANCES ARE YOU'LL WIN EVERY FUCKING TIME.
C2
"SO WHILE YOU'RE DOING TIME, GIVE YOURSELF A CHANCE TO THINK ABOUT THAT..."

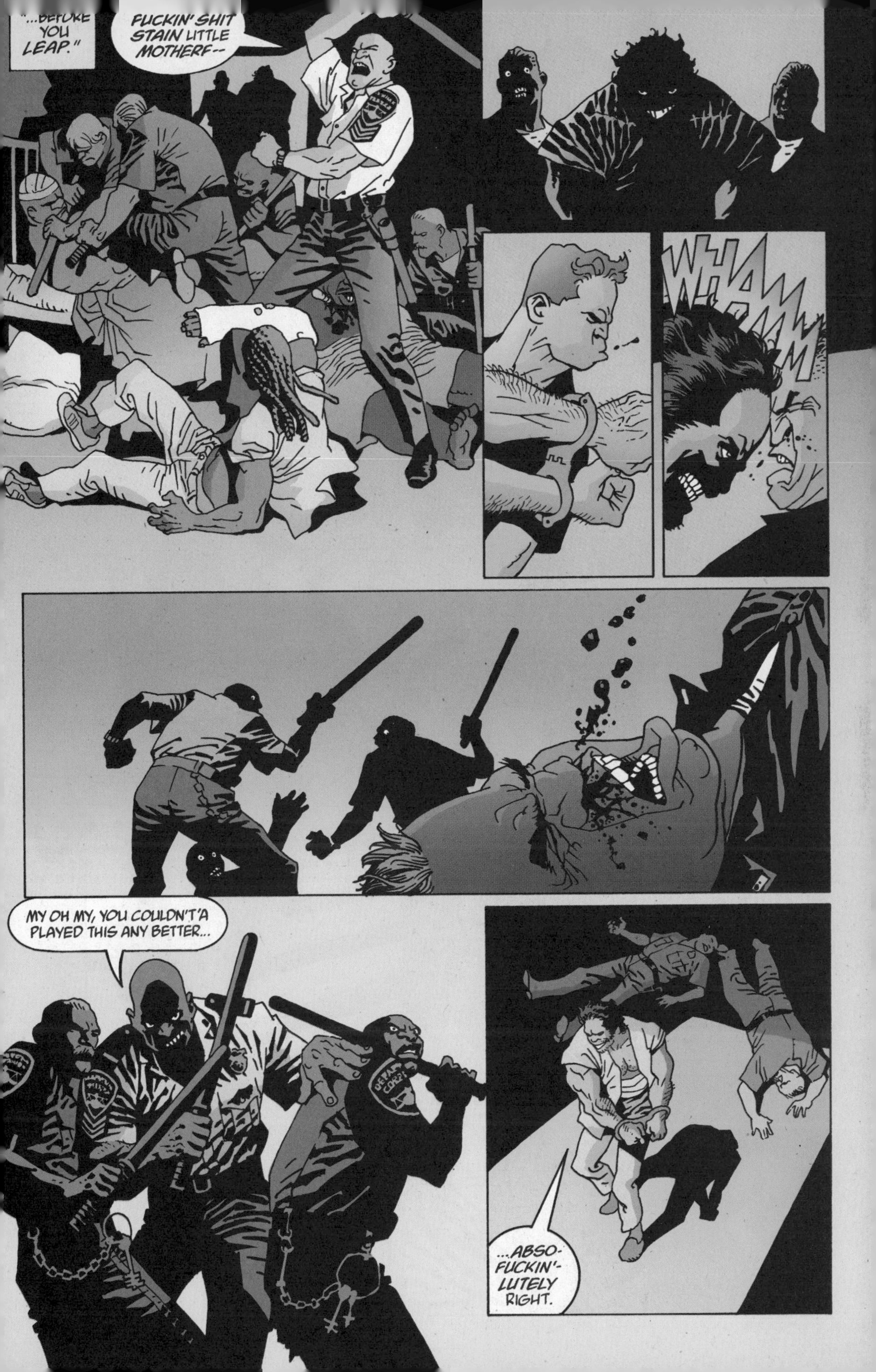
"...BEFORE YOU LEAP."
FUCKIN' SHIT STAIN LITTLE MOTHERF--
WHAM
MY OH MY, YOU COULDN'T'A PLAYED THIS ANY BETTER...
...ABSO-FUCKIN'-LUTELY RIGHT.

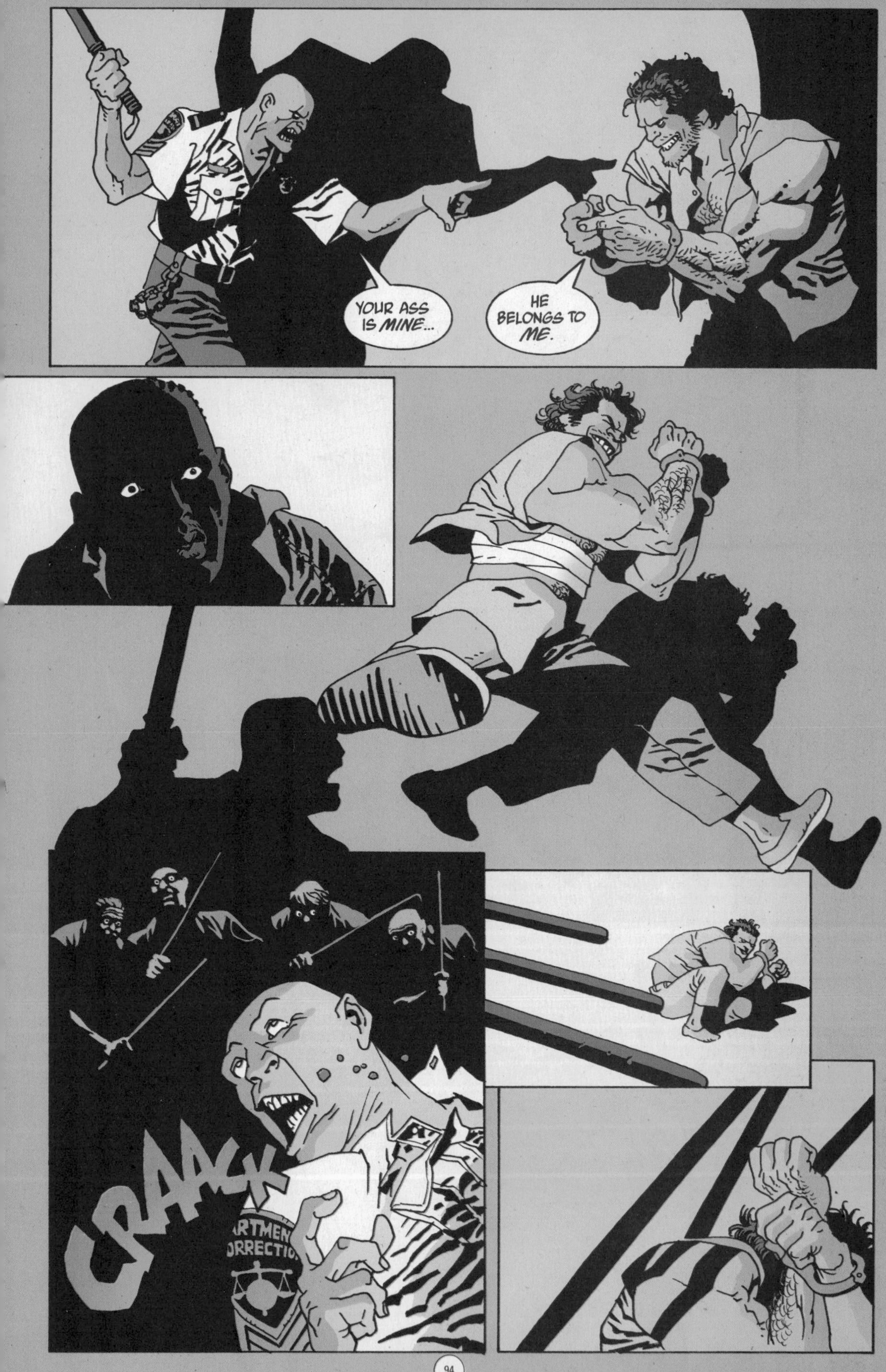
YOUR ASS IS MINE...
HE BELONGS TO ME.
CRAACK
ARTMENT
ORRECTIO

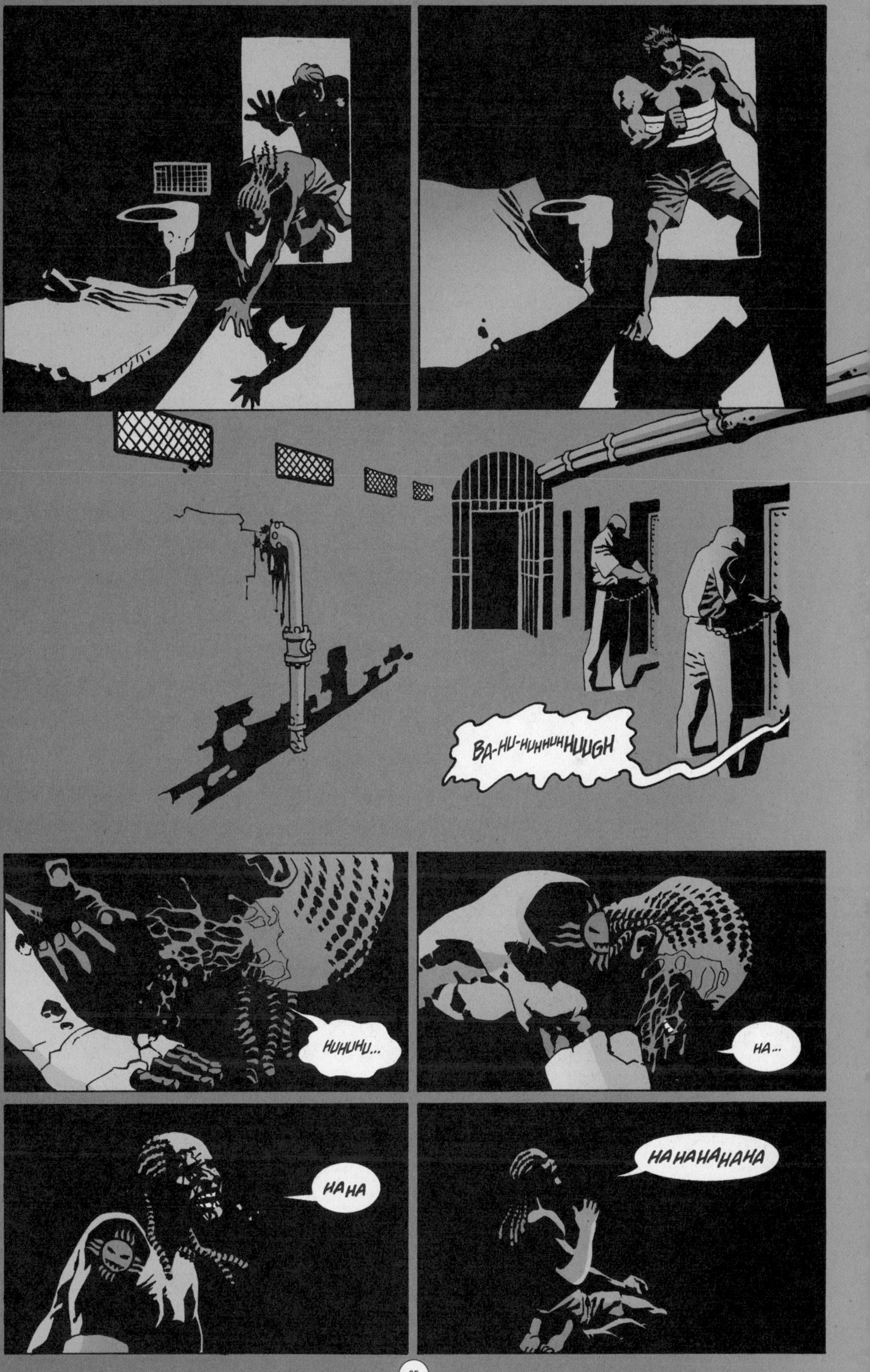
BA-HU-HUHHUHHUUGH
HUHUHU...
HA...
HAHA
HAHAHAHAHA

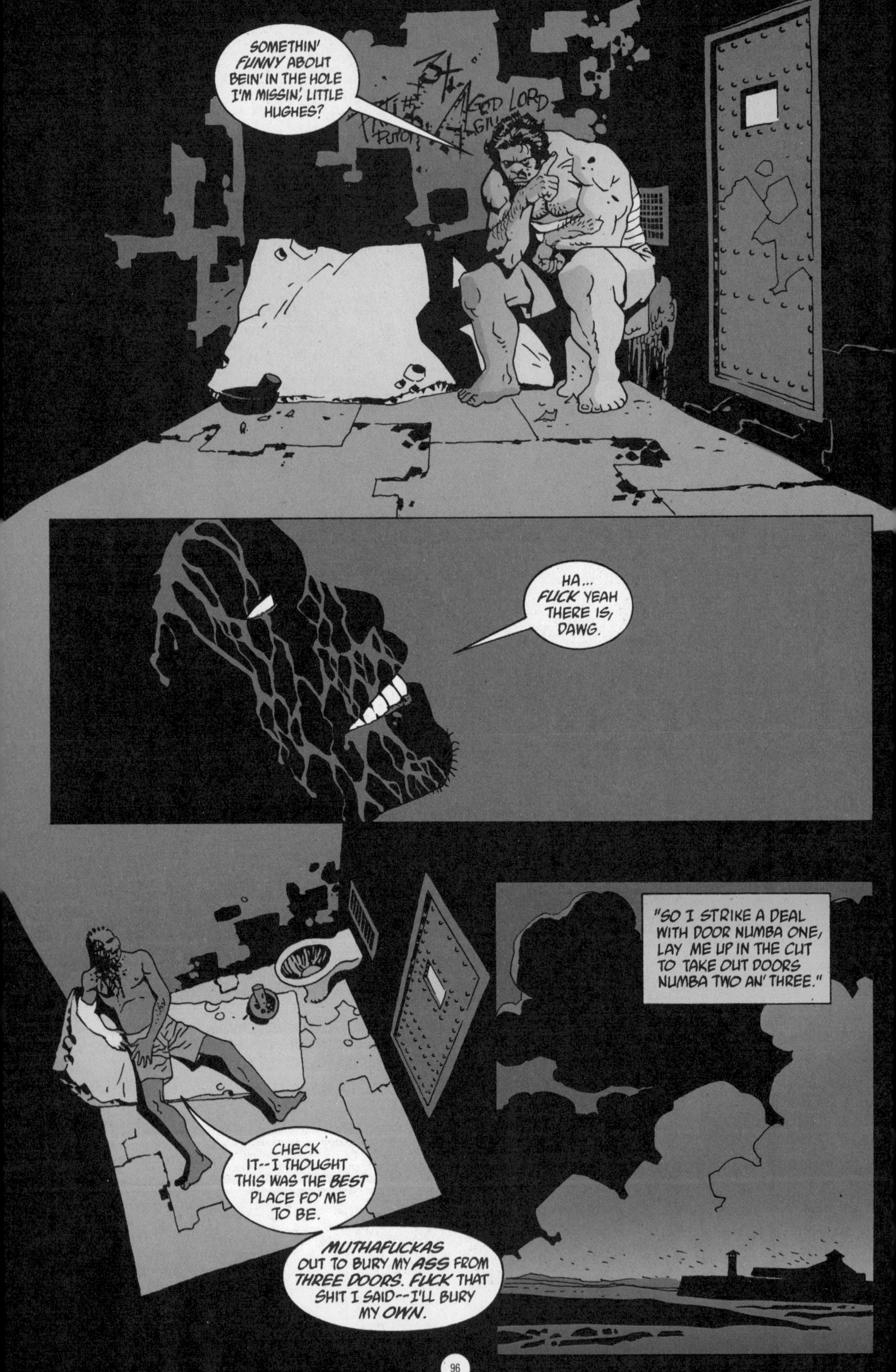
SOMETHIN' FUNNY ABOUT BEIN' IN THE HOLE I'M MISSIN', LITTLE HUGHES?
GOD LORD
HA... FUCK YEAH THERE IS, DAWG.
"SO I STRIKE A DEAL WITH DOOR NUMBA ONE, LAY ME UP IN THE CUT TO TAKE OUT DOORS NUMBA TWO AN' THREE."
CHECK IT--I THOUGHT THIS WAS THE BEST PLACE FO' ME TO BE.
MUTHAFUCKAS OUT TO BURY MY ASS FROM THREE DOORS. FUCK THAT SHIT I SAID--I'LL BURY MY OWN.

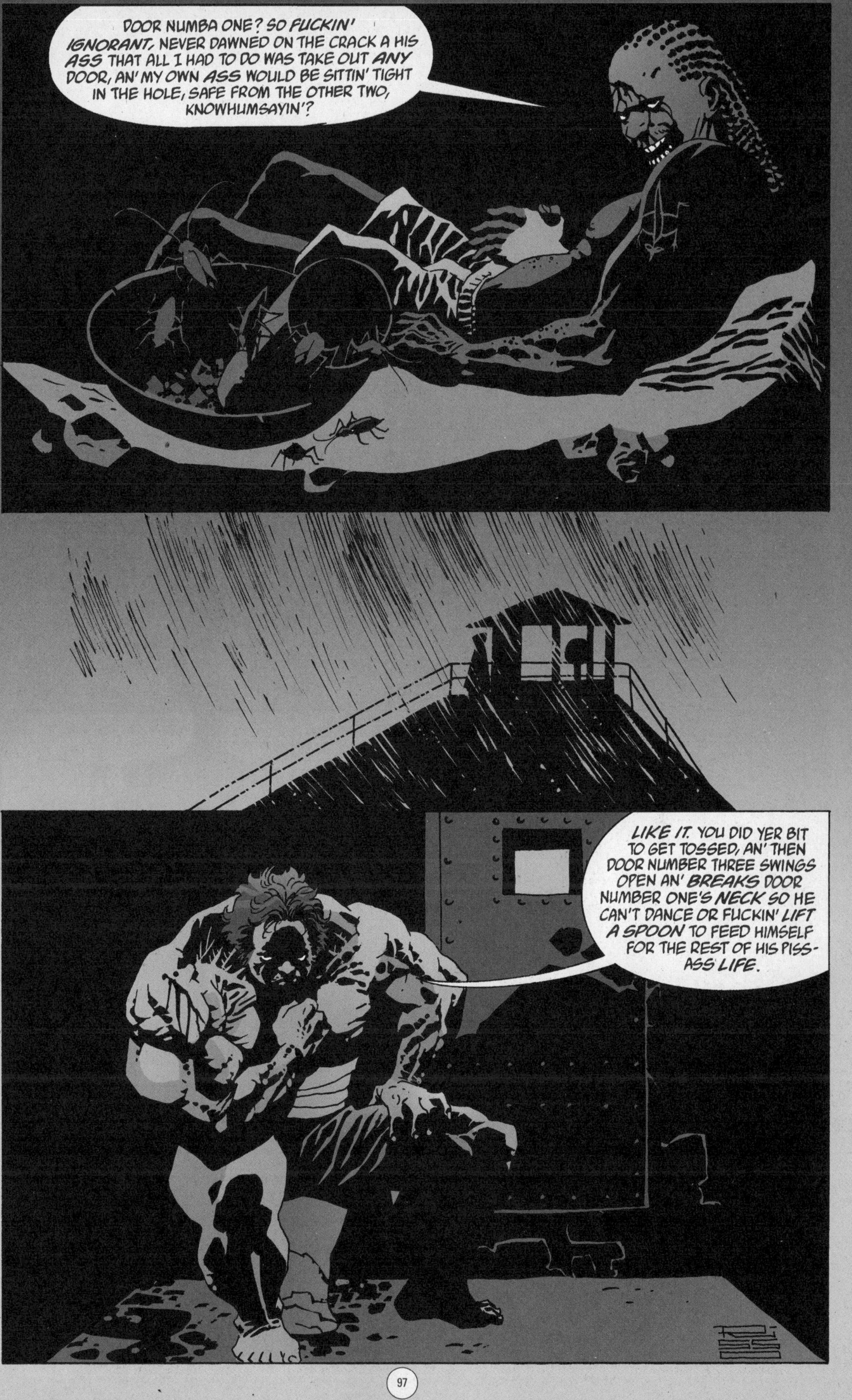
DOOR NUMBA ONE? SO FUCKIN' IGNORANT, NEVER DAWNED ON THE CRACK A HIS ASS THAT ALL I HAD TO DO WAS TAKE OUT ANY DOOR, AN' MY OWN ASS WOULD BE SITTIN' TIGHT IN THE HOLE, SAFE FROM THE OTHER TWO, KNOWHUMSAYIN'?
LIKE IT. YOU DID YER BIT TO GET TOSSED, AN' THEN DOOR NUMBER THREE SWINGS OPEN AN' BREAKS DOOR NUMBER ONE'S NECK SO HE CAN'T DANCE OR FUCKIN' LIFT A SPOON TO FEED HIMSELF FOR THE REST OF HIS PISS-ASS LIFE.

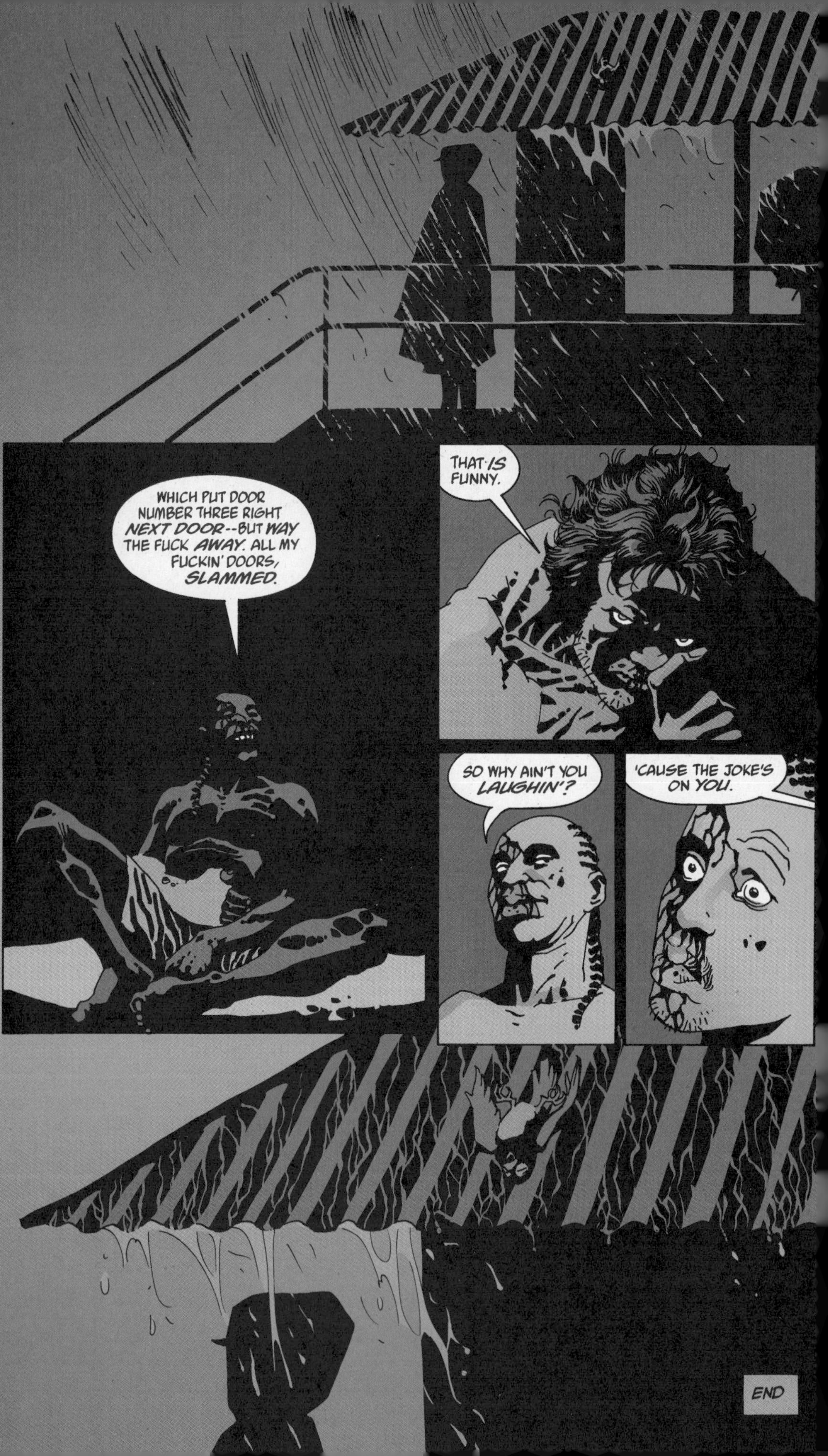
WHICH PUT DOOR NUMBER THREE RIGHT NEXT DOOR--BUT WAY THE FUCK AWAY. ALL MY FUCKIN' DOORS, SLAMMED.
THAT IS FUNNY.
SO WHY AIN'T YOU LAUGHIN'?
'CAUSE THE JOKE'S ON YOU.
END

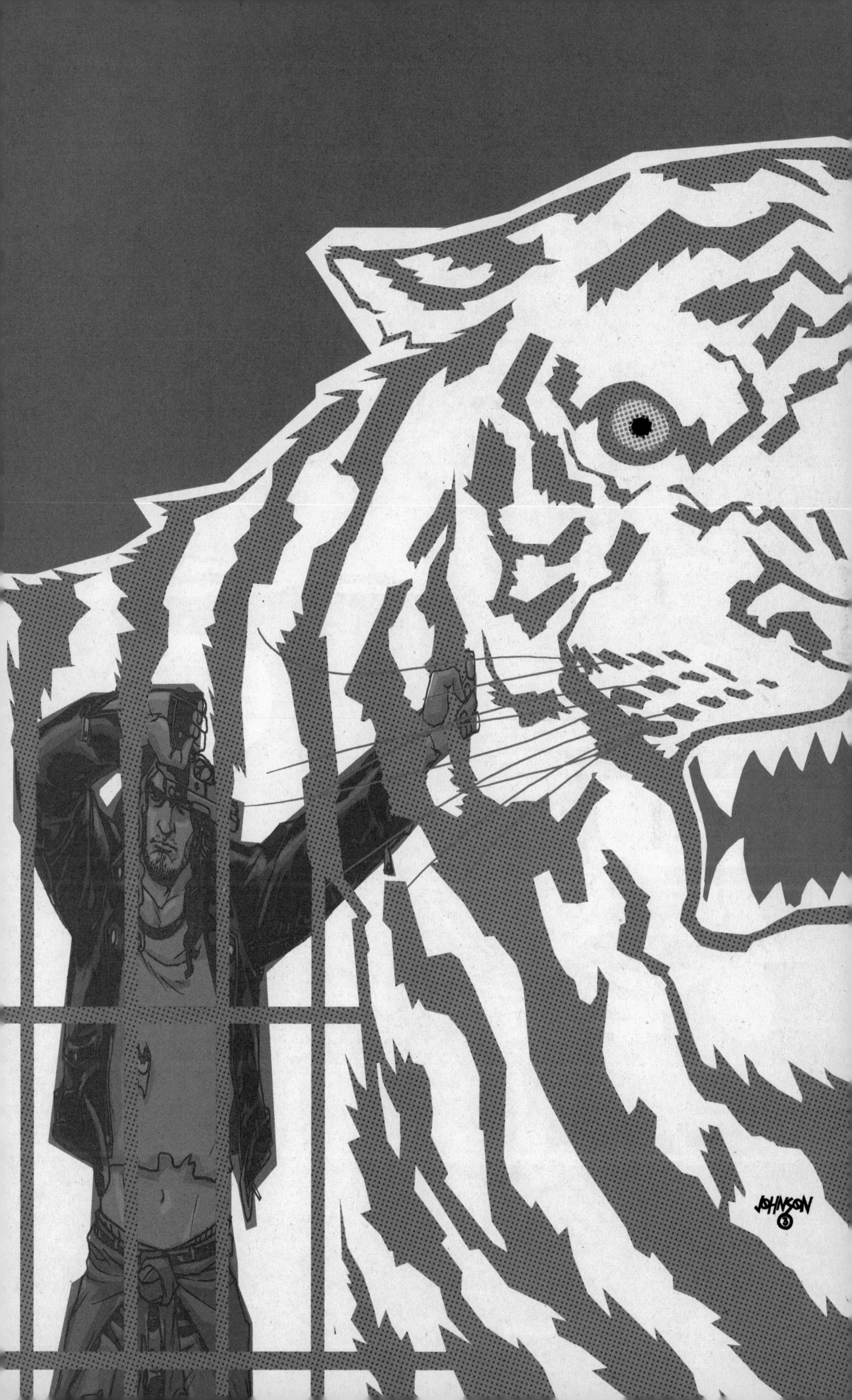
JOHNSON

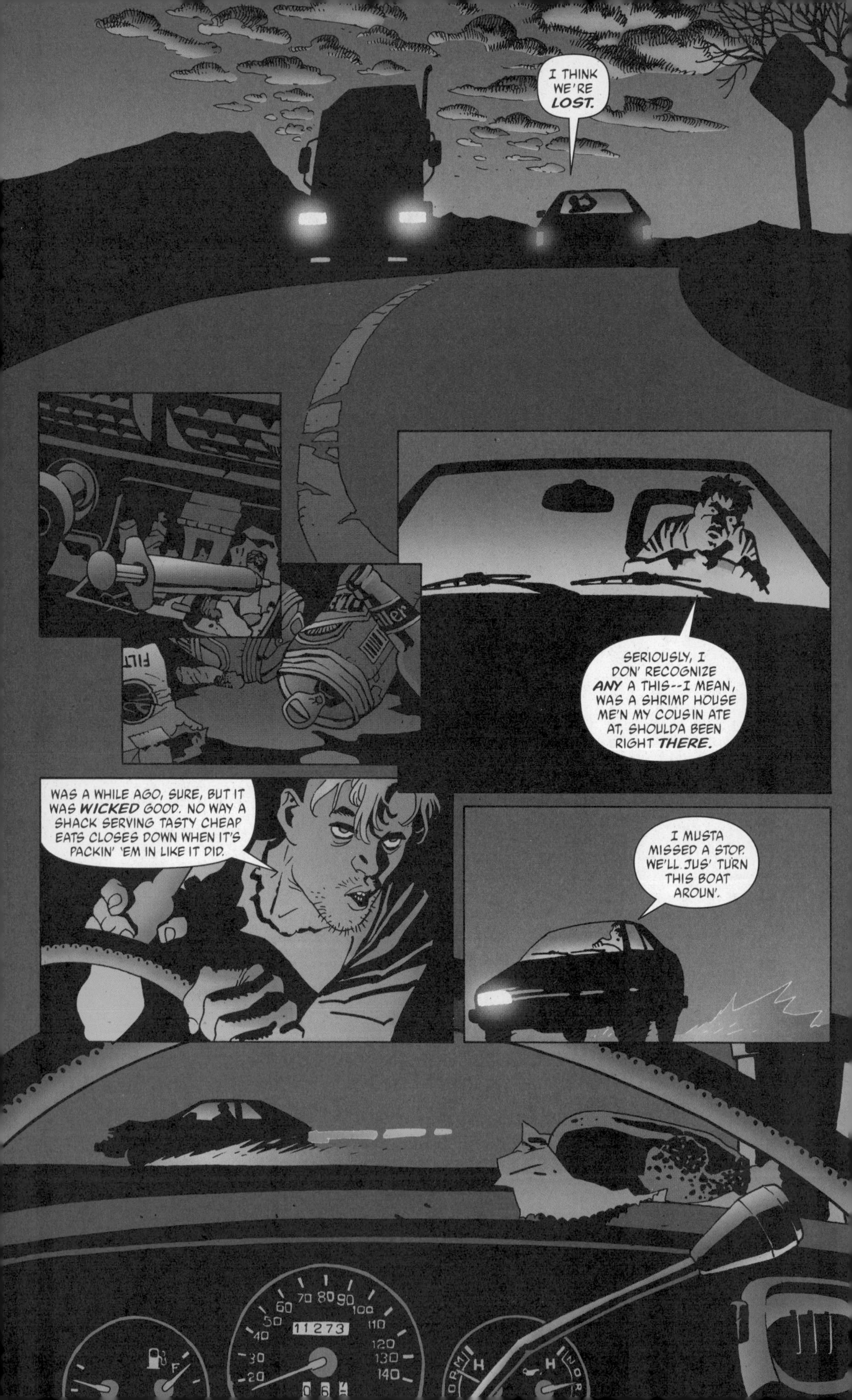
I THINK WE'RE LOST.
SERIOUSLY, I DON' RECOGNIZE ANY A THIS--I MEAN, WAS A SHRIMP HOUSE ME'N MY COUSIN ATE AT, SHOULDA BEEN RIGHT THERE.
WAS A WHILE AGO, SURE, BUT IT WAS WICKED GOOD. NO WAY A SHACK SERVING TASTY CHEAP EATS CLOSES DOWN WHEN IT'S PACKIN' 'EM IN LIKE IT DID.
I MUSTA MISSED A STOP. WE'LL JUS' TURN THIS BOAT AROUN'.

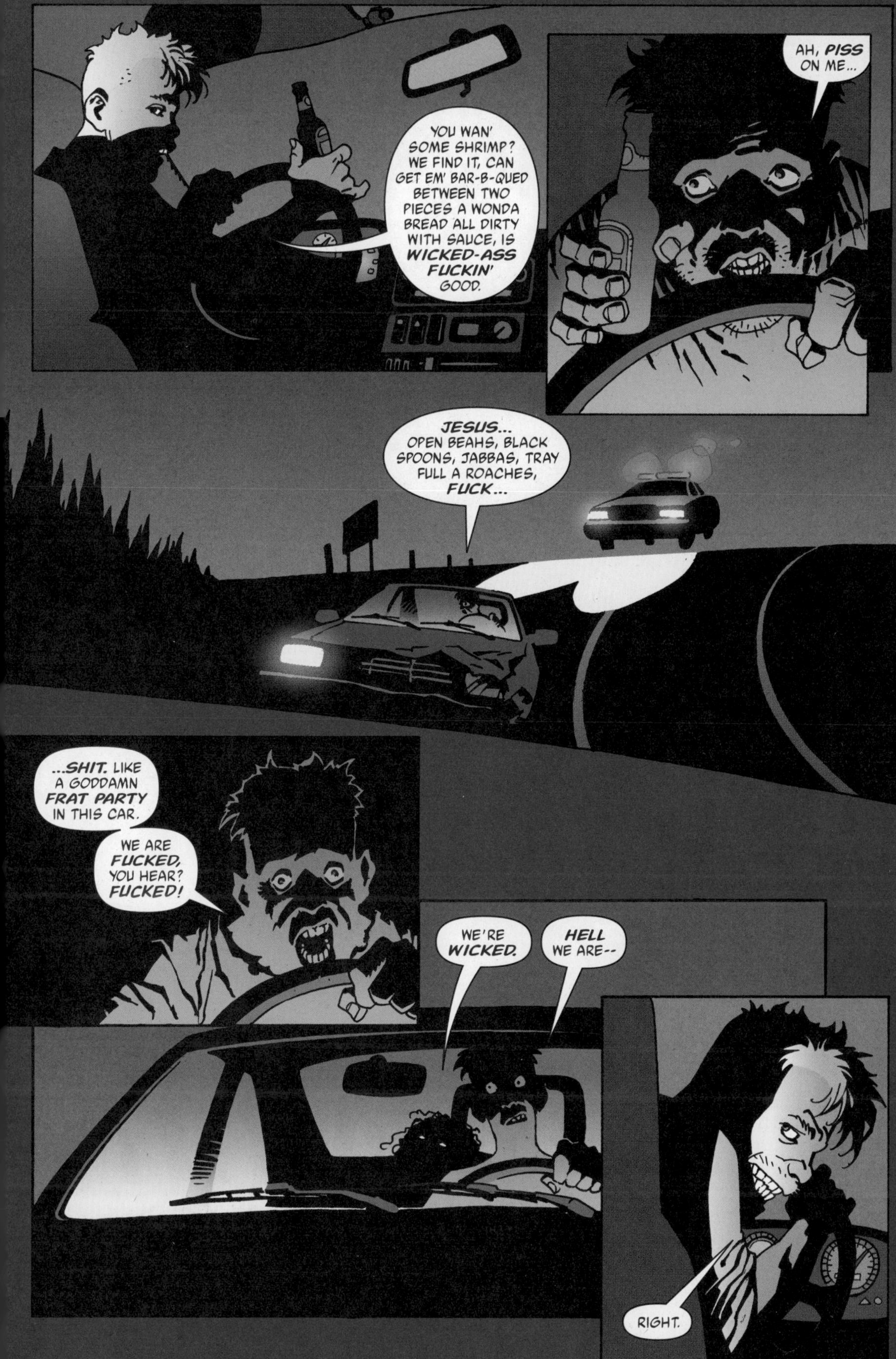

YOU WAN' SOME SHRIMP? WE FIND IT, CAN GET EM' BAR-B-QUED BETWEEN TWO PIECES A WONDA BREAD ALL DIRTY WITH SAUCE, IS WICKED-ASS FUCKIN' GOOD.
AH, PISS ON ME...
JESUS... OPEN BEAHS, BLACK SPOONS, JABBAS, TRAY FULL A ROACHES, FUCK...
...SHIT. LIKE A GODDAMN FRAT PARTY IN THIS CAR.
WE ARE FUCKED, YOU HEAR? FUCKED!
WE'RE WICKED.
HELL WE ARE--
RIGHT.

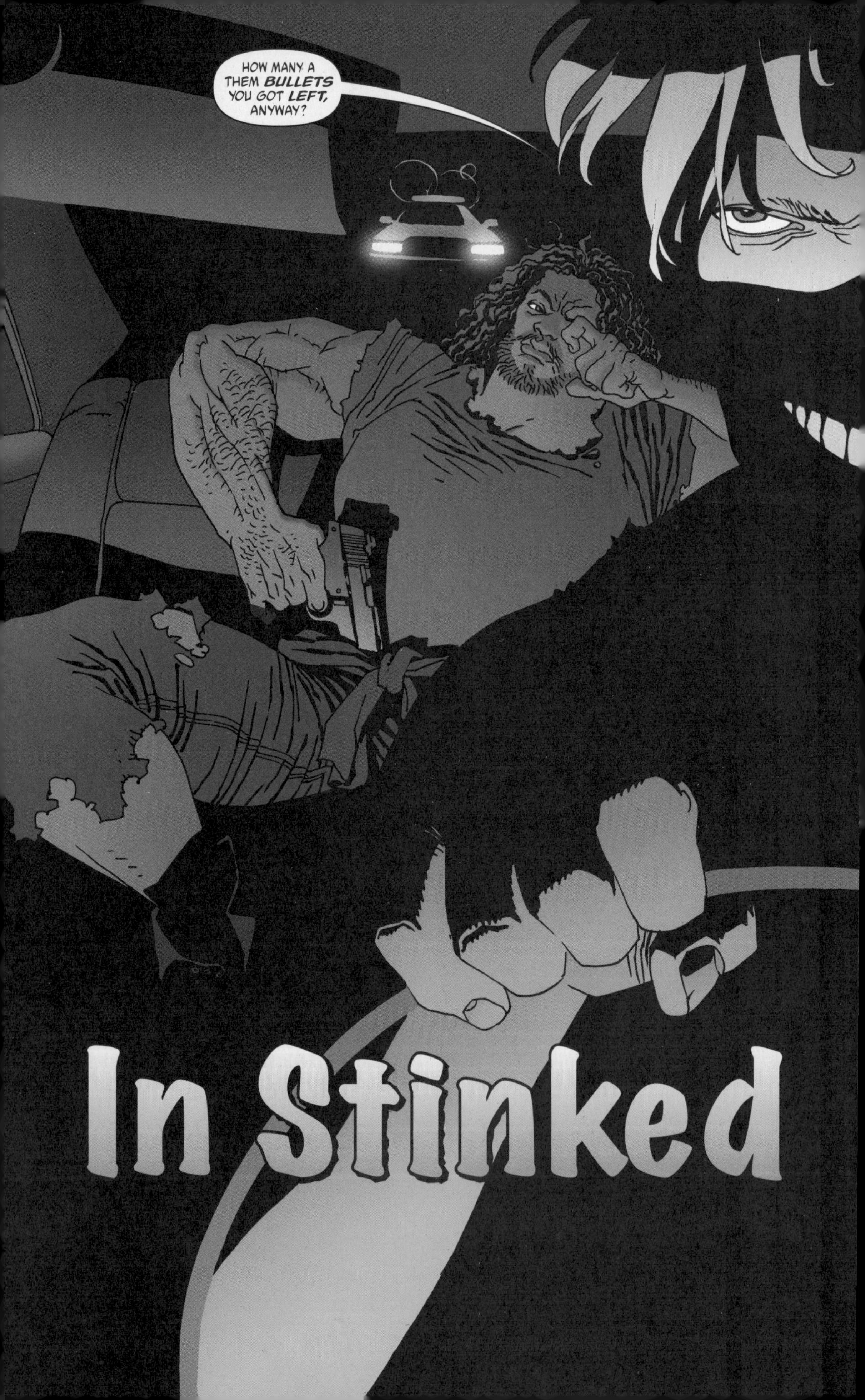

In Stinked

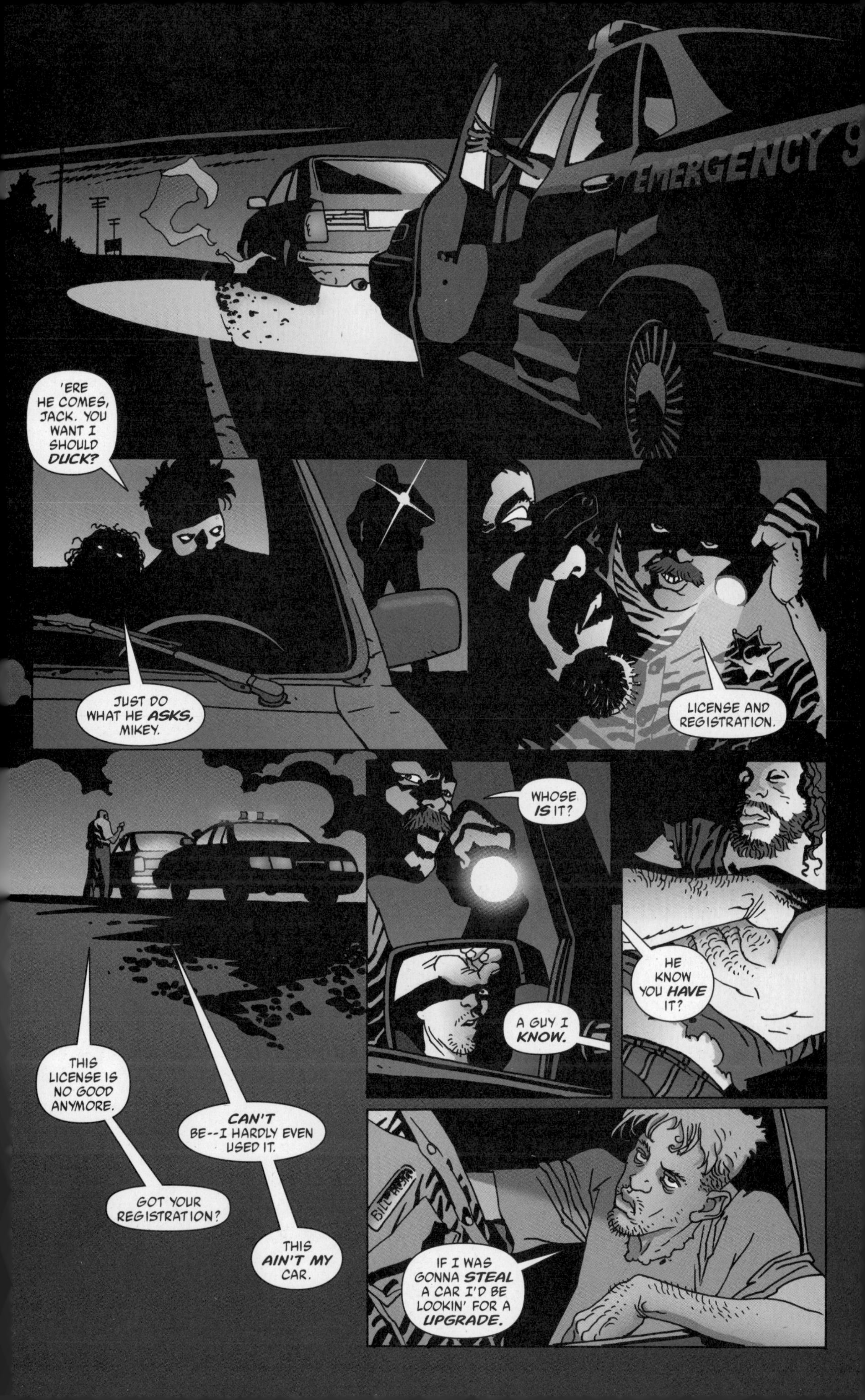
EMERGENCY 9
'ERE HE COMES, JACK. YOU WANT I SHOULD DUCK?
JUST DO WHAT HE ASKS, MIKEY.
LICENSE AND REGISTRATION.
THIS LICENSE IS NO GOOD ANYMORE.
CAN'T BE--I HARDLY EVEN USED IT.
GOT YOUR REGISTRATION?
THIS AIN'T MY CAR.
WHOSE IS IT?
A GUY I KNOW.
HE KNOW YOU HAVE IT?
IF I WAS GONNA STEAL A CAR I'D BE LOOKIN' FOR A UPGRADE.

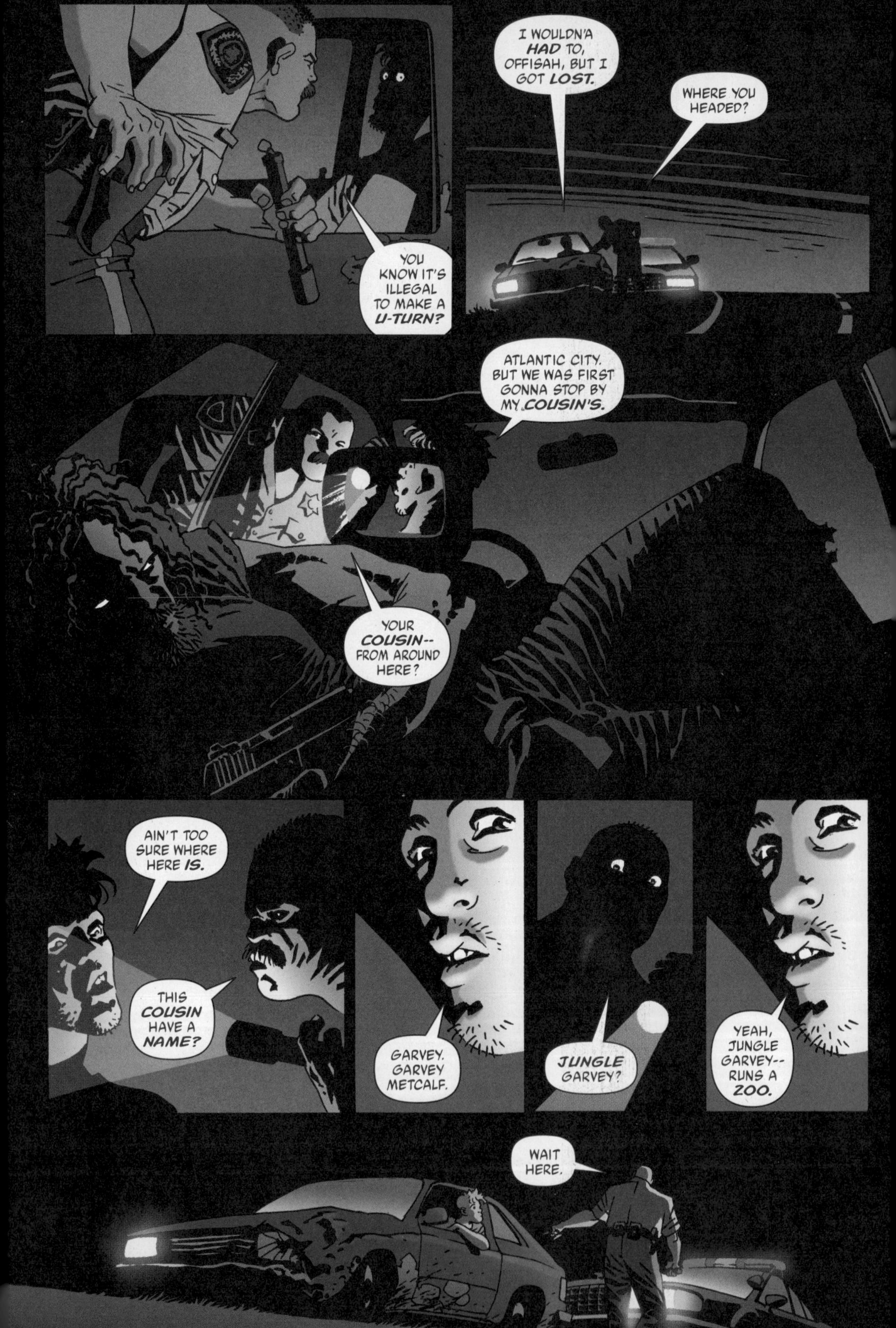
I WOULDN'A HAD TO, OFFISAH, BUT I GOT LOST.
WHERE YOU HEADED?
YOU KNOW IT'S ILLEGAL TO MAKE A U-TURN?
ATLANTIC CITY. BUT WE WAS FIRST GONNA STOP BY MY COUSIN'S.
YOUR COUSIN-- FROM AROUND HERE?
AIN'T TOO SURE WHERE HERE IS.
THIS COUSIN HAVE A NAME?
GARVEY. GARVEY METCALF.
JUNGLE GARVEY?
YEAH, JUNGLE GARVEY-- RUNS A ZOO.
WAIT HERE.

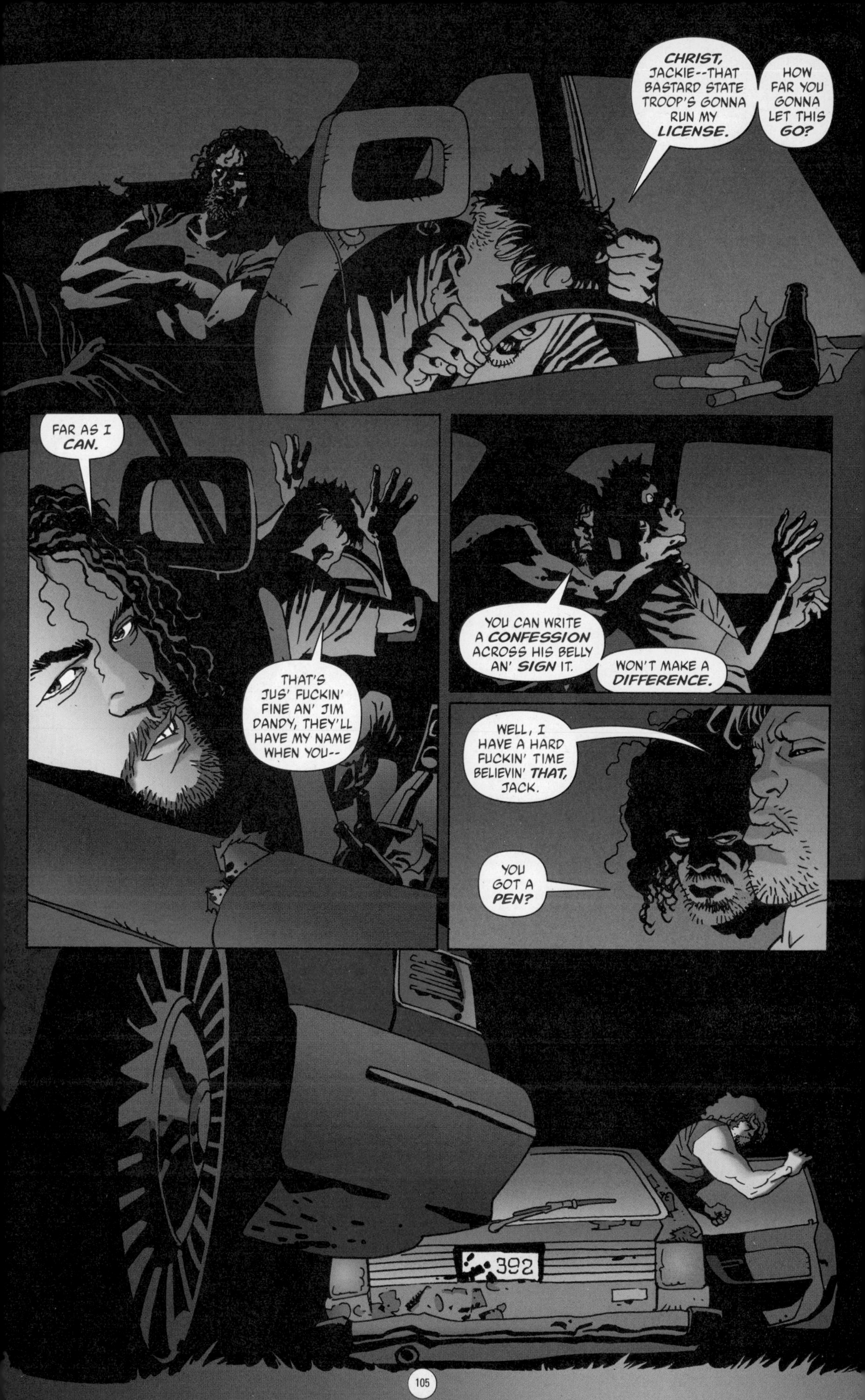
CHRIST, JACKIE--THAT BASTARD STATE TROOP'S GONNA RUN MY LICENSE.
HOW FAR YOU GONNA LET THIS GO?
FAR AS I CAN.
THAT'S JUS' FUCKIN' FINE AN' JIM DANDY, THEY'LL HAVE MY NAME WHEN YOU--
YOU CAN WRITE A CONFESSION ACROSS HIS BELLY AN' SIGN IT.
WON'T MAKE A DIFFERENCE.
WELL, I HAVE A HARD FUCKIN' TIME BELIEVIN' THAT, JACK.
YOU GOT A PEN?
392

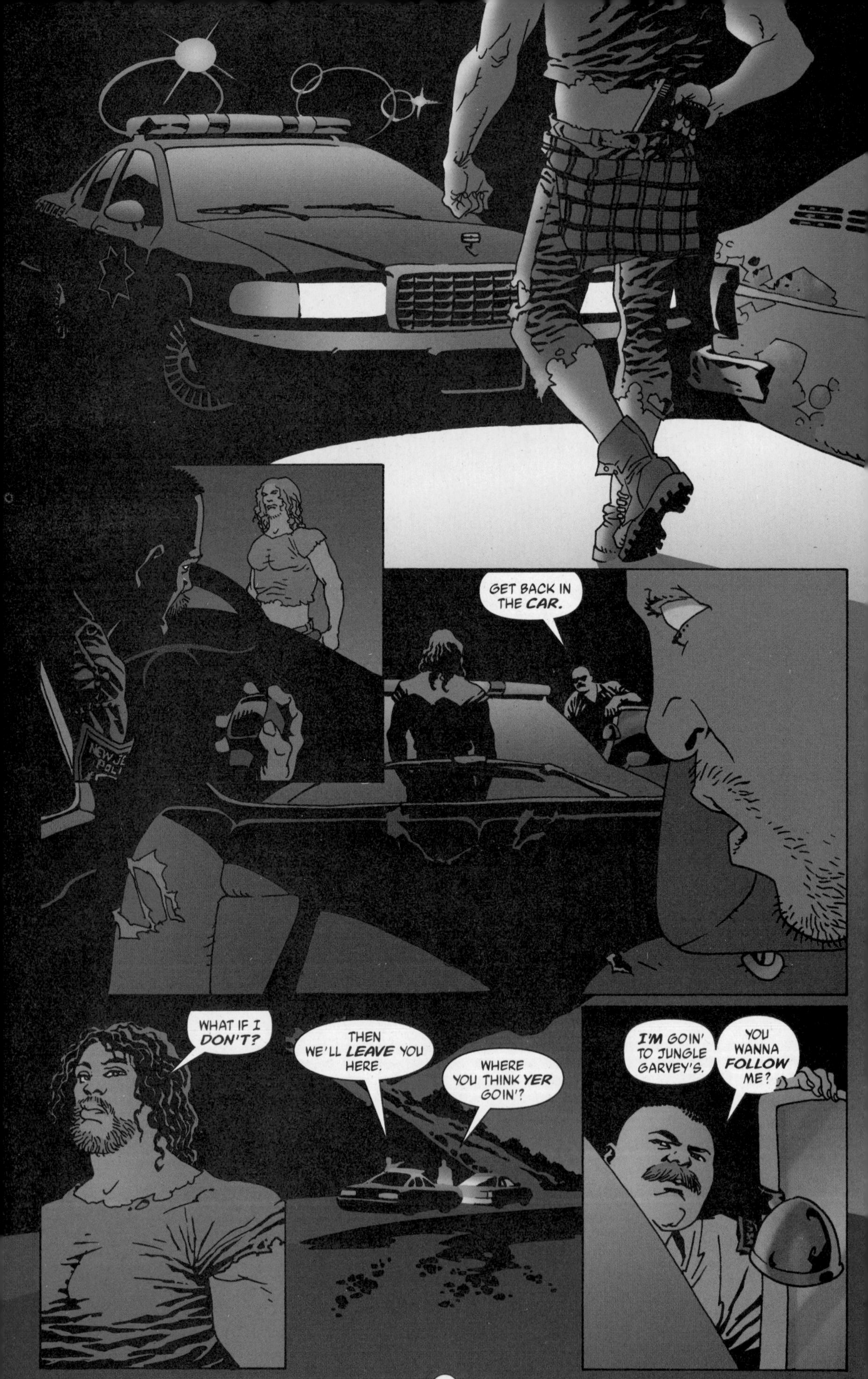
GET BACK IN THE CAR.
WHAT IF I DON'T?
THEN WE'LL LEAVE YOU HERE.
WHERE YOU THINK YER GOIN'?
I'M GOIN' TO JUNGLE GARVEY'S.
YOU WANNA FOLLOW ME?

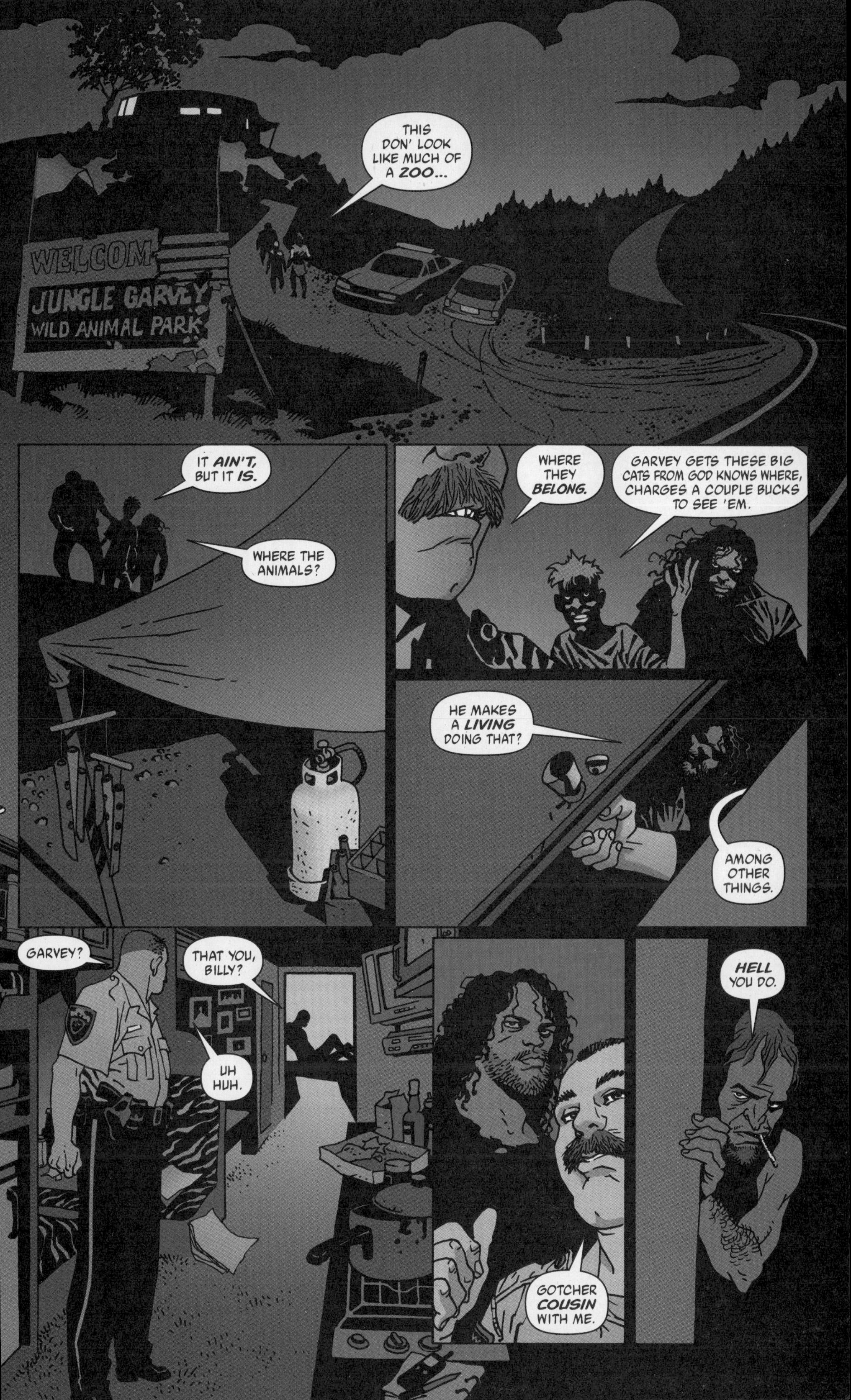
WELCOM
JUNGLE GARVEY
WILD ANIMAL PARK
THIS DON' LOOK LIKE MUCH OF A ZOO...
IT AIN'T, BUT IT IS.
WHERE THE ANIMALS?
WHERE THEY BELONG.
GARVEY GETS THESE BIG CATS FROM GOD KNOWS WHERE, CHARGES A COUPLE BUCKS TO SEE 'EM.
HE MAKES A LIVING DOING THAT?
AMONG OTHER THINGS.
GARVEY?
THAT YOU, BILLY?
UH HUH.
GOTCHER COUSIN WITH ME.
HELL YOU DO.

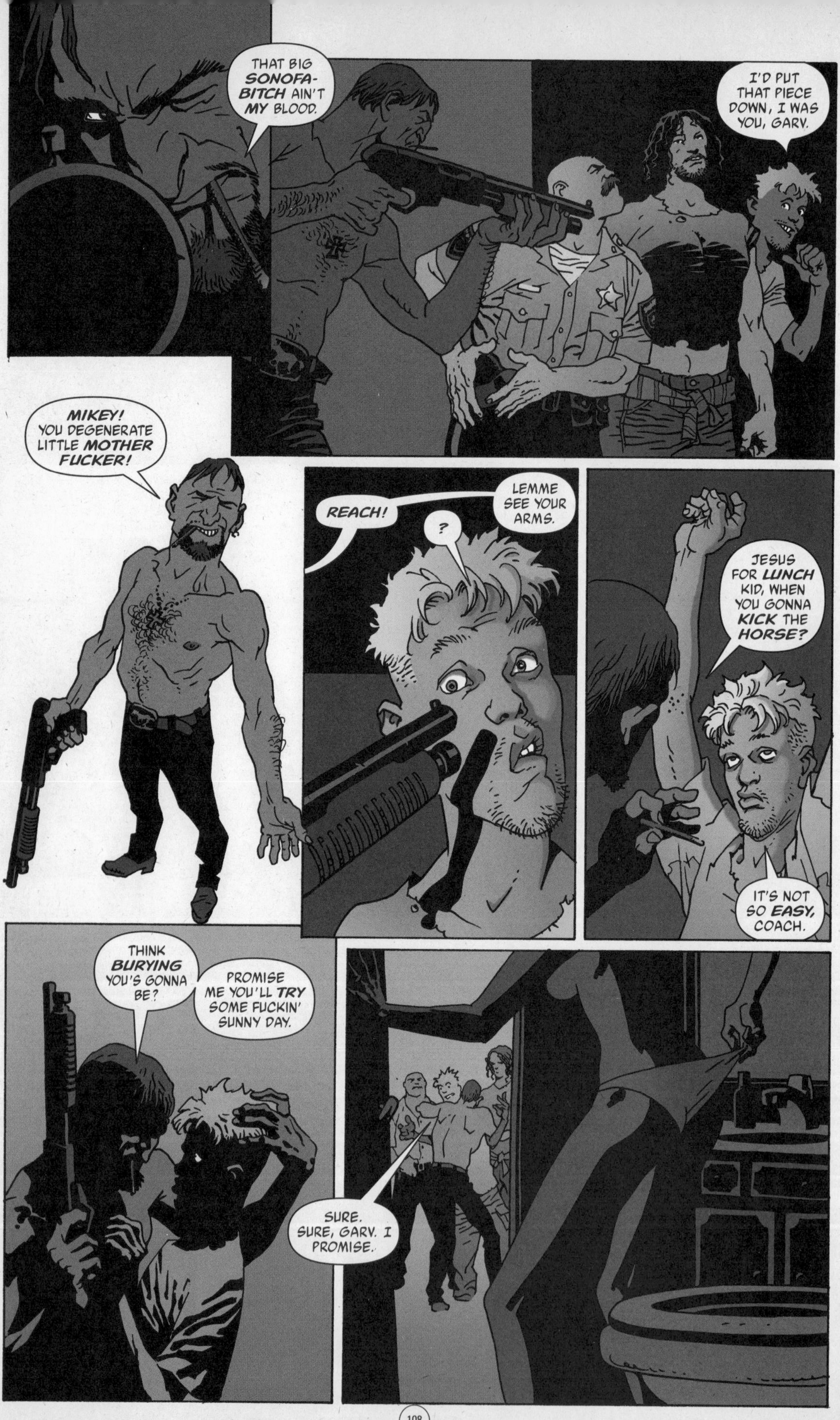
THAT BIG SONOFA-BITCH AIN'T MY BLOOD.
I'D PUT THAT PIECE DOWN, I WAS YOU, GARV.
MIKEY! YOU DEGENERATE LITTLE MOTHER FUCKER!
REACH!
LEMME SEE YOUR ARMS.
?
JESUS FOR LUNCH KID, WHEN YOU GONNA KICK THE HORSE?
IT'S NOT SO EASY, COACH.
THINK BURYING YOU'S GONNA BE?
PROMISE ME YOU'LL TRY SOME FUCKIN' SUNNY DAY.
SURE. SURE, GARV. I PROMISE.

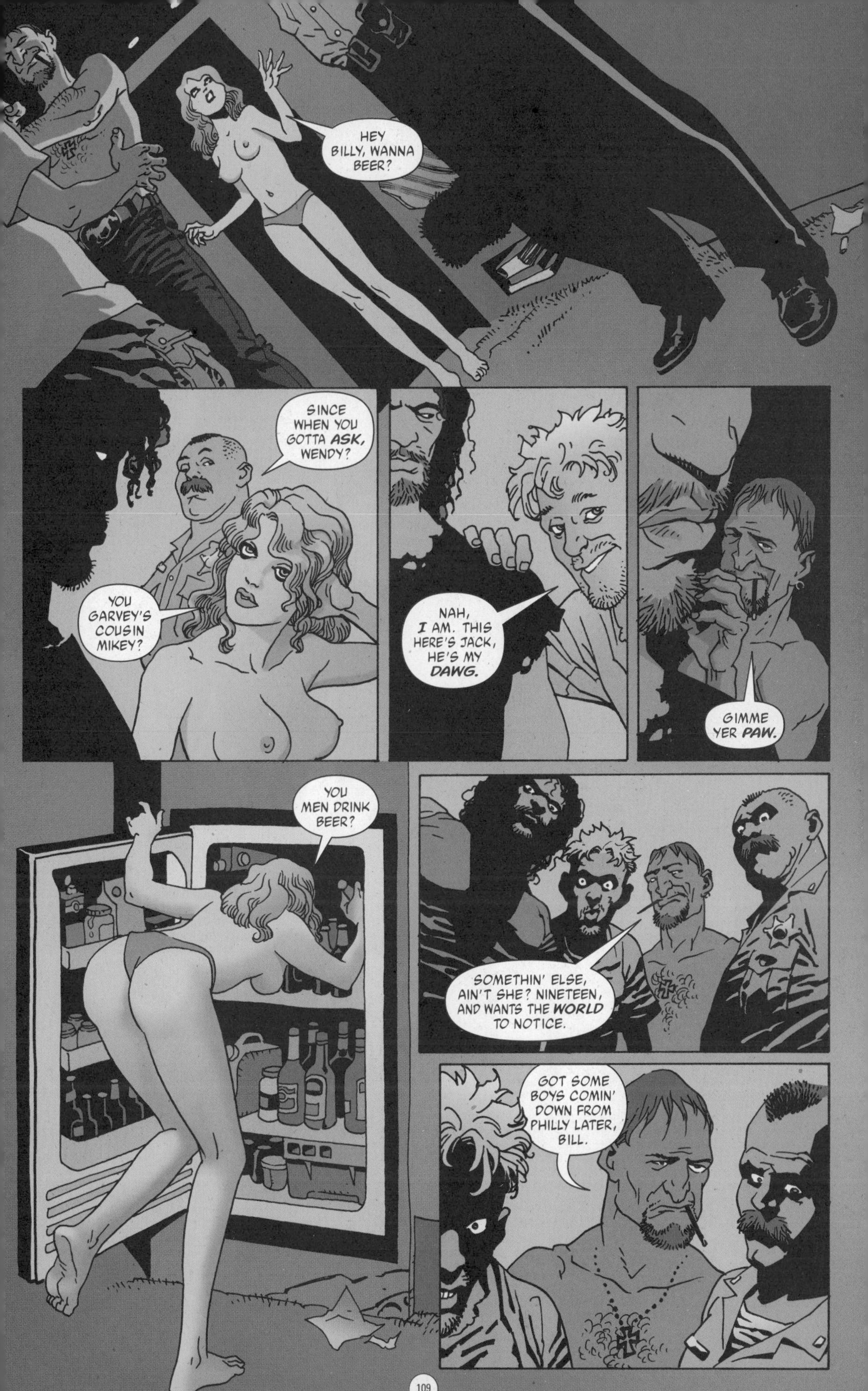
HEY BILLY, WANNA BEER?
SINCE WHEN YOU GOTTA ASK, WENDY?
YOU GARVEY'S COUSIN MIKEY?
NAH, I AM. THIS HERE'S JACK, HE'S MY DAWG.
GIMME YER PAW.
YOU MEN DRINK BEER?
SOMETHIN' ELSE, AIN'T SHE? NINETEEN, AND WANTS THE WORLD TO NOTICE.
GOT SOME BOYS COMIN' DOWN FROM PHILLY LATER, BILL.

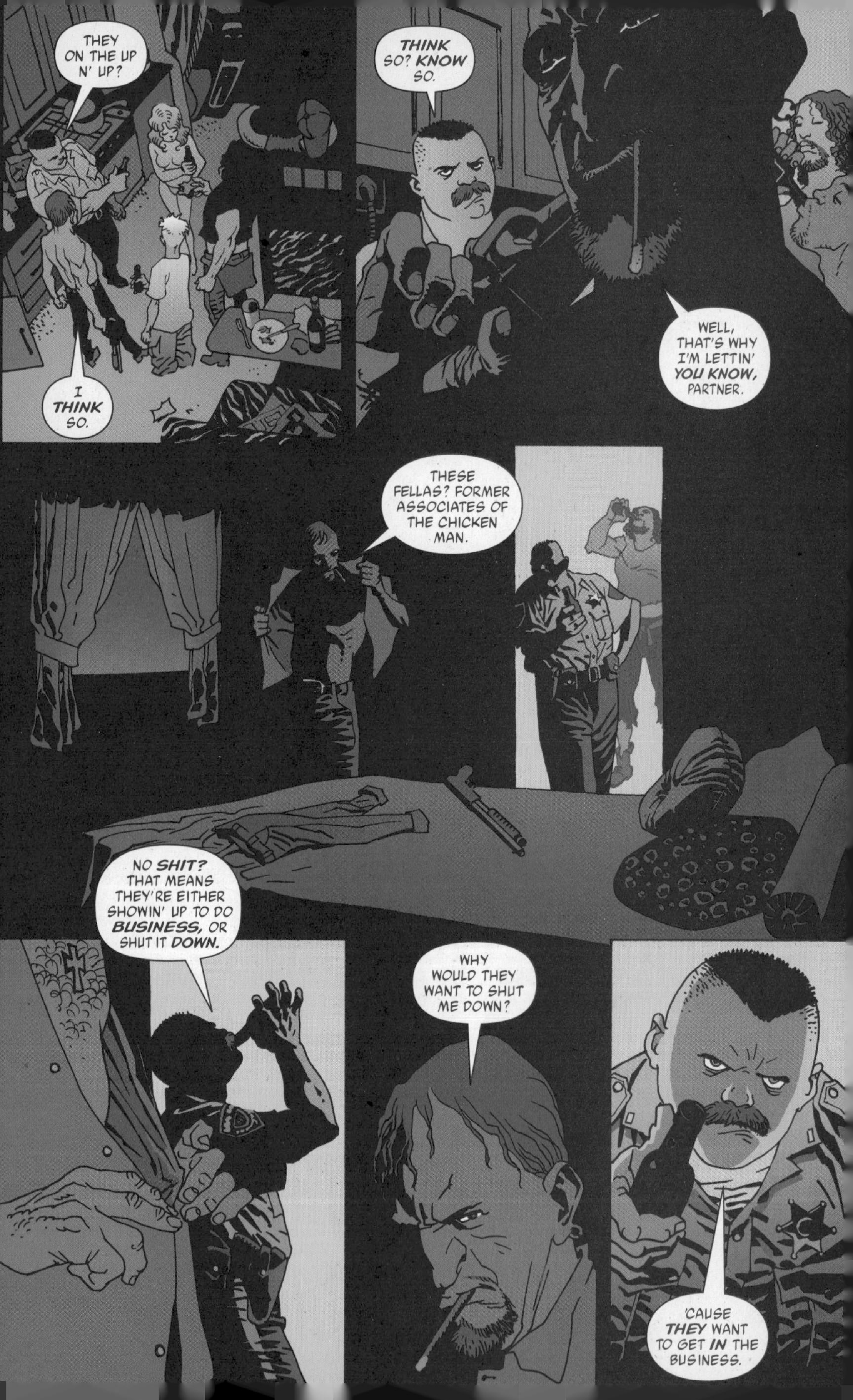
THEY ON THE UP N' UP?
I THINK SO.
THINK SO? KNOW SO.
WELL, THAT'S WHY I'M LETTIN' YOU KNOW, PARTNER.
THESE FELLAS? FORMER ASSOCIATES OF THE CHICKEN MAN.
NO SHIT? THAT MEANS THEY'RE EITHER SHOWIN' UP TO DO BUSINESS, OR SHUT IT DOWN.
WHY WOULD THEY WANT TO SHUT ME DOWN?
'CAUSE THEY WANT TO GET IN THE BUSINESS.

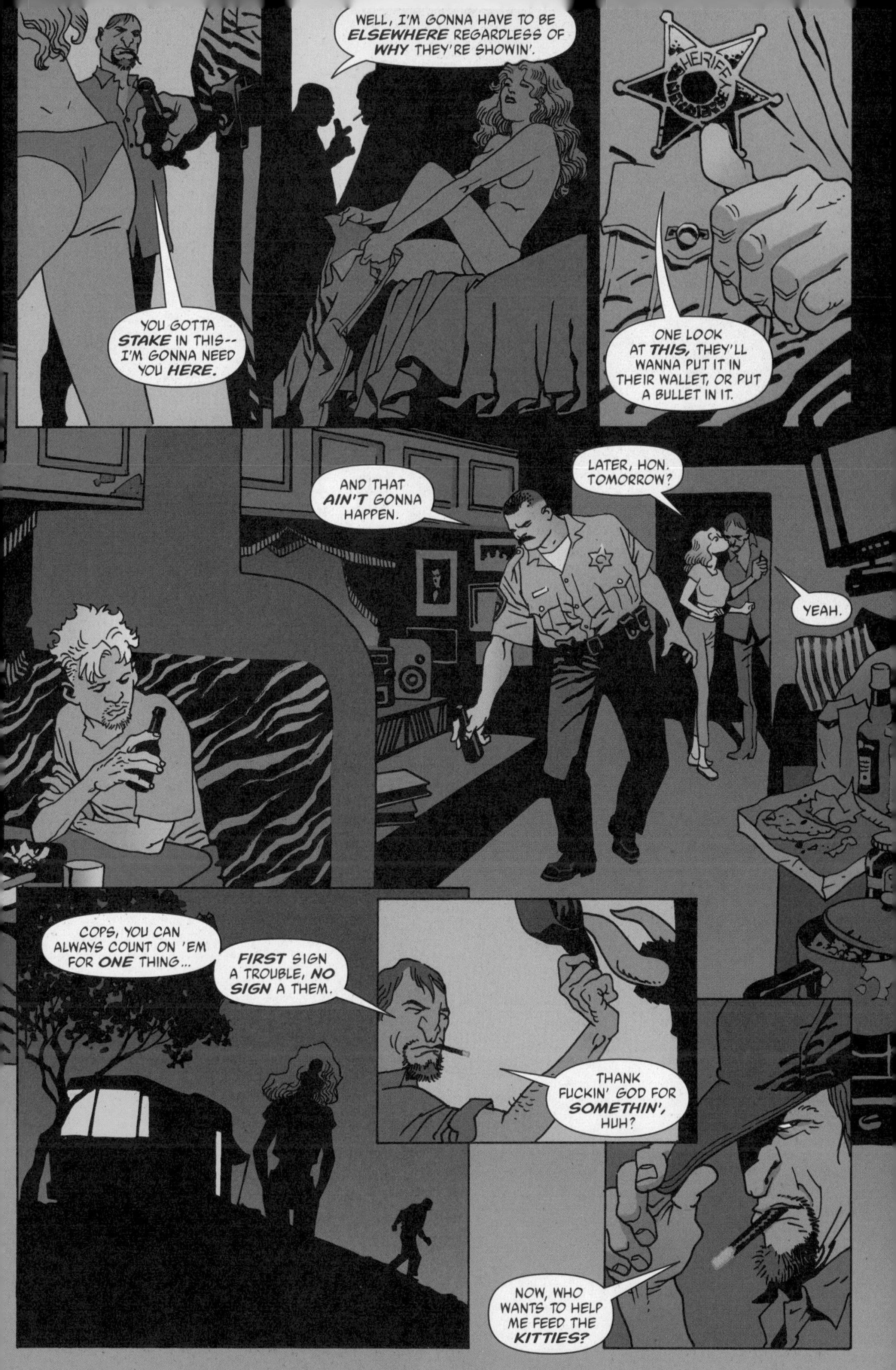
YOU GOTTA
STAKE IN THIS--
I'M GONNA NEED
YOU HERE.
WELL, I'M GONNA HAVE TO BE
ELSEWHERE REGARDLESS OF
WHY THEY'RE SHOWIN'.
SHERIFF
ONE LOOK
AT THIS, THEY'LL
WANNA PUT IT IN
THEIR WALLET, OR PUT
A BULLET IN IT.
AND THAT
AIN'T GONNA
HAPPEN.
LATER, HON.
TOMORROW?
YEAH.
COPS, YOU CAN
ALWAYS COUNT ON 'EM
FOR ONE THING...
FIRST SIGN
A TROUBLE, NO
SIGN A THEM.
THANK
FUCKIN' GOD FOR
SOMETHIN',
HUH?
NOW, WHO
WANTS TO HELP
ME FEED THE
KITTIES?

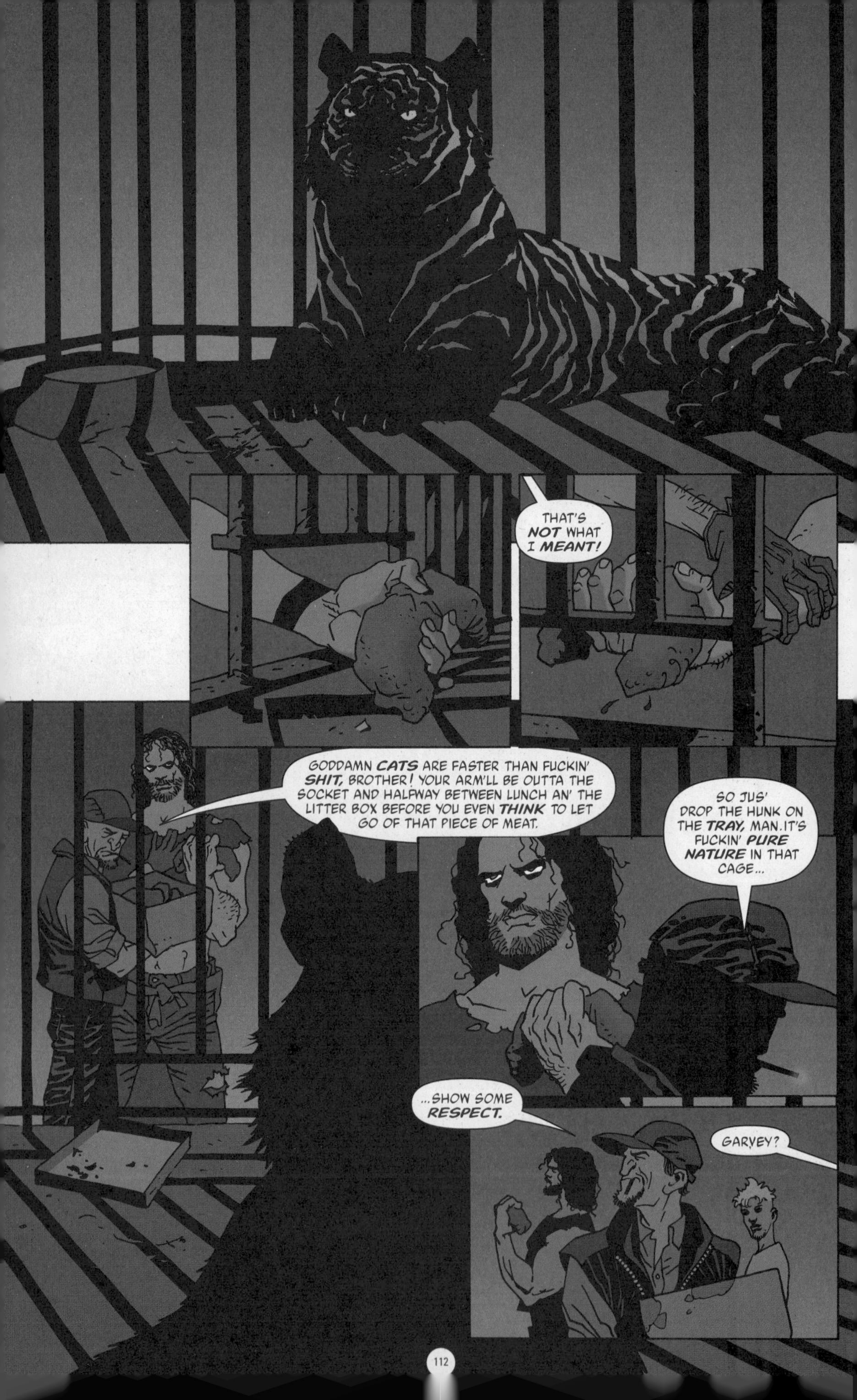
THAT'S NOT WHAT I MEANT!
GODDAMN CATS ARE FASTER THAN FUCKIN' SHIT, BROTHER! YOUR ARM'LL BE OUTTA THE SOCKET AND HALFWAY BETWEEN LUNCH AN' THE LITTER BOX BEFORE YOU EVEN THINK TO LET GO OF THAT PIECE OF MEAT.
SO JUS' DROP THE HUNK ON THE TRAY, MAN. IT'S FUCKIN' PURE NATURE IN THAT CAGE...
...SHOW SOME RESPECT.
GARVEY?

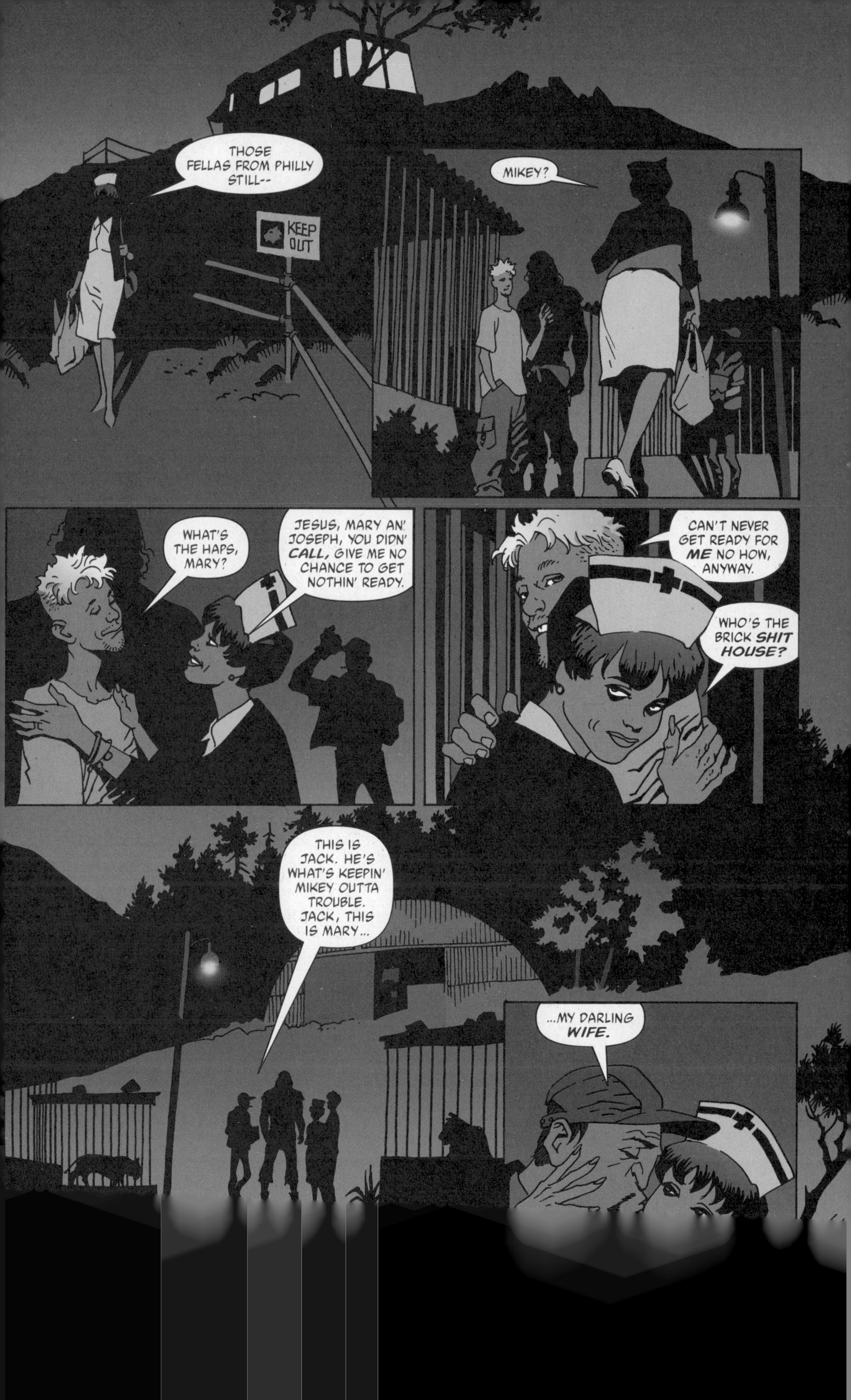
THOSE FELLAS FROM PHILLY STILL--
KEEP OUT
MIKEY?
WHAT'S THE HAPS, MARY?
JESUS, MARY AN' JOSEPH, YOU DIDN' CALL, GIVE ME NO CHANCE TO GET NOTHIN' READY.
CAN'T NEVER GET READY FOR ME NO HOW, ANYWAY.
WHO'S THE BRICK SHIT HOUSE?
THIS IS JACK. HE'S WHAT'S KEEPIN' MIKEY OUTTA TROUBLE. JACK, THIS IS MARY...
...MY DARLING WIFE.

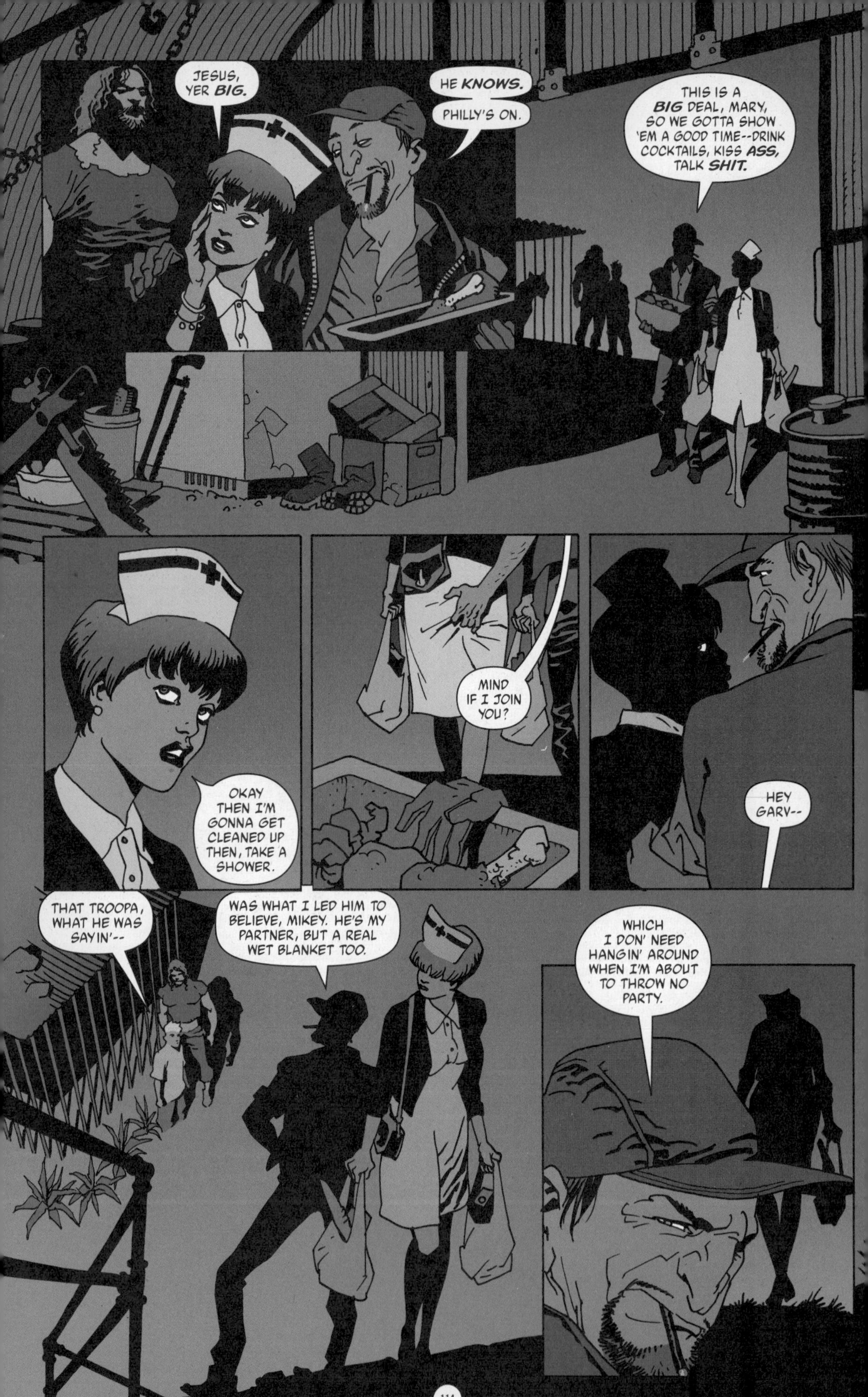
JESUS, YER BIG.
HE KNOWS.
PHILLY'S ON.
THIS IS A BIG DEAL, MARY, SO WE GOTTA SHOW 'EM A GOOD TIME--DRINK COCKTAILS, KISS ASS, TALK SHIT.
OKAY THEN I'M GONNA GET CLEANED UP THEN, TAKE A SHOWER.
MIND IF I JOIN YOU?
HEY GARV--
THAT TROOPA, WHAT HE WAS SAYIN'--
WAS WHAT I LED HIM TO BELIEVE, MIKEY. HE'S MY PARTNER, BUT A REAL WET BLANKET TOO.
WHICH I DON' NEED HANGIN' AROUND WHEN I'M ABOUT TO THROW NO PARTY.

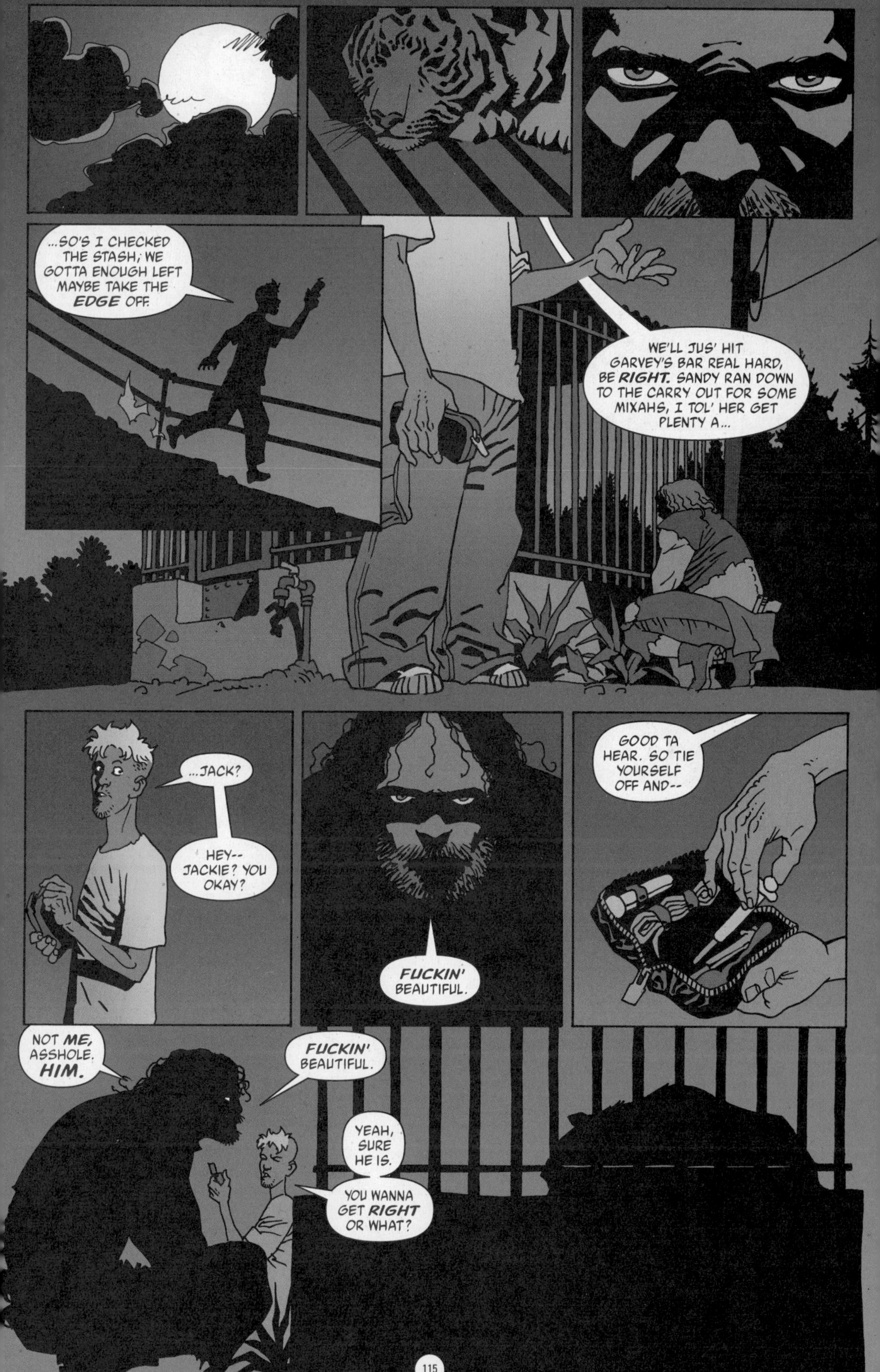
...SO'S I CHECKED THE STASH; WE GOTTA ENOUGH LEFT MAYBE TAKE THE EDGE OFF.
WE'LL JUS' HIT GARVEY'S BAR REAL HARD, BE RIGHT. SANDY RAN DOWN TO THE CARRY OUT FOR SOME MIXAHS, I TOL' HER GET PLENTY A...
...JACK?
HEY-- JACKIE? YOU OKAY?
FUCKIN' BEAUTIFUL.
GOOD TA HEAR. SO TIE YOURSELF OFF AND--
NOT ME, ASSHOLE. HIM.
FUCKIN' BEAUTIFUL.
YEAH, SURE HE IS.
YOU WANNA GET RIGHT OR WHAT?

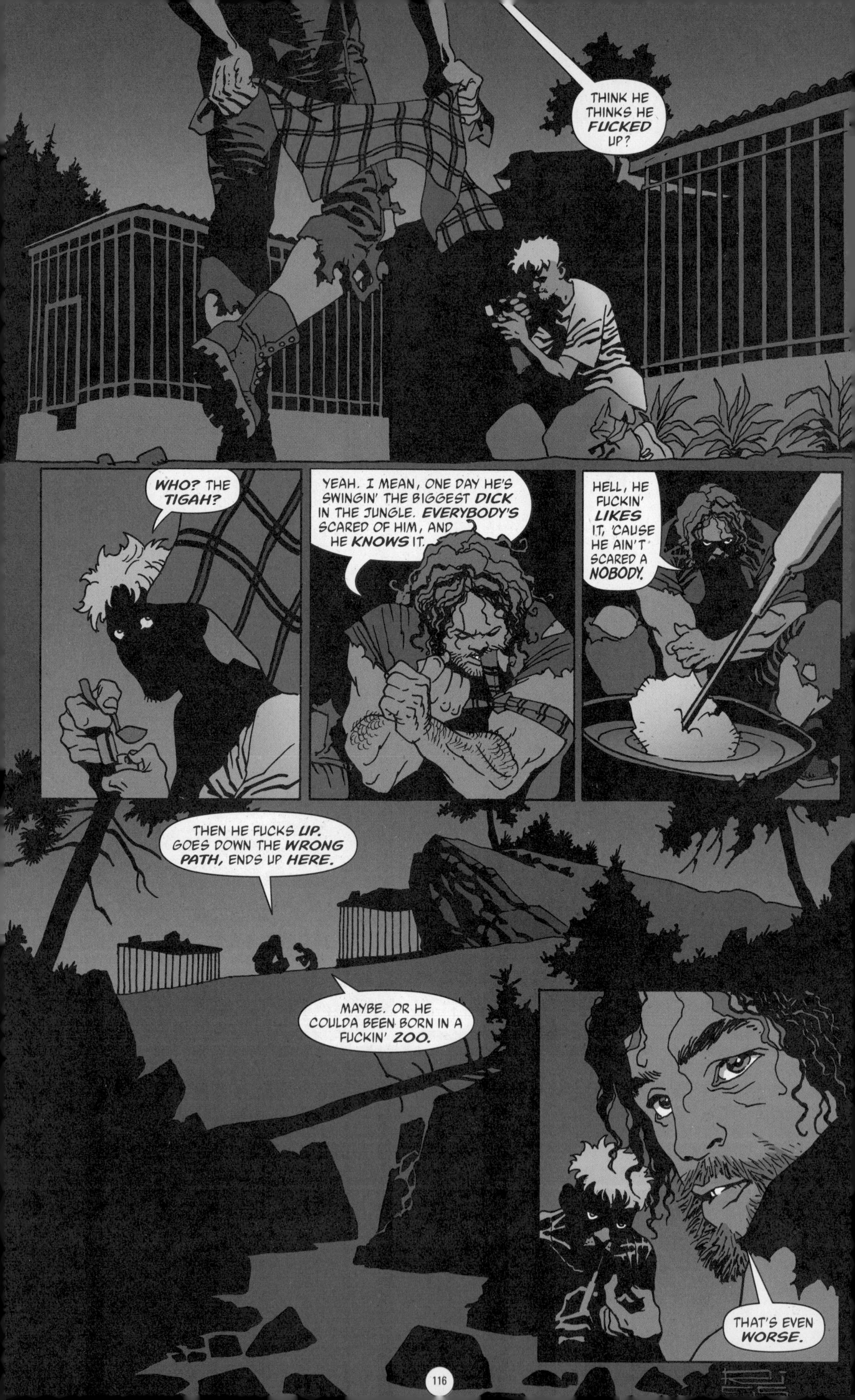
THINK HE THINKS HE FUCKED UP?
WHO? THE TIGAH?
YEAH. I MEAN, ONE DAY HE'S SWINGIN' THE BIGGEST DICK IN THE JUNGLE. EVERYBODY'S SCARED OF HIM, AND HE KNOWS IT.
HELL, HE FUCKIN' LIKES IT, 'CAUSE HE AIN'T SCARED A NOBODY.
THEN HE FUCKS UP. GOES DOWN THE WRONG PATH, ENDS UP HERE.
MAYBE. OR HE COULDA BEEN BORN IN A FUCKIN' ZOO.
THAT'S EVEN WORSE.

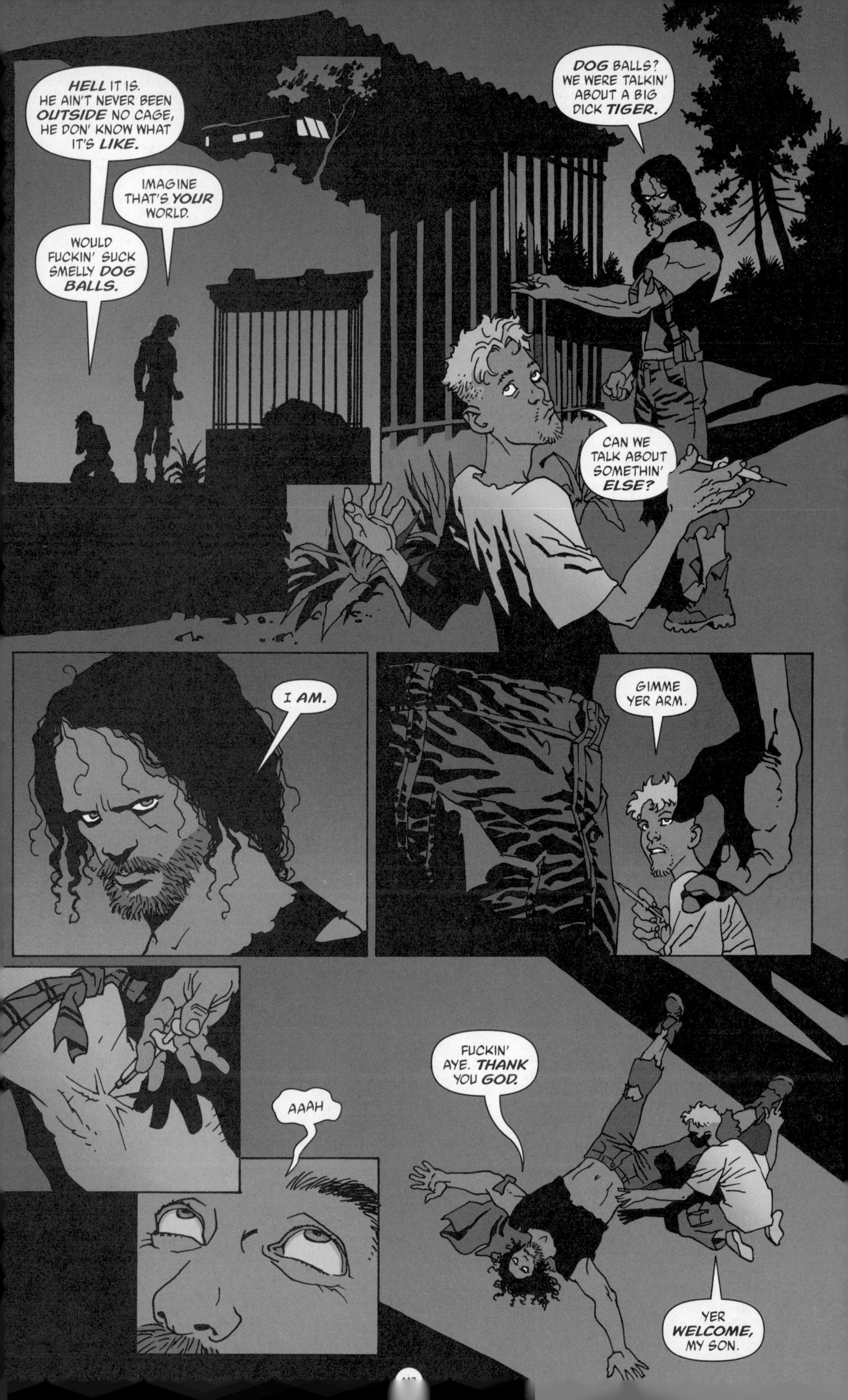
HELL IT IS. HE AIN'T NEVER BEEN OUTSIDE NO CAGE, HE DON' KNOW WHAT IT'S LIKE.
IMAGINE THAT'S YOUR WORLD.
WOULD FUCKIN' SUCK SMELLY DOG BALLS.
DOG BALLS? WE WERE TALKIN' ABOUT A BIG DICK TIGER.
CAN WE TALK ABOUT SOMETHIN' ELSE?
I AM.
GIMME YER ARM.
AAAH
FUCKIN' AYE. THANK YOU GOD.
YER WELCOME, MY SON.

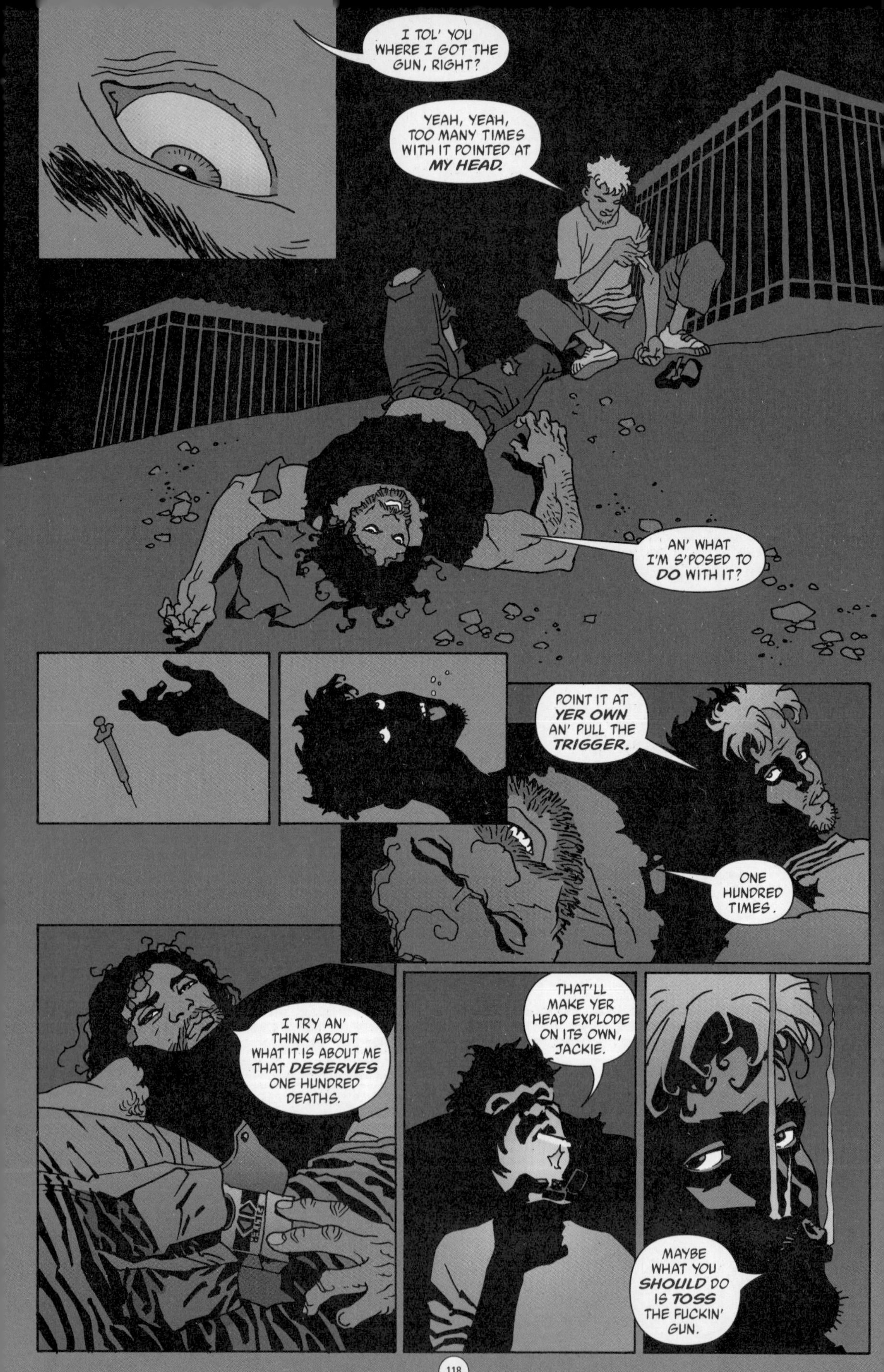

I TOL' YOU WHERE I GOT THE GUN, RIGHT?
YEAH, YEAH, TOO MANY TIMES WITH IT POINTED AT MY HEAD.
AN' WHAT I'M S'POSED TO DO WITH IT?
POINT IT AT YER OWN AN' PULL THE TRIGGER.
ONE HUNDRED TIMES.
I TRY AN' THINK ABOUT WHAT IT IS ABOUT ME THAT DESERVES ONE HUNDRED DEATHS.
THAT'LL MAKE YER HEAD EXPLODE ON ITS OWN, JACKIE.
MAYBE WHAT YOU SHOULD DO IS TOSS THE FUCKIN' GUN.

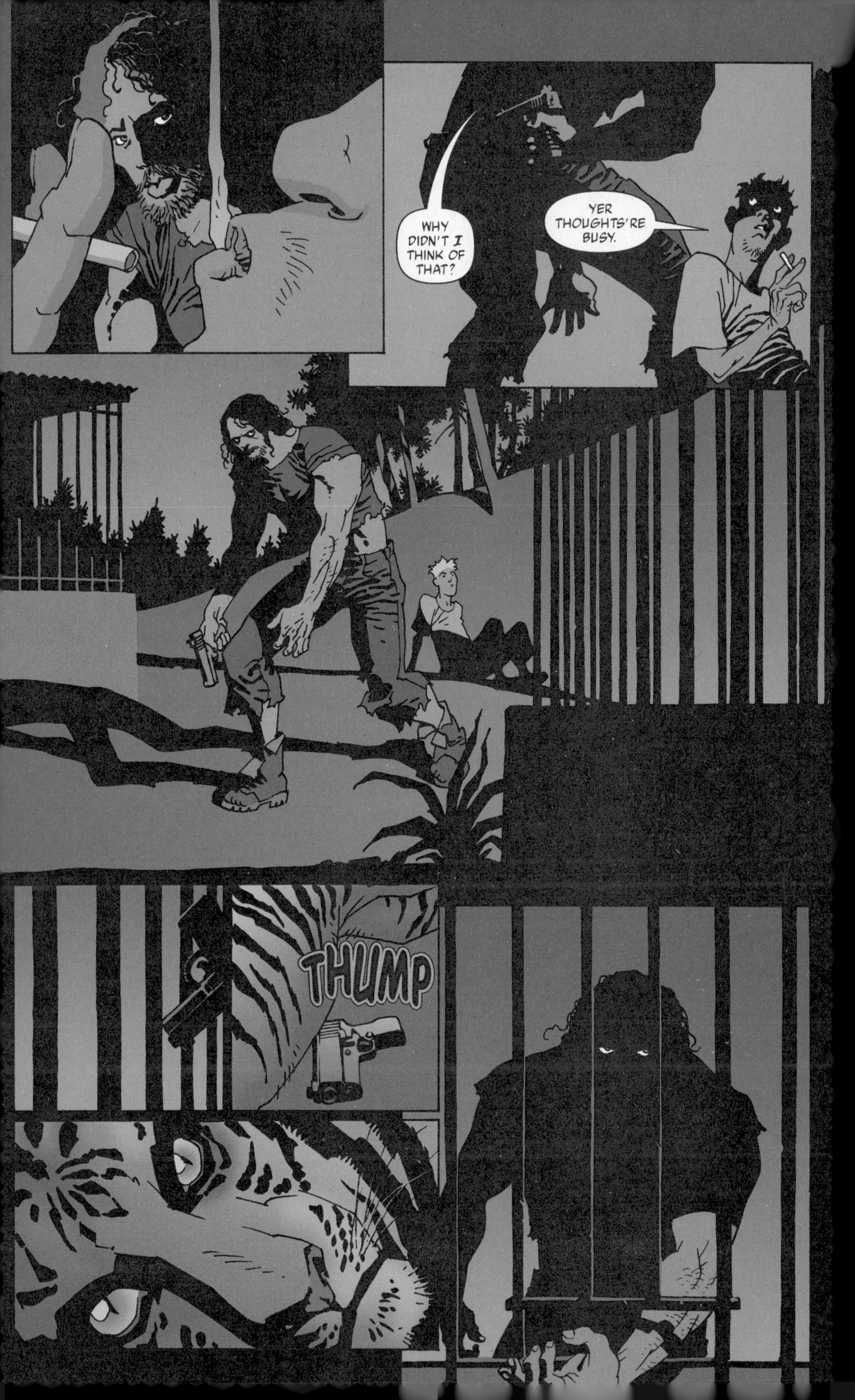
WHY DIDN'T I THINK OF THAT?
YER THOUGHTS'RE BUSY.
THUMP

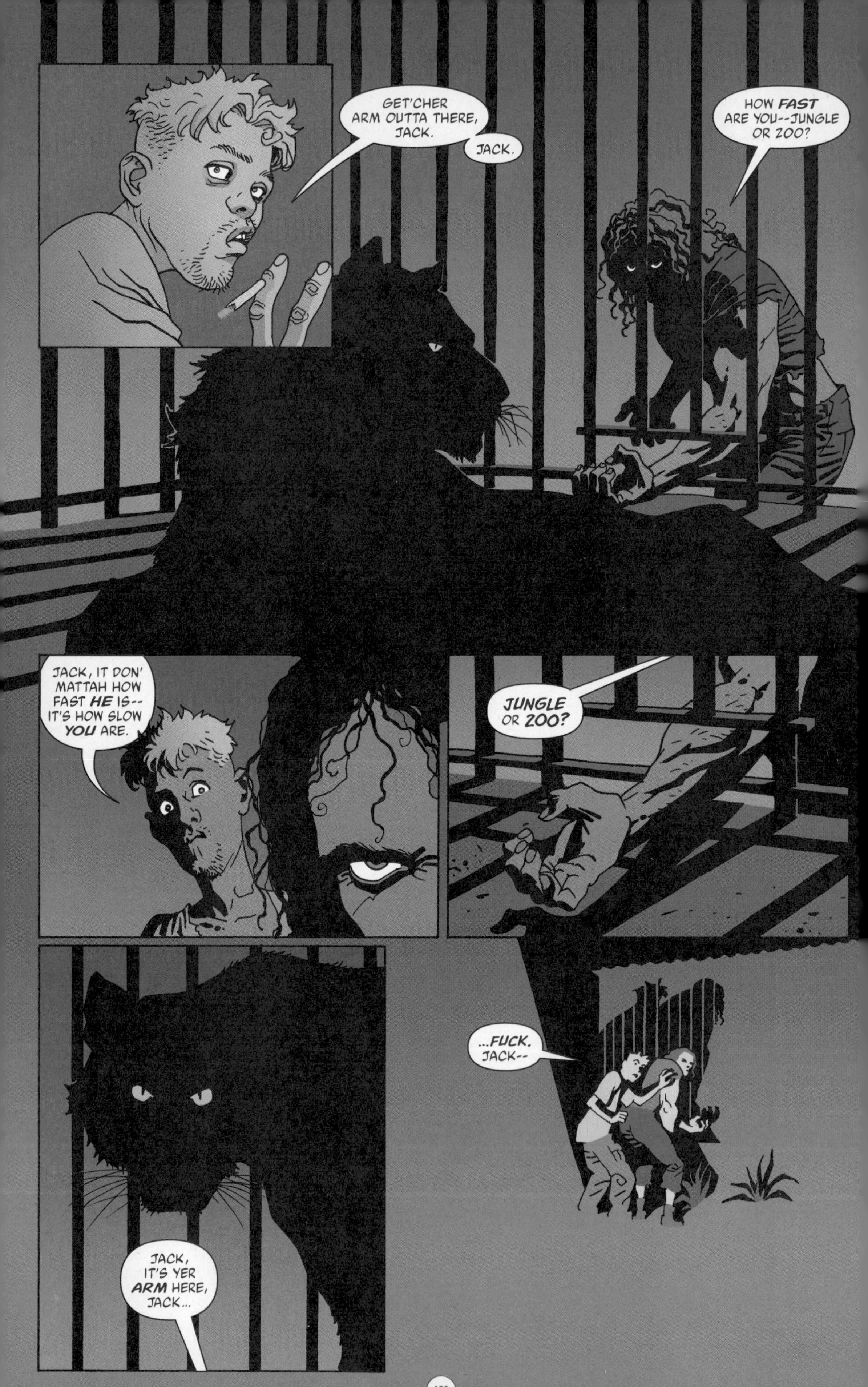
GET'CHER ARM OUTTA THERE, JACK.
JACK.
HOW **FAST** ARE YOU--JUNGLE OR ZOO?
JACK, IT DON' MATTAH HOW FAST **HE** IS-- IT'S HOW SLOW **YOU** ARE.
JUNGLE OR **ZOO?**
...**FUCK.** JACK--
JACK, IT'S YER **ARM** HERE, JACK...

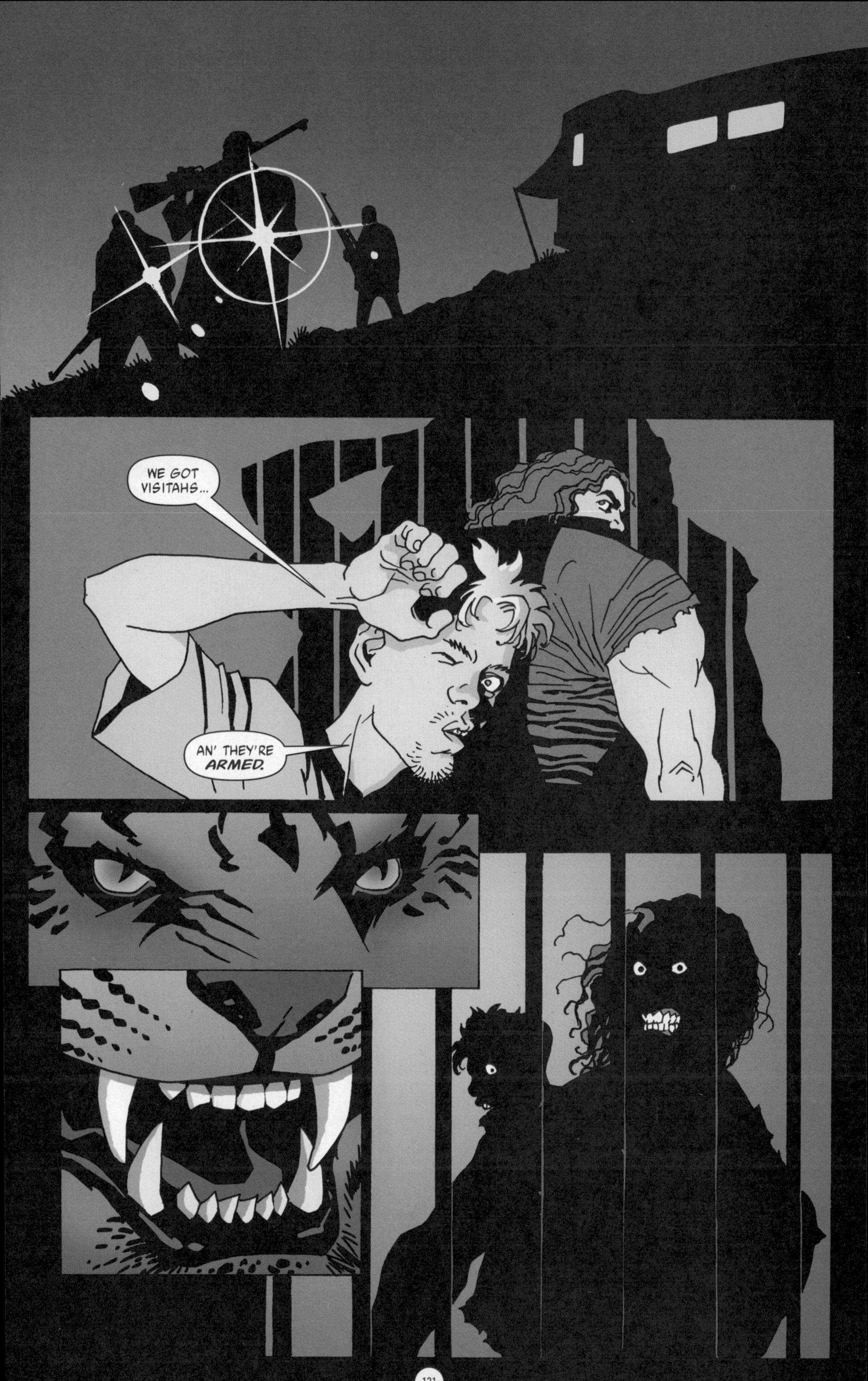
WE GOT VISITAHS...
AN' THEY'RE ARMED.

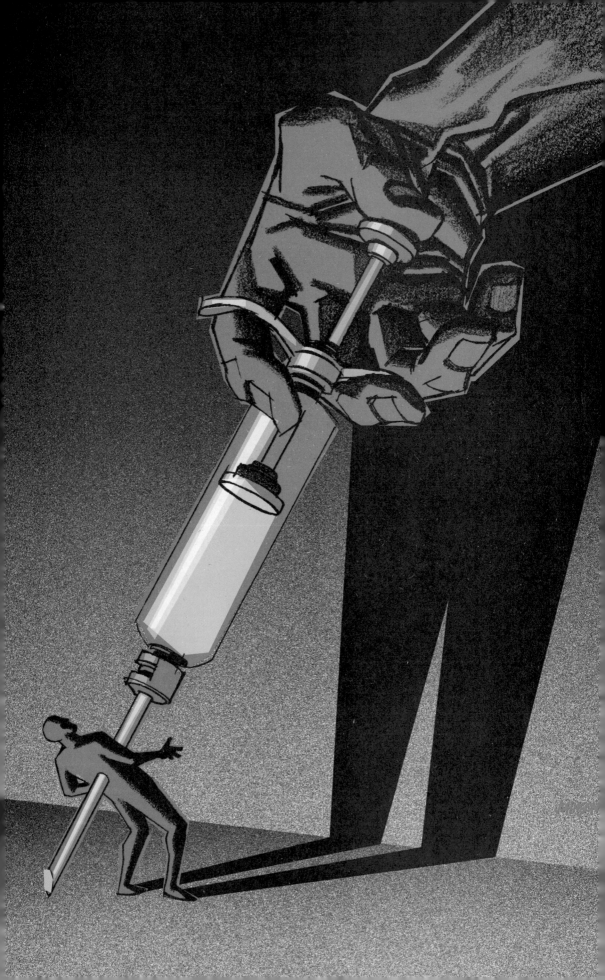

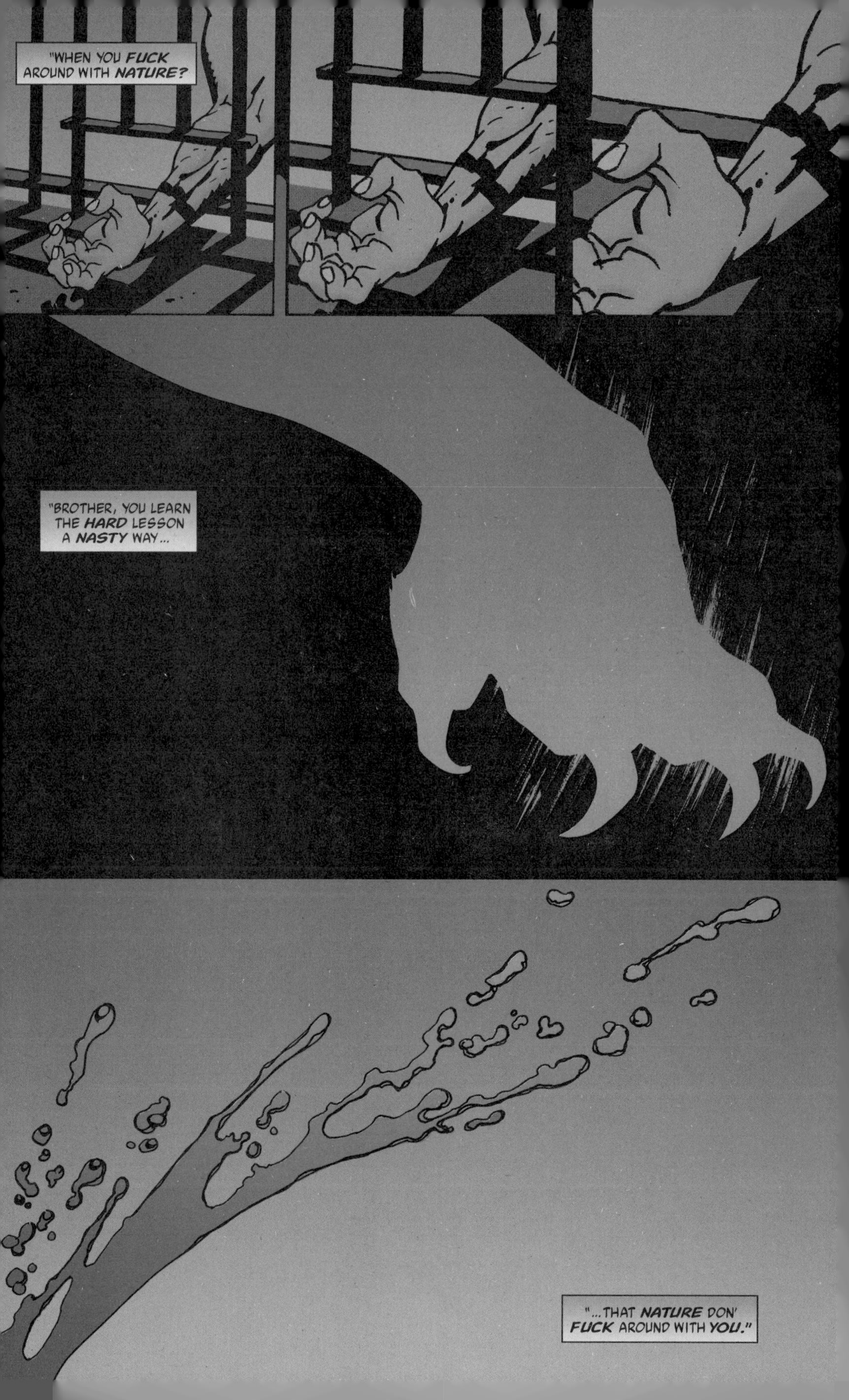
"WHEN YOU FUCK AROUND WITH NATURE?
"BROTHER, YOU LEARN THE HARD LESSON A NASTY WAY...
"...THAT NATURE DON' FUCK AROUND WITH YOU."

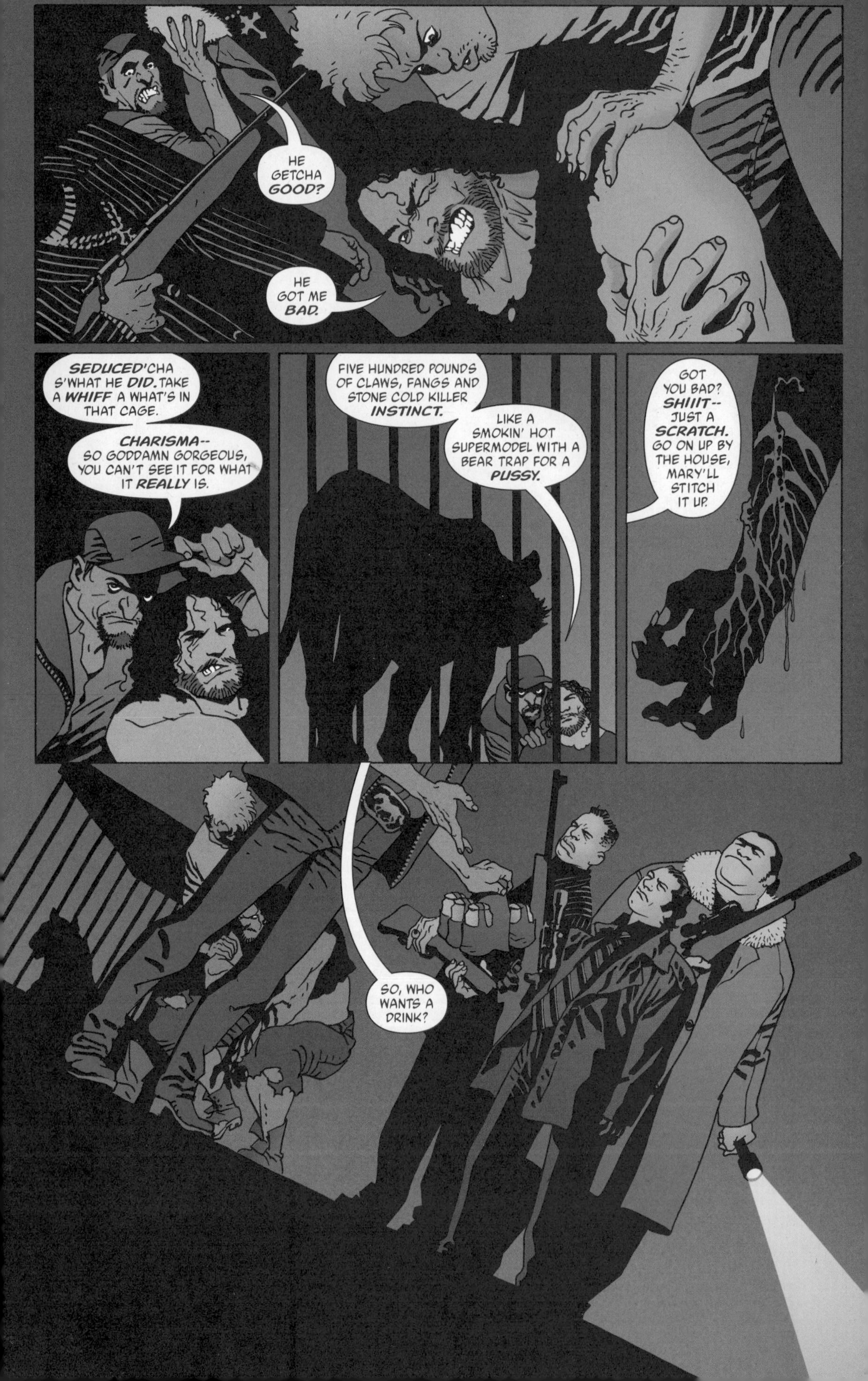

HE GETCHA GOOD?
HE GOT ME BAD.
SEDUCED'CHA S'WHAT HE DID. TAKE A WHIFF A WHAT'S IN THAT CAGE.
CHARISMA-- SO GODDAMN GORGEOUS, YOU CAN'T SEE IT FOR WHAT IT REALLY IS.
FIVE HUNDRED POUNDS OF CLAWS, FANGS AND STONE COLD KILLER INSTINCT.
LIKE A SMOKIN' HOT SUPERMODEL WITH A BEAR TRAP FOR A PUSSY.
GOT YOU BAD? SHIIIT-- JUST A SCRATCH. GO ON UP BY THE HOUSE, MARY'LL STITCH IT UP.
SO, WHO WANTS A DRINK?

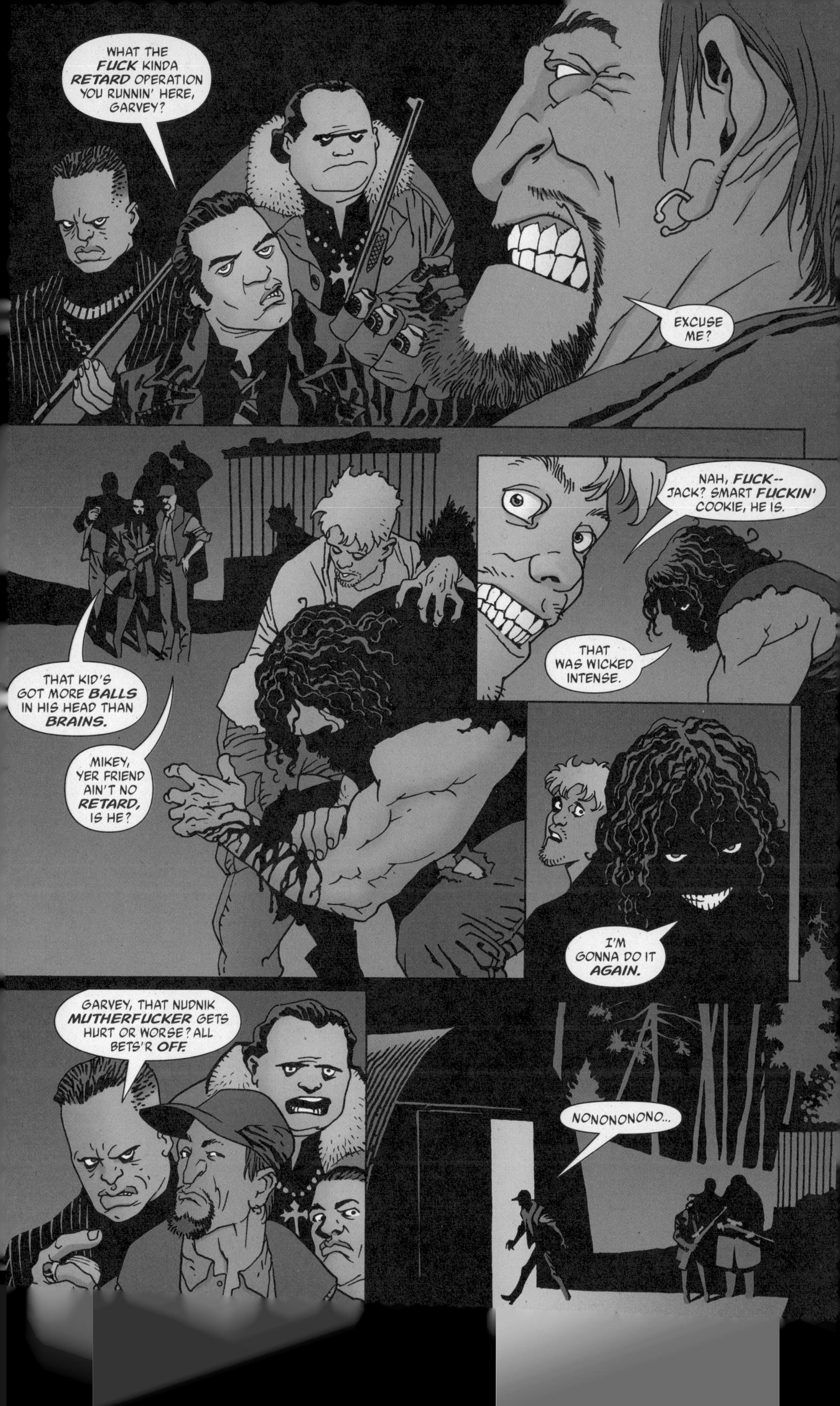
WHAT THE **FUCK** KINDA **RETARD** OPERATION YOU RUNNIN' HERE, GARVEY?
EXCUSE ME?
THAT KID'S GOT MORE **BALLS** IN HIS HEAD THAN **BRAINS.**
MIKEY, YER FRIEND AIN'T NO **RETARD,** IS HE?
NAH, **FUCK**-- JACK? SMART **FUCKIN'** COOKIE, HE IS.
THAT WAS WICKED INTENSE.
I'M GONNA DO IT **AGAIN.**
GARVEY, THAT NUDNIK **MUTHERFUCKER** GETS HURT OR WORSE? ALL BETS'R **OFF.**
NONONONONO...

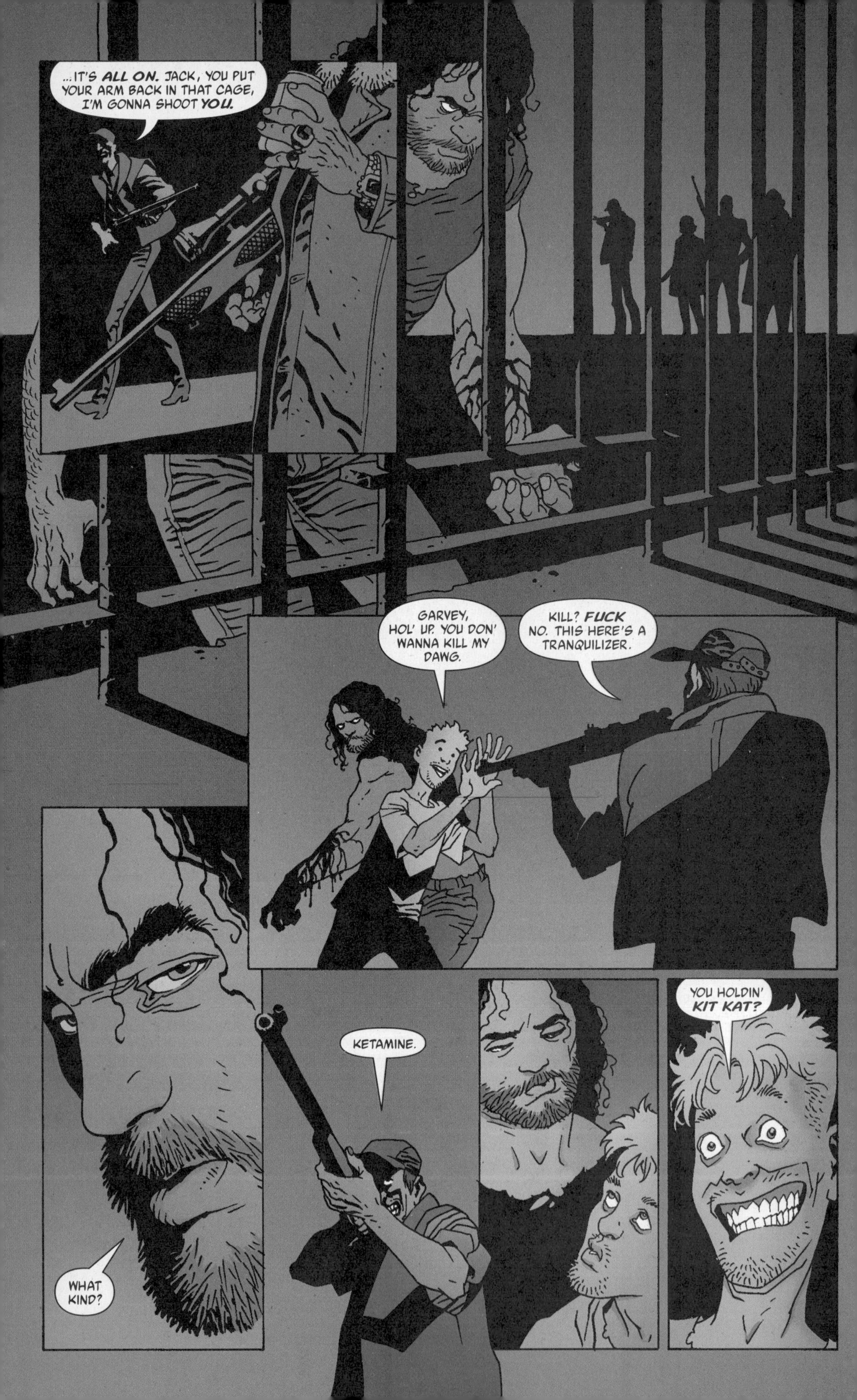

...IT'S **ALL ON.** JACK, YOU PUT YOUR ARM BACK IN THAT CAGE, I'M GONNA SHOOT **YOU.**
GARVEY, HOL' UP. YOU DON' WANNA KILL MY DAWG.
KILL? **FUCK** NO. THIS HERE'S A TRANQUILIZER.
WHAT KIND?
KETAMINE.
YOU HOLDIN' **KIT KAT?**

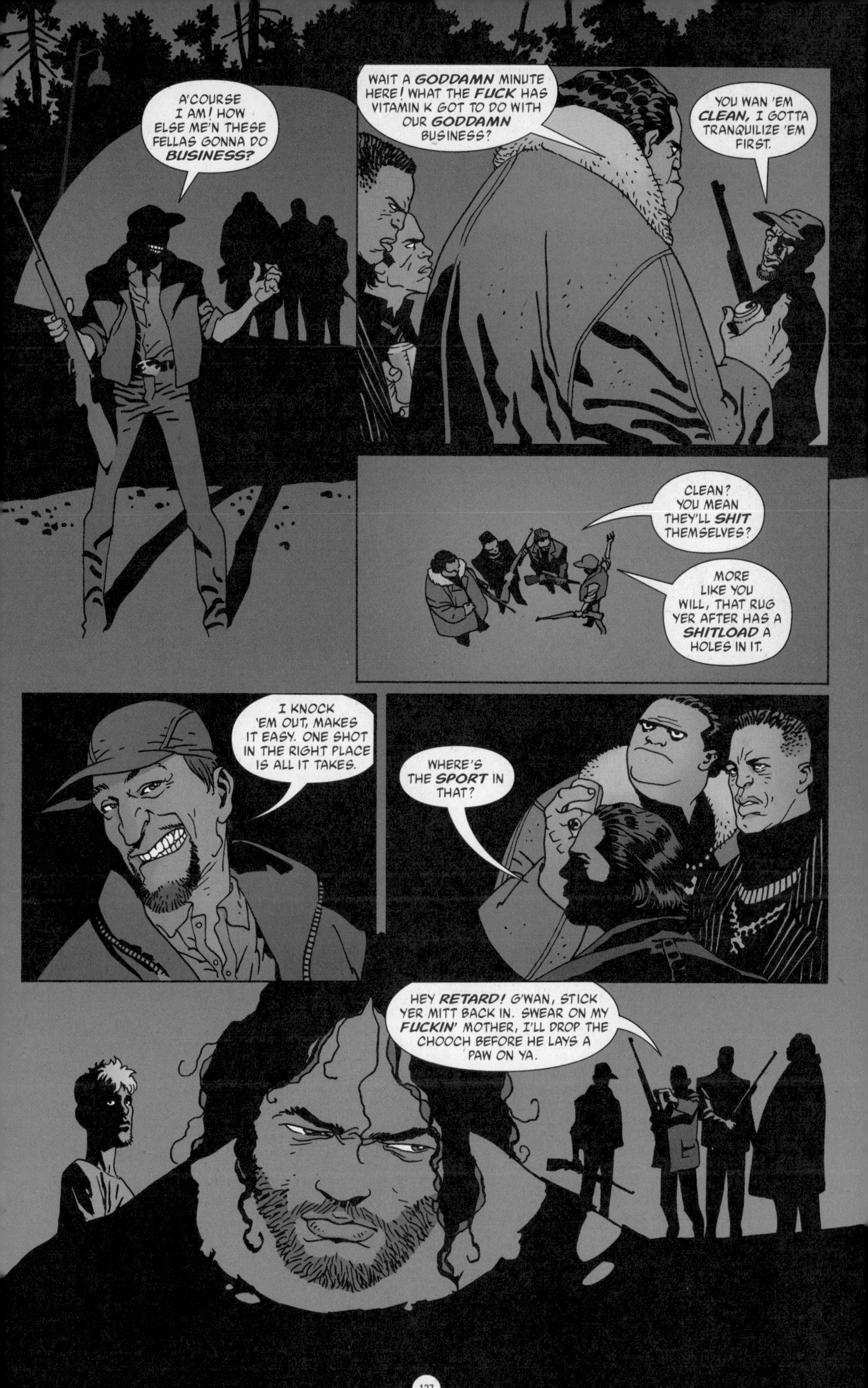
A'COURSE I AM! HOW ELSE ME'N THESE FELLAS GONNA DO BUSINESS?
WAIT A GODDAMN MINUTE HERE! WHAT THE FUCK HAS VITAMIN K GOT TO DO WITH OUR GODDAMN BUSINESS?
YOU WAN 'EM CLEAN, I GOTTA TRANQUILIZE 'EM FIRST.
CLEAN? YOU MEAN THEY'LL SHIT THEMSELVES?
MORE LIKE YOU WILL, THAT RUG YER AFTER HAS A SHITLOAD A HOLES IN IT.
I KNOCK 'EM OUT, MAKES IT EASY. ONE SHOT IN THE RIGHT PLACE IS ALL IT TAKES.
WHERE'S THE SPORT IN THAT?
HEY RETARD! G'WAN, STICK YER MITT BACK IN. SWEAR ON MY FUCKIN' MOTHER, I'LL DROP THE CHOOCH BEFORE HE LAYS A PAW ON YA.

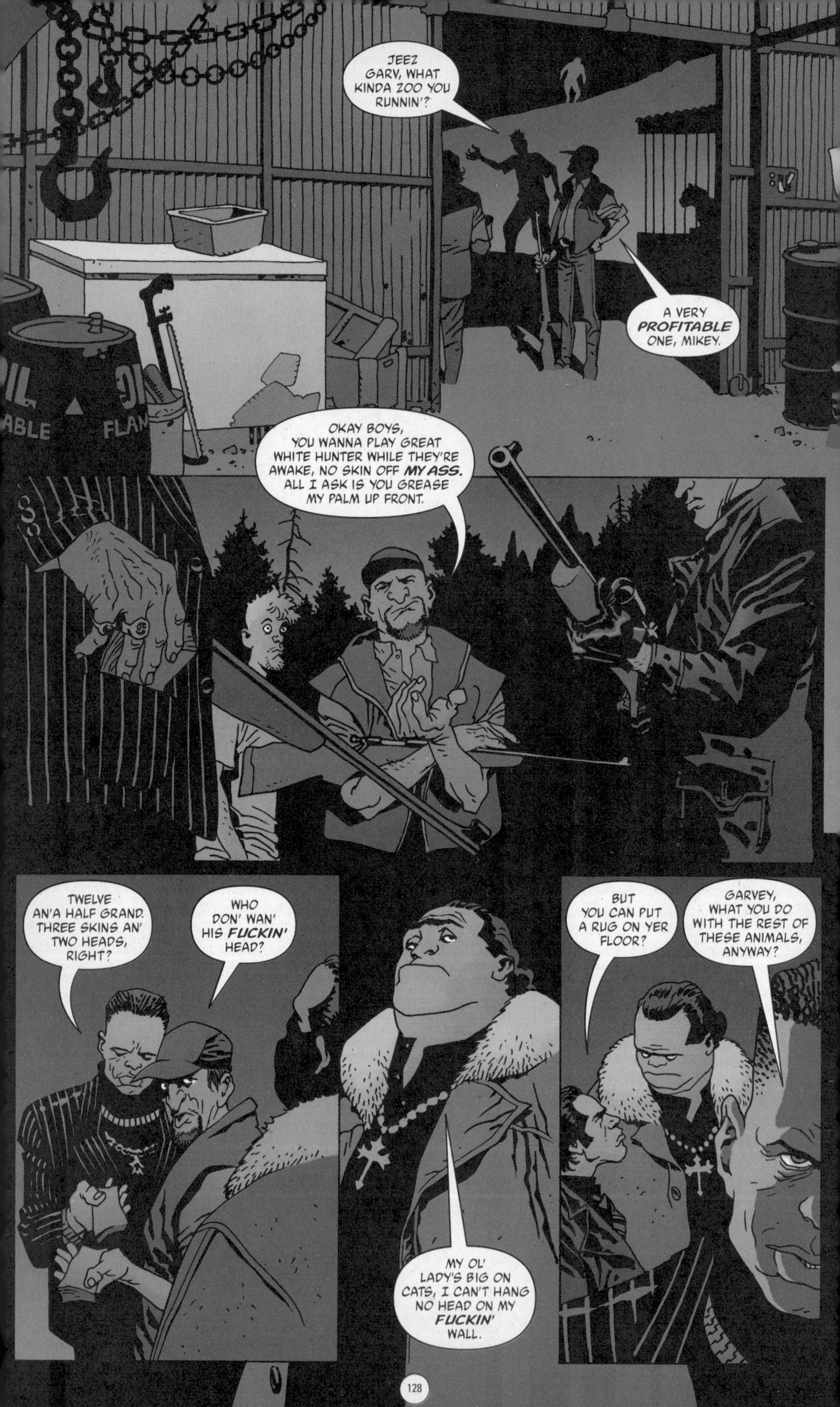

JEEZ GARV, WHAT KINDA ZOO YOU RUNNIN'?
A VERY PROFITABLE ONE, MIKEY.
OKAY BOYS, YOU WANNA PLAY GREAT WHITE HUNTER WHILE THEY'RE AWAKE, NO SKIN OFF MY ASS. ALL I ASK IS YOU GREASE MY PALM UP FRONT.
TWELVE AN'A HALF GRAND. THREE SKINS AN' TWO HEADS, RIGHT?
WHO DON' WAN' HIS FUCKIN' HEAD?
MY OL' LADY'S BIG ON CATS, I CAN'T HANG NO HEAD ON MY FUCKIN' WALL.
BUT YOU CAN PUT A RUG ON YER FLOOR?
GARVEY, WHAT YOU DO WITH THE REST OF THESE ANIMALS, ANYWAY?

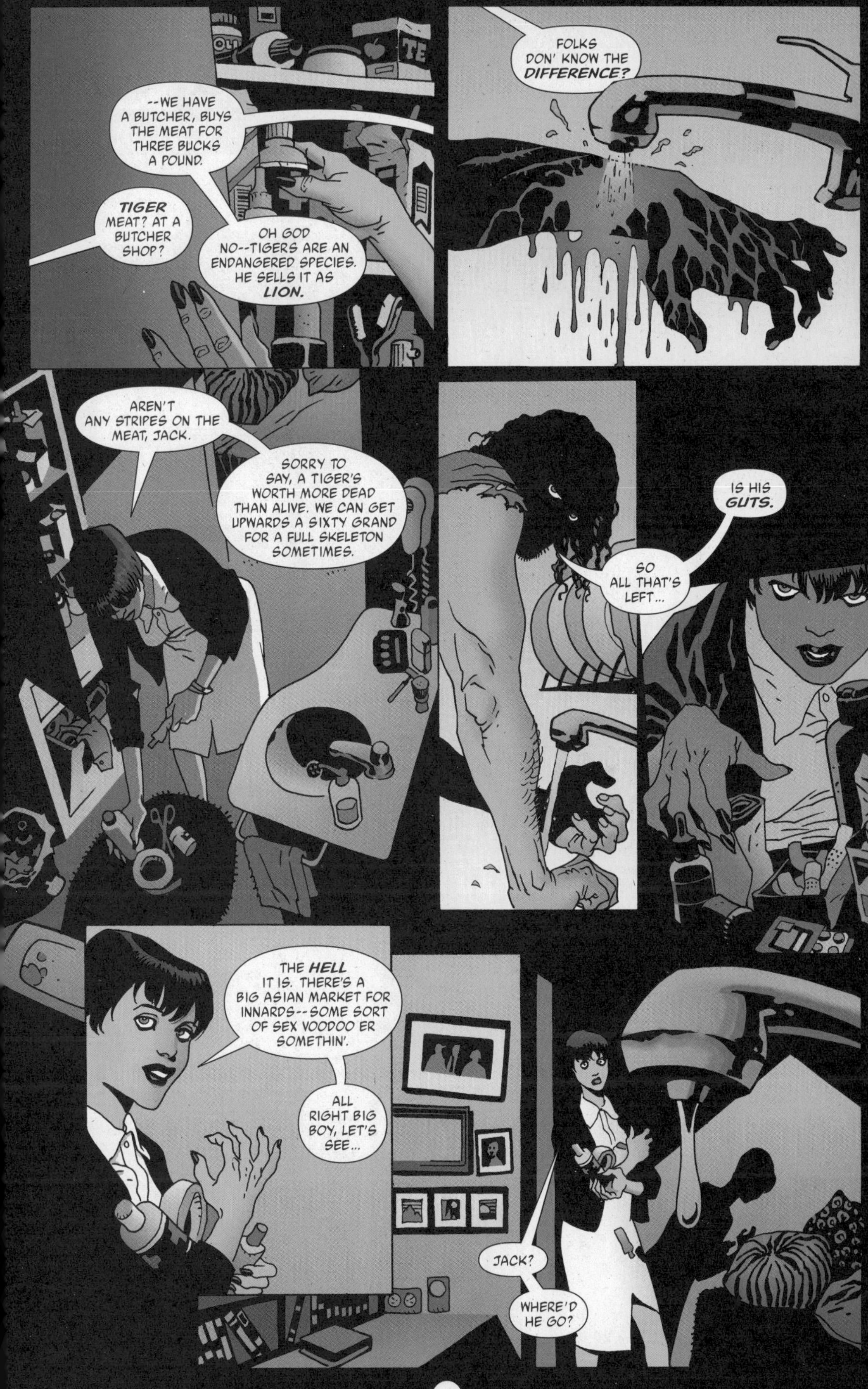
--WE HAVE A BUTCHER, BUYS THE MEAT FOR THREE BUCKS A POUND.
TIGER MEAT? AT A BUTCHER SHOP?
OH GOD NO--TIGERS ARE AN ENDANGERED SPECIES. HE SELLS IT AS LION.
FOLKS DON' KNOW THE DIFFERENCE?
AREN'T ANY STRIPES ON THE MEAT, JACK.
SORRY TO SAY, A TIGER'S WORTH MORE DEAD THAN ALIVE. WE CAN GET UPWARDS A SIXTY GRAND FOR A FULL SKELETON SOMETIMES.
SO ALL THAT'S LEFT...
IS HIS GUTS.
THE HELL IT IS. THERE'S A BIG ASIAN MARKET FOR INNARDS--SOME SORT OF SEX VOODOO ER SOMETHIN'.
ALL RIGHT BIG BOY, LET'S SEE...
JACK?
WHERE'D HE GO?

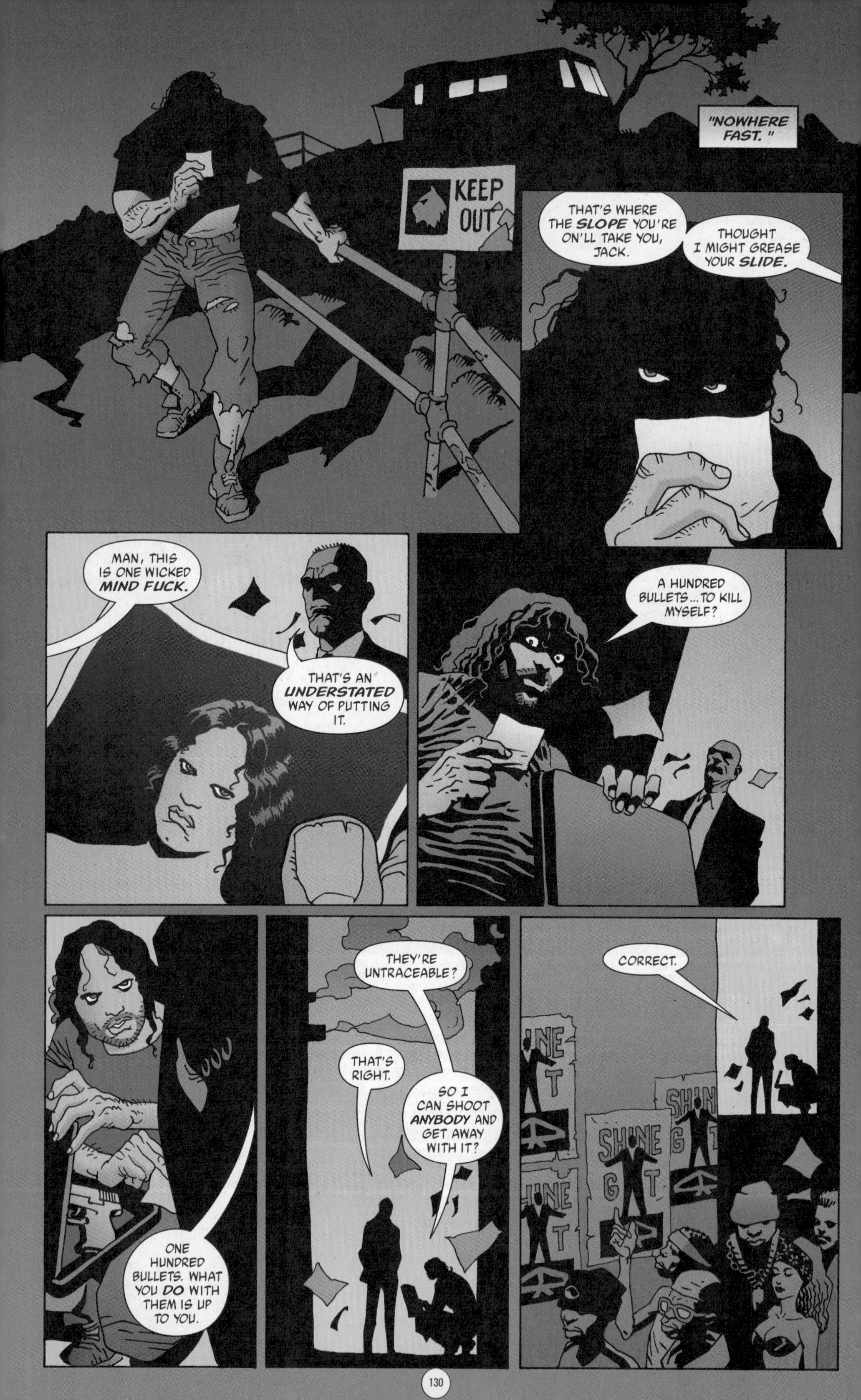
"NOWHERE FAST."
KEEP OUT
THAT'S WHERE THE SLOPE YOU'RE ON'LL TAKE YOU, JACK.
THOUGHT I MIGHT GREASE YOUR SLIDE.
MAN, THIS IS ONE WICKED MIND FUCK.
THAT'S AN UNDERSTATED WAY OF PUTTING IT.
A HUNDRED BULLETS... TO KILL MYSELF?
ONE HUNDRED BULLETS. WHAT YOU DO WITH THEM IS UP TO YOU.
THEY'RE UNTRACEABLE?
THAT'S RIGHT.
SO I CAN SHOOT ANYBODY AND GET AWAY WITH IT?
CORRECT.

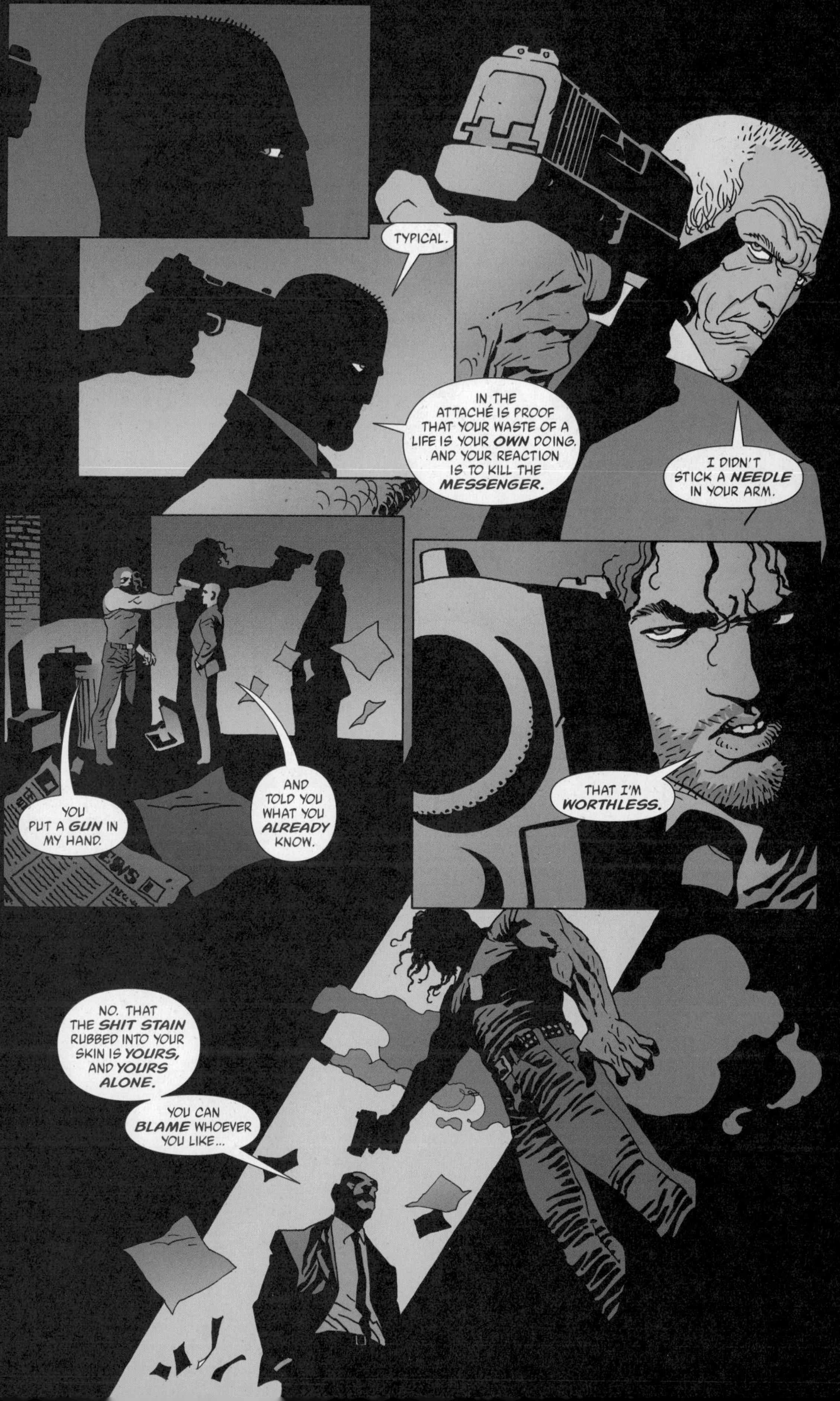
TYPICAL.
IN THE ATTACHÉ IS PROOF THAT YOUR WASTE OF A LIFE IS YOUR OWN DOING. AND YOUR REACTION IS TO KILL THE MESSENGER.
I DIDN'T STICK A NEEDLE IN YOUR ARM.
YOU PUT A GUN IN MY HAND.
AND TOLD YOU WHAT YOU ALREADY KNOW.
THAT I'M WORTHLESS.
NO. THAT THE SHIT STAIN RUBBED INTO YOUR SKIN IS YOURS, AND YOURS ALONE.
YOU CAN BLAME WHOEVER YOU LIKE...

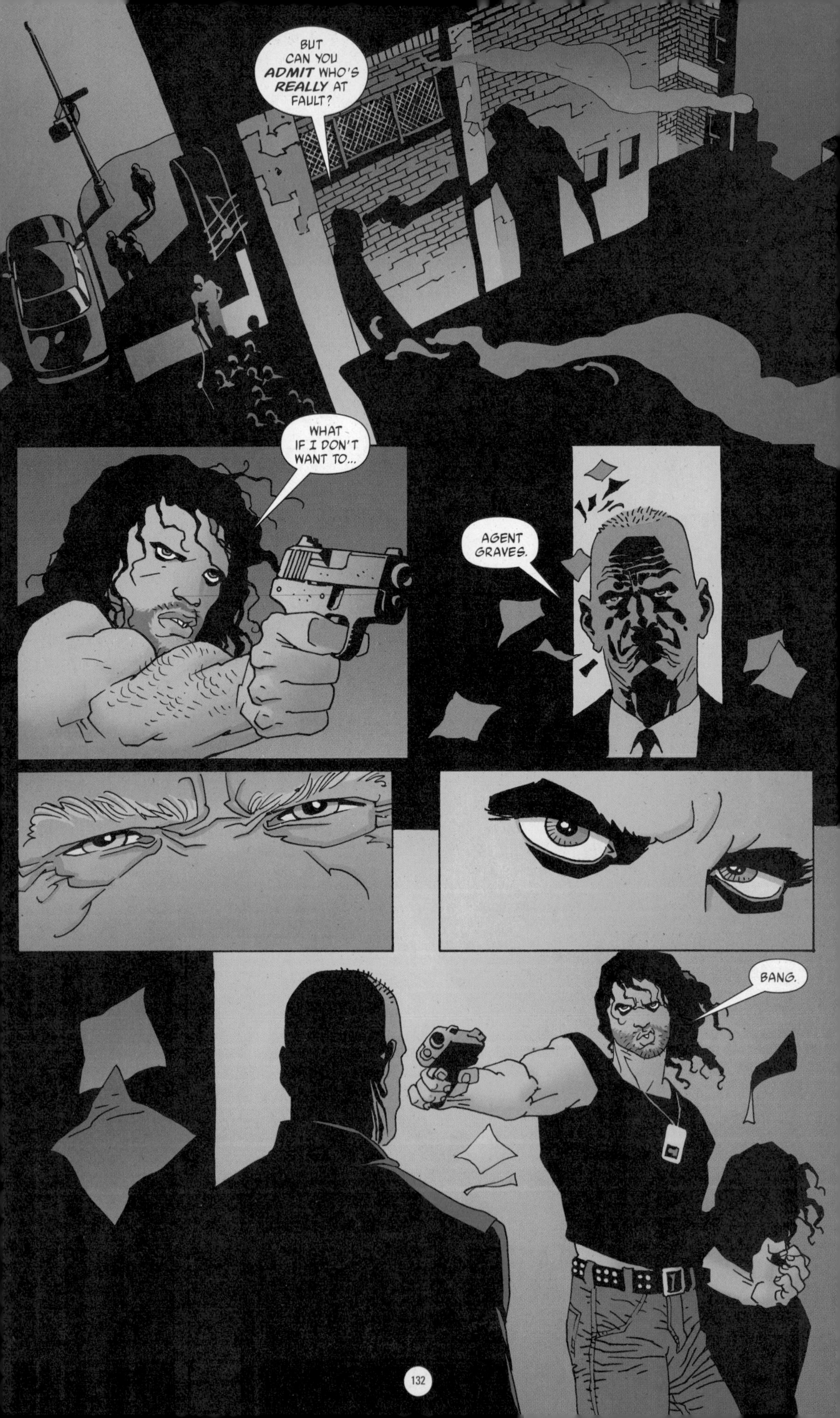
BUT CAN YOU ADMIT WHO'S REALLY AT FAULT?
WHAT IF I DON'T WANT TO...
AGENT GRAVES.
BANG.

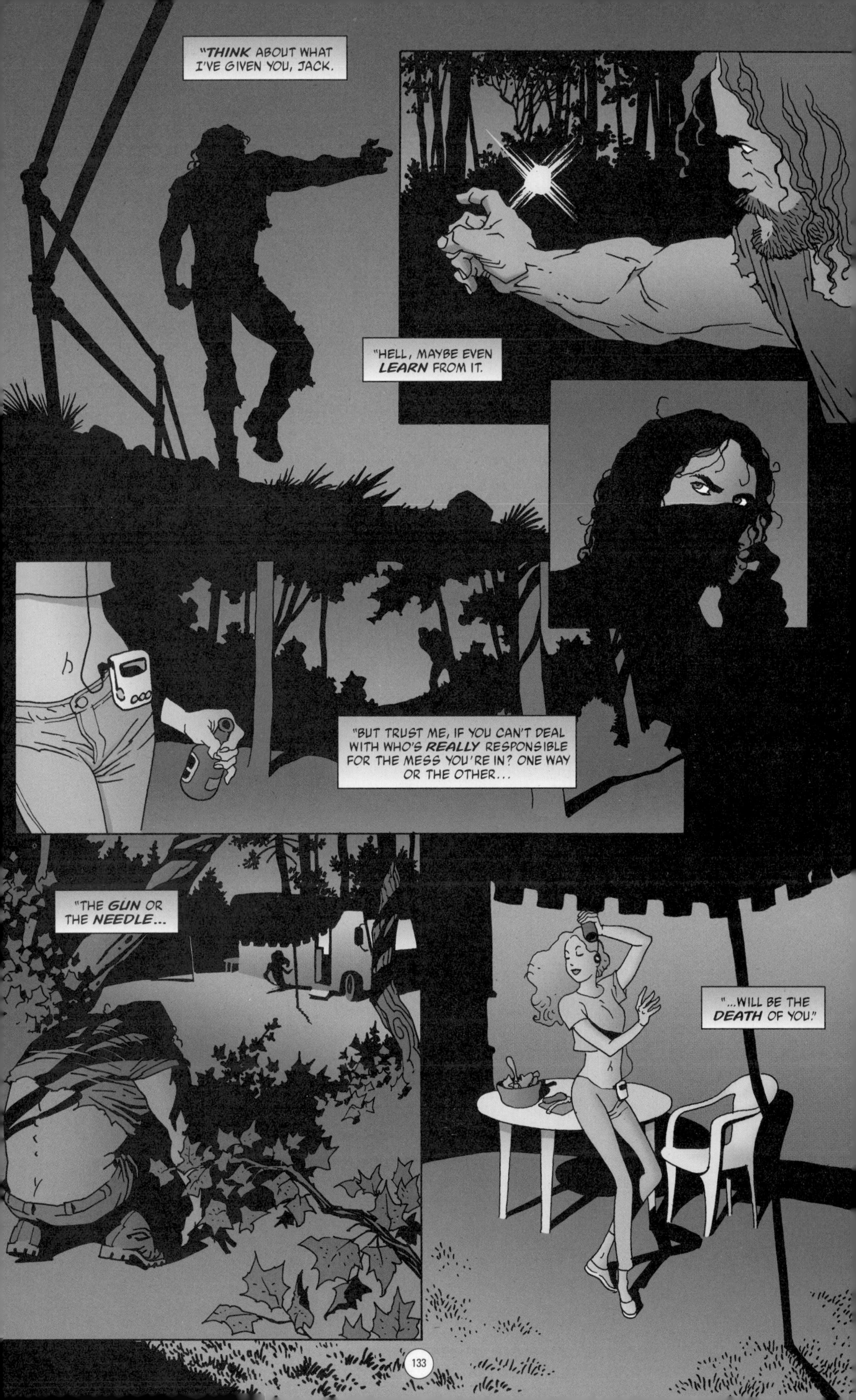
"THINK ABOUT WHAT I'VE GIVEN YOU, JACK.
"HELL, MAYBE EVEN LEARN FROM IT.
"BUT TRUST ME, IF YOU CAN'T DEAL WITH WHO'S REALLY RESPONSIBLE FOR THE MESS YOU'RE IN? ONE WAY OR THE OTHER...
"THE GUN OR THE NEEDLE...
"...WILL BE THE DEATH OF YOU."

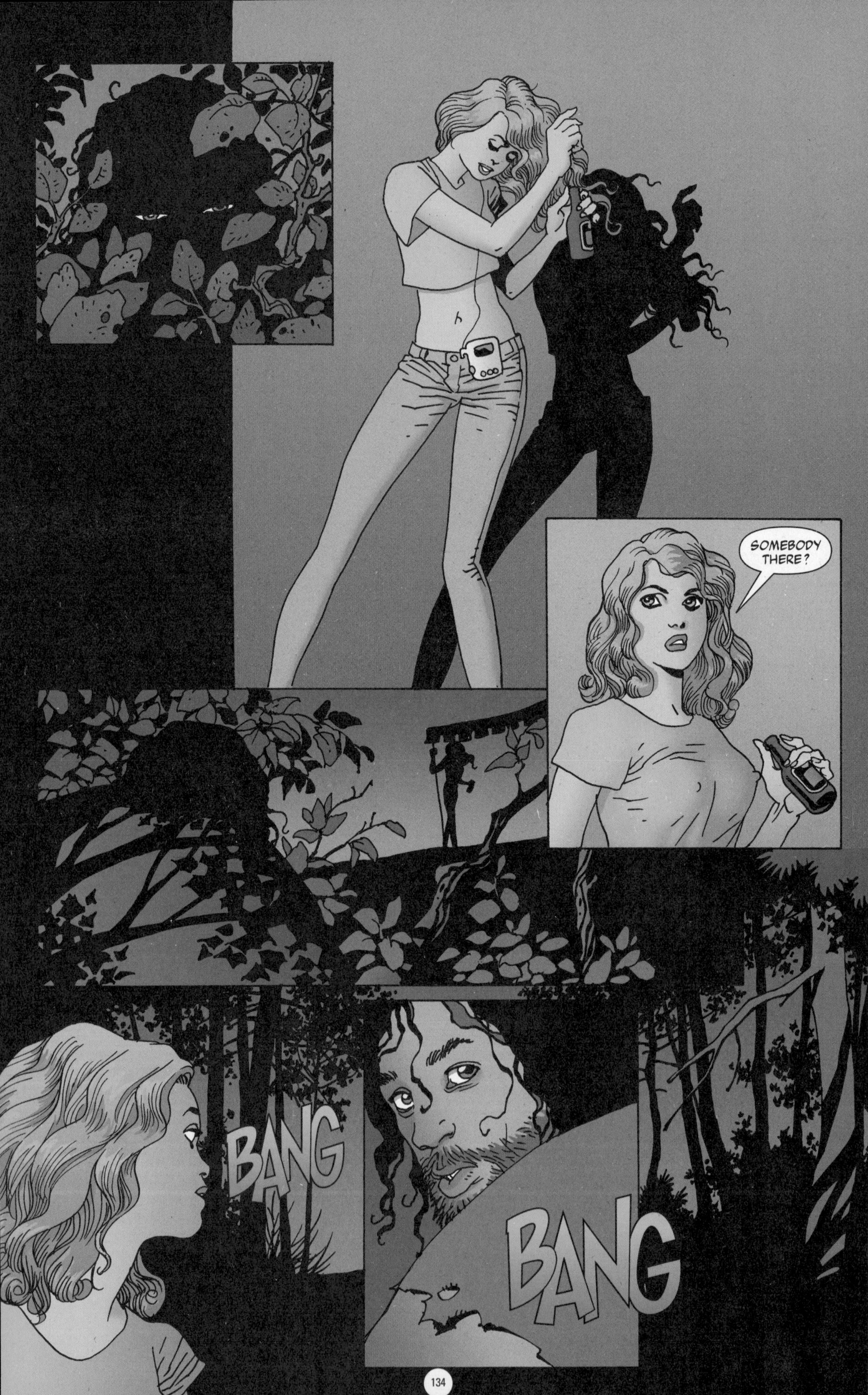
SOMEBODY THERE?
BANG
BANG

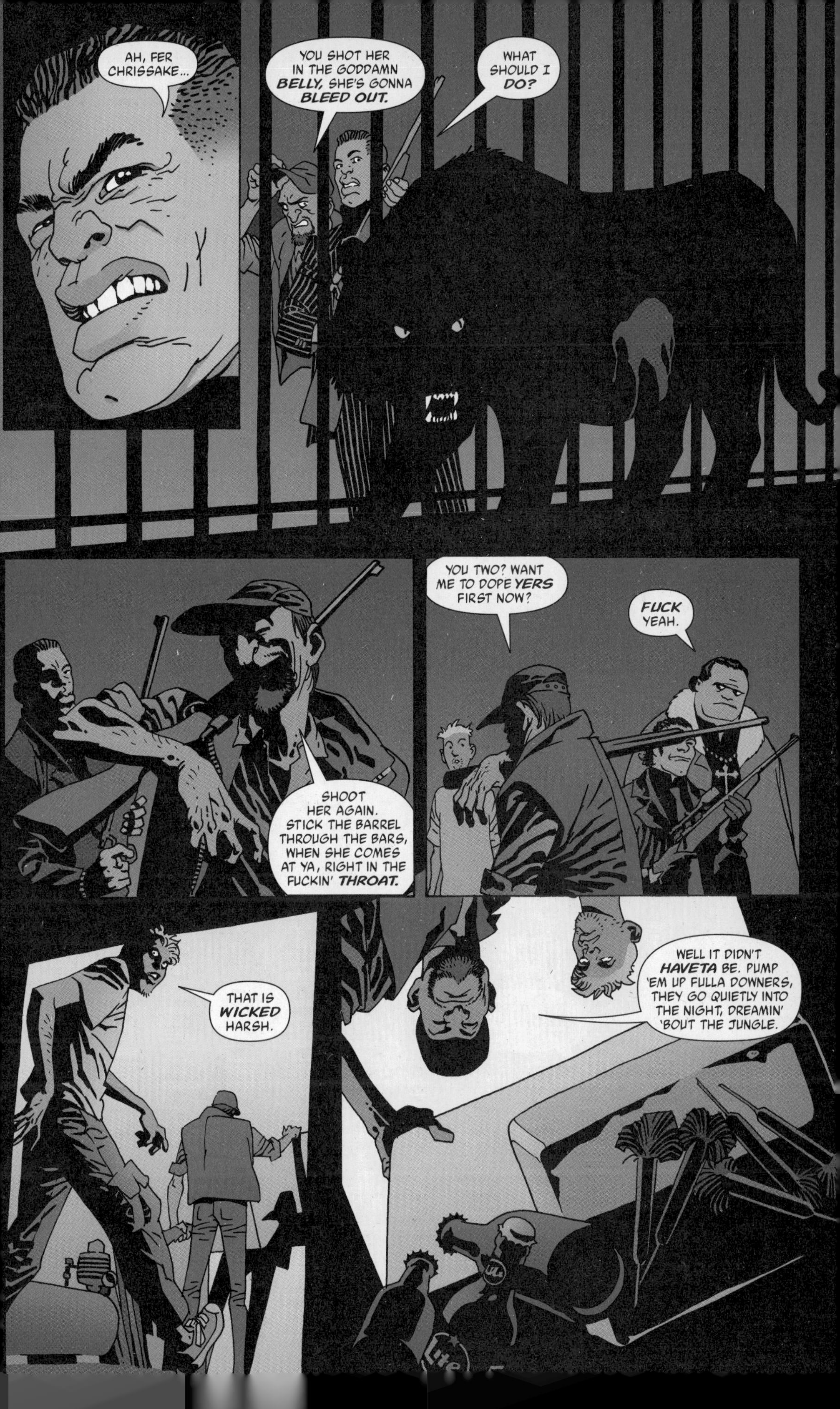
AH, FER CHRISSAKE...
YOU SHOT HER IN THE GODDAMN BELLY, SHE'S GONNA BLEED OUT.
WHAT SHOULD I DO?
SHOOT HER AGAIN. STICK THE BARREL THROUGH THE BARS, WHEN SHE COMES AT YA, RIGHT IN THE FUCKIN' THROAT.
YOU TWO? WANT ME TO DOPE YERS FIRST NOW?
FUCK YEAH.
THAT IS WICKED HARSH.
WELL IT DIDN'T HAVETA BE. PUMP 'EM UP FULLA DOWNERS, THEY GO QUIETLY INTO THE NIGHT, DREAMIN' 'BOUT THE JUNGLE.

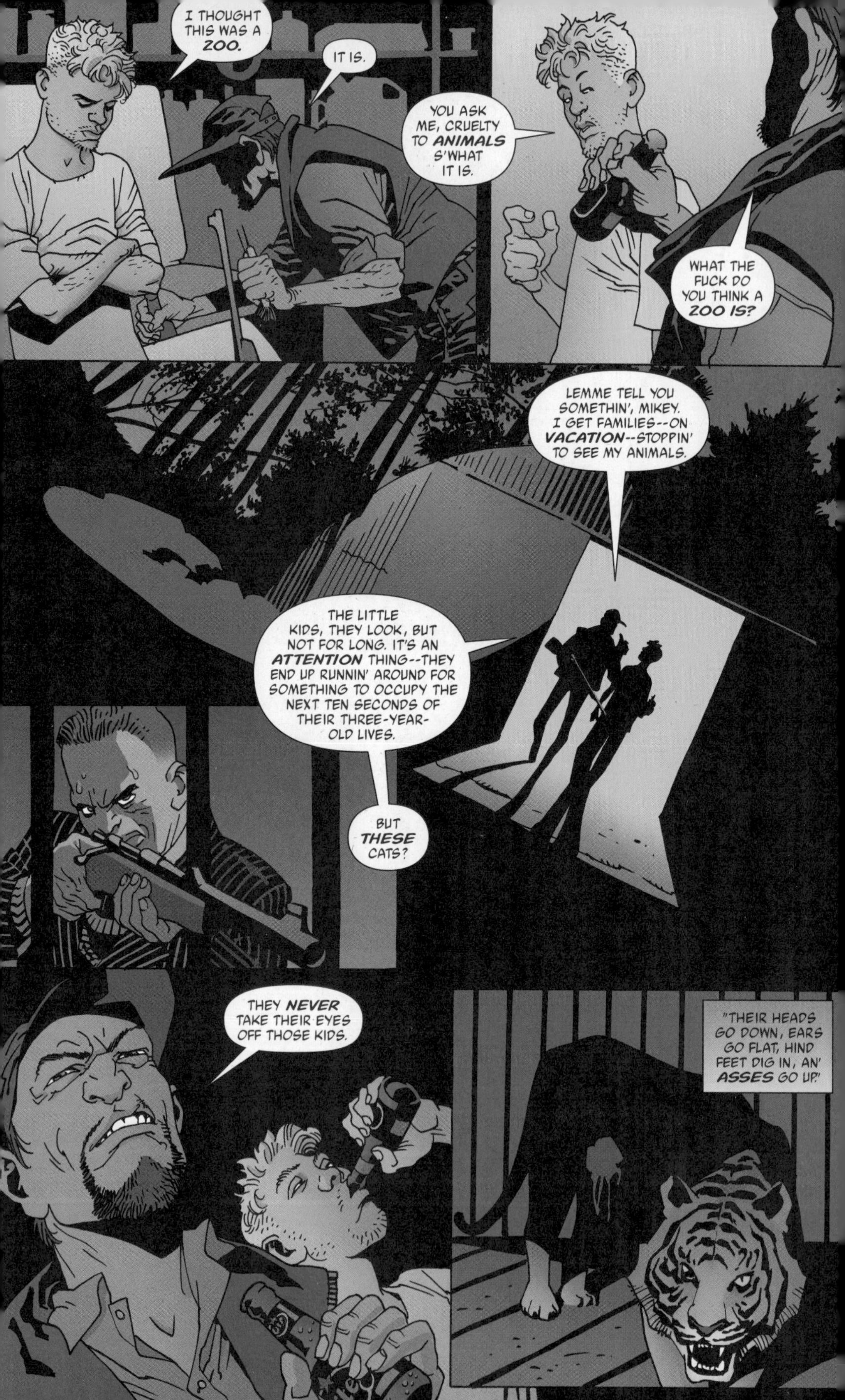
I THOUGHT THIS WAS A ZOO.
IT IS.
YOU ASK ME, CRUELTY TO ANIMALS S'WHAT IT IS.
WHAT THE FUCK DO YOU THINK A ZOO IS?
LEMME TELL YOU SOMETHIN', MIKEY. I GET FAMILIES--ON VACATION--STOPPIN' TO SEE MY ANIMALS.
THE LITTLE KIDS, THEY LOOK, BUT NOT FOR LONG. IT'S AN ATTENTION THING--THEY END UP RUNNIN' AROUND FOR SOMETHING TO OCCUPY THE NEXT TEN SECONDS OF THEIR THREE-YEAR-OLD LIVES.
BUT THESE CATS?
THEY NEVER TAKE THEIR EYES OFF THOSE KIDS.
"THEIR HEADS GO DOWN, EARS GO FLAT, HIND FEET DIG IN, AN' ASSES GO UP.'

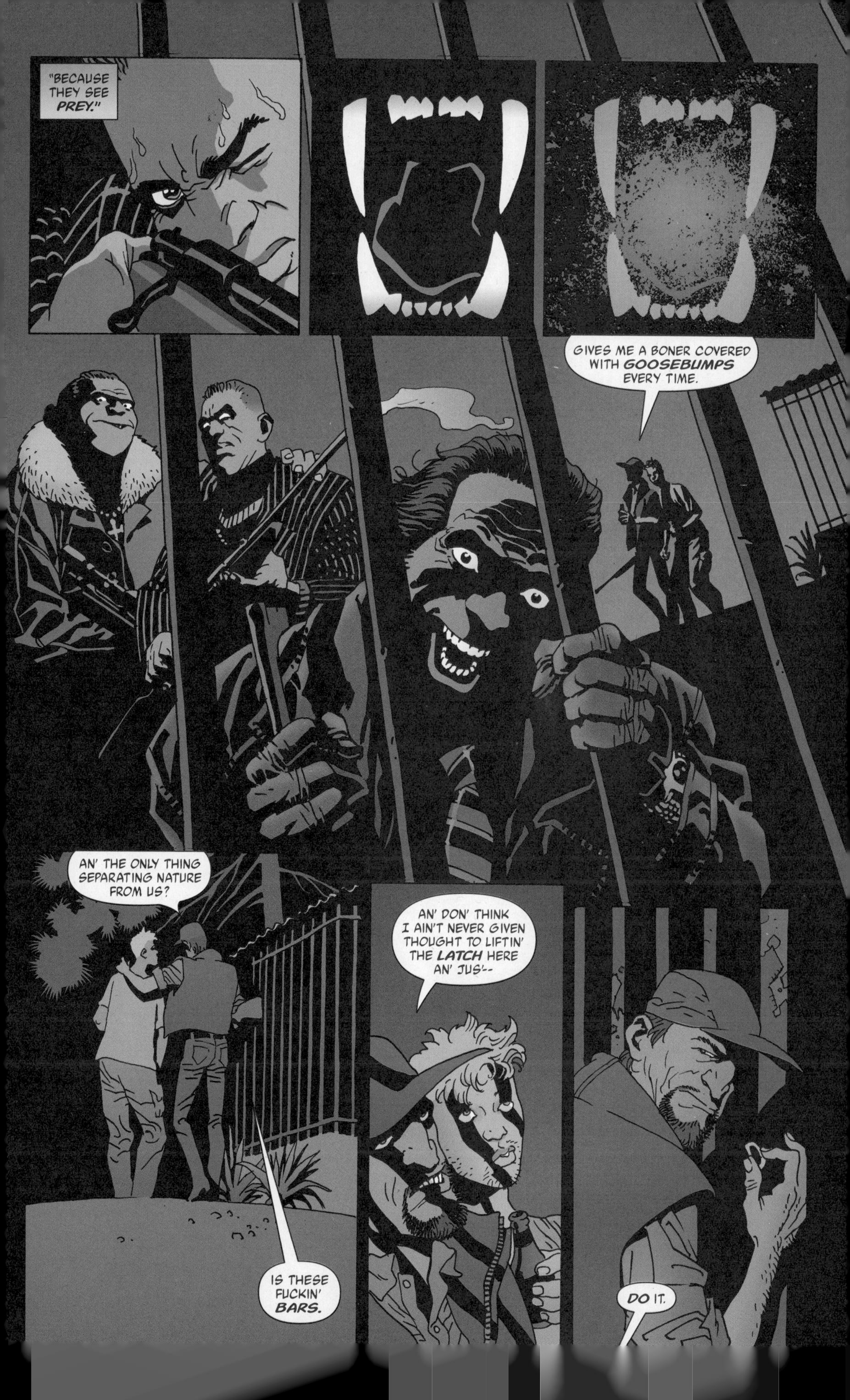
"BECAUSE THEY SEE PREY."
GIVES ME A BONER COVERED WITH GOOSEBUMPS EVERY TIME.
AN' THE ONLY THING SEPARATING NATURE FROM US?
IS THESE FUCKIN' BARS.
AN' DON' THINK I AIN'T NEVER GIVEN THOUGHT TO LIFTIN' THE LATCH HERE AN' JUS'--
DO IT.

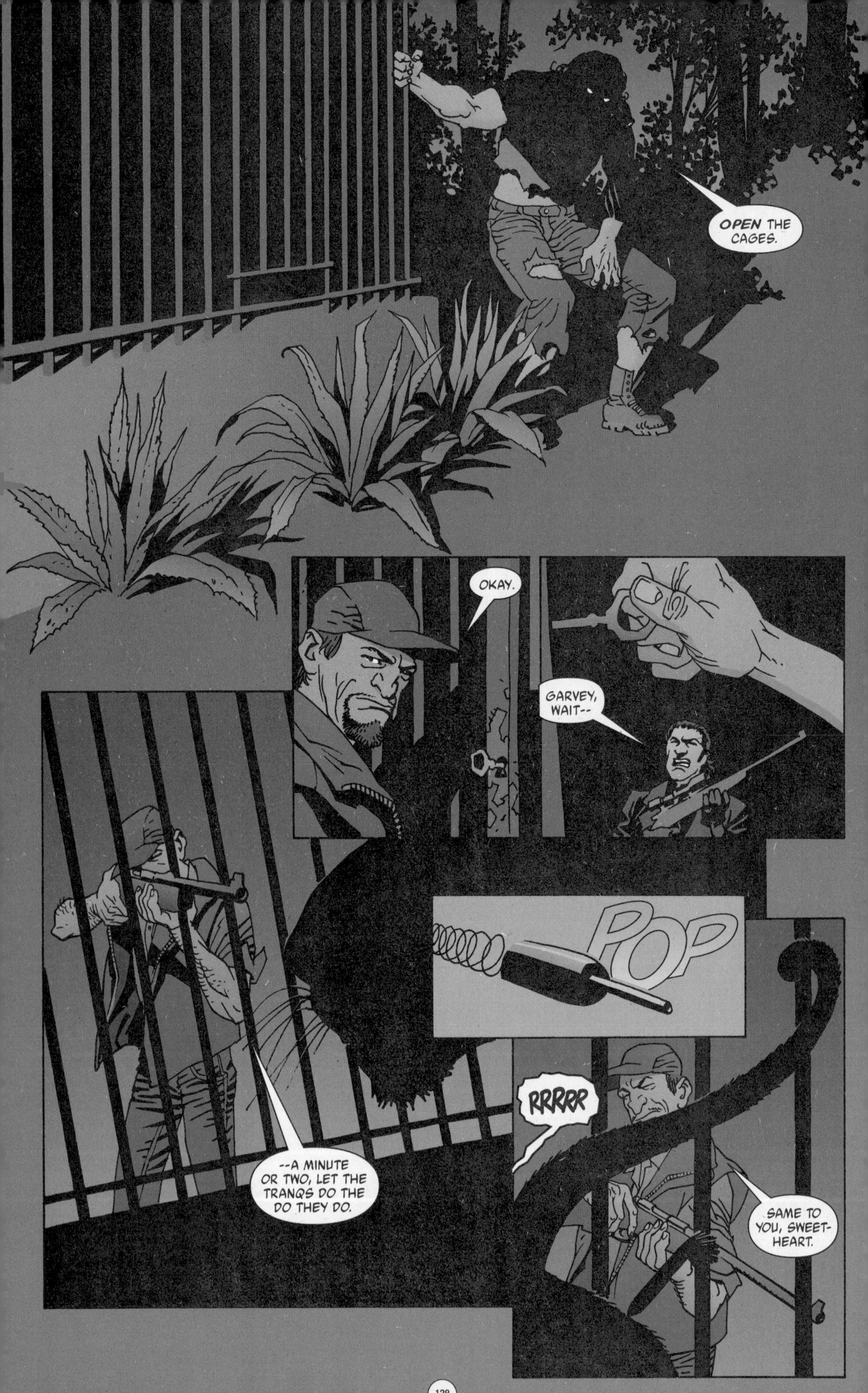

OPEN THE CAGES.
OKAY.
GARVEY, WAIT--
--A MINUTE OR TWO, LET THE TRANQS DO THE DO THEY DO.
POP
RRRRR
SAME TO YOU, SWEET-HEART.

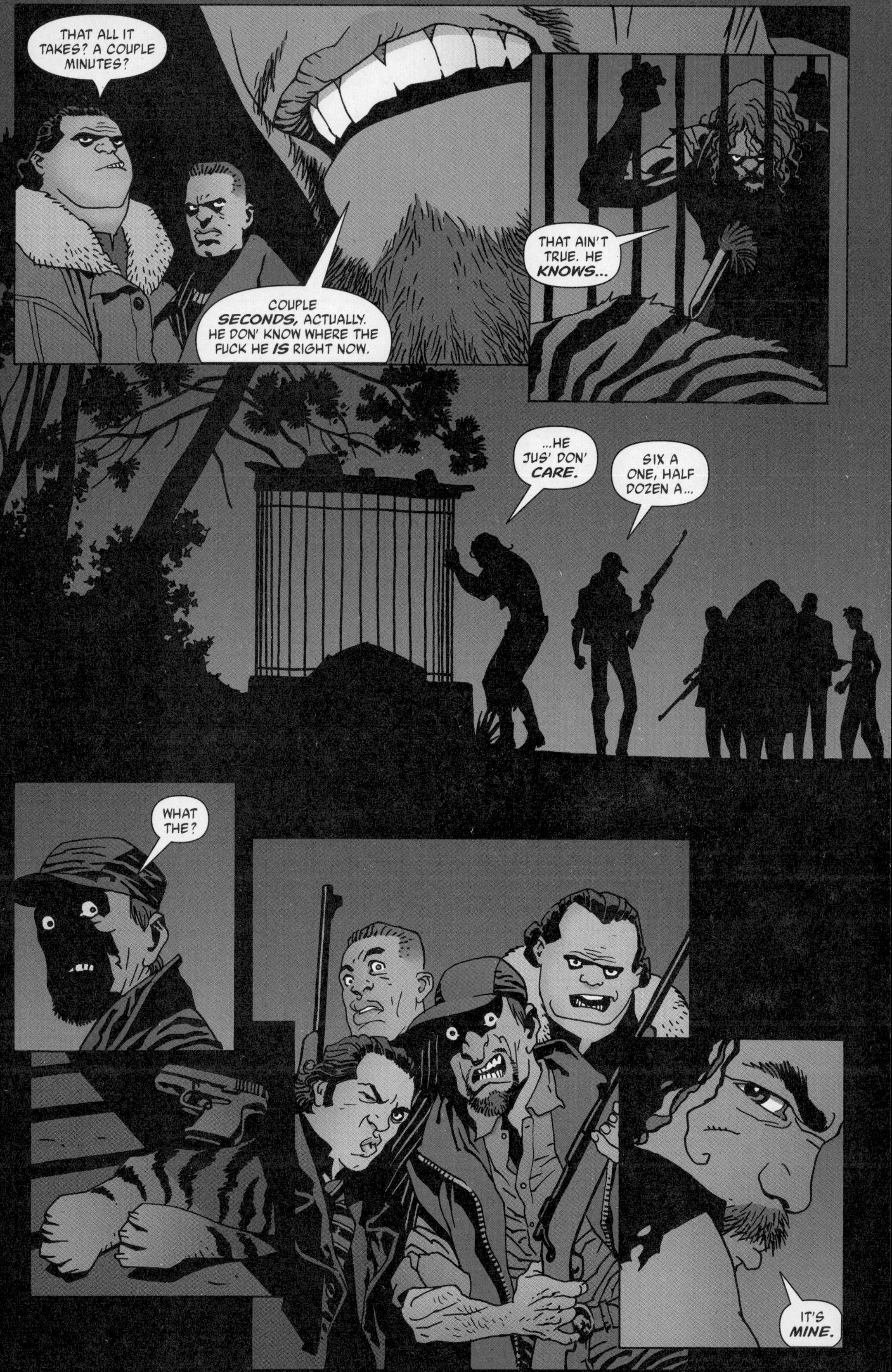
THAT ALL IT TAKES? A COUPLE MINUTES?
COUPLE SECONDS, ACTUALLY. HE DON' KNOW WHERE THE FUCK HE IS RIGHT NOW.
THAT AIN'T TRUE. HE KNOWS...
...HE JUS' DON' CARE.
SIX A ONE, HALF DOZEN A...
WHAT THE?
IT'S MINE.

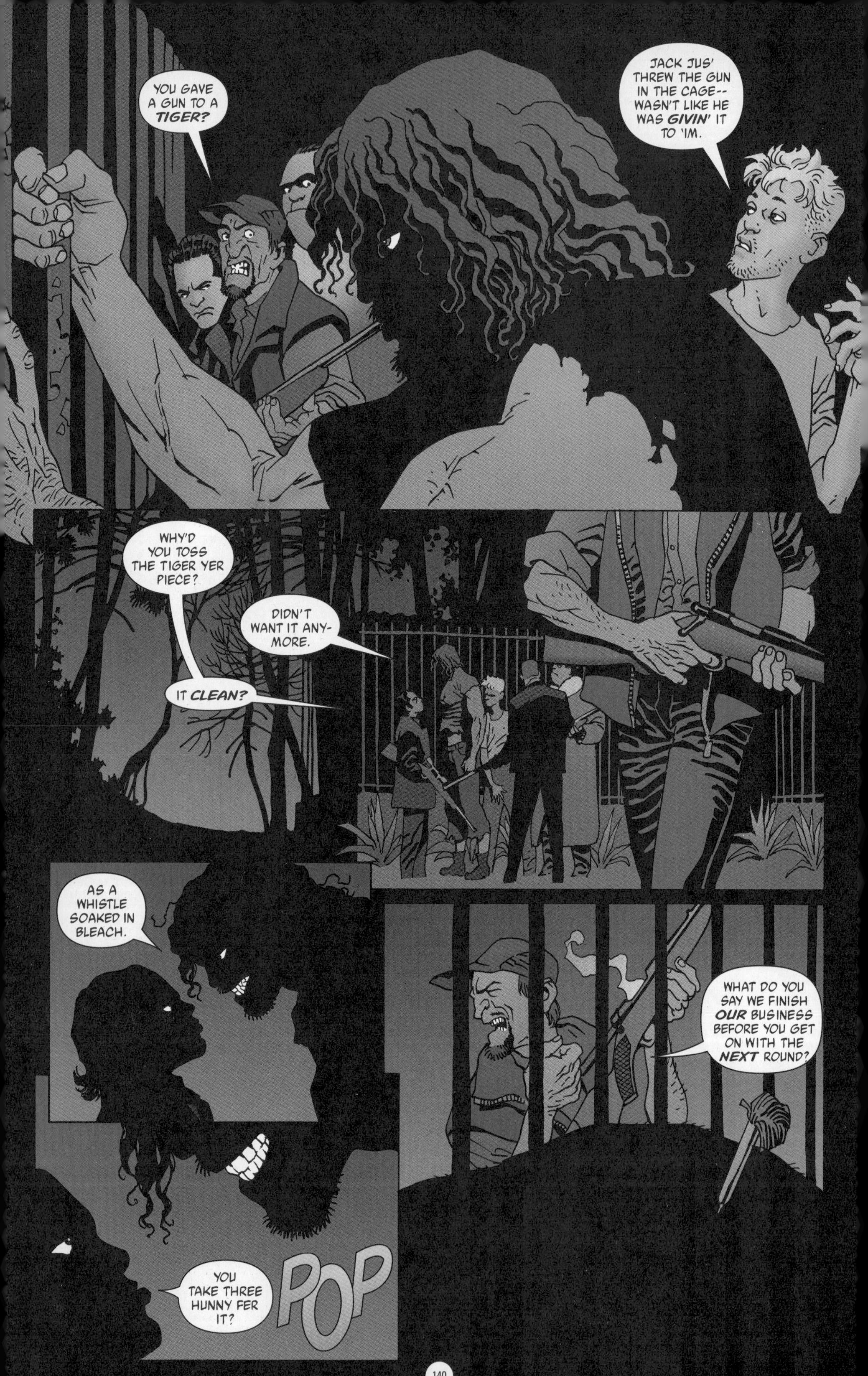
YOU GAVE A GUN TO A TIGER?
JACK JUS' THREW THE GUN IN THE CAGE-- WASN'T LIKE HE WAS GIVIN' IT TO 'IM.
WHY'D YOU TOSS THE TIGER YER PIECE?
DIDN'T WANT IT ANY-MORE.
IT CLEAN?
AS A WHISTLE SOAKED IN BLEACH.
WHAT DO YOU SAY WE FINISH OUR BUSINESS BEFORE YOU GET ON WITH THE NEXT ROUND?
YOU TAKE THREE HUNNY FER IT?
POP

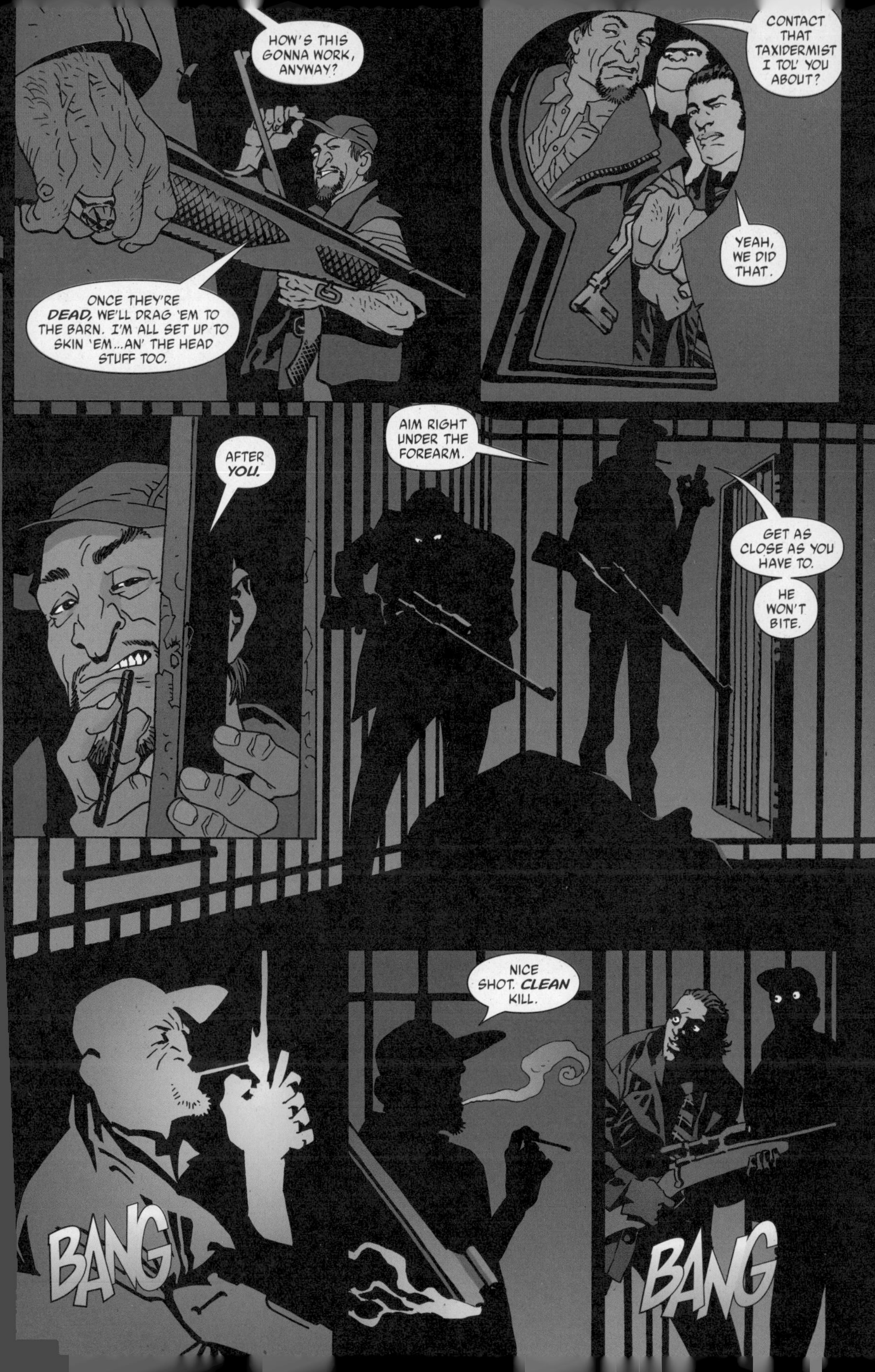
HOW'S THIS GONNA WORK, ANYWAY?
ONCE THEY'RE DEAD, WE'LL DRAG 'EM TO THE BARN. I'M ALL SET UP TO SKIN 'EM...AN' THE HEAD STUFF TOO.
CONTACT THAT TAXIDERMIST I TOL' YOU ABOUT?
YEAH, WE DID THAT.
AFTER YOU.
AIM RIGHT UNDER THE FOREARM.
GET AS CLOSE AS YOU HAVE TO.
HE WON'T BITE.
BANG
NICE SHOT. CLEAN KILL.
BANG

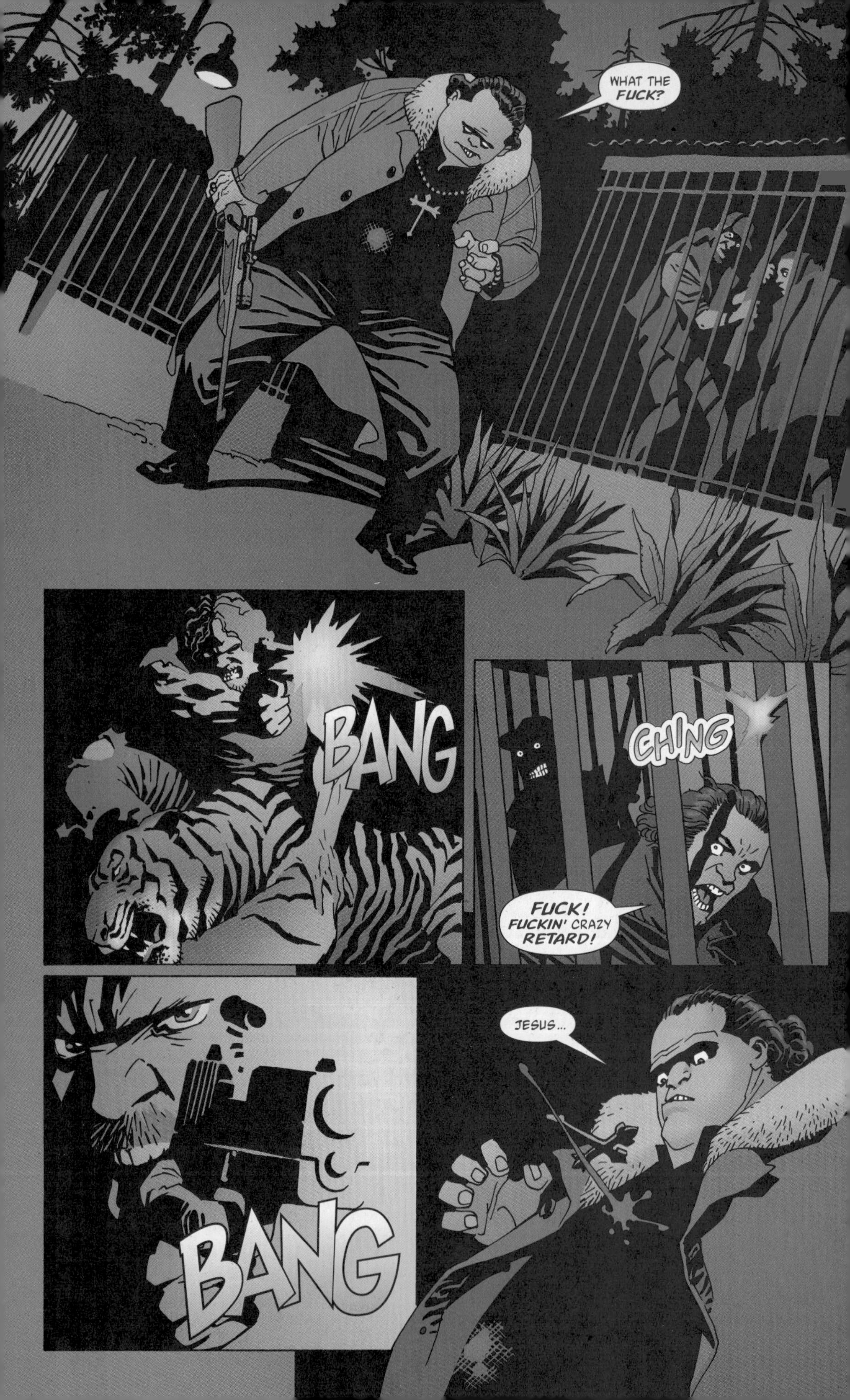
WHAT THE FUCK?
BANG
CHING
FUCK! FUCKIN' CRAZY RETARD!
BANG
JESUS...

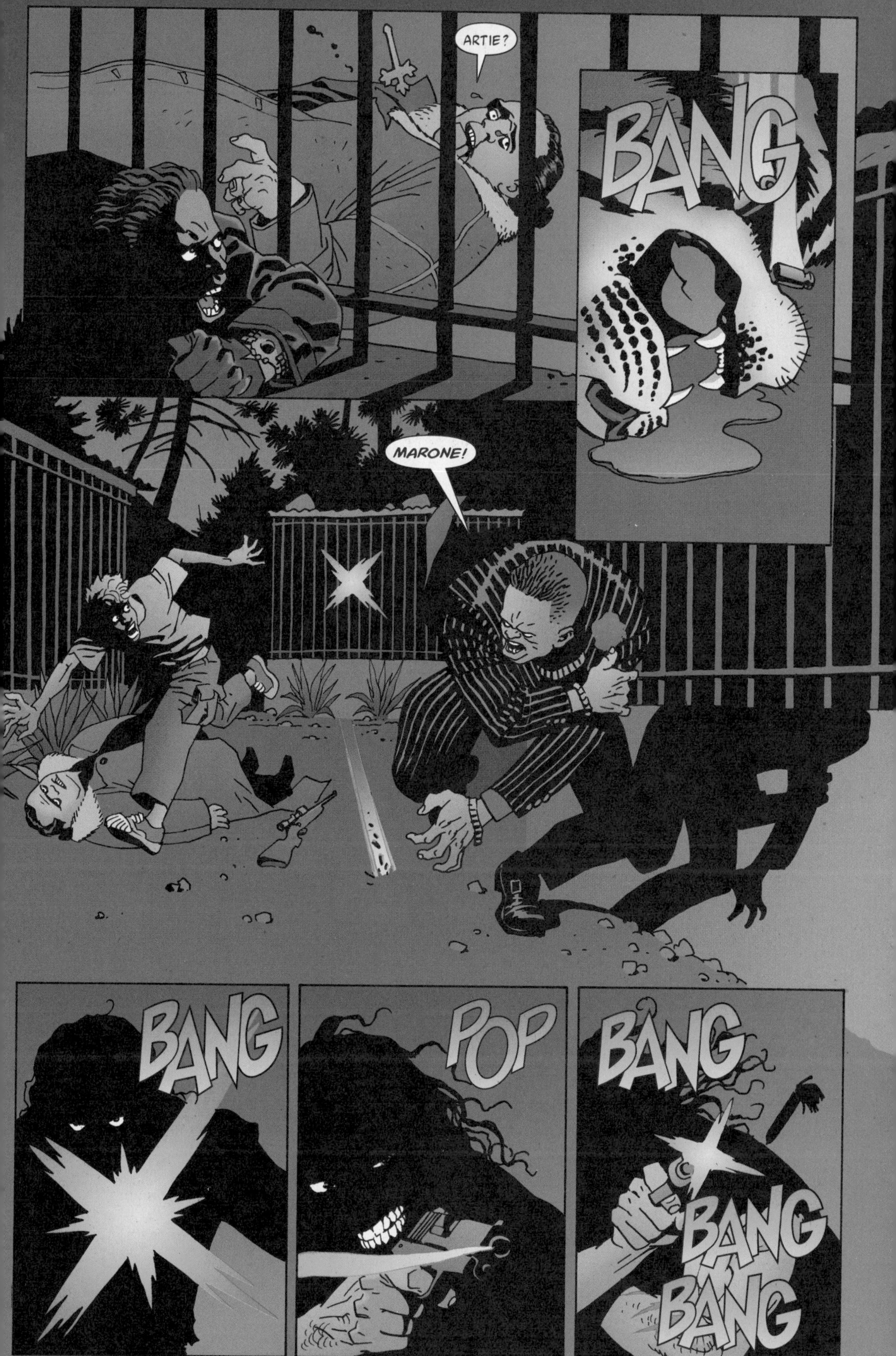
ARTIE?
BANG
MARONE!
BANG
POP
BANG
BANG
BANG

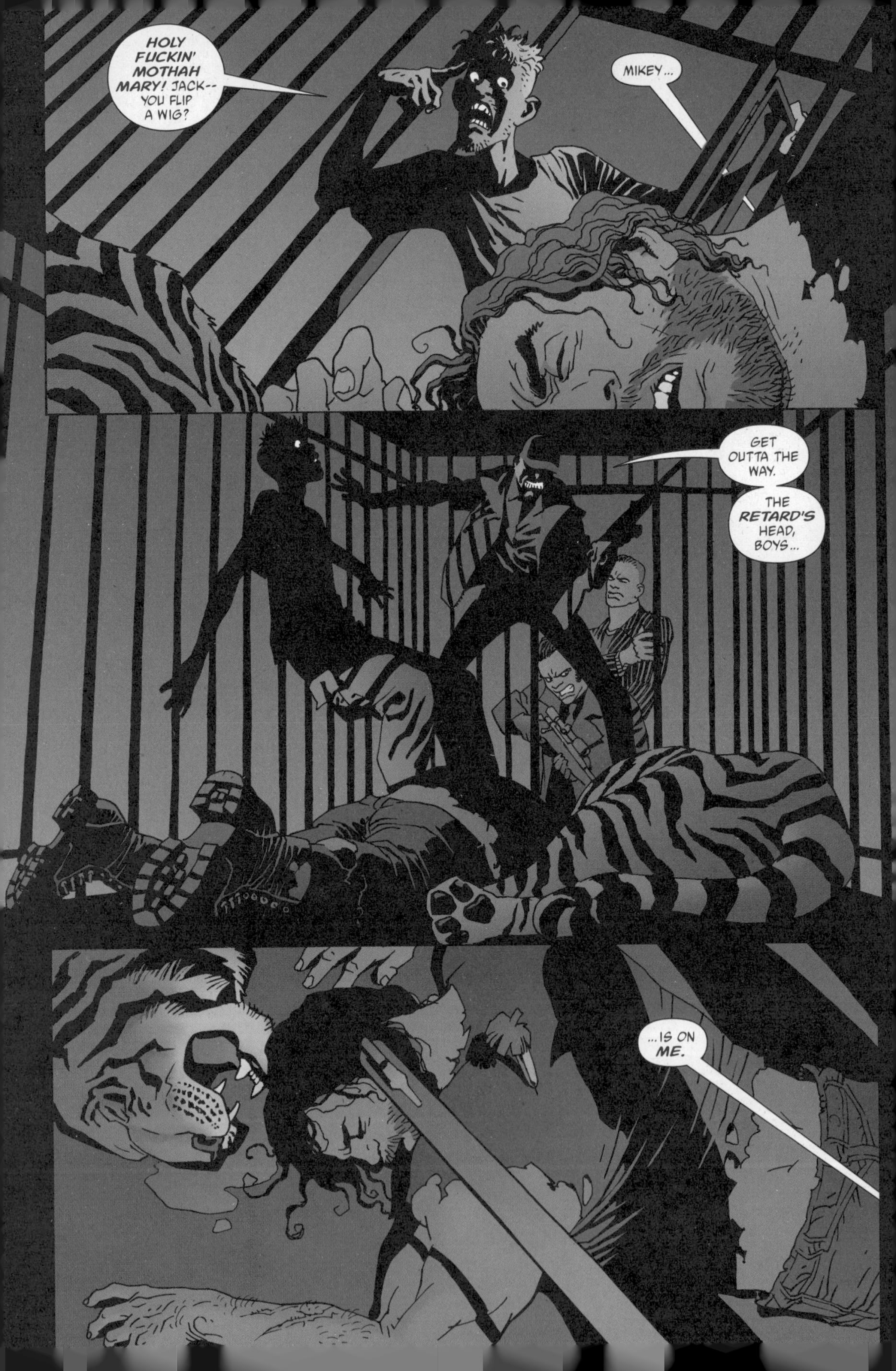
HOLY FUCKIN' MOTHAH MARY! JACK-- YOU FLIP A WIG?
MIKEY...
GET OUTTA THE WAY.
THE RETARD'S HEAD, BOYS...
...IS ON ME.

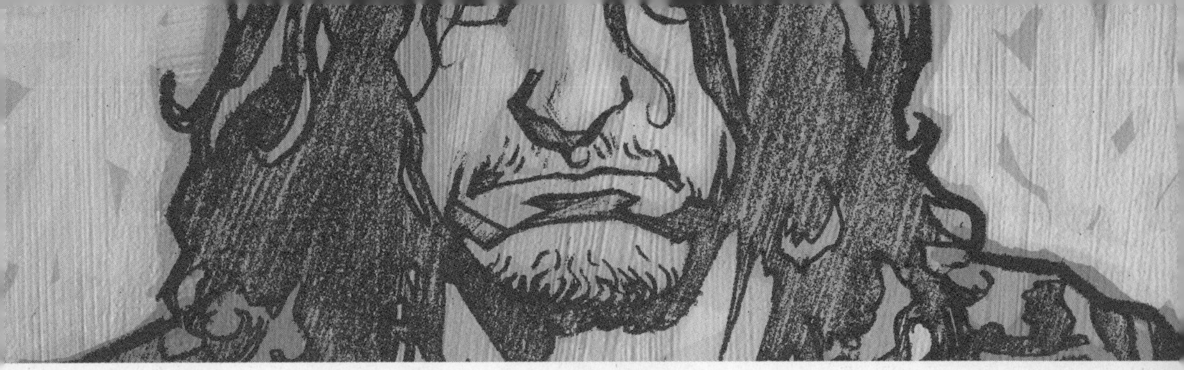

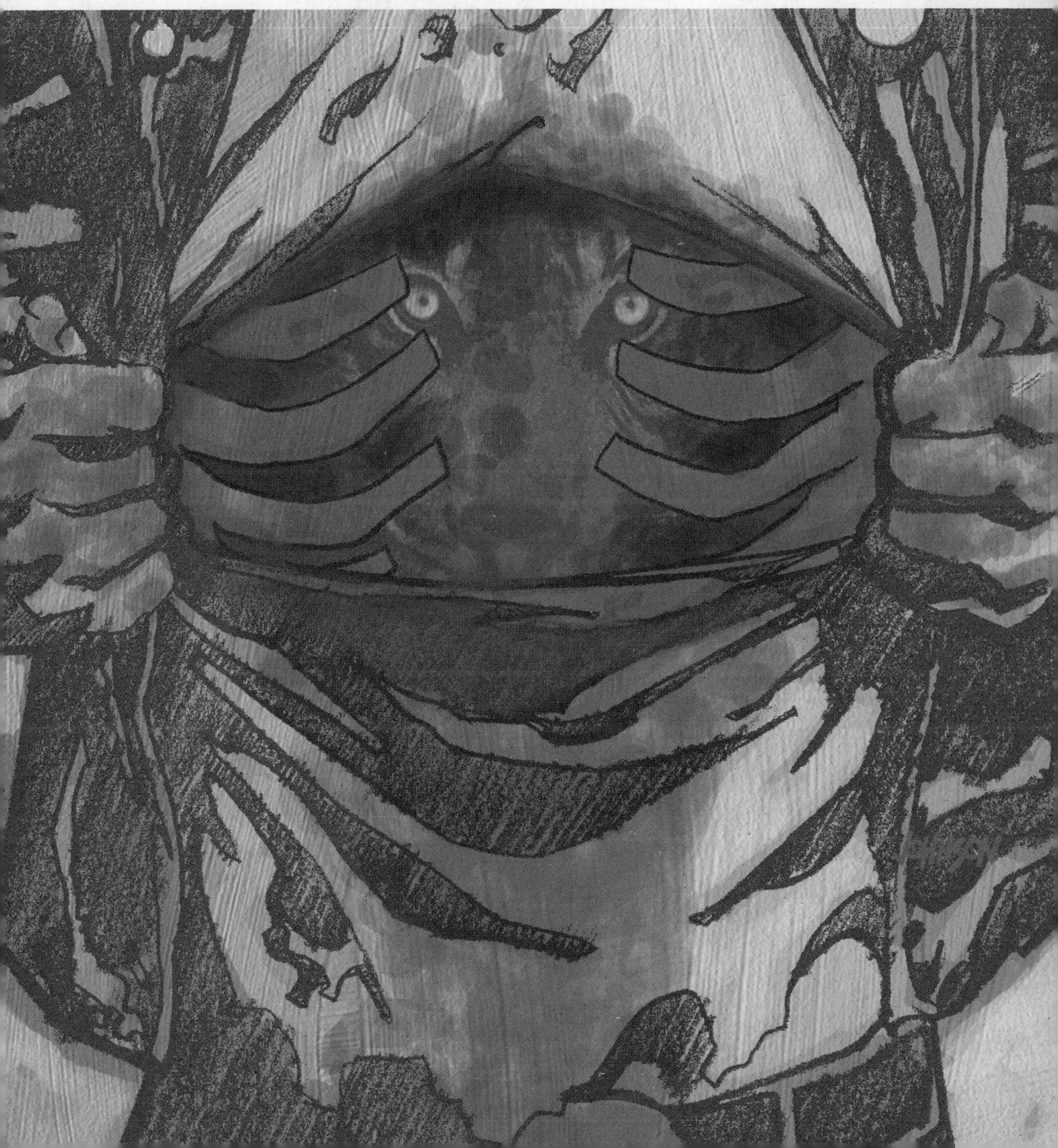

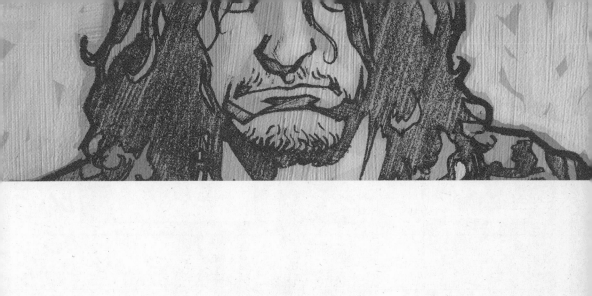

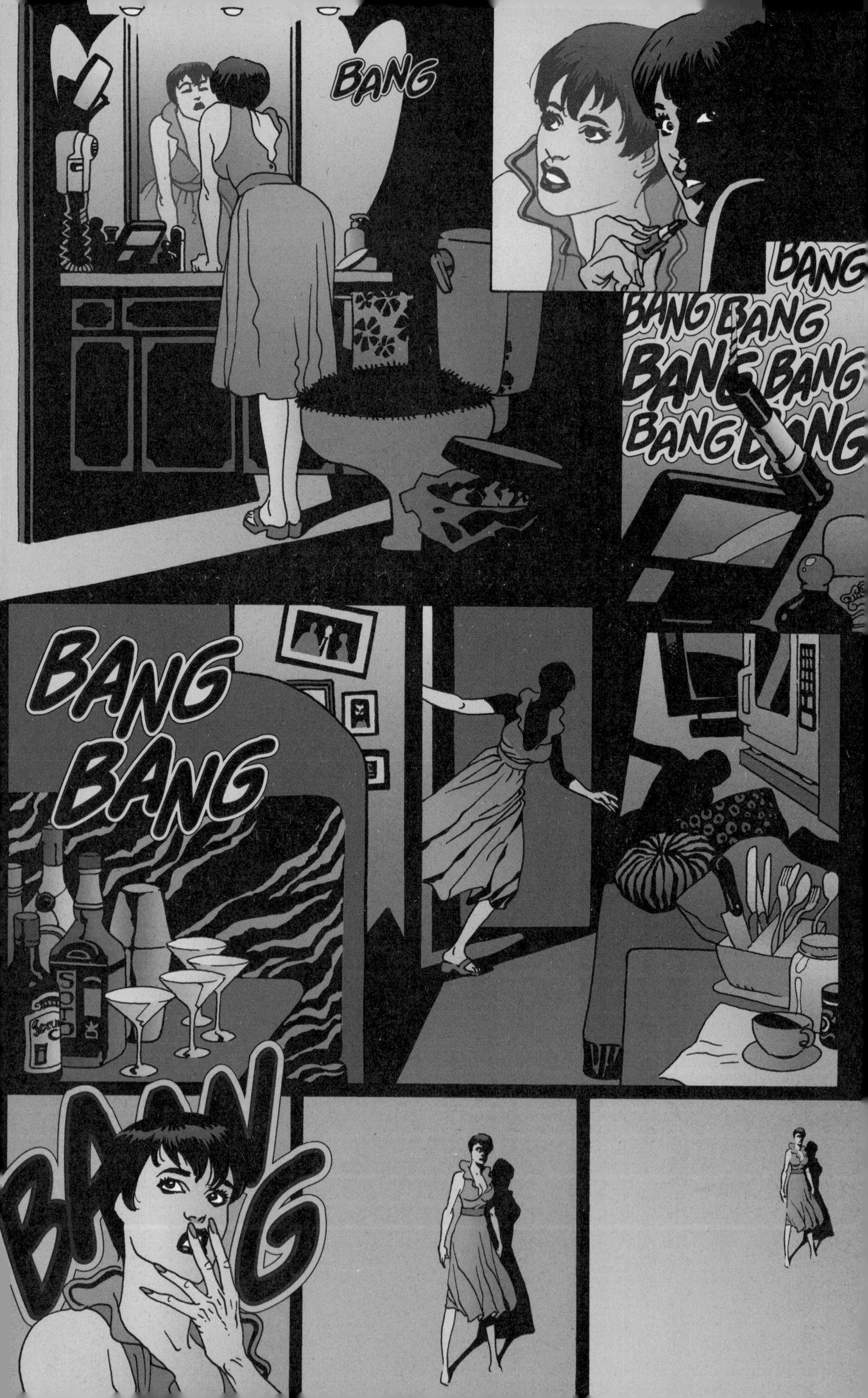
BANG
BANG
BANG BANG
BANG BANG
BANG
BANG
BANG
BANG

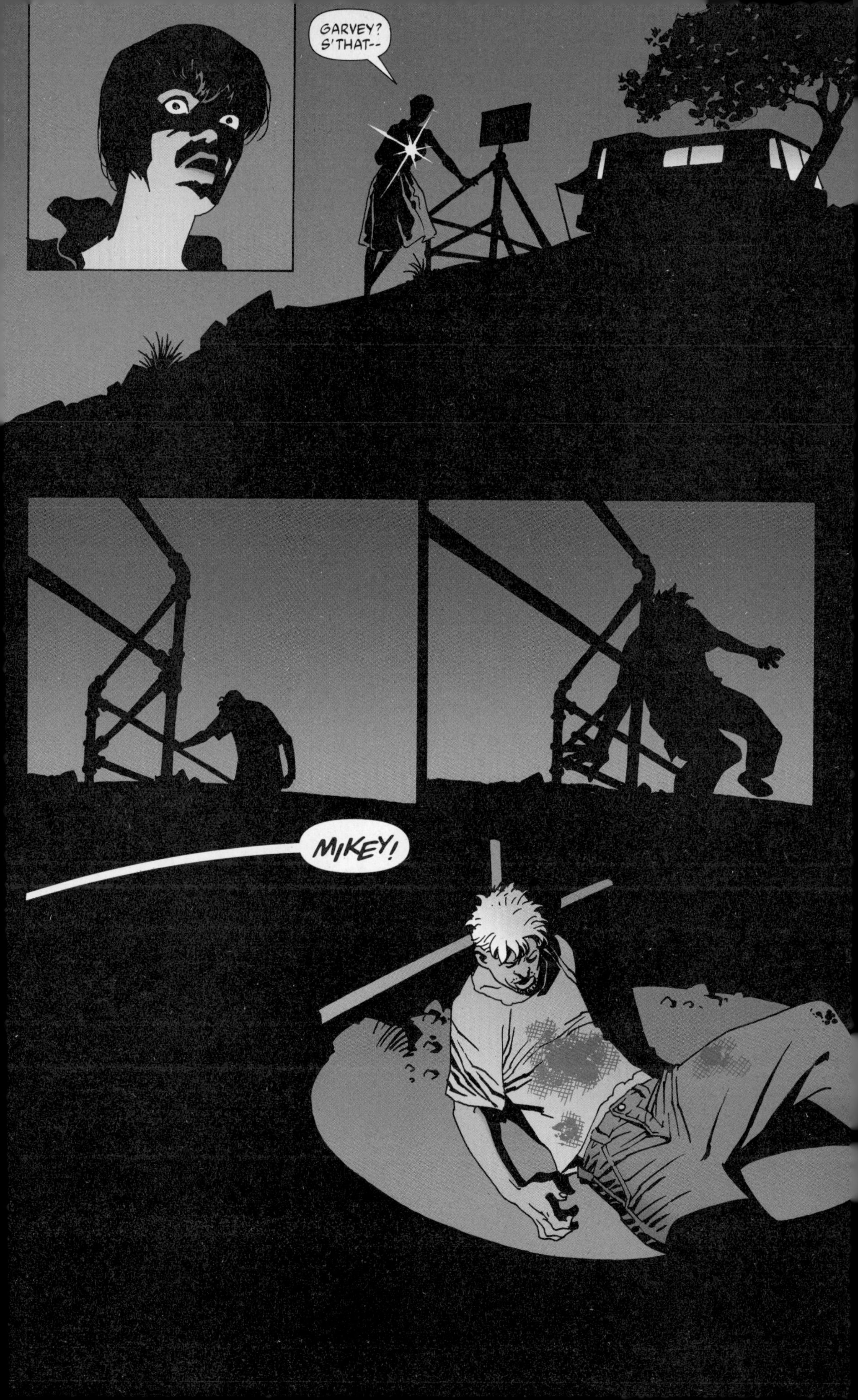
GARVEY? S'THAT--
MIKEY!

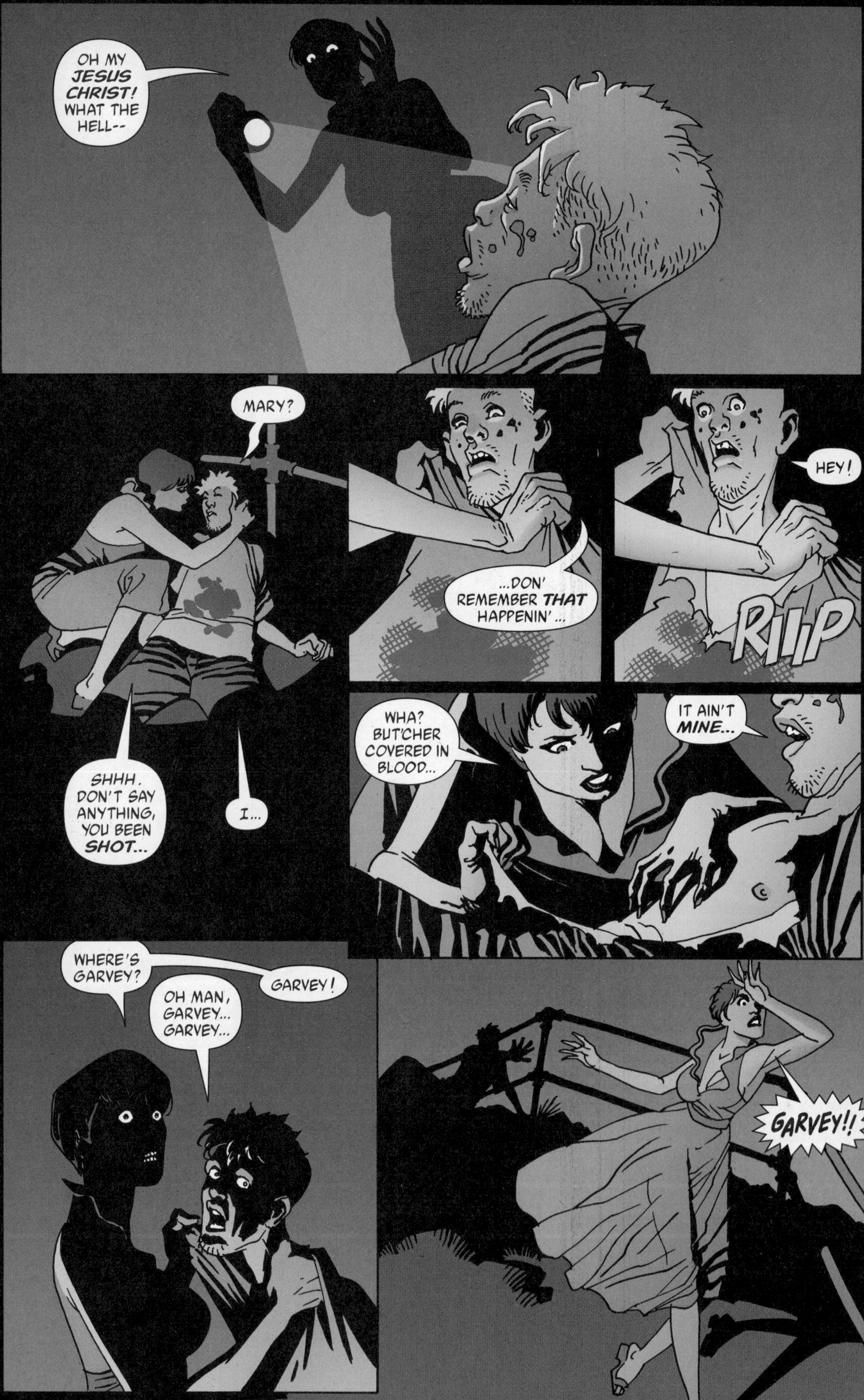
OH MY JESUS CHRIST! WHAT THE HELL--
MARY?
SHHH. DON'T SAY ANYTHING, YOU BEEN SHOT...
I...
...DON' REMEMBER THAT HAPPENIN'...
HEY!
RIIIP
WHA? BUT'CHER COVERED IN BLOOD...
IT AIN'T MINE...
WHERE'S GARVEY?
GARVEY!
OH MAN, GARVEY... GARVEY...
GARVEY!!

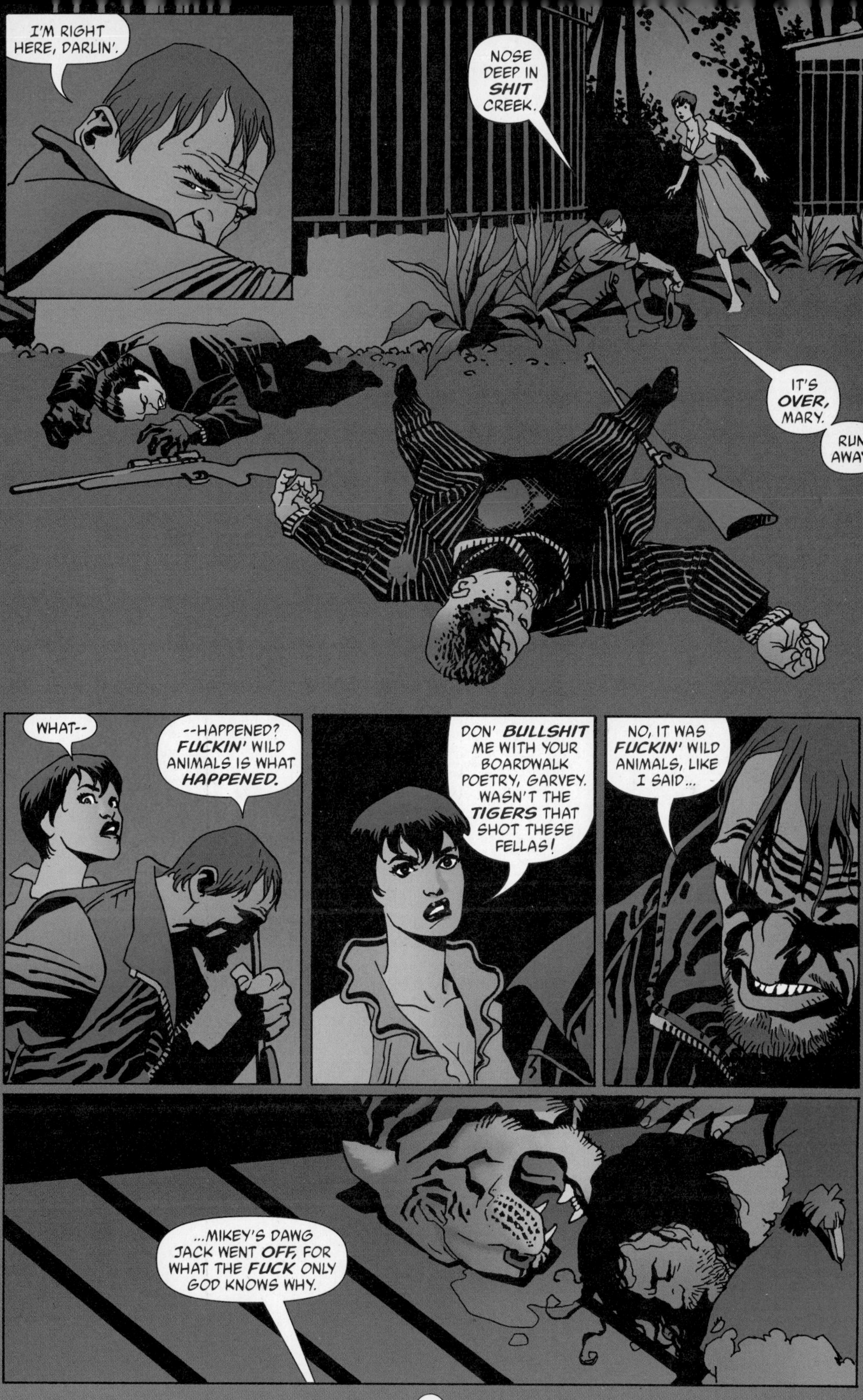
I'M RIGHT HERE, DARLIN'.
NOSE DEEP IN SHIT CREEK.
IT'S OVER, MARY.
RUN AWAY.
WHAT--
--HAPPENED? FUCKIN' WILD ANIMALS IS WHAT HAPPENED.
DON' BULLSHIT ME WITH YOUR BOARDWALK POETRY, GARVEY. WASN'T THE TIGERS THAT SHOT THESE FELLAS!
NO, IT WAS FUCKIN' WILD ANIMALS, LIKE I SAID...
...MIKEY'S DAWG JACK WENT OFF, FOR WHAT THE FUCK ONLY GOD KNOWS WHY.

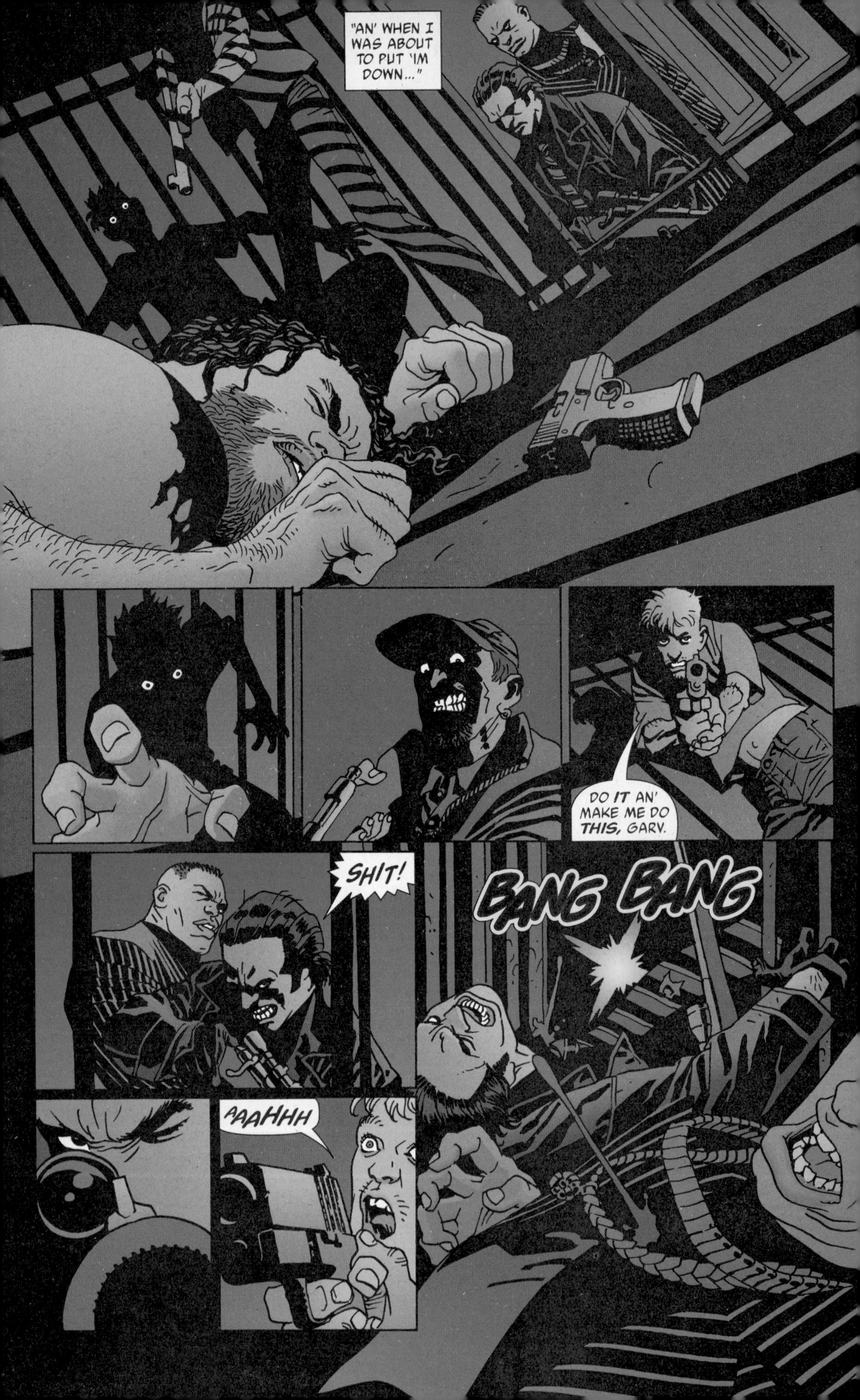
"AN' WHEN I WAS ABOUT TO PUT 'IM DOWN..."
DO IT AN' MAKE ME DO THIS, GARV.
SHIT!
BANG BANG
AAAHHH

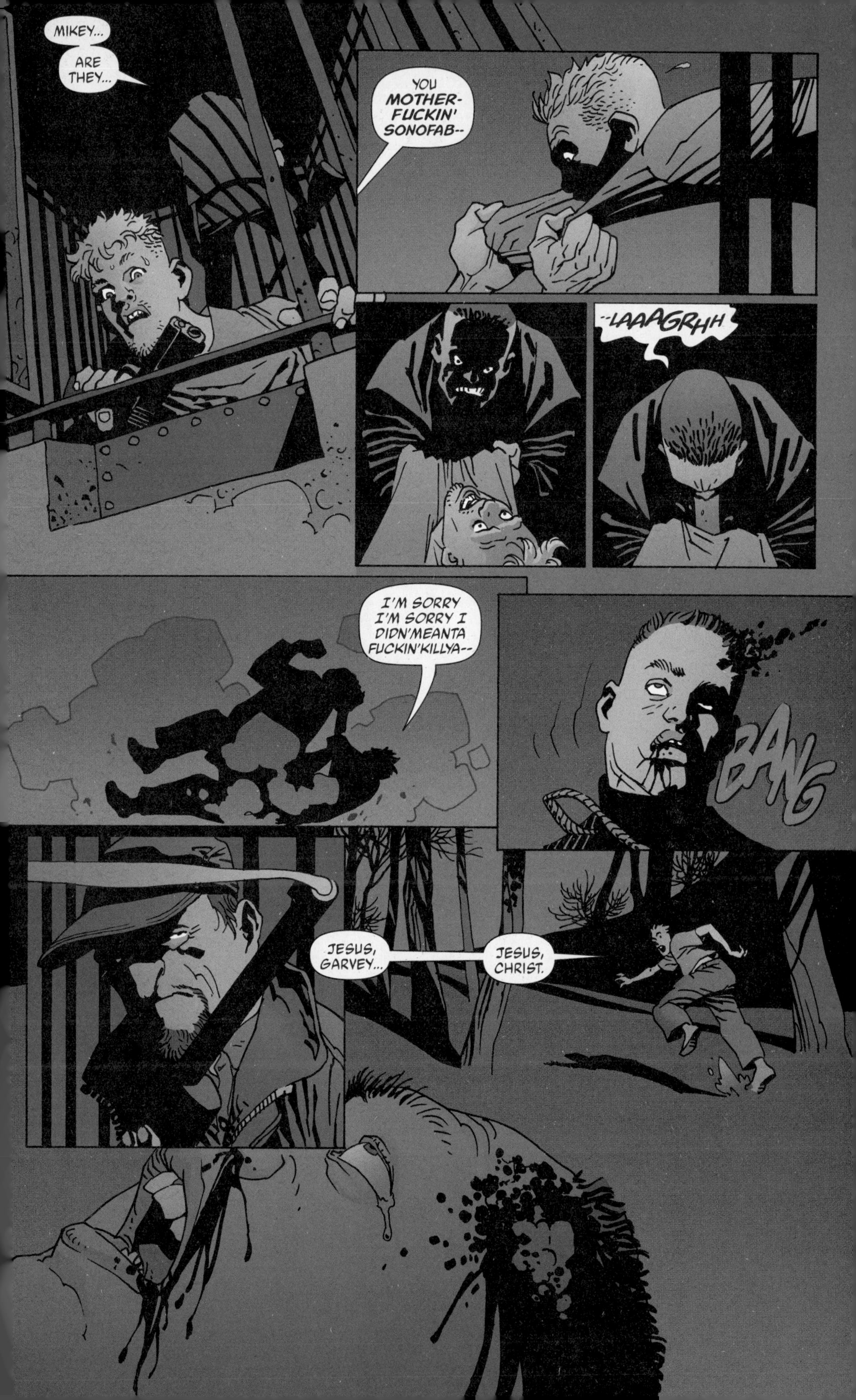
MIKEY...
ARE THEY...
YOU MOTHER-FUCKIN' SONOFAB--
--LAAAGRHH
I'M SORRY I'M SORRY I DIDN'MEANTA FUCKIN'KILLYA--
BANG
JESUS, GARVEY...
JESUS, CHRIST.

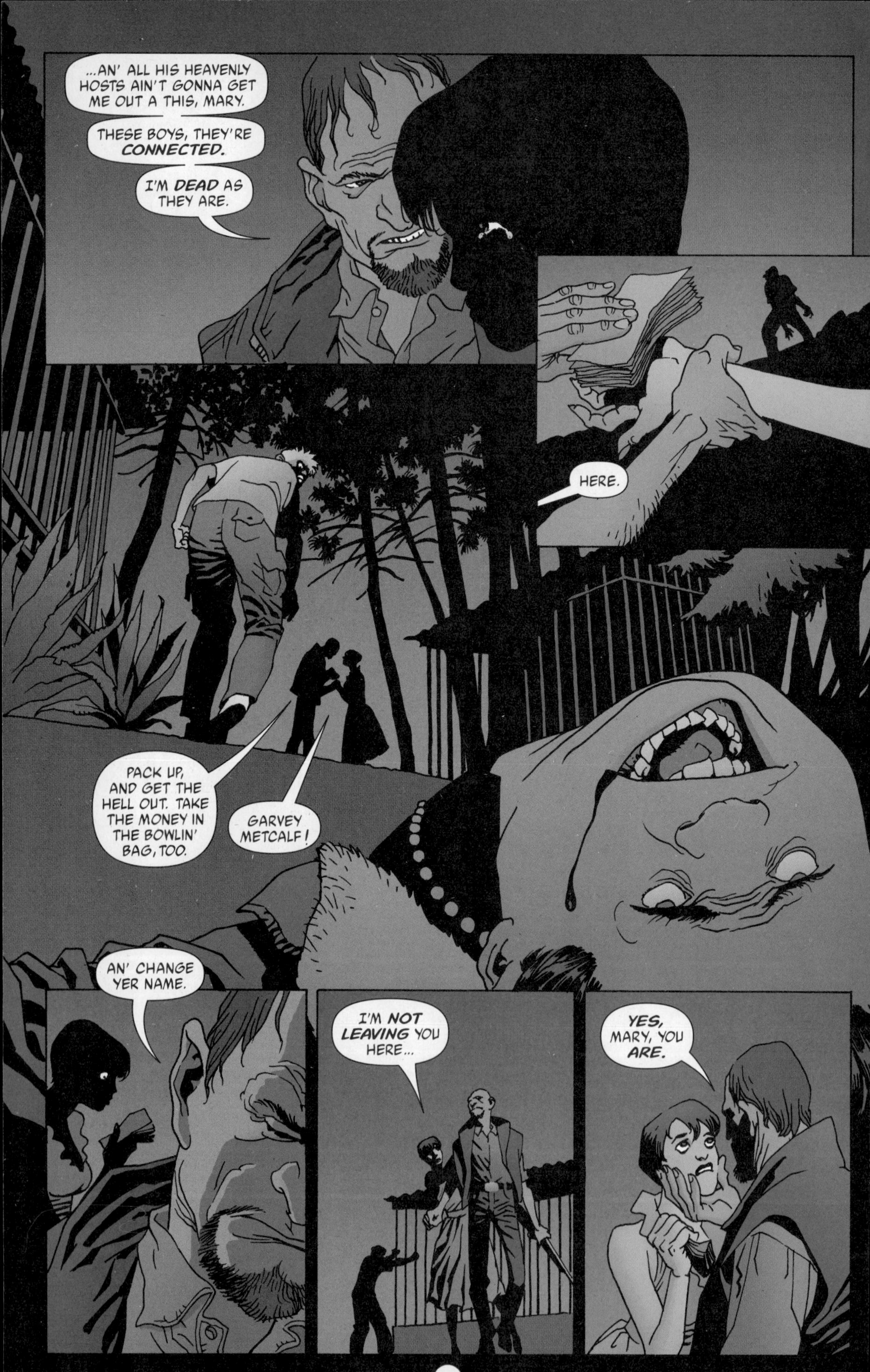
...AN' ALL HIS HEAVENLY HOSTS AIN'T GONNA GET ME OUT A THIS, MARY.
THESE BOYS, THEY'RE CONNECTED.
I'M DEAD AS THEY ARE.
HERE.
PACK UP, AND GET THE HELL OUT. TAKE THE MONEY IN THE BOWLIN' BAG, TOO.
GARVEY METCALF!
AN' CHANGE YER NAME.
I'M NOT LEAVING YOU HERE...
YES, MARY, YOU ARE.

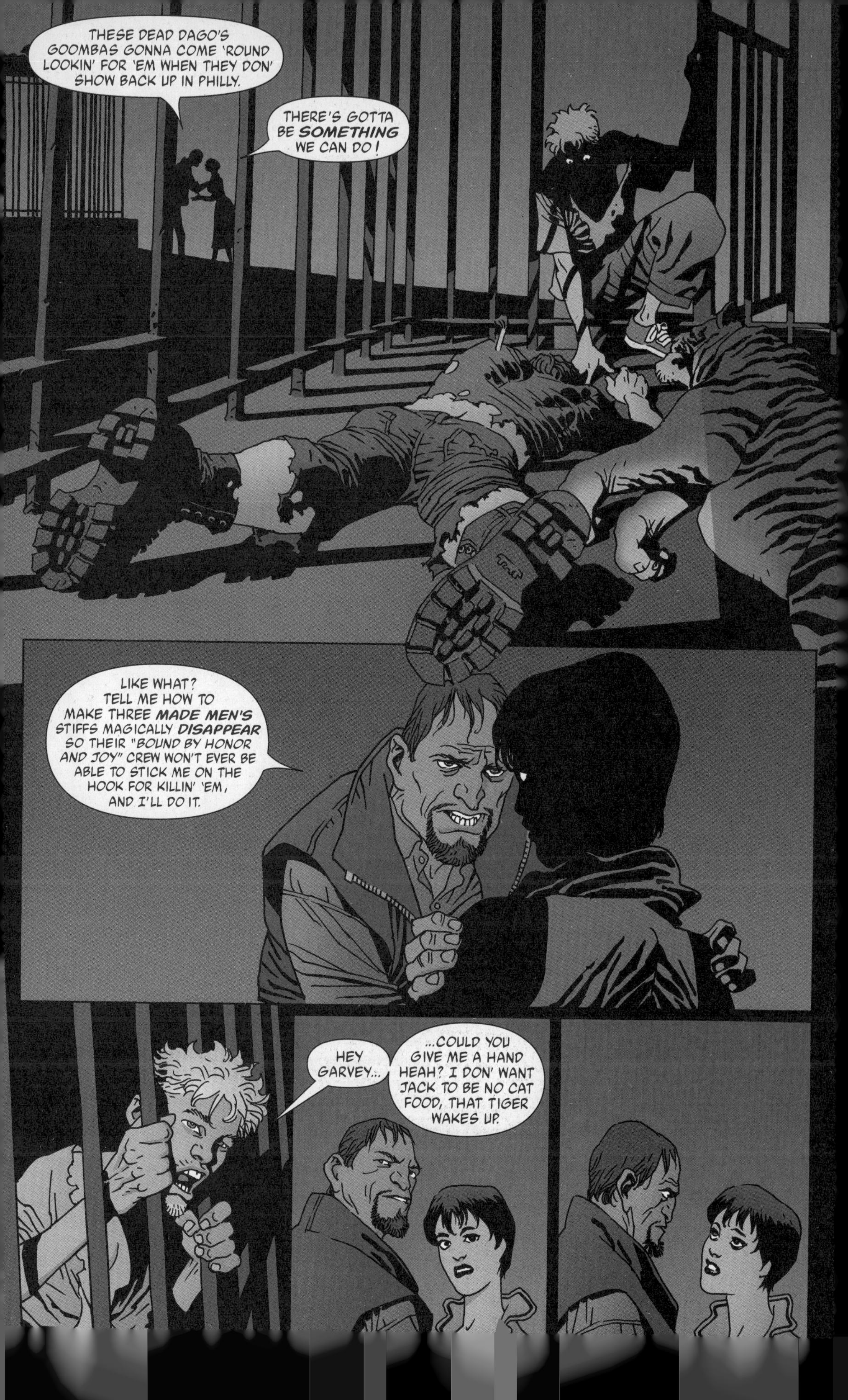
THESE DEAD DAGO'S GOOMBAS GONNA COME 'ROUND LOOKIN' FOR 'EM WHEN THEY DON' SHOW BACK UP IN PHILLY.
THERE'S GOTTA BE SOMETHING WE CAN DO!
LIKE WHAT? TELL ME HOW TO MAKE THREE MADE MEN'S STIFFS MAGICALLY DISAPPEAR SO THEIR "BOUND BY HONOR AND JOY" CREW WON'T EVER BE ABLE TO STICK ME ON THE HOOK FOR KILLIN' 'EM, AND I'LL DO IT.
HEY GARVEY...
...COULD YOU GIVE ME A HAND HEAH? I DON' WANT JACK TO BE NO CAT FOOD, THAT TIGER WAKES UP.

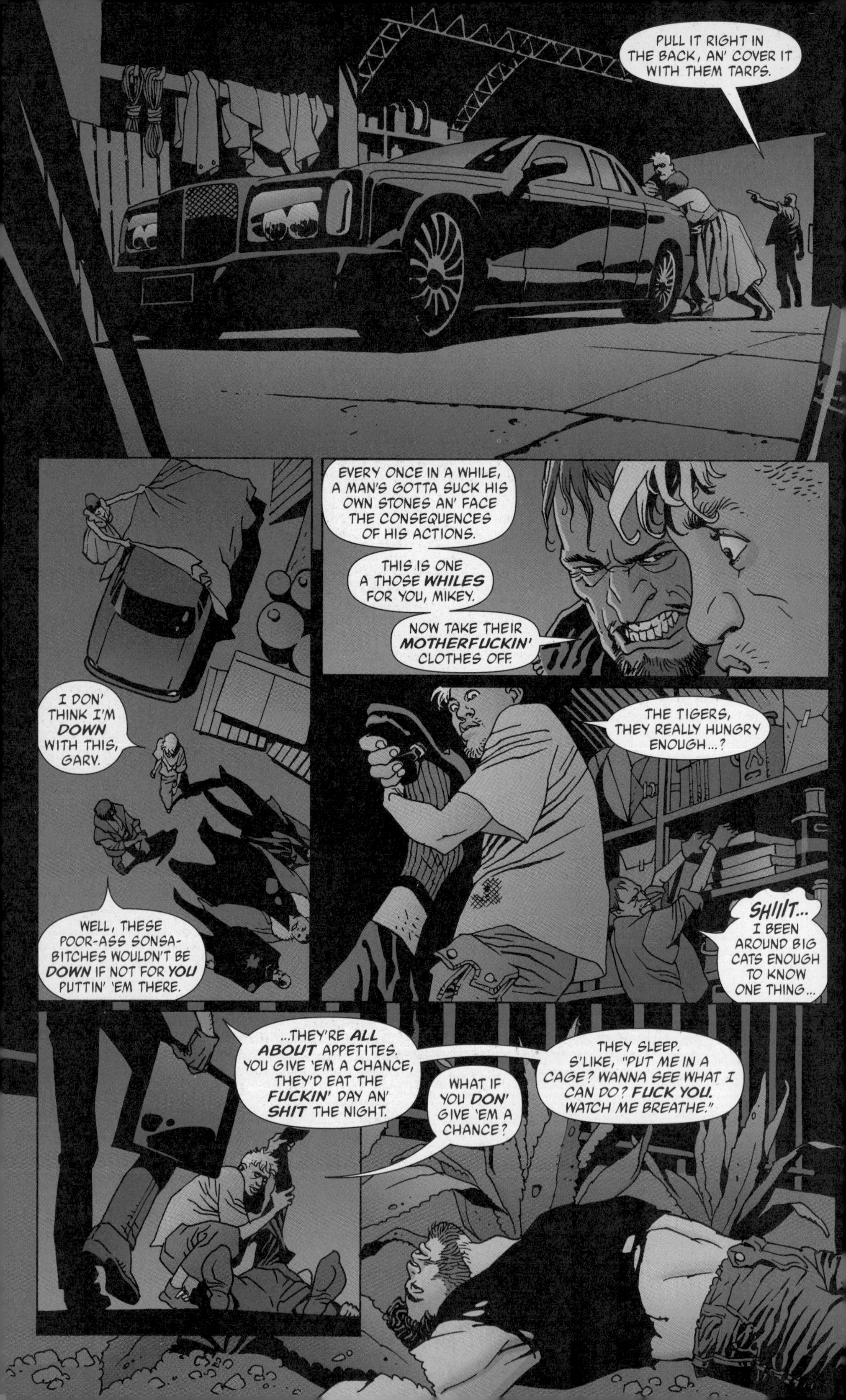
PULL IT RIGHT IN THE BACK, AN' COVER IT WITH THEM TARPS.
EVERY ONCE IN A WHILE, A MAN'S GOTTA SUCK HIS OWN STONES AN' FACE THE CONSEQUENCES OF HIS ACTIONS.
THIS IS ONE A THOSE WHILES FOR YOU, MIKEY.
NOW TAKE THEIR MOTHERFUCKIN' CLOTHES OFF.
I DON' THINK I'M DOWN WITH THIS, GARV.
WELL, THESE POOR-ASS SONSA-BITCHES WOULDN'T BE DOWN IF NOT FOR YOU PUTTIN' 'EM THERE.
THE TIGERS, THEY REALLY HUNGRY ENOUGH...?
SHIIIT... I BEEN AROUND BIG CATS ENOUGH TO KNOW ONE THING...
...THEY'RE ALL ABOUT APPETITES. YOU GIVE 'EM A CHANCE, THEY'D EAT THE FUCKIN' DAY AN' SHIT THE NIGHT.
WHAT IF YOU DON' GIVE 'EM A CHANCE?
THEY SLEEP. S'LIKE, "PUT ME IN A CAGE? WANNA SEE WHAT I CAN DO? FUCK YOU. WATCH ME BREATHE."

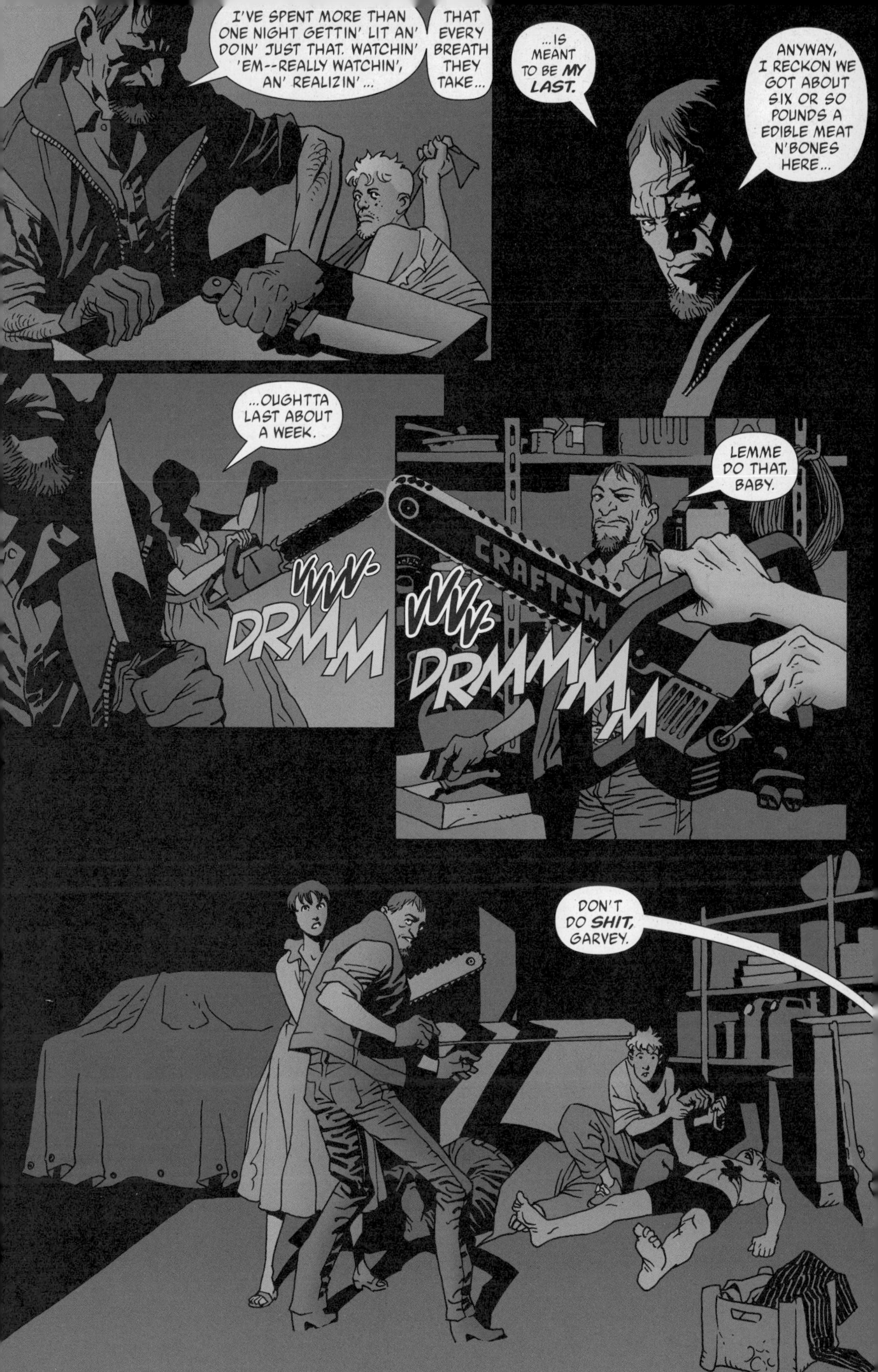
I'VE SPENT MORE THAN ONE NIGHT GETTIN' LIT AN' DOIN' JUST THAT. WATCHIN' 'EM--REALLY WATCHIN', AN' REALIZIN'...
THAT EVERY BREATH THEY TAKE...
...IS MEANT TO BE MY LAST.
ANYWAY, I RECKON WE GOT ABOUT SIX OR SO POUNDS A EDIBLE MEAT N'BONES HERE...
...OUGHTTA LAST ABOUT A WEEK.
VVVV-
DRMM
LEMME DO THAT, BABY.
CRAFTSM
VVVV-
DRMMMMM
DON'T DO SHIT, GARVEY.

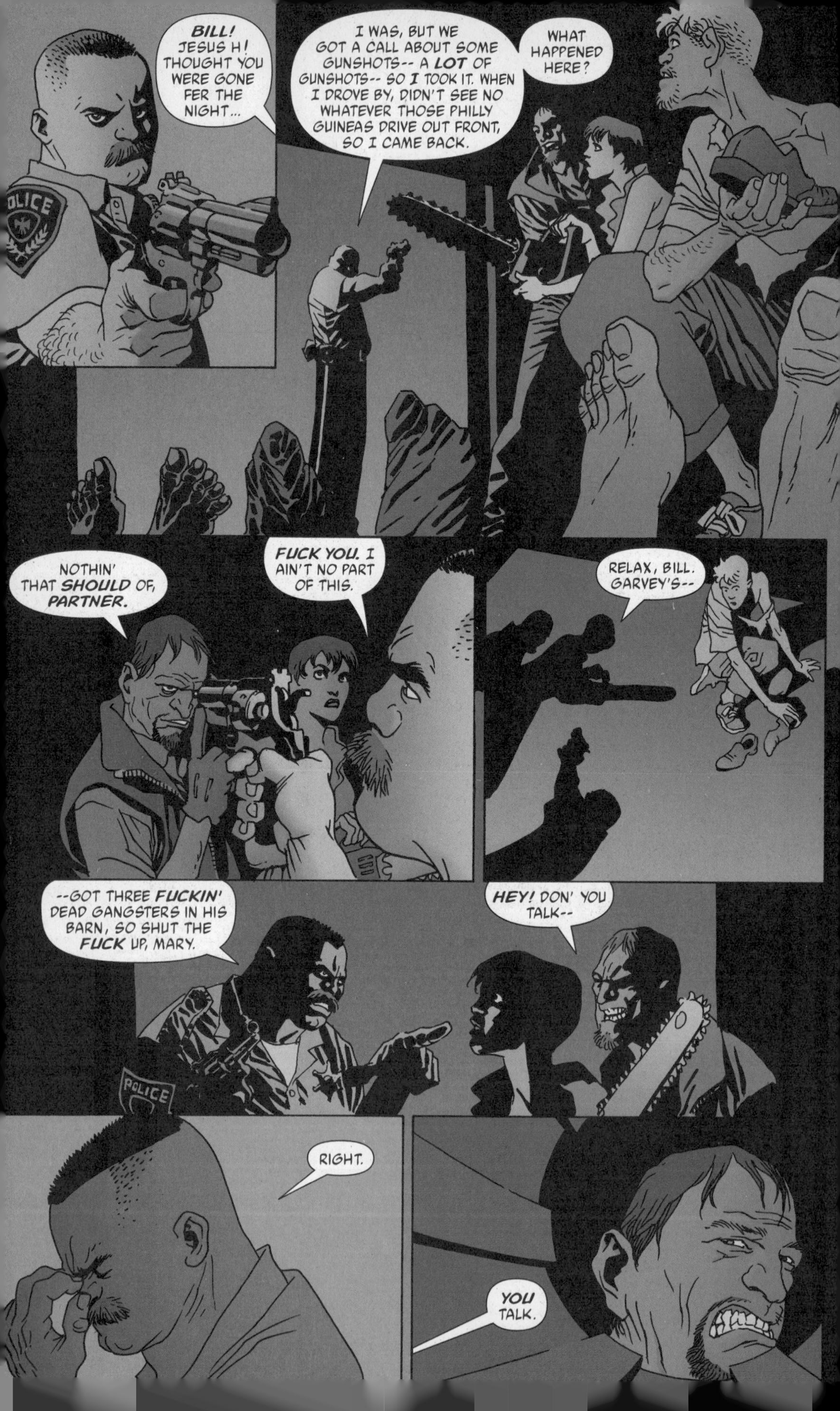
BILL! JESUS H! THOUGHT YOU WERE GONE FER THE NIGHT...
I WAS, BUT WE GOT A CALL ABOUT SOME GUNSHOTS-- A LOT OF GUNSHOTS-- SO I TOOK IT. WHEN I DROVE BY, DIDN'T SEE NO WHATEVER THOSE PHILLY GUINEAS DRIVE OUT FRONT, SO I CAME BACK.
WHAT HAPPENED HERE?
POLICE
NOTHIN' THAT SHOULD OF, PARTNER.
FUCK YOU. I AIN'T NO PART OF THIS.
RELAX, BILL. GARVEY'S--
--GOT THREE FUCKIN' DEAD GANGSTERS IN HIS BARN, SO SHUT THE FUCK UP, MARY.
HEY! DON' YOU TALK--
POLICE
RIGHT.
YOU TALK.

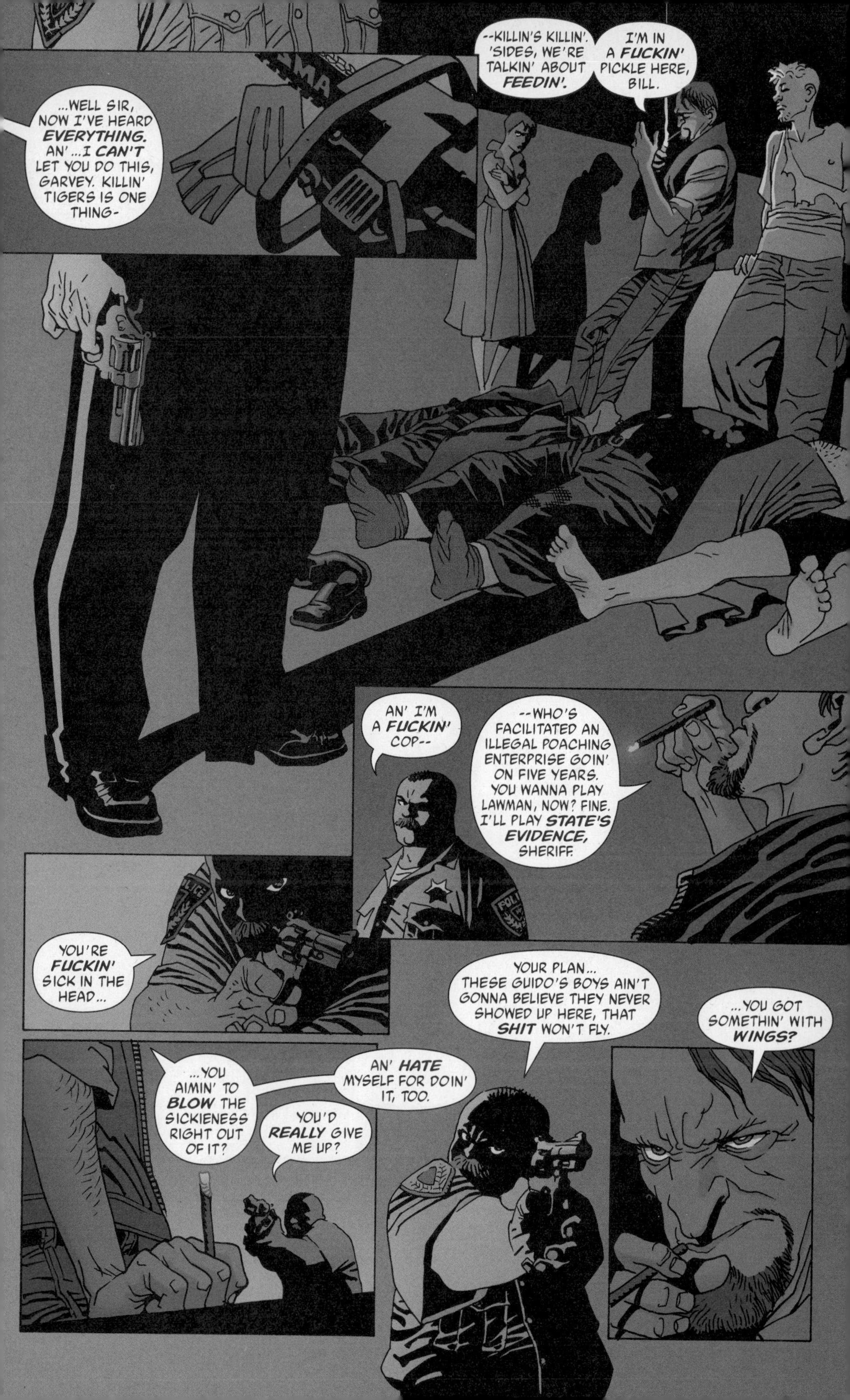
...WELL SIR, NOW I'VE HEARD EVERYTHING. AN' ...I CAN'T LET YOU DO THIS, GARVEY. KILLIN' TIGERS IS ONE THING-
--KILLIN'S KILLIN'. 'SIDES, WE'RE TALKIN' ABOUT FEEDIN'.
I'M IN A FUCKIN' PICKLE HERE, BILL.
AN' I'M A FUCKIN' COP--
--WHO'S FACILITATED AN ILLEGAL POACHING ENTERPRISE GOIN' ON FIVE YEARS. YOU WANNA PLAY LAWMAN, NOW? FINE. I'LL PLAY STATE'S EVIDENCE, SHERIFF.
YOU'RE FUCKIN' SICK IN THE HEAD...
...YOU AIMIN' TO BLOW THE SICKIENESS RIGHT OUT OF IT?
AN' HATE MYSELF FOR DOIN' IT, TOO.
YOU'D REALLY GIVE ME UP?
YOUR PLAN... THESE GUIDO'S BOYS AIN'T GONNA BELIEVE THEY NEVER SHOWED UP HERE, THAT SHIT WON'T FLY.
...YOU GOT SOMETHIN' WITH WINGS?

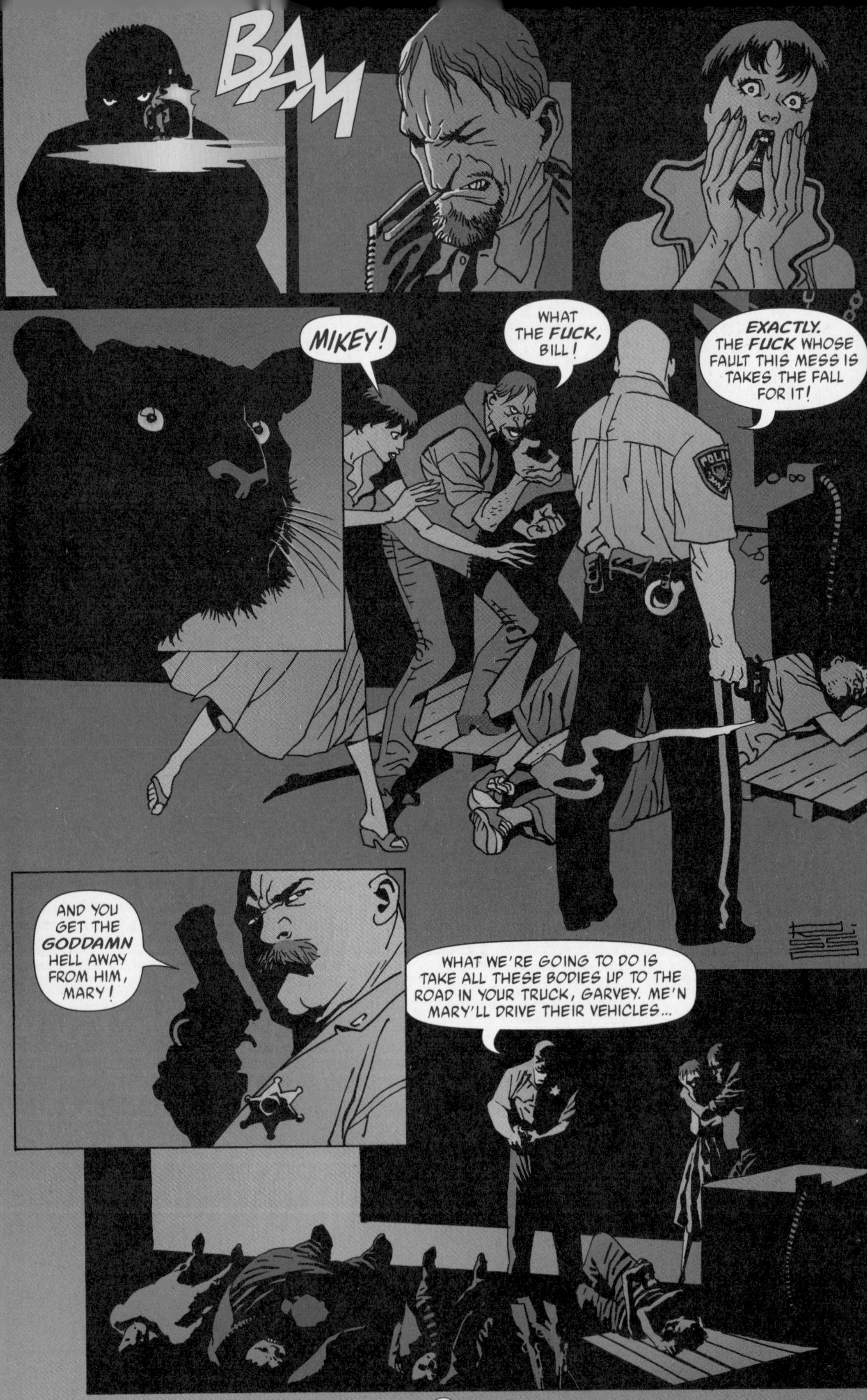
BAM
MIKEY!
WHAT THE FUCK, BILL!
EXACTLY. THE FUCK WHOSE FAULT THIS MESS IS TAKES THE FALL FOR IT!
AND YOU GET THE GODDAMN HELL AWAY FROM HIM, MARY!
WHAT WE'RE GOING TO DO IS TAKE ALL THESE BODIES UP TO THE ROAD IN YOUR TRUCK, GARVEY. ME'N MARY'LL DRIVE THEIR VEHICLES...

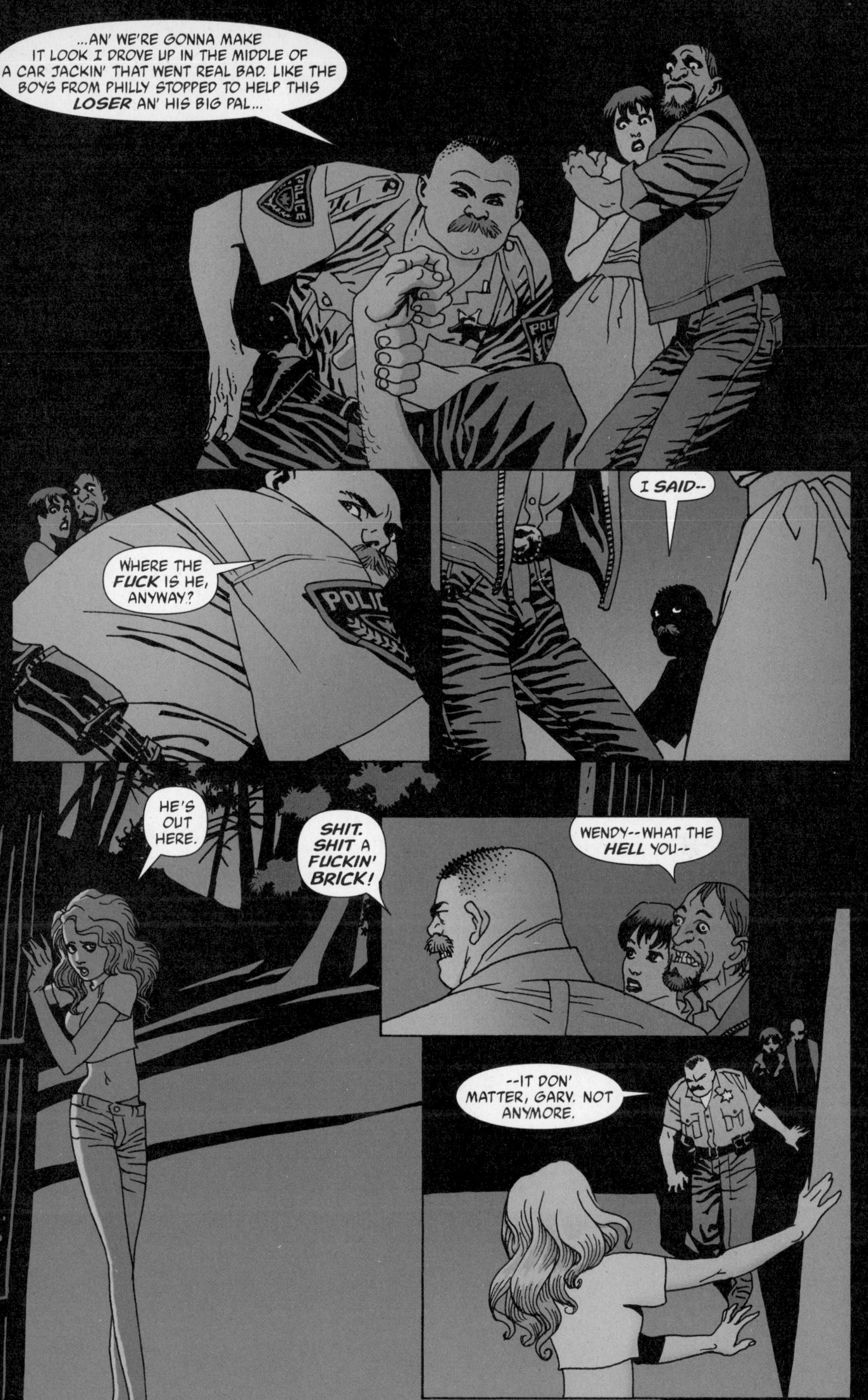
...AN' WE'RE GONNA MAKE IT LOOK I DROVE UP IN THE MIDDLE OF A CAR JACKIN' THAT WENT REAL BAD. LIKE THE BOYS FROM PHILLY STOPPED TO HELP THIS LOSER AN' HIS BIG PAL...
POLICE
WHERE THE FUCK IS HE, ANYWAY?
POLICE
I SAID--
HE'S OUT HERE.
SHIT. SHIT A FUCKIN' BRICK!
WENDY--WHAT THE HELL YOU--
--IT DON' MATTER, GARV. NOT ANYMORE.

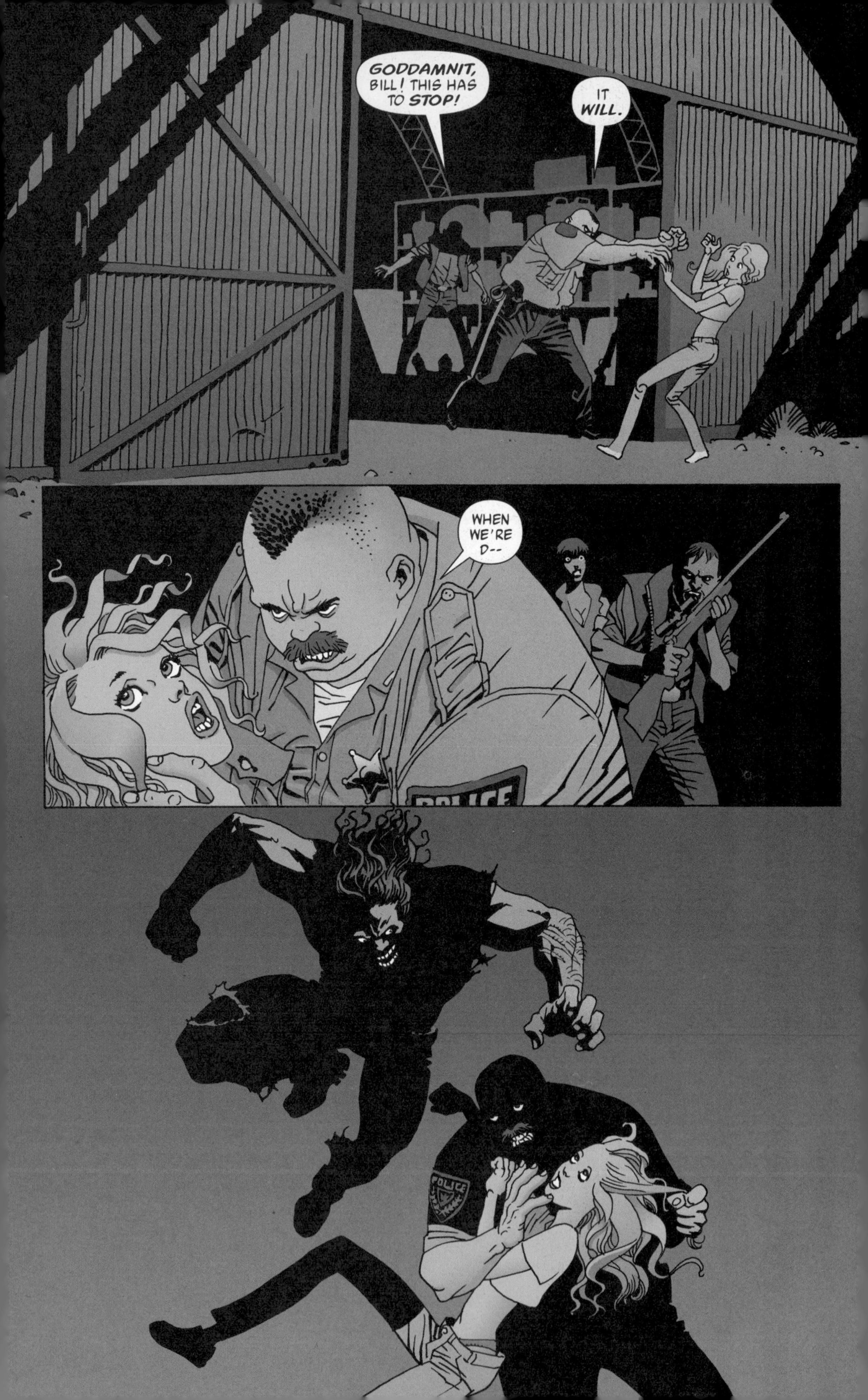
GODDAMNIT, BILL! THIS HAS TO STOP!
IT WILL.
WHEN WE'RE D--
POLICE

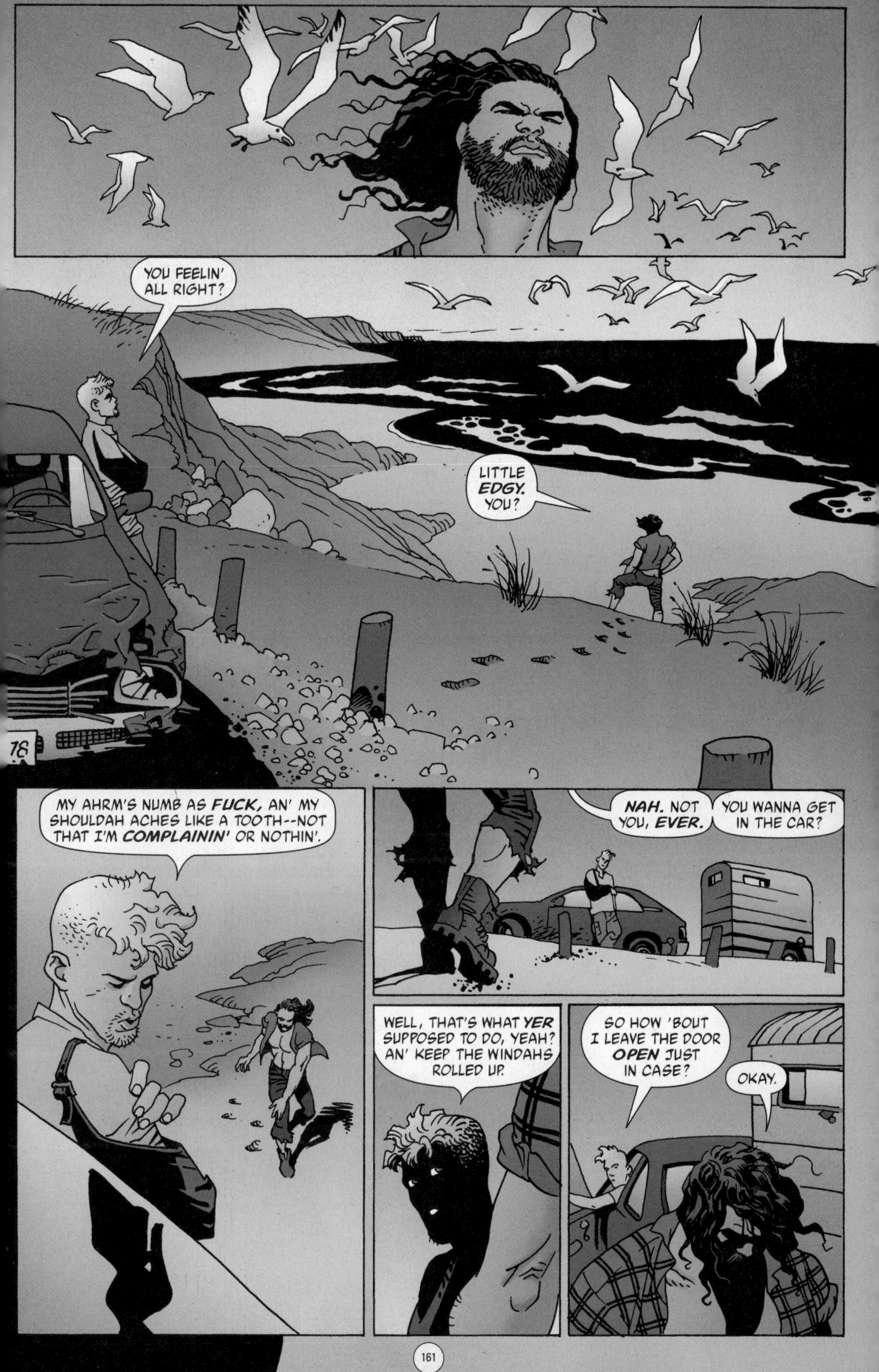
YOU FEELIN' ALL RIGHT?
LITTLE EDGY. YOU?
MY AHRM'S NUMB AS FUCK, AN' MY SHOULDAH ACHES LIKE A TOOTH--NOT THAT I'M COMPLAININ' OR NOTHIN'.
NAH. NOT YOU, EVER.
YOU WANNA GET IN THE CAR?
WELL, THAT'S WHAT YER SUPPOSED TO DO, YEAH? AN' KEEP THE WINDAHS ROLLED UP.
SO HOW 'BOUT I LEAVE THE DOOR OPEN JUST IN CASE?
OKAY.

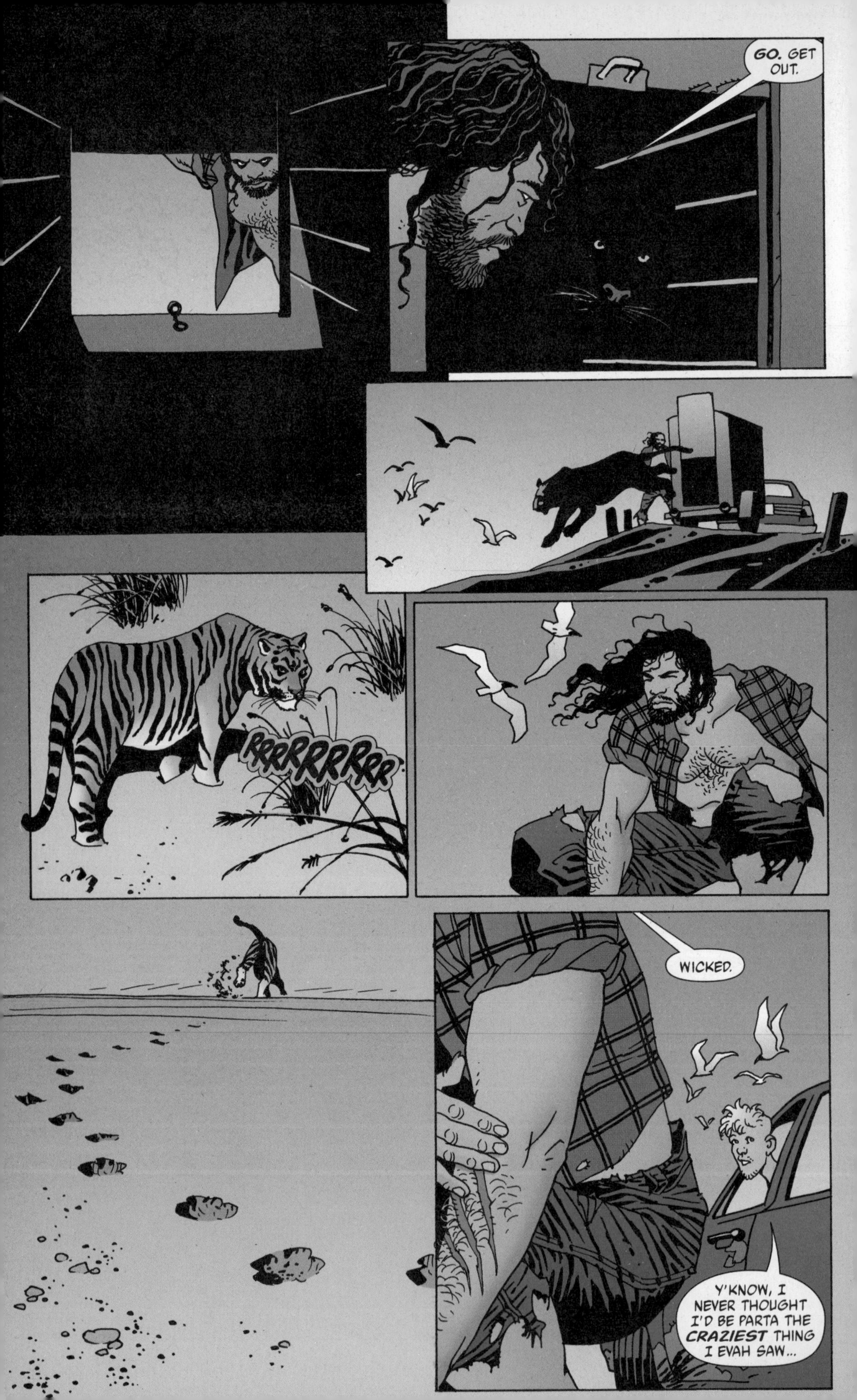
GO. GET OUT.
RRRRRRRRRR
WICKED.
Y'KNOW, I NEVER THOUGHT I'D BE PARTA THE CRAZIEST THING I EVAH SAW...

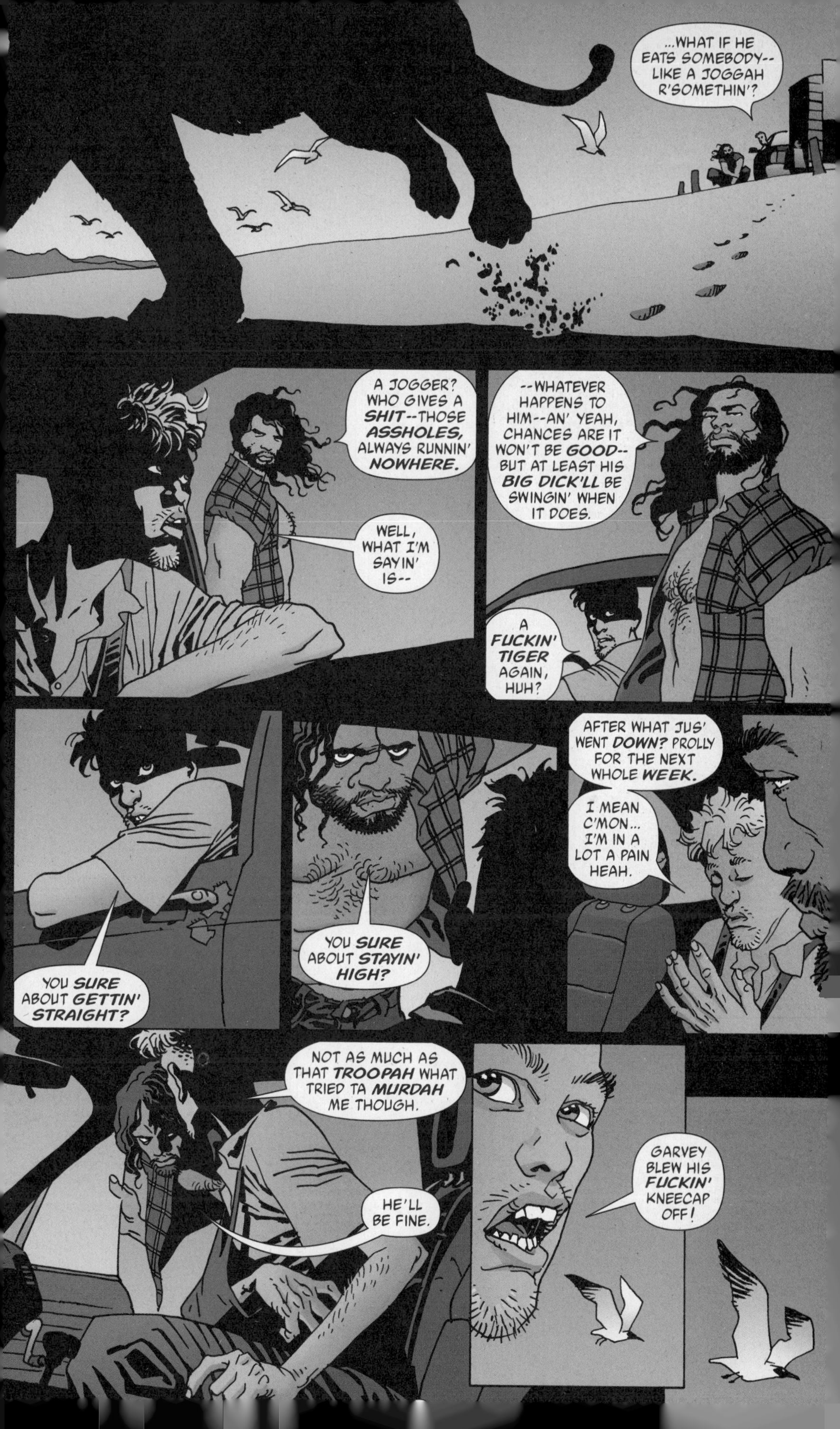
...WHAT IF HE EATS SOMEBODY-- LIKE A JOGGAH R'SOMETHIN'?
A JOGGER? WHO GIVES A SHIT--THOSE ASSHOLES, ALWAYS RUNNIN' NOWHERE.
WELL, WHAT I'M SAYIN' IS--
--WHATEVER HAPPENS TO HIM--AN' YEAH, CHANCES ARE IT WON'T BE GOOD-- BUT AT LEAST HIS BIG DICK'LL BE SWINGIN' WHEN IT DOES.
A FUCKIN' TIGER AGAIN, HUH?
YOU SURE ABOUT GETTIN' STRAIGHT?
YOU SURE ABOUT STAYIN' HIGH?
AFTER WHAT JUS' WENT DOWN? PROLLY FOR THE NEXT WHOLE WEEK.
I MEAN C'MON... I'M IN A LOT A PAIN HEAH.
NOT AS MUCH AS THAT TROOPAH WHAT TRIED TA MURDAH ME THOUGH.
HE'LL BE FINE.
GARVEY BLEW HIS FUCKIN' KNEECAP OFF!

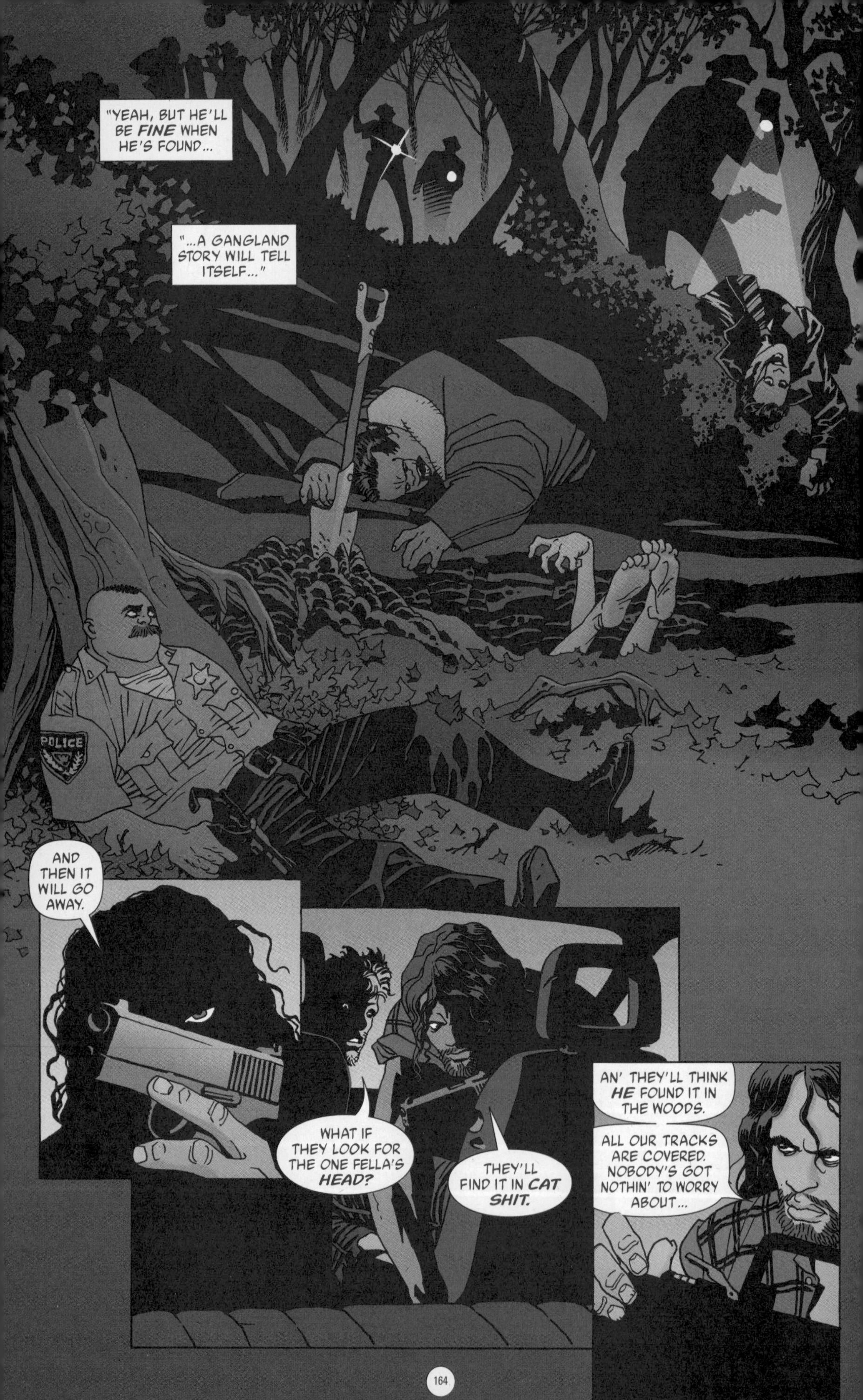
"YEAH, BUT HE'LL BE FINE WHEN HE'S FOUND...
"...A GANGLAND STORY WILL TELL ITSELF..."
POLICE
AND THEN IT WILL GO AWAY.
WHAT IF THEY LOOK FOR THE ONE FELLA'S HEAD?
THEY'LL FIND IT IN CAT SHIT.
AN' THEY'LL THINK HE FOUND IT IN THE WOODS.
ALL OUR TRACKS ARE COVERED. NOBODY'S GOT NOTHIN' TO WORRY ABOUT...

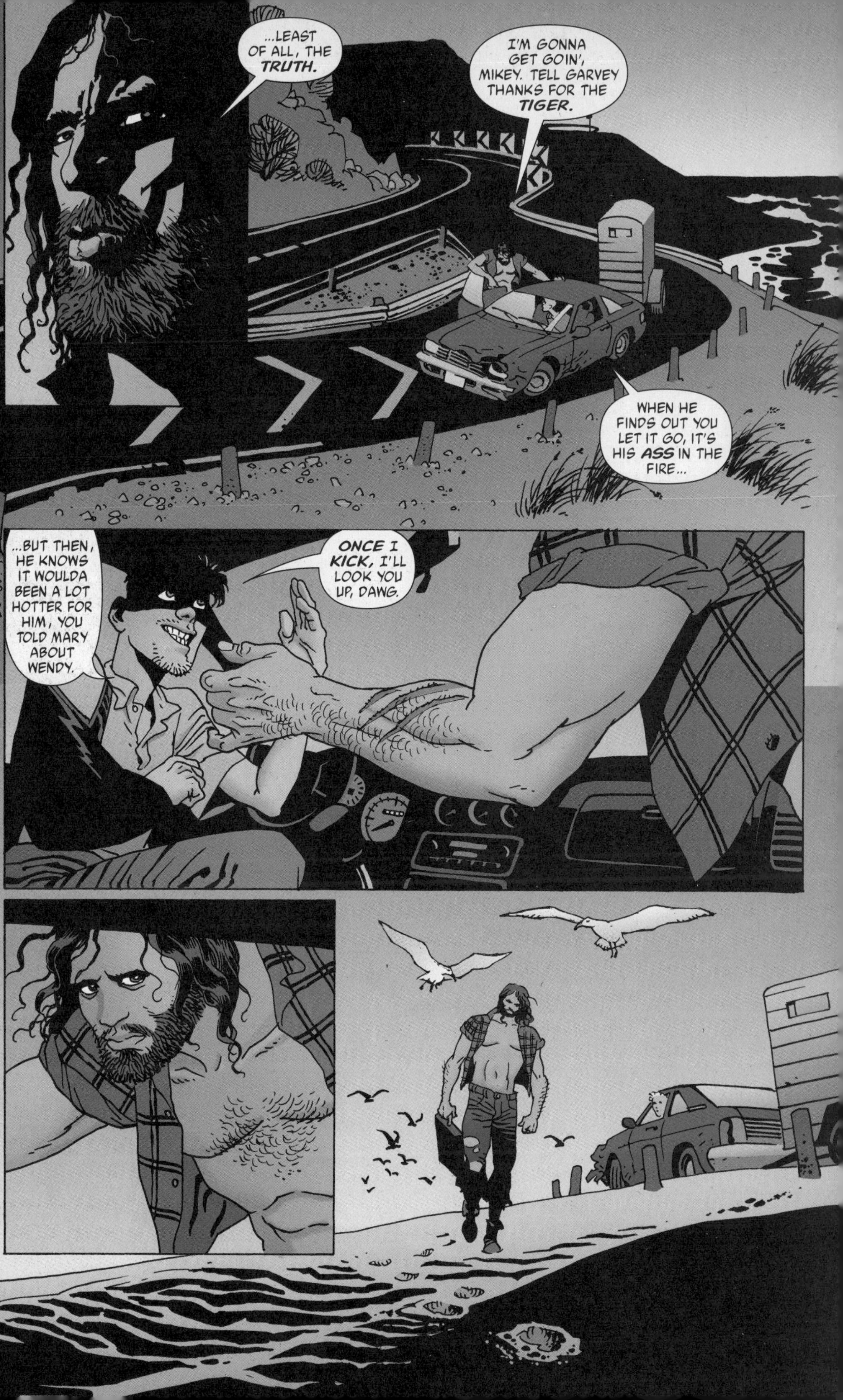

...LEAST OF ALL, THE TRUTH.
I'M GONNA GET GOIN', MIKEY. TELL GARVEY THANKS FOR THE TIGER.
WHEN HE FINDS OUT YOU LET IT GO, IT'S HIS ASS IN THE FIRE...
...BUT THEN, HE KNOWS IT WOULDA BEEN A LOT HOTTER FOR HIM, YOU TOLD MARY ABOUT WENDY.
ONCE I KICK, I'LL LOOK YOU UP, DAWG.

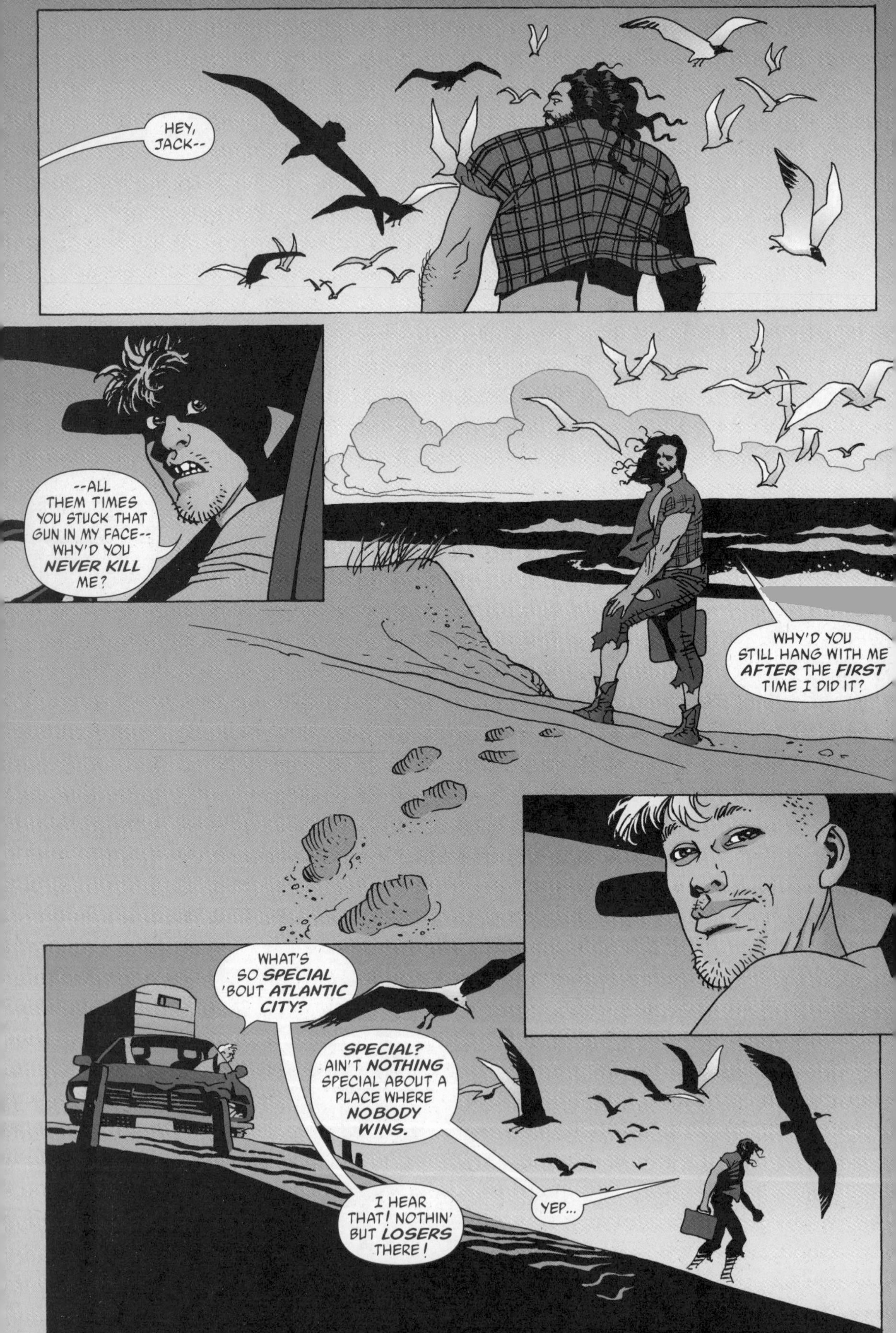
HEY, JACK--
--ALL THEM TIMES YOU STUCK THAT GUN IN MY FACE-- WHY'D YOU NEVER KILL ME?
WHY'D YOU STILL HANG WITH ME AFTER THE FIRST TIME I DID IT?
WHAT'S SO SPECIAL 'BOUT ATLANTIC CITY?
SPECIAL? AIN'T NOTHING SPECIAL ABOUT A PLACE WHERE NOBODY WINS.
I HEAR THAT! NOTHIN' BUT LOSERS THERE!
YEP...